JOURNALS

of

GEORGE

WHITEFIELD

CHRISTIAN CLASSICS
P.O. Box 2722, Grand Rapids, Michigan 49501

A
SHORT
ACCOUNT

OF

GOD'S DEALINGS

With
GEORGE WHITEFIELD

(1714 — 1736)

Written by HIMSELF, on board the *Elizabeth*, Captain Stephenson, bound from London to Philadelphia, and sent over by HIM to be published for the Benefit of the Orphan-house in Georgia.

From Whitefield's Preface to The
1756 Edition of His Journals

Since it hath pleased our heavenly Father to protract my worthless life to such an expected period, I desire to thank Him from my inmost soul, that He hath given me to see the gospel seed, that was sown upwards of twenty years ago, now grown into a great tree.

Glory be to His holy Name! Multitudes both in England, Scotland, Wales, Ireland, and various parts of North America, have been brought to lodge under the branches of it. How far it is yet to spread can be known only to Him with whom the residue of the Spirit is.

At present, thanks be to God, the prospect is promising. A new set of instruments seem to be rising up, by whom, I trust, those that were first sent forth will not only be succeeded, but eclipsed, as the stars are succeeded and eclipsed by the rising sun. May they go on and prosper; and in the strength of their common Lord, be made happily instrumental to direct a careless unthinking world into a *holy Method* of dying unto themselves, and living unto God!

This is the only Methodism I desire to know. And that this may meet with an universal flow amongst Ministers and people of all denominations I am sure thou wilt join in praying with,

Christian Reader,

Thy ready Servant for our common Master's Sake,

G. WHITEFIELD.

London,
June 4, 1756

Although the following Account of what God has done for my soul, will undoubtedly be differently judged of by different people; yet, since I believe a single eye to God's glory moves me to write, and I find myself much pressed in spirit to publish it at this time, I am not in the least solicitous about the reception it will meet with in the world.

The benefit I have received from reading the Lives of others, the examples we have in Scripture of the sacred authors composing their own histories, and more especially the assistance I have had from the Holy Spirit, in bringing many things to my remembrance, which otherwise I would have forgotten, seemed to me reasons sufficient to justify my conduct in the sight of God and good men.

Further, as God has been pleased of late to call me to a public work, I thought His children would be glad to know how I was trained up for it. And though some may think this had been as well deferred till after my death, or written by some other person, yet I thought it might be more beneficial, and be better credited, if written with my own hand, and published whilst I was yet alive.

In the accounts of good men which I have read, I have observed that the writers of them have been partial. They have given us the bright, but not the dark side of their character. This, I think, proceeded from a kind of pious fraud, lest mentioning persons' faults should encourage others in sin. It cannot, I am sure, proceed from the wisdom which cometh from above. The sacred writers given an account of their failings as well as their virtues. Peter is not ashamed to confess that with oaths and curses he thrice denied his Master; nor do the Evangelists make any scruple of telling us, that out of Mary Magdalene Jesus Christ cast seven devils.

I have therefore endeavored to follow their good example. I have simply told what I was by nature, as well as what I am by grace. I am not over cautious as to any supposed consequences, since none can be hurt by these but such as hold the truth in unrighteousness. To the pure all things will be pure.

As I have often wished, when in my best frames, that the first years of my life might be put down as a blank, and had no more in remembrance, so I could almost wish now to pass them over in silence. But as they will, in some degree, illustrate God's dealings with me in my riper years, I shall, as I am able, give the following brief account of them.

I. FROM MY INFANCY, TILL MY BEING FOR SOME TIME AT THE UNIVERSITY

I was born in Gloucester, in the month of December, 1714. My father and mother kept the Bell Inn. The former died when I was two years old; the latter is now alive, and has often told me how she endured fourteen weeks' sickness after she brought me into the world; but was used to say, even when I was an infant, that she expected more comfort from me than any other of her children. This, with the circumstance of my being born in an inn, has been often of service to me in exciting my endeavors to make good my mother's expectations, and so follow the example of my dear

Savior, who was born in a manger belonging to an inn.

My very infant years must necessarily not be mentioned; yet I can remember such early stirrings of corruption in my heart, as abundantly convinces me that I was conceived and born in sin; that in me dwelleth no good thing by nature, and that if God had not freely prevented me by His grace, I must have been forever banished from His Divine presence.

I can truly say I was froward from my mother's womb. I was so brutish as to hate instruction, and used purposely to shun all opportunities of receiving it. I can date some very early acts of uncleanness. I soon gave pregnant proofs of an impudent temper. Lying, filthy talking, and foolish jesting I was much addicted to, even when very young. Sometimes I used to curse, if not swear. Stealing from my mother I thought no theft at all, and used to make no scruple of taking money out of her pocket before she was up. I have frequently betrayed my trust, and have more than once spent money I took in the house, in buying fruits, tarts, &c. to satisfy my sensual appetite. Numbers of Sabbaths have I broken, and generally used to behave myself very irreverently in God's sanctuary. Much money have I spent in plays, and in the common entertainments of the age. Cards, and reading romances, were my heart's delight. Often have I joined with others in playing roguish tricks, but was generally, if not always, *happily detected*. For this, I have often since, and do now bless and praise God.

It would be endless to recount the sins and offenses of my younger days. They are more in number than the hairs of my head. My heart would fail me at the remembrance of them, was I not assured that my Redeemer liveth, ever to make intercession for me. However the young man in the Gospel might boast how he had kept the commandments from his youth, with shame and confusion of face I confess that I have broken them all from my youth. Whatever foreseen fitness for salvation others may talk of and glory in, I disclaim any such thing. If I trace myself from my cradle to my manhood, I can see nothing in me but a fitness to be damned. I speak the truth in Christ, I lie not. If the Almighty had not prevented me by His grace, and wrought most powerfully upon my soul, quickening me by His free Spirit when dead in trespasses and sins, I had now either been sitting in darkness, and in the shadow of death, or condemned, as the due reward of my crimes, to be forever lifting up my eyes in torments.

But such was the free grace of God to me, that though corruption worked so strongly in my soul, and produced such early and bitter fruits, yet I can recollect very early movings of the blessed Spirit upon my heart, sufficient to satisfy me that God loved me with an everlasting love, and separated me even from my mother's womb, for the work to which He afterwards was pleased to call me.

I had some early convictions of sin; and once, I remember when some persons (as they frequently did) made it their business to tease me, I immediately retired to my room, and kneeling down, with many tears, prayed over that Psalm wherein David so often repeats these words — *"But in the Name of the Lord will I destroy them."* I was always fond of being a clergyman, used frequently to imitate the ministers reading prayers, &c. Part of the money I used to steal from my parent I gave to the poor, and some books I privately took from others, for which I have since restored fourfold, I remember were books of devotion.

My mother was very careful of my education, and always kept me in my tender years, for which I can never sufficiently thank her, from intermeddling in the least with the public business.

About the tenth year of my age, it pleased God to permit my mother to marry a second time. It proved what the world would call an unhappy match as for temporals, but God overruled it for good. It set my brethren upon thinking more than otherwise they would have done, and made an uncommon impression upon my own heart in particular.

When I was about twelve, I was placed at a school called St. Mary de Crypt, in Gloucester, — the last grammar school I ever went to. Having a good elocution and memory, I was remarked for making speeches before the corporation at their annual visitation. But I cannot say I felt any drawings of God upon my soul for a year or two, saving that I laid out some of the money that was given me on one of those forementioned occasions, in buying Ken's *Manual for Winchester Scholars* — a book that had much affected me when my brother used to read it in my mother's troubles, and which, for some time after I bought it, was of great benefit to my soul.

During the time of my being at school, I was very fond of reading plays, and have kept from school for days together to prepare myself for acting them. My master seeing how mine and my schoolfellows' vein ran, composed something of this kind for us himself, and caused me to dress myself in girls' clothes, which I had often done, to act a part before the corporation. The remembrance of this has often covered me with confusion of face, and I hope will do so, even to the end of my life.

And I cannot but here observe, with much concern of mind, how this way of training up youth has a natural tendency to debauch the mind, to raise ill passions, and to stuff the memory with things as contrary to the Gospel of Jesus Christ, as light to darkness, Heaven to Hell. However, though the first thing I had to repent of was my education in general, yet I must always acknowledge my particular thanks are due to my master, for the great pains he took with me and his other scholars, in teaching us to speak and write correctly.

Before I was fifteen, having, as I thought, made a sufficient progress in the classics, and, at the bottom, longing to be set at liberty from the confinement of a school, I one day told my mother, "Since her circumstances would not permit her to give me an University education, more learning I thought would spoil me for a tradesman; and, therefore, I judged it best not to learn Latin any longer." She at first refused to consent, but my corruptions soon got the better of her good nature. Hereupon, for some time I went to learn to write only. But my mother's circumstances being much on the decline, and being tractable that way, I from time to time began to assist her occasionally in the public-house, till at length I put on my blue apron and my snuffers, washed mops, cleaned rooms, and, in one word, became professed and common drawer for nigh a year and a half.

But He Who was with David when he was following the sheep big with young, was with me even here. For notwithstanding I was thus employed in a common inn, and had sometimes the care of the whole house upon my hands, yet I composed two or three sermons, and dedicated one of them in particular to my elder brother. One time, I remember I was much pressed to self-examination, and found myself very unwilling to look into my heart. Frequently I read the Bible when sitting up at night. Seeing the boys go by to school has often cut me to the heart. And a dear youth, now with God, would often come entreating me when serving at the bar, to go to Oxford. My general answer was, "I wish I could."

After I had continued about a year in this servile employment, my mother was obliged to leave the inn. My brother, who had been bred up for the business, married; whereupon all was made over to him; and, I, being accustomed to the house, it was agreed that I should continue there as an assistant. But God's thoughts were not as our thoughts. By His good Providence it happened that my sister-in-law and I could by no means agree; and at length the resentment grew to such a height, that my proud heart would scarce suffer me to speak to her for three weeks together. But notwithstanding I was much to blame, yet I used to retire and weep before the Lord, as Hagar when flying from her mistress Sarah — little thinking that God by this means was forcing me out of the public business, and calling me from drawing wine for drunkards, to draw water out of the wells of salvation for the refreshment of His spiritual Israel.

After continuing for a long while under this burden of mind, I at length resolved, thinking my absence would make all things easy, to go away. Accordingly, by the advice of my brother, and consent of my mother, I went to see my elder brother then settled at Bristol.

Here God was pleased to give me great foretastes of His love, and fill me with such unspeakable raptures, particularly once in St. John's Church, that I was carried out beyond myself. I felt great hungerings and thirstings after the blessed Sacrament, and wrote many letters to my mother, telling her I would never go into the public employment again. Thomas a Kempis was my great delight, and I was always impatient till the bell rang to call me to tread the courts of the Lord's House. But in the midst of these illuminations something surely whispered, "This will not last."

And, indeed, so it happened. For — oh that I could write it in tears of blood! — when I left Bristol, as I did in about two months, and returned to Gloucester, I changed my devotion with my place. Alas! all my fervor went off: I had no inclination to go to Church, or draw nigh unto God. In short, my heart, though I had so lately tasted of His love, was far from Him.

However, I had so much religion left, as to persist in my resolution not to live in the inn; and therefore my mother gave me leave, though she had but a little income, to have a bed upon the ground, and live at her house, till Providence should point out a place for me.

Having now, as I thought, nothing to do, it was a proper season for Satan to tempt me. Much of my time I spent in reading plays, and in sauntering from place to place. I was careful to adorn my body, but took little pains to deck and beautify my soul. Evil communications with my old schoolfellows soon corrupted my good manners. By seeing their evil practices, the sense of the Divine Presence I had vouchsafed unto me insensibly wore off my mind, and I at length fell into abominable secret sin, the dismal effects of which I have felt, and groaned under ever since.

But God, whose gifts and callings are without repentance, would let nothing pluck me out of His hands, though I was continually doing despite to the Spirit of Grace. He saw me with pity and compassion, when lying in my blood. He passed by me; He said unto me, *Live*; and even gave me some foresight of His providing for me.

One morning, as I was reading a play to my sister, said I, "Sister, God intends something for me which we know not of. As I have been diligent in business, I believe many would gladly have me for an apprentice, but every way seems to be barred up, so that I think God will provide for me some way or other that we cannot apprehend."

How I came to say these words I know not. God afterwards showed me they came from Him. Having thus lived with my mother for some considerable time, a young student, who was once my schoolfellow, and then a servitor of Pembroke College, Oxford, came to pay my mother a visit. Amongst other conversation, he told her how he had discharged all college expenses that quarter, and received a penny. Upon that my mother immediately cried out, "This will do for my son." Then turning to me, she said, "Will you go to Oxford, George?" I replied, "With all my heart." Whereupon, having the same friends that this young student had, my mother, without delay, waited on them. They promised their interest to get me a servitor's place in the same college. She then applied to my old master, who much approved of my coming to school again.

In about a week I went and re-entered myself, and being grown much in stature, my master addressed me thus: "I see, George, you are advanced in stature, but your better part must needs have gone backwards." This made me blush. He set me something to translate into Latin; and though I had made no application to my classics for so long a time, yet I had but one inconsiderable fault in my exercises. This, I believe, somewhat surprised my master then, and has afforded me matter of thanks and praise ever since.

Being resettled at school, I spared no pains to go forward in my book. God was pleased to give me His blessing, and I learned much faster than I did before. But all this while I continued in secret sin; and, at length, got acquainted with such a set of debauched, abandoned, atheistical youths, that if God, by His free, unmerited, and especial grace, had not delivered me out of their hands, I should have long since sat in the scorner's chair, and made a mock at sin. By keeping company with them, my thoughts of religion grew more and more like theirs. I went to public service only to make sport and walk about. I took pleasure in their lewd conversation. I began to reason as they did, and to ask why God had given me passions, and not permitted me to gratify them? Not considering that God did not originally give us these *corrupt* passions, and that He had promised help to withstand them, if we would ask it of Him. In short, I soon made a great proficiency in the school of the Devil. I affected to look rakish, and was in a fair way of being as infamous as the worst of them.

But, oh stupendous love! God even here stopped me, when running on in a full career to hell. For, just as I was upon the brink of ruin, He gave me such a distaste of their principles and practices, that I discovered them to my master, who soon put a stop to their proceedings.

Being thus delivered out of the snare of the Devil, I began to be more and more serious, and felt God at different times working powerfully and convincingly upon my soul. One day in particular, as I was coming downstairs, and overheard my friends speaking well of me, God so deeply convicted me of hypocrisy, that though I had formed frequent but ineffectual resolutions before, yet I had then power given me over my secret and darling sin. Notwithstanding, some time after being overtaken in liquor, as I have been twice or thrice in my lifetime, Satan gained his usual advantage over me again, — an experimental proof to my poor soul, how that wicked one makes use of men as machines, working them up to just what he pleases, when by intemperance they have chased away the Spirit of God from them.

Being now near the seventeenth year of my age, I was resolved to prepare myself for the holy Sacrament, which I received on Christmas Day. I began now to be more and more watchful over my thoughts, words, and actions. I kept the following Lent, fasting Wednesday and Friday thirty-six hours together. My evenings, when I had done waiting upon my mother, were generally spent in acts of devotion, reading *Drelincourt on Death*, and other practical books, and I constantly went to public worship twice a day. Being now upper-boy, by God's help I made some reformation amongst my schoolfellows. I was very diligent in reading and learning the classics, and in studying my Greek Testament, but was not yet convinced of the absolute unlawfulness of playing at cards, and of reading and seeing plays, though I began to have some scruples about it.

Near this time I dreamed that I was to see God on Mount Sinai, but was afraid to meet Him. This made a great impression upon me; and a gentlewoman to whom I told it, said, "George, this is a call from God."

Still I grew more serious after this dream; but yet hypocrisy crept into every action. As once I affected to look more rakish, I now strove to appear more grave than I really was. However, an uncommon concern and alteration was visible in my behavior, and I often used to find fault with the lightness of others.

One night, as I was going on an errand for my mother, an unaccountable, but very strong impression was made upon my heart that I should preach quickly. When I came home, I innocently told my mother what had befallen me; but she, like Joseph's parents, when he told them his dream, turned short upon me, crying out, "What does the boy mean? Prithee hold thy tongue," or something to that purpose. God has since shown her from Whom that impression came.

For a twelve month, I went on in a round of duties, receiving the Sacrament monthly, fasting frequently, attending constantly on public worship, and praying often more than twice a day in private. One of my brothers used to tell me, he feared this would not hold long, and that I should forget all when I came to Oxford. This caution did me much service, for it set me upon praying for perseverance; and, under God, the preparation I made in the country was a preservative against the manifold temptations which beset me at my first coming to that seat of learning.

Being now near eighteen years old, it was judged proper for me to go to the University. God had sweetly prepared my way. The friends before applied to recommended me to the Master of Pembroke College. Another friend took us 10 pounds upon bond, which I have since repaid, to defray the first expense of entering; and the Master, contrary to all expectations, admitted me servitor immediately.

Soon after my admission I went and resided, and found my having been used to a public-house was now of service to me. For many of the servitors being sick at my first coming up, by my diligent and ready attendance, I ingratiated myself into the gentlemen's favor so far, that many, who had it in their power, chose me to be their servitor.

This much lessened my expense; and indeed, God was so gracious, that with the profits of my place, and some little presents made me by my kind tutor, for almost the first three years I did not put all my relations together to above 24 pounds expense. And it has often grieved my soul to see so many young students spending their substance in extravagant living, and thereby entirely unfitting themselves for the prosecution of their studies.

I had not been long at the University, before I found the benefit of the foundation I had laid in the country for a holy life. I was quickly solicited to join in their excess of riot with several who lay in the same room. God, in answer to prayers before put up, gave me grace to withstand them; and once in particular, it being cold, my limbs were so benumbed by sitting alone in my study, because I would not go out amongst them, that I could scarce sleep all night. But I soon found the benefit of not yielding: for when they perceived they could not prevail, they let me alone as a singular odd fellow.

All this while I was not fully satisfied of the sin of playing at cards and reading plays, till God upon a fast-day was pleased to convince me. For, taking a play, to read a passage out of it to a friend, God struck my heart with such power, that I was obliged to lay it down again; and, blessed be His Name, I have not read any such book since.

Before I went to the University, I met with Mr. Law's *Serious Call to a Devout Life*, but had not then money to purchase it. Soon after my coming up to the University, seeing a small edition of it in a friend's hand, I soon procured it. God worked powerfully upon my soul, as He has since upon many others, by that and his other excellent treatise upon *Christian Perfection*.

I now began to pray and sing psalms thrice every day, besides morning and evening, and to fast every Friday, and to receive the Sacrament at a parish church near our college, and at the castle, where the despised Methodists used to receive once a month.

The young men so called were then much talked of at Oxford. I had heard of, and loved them before I came to the University; and so strenuously defended them when I heard them reviled by the students, that they began to think that I also in time should be one of them.

For above a year my soul longed to be acquainted with some of them, and I was strongly pressed to follow their good example, when I saw them go through a ridiculing crowd to receive the Holy Eucharist at St. Mary's. At length, God was pleased to open a door. It happened that a poor woman in one of the workhouses had attempted to cut her throat, but was happily prevented. Upon hearing of this, and knowing that both the Mr. Wesleys were ready to every good work, I sent a poor apple-woman of our college to inform Mr. Charles Wesley of it, charging her not to discover who sent her. She went; but, contrary to my orders, told my name. He having heard of my coming to the castle and a parish-church sacrament, and having met me frequently walking by myself, followed the woman when she was gone away, and sent an invitation to me by her, to come to breakfast with him the next morning.

I thankfully embraced the opportunity; and, blessed be God! it was one of the most profitable visits I ever made in my life. My soul, at that time, was athirst for some spiritual friends to lift up my hands when they hung down, and to strengthen my feeble knees. He soon discovered it, and, like a wise winner of souls, made all his discourses tend that way. And when he had put into my hands Professor Francke's treatise *Against the Fear of Man*, and a book, entitled, *The Country Parson's Advice to His Parishioners* (the last of which was wonderfully blessed to my soul) I took my leave.

In a short time he let me have another book, entitled, *The Life of God in the Soul of Man*; and, though I had fasted, watched and prayed, and received the Sacrament so long, yet I never knew what true religion was, till God sent me that excellent treatise by the hands of my never-to-be-forgotten friend.

At my first reading it, I wondered what the author meant by saying, "That some falsely placed religion in going to church, doing hurt to no one, being constant in the duties of the closet, and now and then reaching out their hands to give alms to their poor neighbors," "Alas!" thought I, "if this be not true religion, what is?" God soon showed me; for in reading a few lines further, that "true religion was union of the soul with God, and Christ formed within us," a ray of Divine light was instantaneously darted in upon my soul, and from that moment, but not till then, did I know that I must be a new creature.

Upon this, like the woman of Samaria, when Christ revealed Himself to her at the well I had no rest in my soul till I wrote letters to my relations, telling them there was such a thing as the new birth. I imagined they would have gladly received it. But, alas! my words seemed to them as idle tales. They thought that I was going beside myself, and by their letters, confirmed me in the resolutions I had taken not to go down into the country, but continue where I was, lest that, by any means the good work which God had begun in my soul might be made of none effect.

From time to time Mr. Wesley permitted me to come unto him, and instructed me as I was able to bear it. By degrees he introduced me to the rest of his Christian brethren. They built me up daily in the knowledge and fear of God, and taught me to endure hardness like a good soldier of Jesus Christ.

I now began, like them, to live by rule, and to pick up the very fragments of my time, that not a moment of it might be lost. Whether I ate or drank, or whatsoever I did, I endeavored to do all to the glory of God. Like them, having no weekly sacrament, although the Rubric required it, at our own college, I received every Sunday at Christ Church. I joined with them in keeping the stations by fasting Wednesdays and Fridays and left no means unused, which I thought would lead me nearer to Jesus Christ.

Regular retirement, morning and evening, at first I found some difficulty in submitting to; but it soon grew profitable and delightful. As I grew ripe for such exercises, I was from time to time engaged to visit the sick and the prisoners, and to read to poor people, till I made it a custom, as most of us did, to spend an hour every day in doing acts of charity.

The course of my studies I soon entirely changed. Whereas, before, I was busied in studying the dry sciences, and books that went no farther than the surface, I now resolved to read only such as entered into the heart of religion, and which led me directly into an experimental knowledge of Jesus Christ, and Him crucified. The lively oracles of God were my soul's delight. The book of the Divine laws was seldom out of my hands: I meditated therein day and night; and ever since that, God has made my way signally prosperous, and given me abundant success.

God enabled me to do much good to many, as well as to receive much from the despised Methodists, and made me instrumental in converting one who is lately come into the Church, and, I trust, will prove a burning and a shining light.

Several short fits of illness was God pleased to visit and to try me with after my first acquaintance with Mr. Wesley. My new convert was a help-meet for me in those and in all other circumstances; and, in company with him, and several other Christian friends, did I spend many sweet and delightful hours. Never did persons, I believe, strive more earnestly to enter in at the strait gate. They kept their bodies under even to an extreme. They were dead to the world, and willing to be accounted as the dung and offscouring of all things, so that they might win Christ. Their hearts glowed with the love of God, and they never prospered so much in the inward man, as when they had all manner of evil spoken against them falsely without.

Many came amongst them for a while, who, in time of temptation, fell away. The displeasure of a tutor or Head of a College, the changing of a gown from a lower to a higher degree — above all, a thirst for the praise of men, more than that which cometh from God, and servile fear of contempt — caused numbers that had set their hand to the plough, shamefully to look back. The world, and not themselves, gave them the title of Methodists, I suppose, from their custom of regulating their time, and planning the business of the day every morning. Mr. John and Charles

Wesley, were two of the first that thus openly dared to confess Christ; and they, under God, were the spiritual fathers of most of them. They had the pleasure of seeing the work of the Lord prosper in their hands before they went to Georgia. Since their return, the small grain of mustard-seed has sprung up apace. It has taken deep root. It is growing into a great tree. Ere long, I trust, it will fill the land, and numbers of souls will come from the East and from the West, from the North and from the South, and lodge under the branches of it.

But to return. Whilst I was thus comforted on every side, by daily conversing with so many Christian friends, God was pleased to permit Satan to sift me like wheat. A general account of which I shall, by the Divine assistance, give in the following section.

II.   A BRIEF AND SUMMARY ACCOUNT OF MY TEMPTATIONS

At my first setting out, in compassion to my weakness, I grew in favor both with God and man, and used to be much lifted up with sensible devotion, especially at the blessed Sacrament. But when religion began to take root in my heart, and I was fully convinced my soul must totally be renewed ere it could see God, I was visited with outward and inward trials.

The first thing I was called to give up for God was what the world calls my fair reputation. I had no sooner received the sacrament publicly on a week-day at St. Mary's, but I was set up as a mark for all the polite students that knew me to shoot at. By this they knew that I was commenced Methodist; for though there is a sacrament at the beginning of every term, at which all, especially the seniors, are by statute, obliged to be present, yet so dreadfully has that once faithful city played the harlot, that very few Masters, and no undergraduates but the Methodists, attended upon it.

Mr. Charles Wesley, whom I must always mention with the greatest deference and respect, walked with me, in order to confirm me, from the church even to the college. I confess, to my shame, I would gladly have excused him; and the next day, going to his room, one of our Fellows passing by, I was ashamed to be seen to knock at his door. But, blessed be God! this fear of man gradually wore off. As I had imitated Nicodemus in his cowardice, so, by the Divine assistance, I followed him in his courage. I confessed the Methodists more and more publicly every day. I walked openly with them, and chose rather to bear contempt with those people of God, than to enjoy the applause of almost-Christians for a season.

Soon after this, I incurred the displeasure of the Master of the College, who frequently chid, and once threatened to expel me, if I ever visited the poor again. Being surprised at this treatment, and overawed by his authority, I spake unadvisedly with my lips, and said, if it displeased him, I would not. My conscience soon pricked me for this sinful compliance. I immediately repented, and visited the poor the first opportunity, and told my companions, if ever I was called to a stake for Christ's sake, I would serve my tongue as Archbishop Cranmer served his hand, viz., make that burn first.

My tutor, being a moderate man, did not oppose me much, but thought, I believe, that I went a little too far. He lent me books, gave me money, visited me, and furnished me with a physician when sick. In short, he behaved in all respects like a father; and I trust God will remember him for good, in answer to the many prayers I have put up in his behalf.

My relations were quickly alarmed at the alteration of my behavior, conceived strong prejudices against me, and, for some time, counted my life madness. I daily underwent some contempt at college. Some have thrown dirt at me; others, by degrees, took away their pay from me; and two friends, that were dear unto me, grew shy of and forsook me, when they saw me resolved to deny myself, take up my cross daily, and follow Jesus Christ. But our Lord, by His Spirit, soon convinced me that I must know no one after the flesh; and I soon found that promise literally fulfilled, "That no one hath left father or mother, brethren or sisters, houses or lands, for Christ's sake and the Gospel's, but he shall receive a hundredfold in this life, with persecutions, as well as eternal life in the world to come."

These, though little, were useful trials. They inured me to contempt, lessened self-love, and taught me to die daily. My inward sufferings were of a more uncommon nature. Satan seemed to have desired me in particular to sift me as wheat. God permitted him, for wise reasons I have seen already, *viz.*, that His future blessings might not prove my ruin.

From my first awakenings to the Divine life, I felt a particular hungering and thirsting after the humility of Jesus Christ. Night and day I prayed to be a partaker of that grace, imagining that the habit of humility would be instantaneously infused into my soul. But as Gideon taught the men of Succoth with thorns, so God, if I am yet in any measure blessed with true poverty of spirit, taught it me by the exercise of strong temptations.

I observed before how I used to be favored with sensible devotion; those comforts were soon withdrawn, and a horrible fearfulness and dread permitted to overwhelm my soul. One morning in particular, rising from my bed, I felt an unusual impression and weight upon my breast, attended with inward darkness. I applied to my friend, Mr. Charles Wesley. He advised me to keep upon my watch, and referred me to a chapter in Kempis.

In a short time I perceived this load gradually increase, till it almost weighed me down, and fully convinced me that Satan had as real possession of, and power given over, my body, as he had once over Job's. All power of meditating, or even thinking, was taken from me. My memory quite failed me. My whole soul was barren and dry, and I could fancy myself to be like nothing so much as a man locked up in iron armor.

Whenever I kneeled down, I felt great heavings in my body, and have often prayed under the weight of them till the sweat came through me. At this time, Satan used to terrify me much, and threatened to punish me if I discovered his wiles. It being my duty, as servitor, in my turn to knock at the gentlemen's rooms by ten at night, to see who were in their rooms, I thought the Devil would appear to me every stair I went up. And he so troubled me when I lay down to rest, that for some weeks I scarce slept above three hours at a time.

God only knows how many nights I have lain upon my bed groaning under the weight I felt, and bidding Satan depart from me in the Name of Jesus. Whole days and weeks have I spent in lying prostrate on the ground, and begging for freedom from those proud hellish thoughts that used to crowd in upon and distract my soul. But God made Satan drive out Satan; for these thoughts and suggestions created such a self-abhorrence within me, that I never ceased wrestling with God, till He blessed me with a victory over them. Self-love, self-will, pride and envy, so buffeted me in their turns, that I was resolved either to die or conquer. I wanted to see sin as it was, but feared, at the same time, lest the sight of it should terrify me to death.

Whilst my inward man was thus exercised, my outward man was not unemployed. I soon found what a slave I had been to my sensual appetite, and now resolved to get the mastery over it by the help of Jesus Christ. Accordingly by degrees, I began to leave off eating fruits and such like, and gave the money I usually spent in that way to the poor. Afterward, I always chose the worst sort of food, though my place furnished me with variety. I fasted twice a week. My apparel was mean. I thought it unbecoming a penitent to have his hair powdered. I wore woollen gloves, a patched gown and dirty shoes; and though I was then convinced that the Kingdom of God did not consist in meats and drinks, yet I resolutely persisted in these voluntary acts of self-denial, because I found them great promoters of the spiritual life.

For many months, I went on in this state, faint, yet pursuing, and travelling along in the dark, in hope that the Star I had before once seen, would hereafter appear again. During this season I was very active but finding pride creeping in at the end of almost every thought, word, and action, and meeting with Castaniza's *Spiritual Combat*, in which he says, "that he that is employed in mortifying his will was as well employed as though he were converting Indians," or words to that effect, Satan so imposed upon my understanding, that he persuaded me to shut myself up in my study, till I could do good with a single eye, lest, in endeavoring to save others, as I did now, I should, at last, by pride and self-complacence, lose myself.

Henceforward, he transformed himself into an angel of light, and worked so artfully, that I imagined the good, and not the evil spirit suggested to me every thing that I did.

His main drift was to lead me into a state of quietism, (he generally ploughed with God's heifer); and when the Holy Spirit put into my heart good thoughts or convictions, he always drove them to extremes. For instance, having out of pride, put down in my diary what I gave away, Satan tempted me to lay my diary quite aside. When Castaniza advised to talk but little, Satan said I must not talk at all. So that I, who used to be the most forward in exhorting my companions, have sat whole nights almost without speaking at all. Again, when Castaniza advised to endeavor after a silent recollection and waiting upon God, Satan told me I must leave off all forms, and not use my voice in prayer at all. The time would fail me to recount all the instances of this kind in which he had deceived me. But when matters came to an extreme, God always showed me my error, and by His Spirit, pointed out a way for me to escape.

The Devil also sadly imposed upon me in the matter of my college exercises. Whenever I endeavored to compose my theme, I had no power to write a word, nor so much as tell my Christian friends of my inability to do it. Saturday being come, which is the day the students give up their compositions, it was suggested to me that I must go down into the Hall, and confess I could not make a theme, and so publicly suffer, as if it were for my Master's sake. When the bell rung to call us, I went to open the door to go down stairs, but feeling something give me a violent inward check, I entered my study, and continued instant in prayer, waiting the event. For this my tutor fined me half-a-crown. The next week Satan served me in like manner again; but now having got more strength, and perceiving no inward check, I went into the Hall. My name being called, I stood up, and told my tutor I could not make a theme. I think he fined me a second time; but, imagining that I would not willingly neglect my exercise, he afterwards called me into the Common Room, and kindly enquired whether any misfortune had befallen me, or what was the reason I could not make a theme. I burst into tears, and assured him that it was not out of contempt of authority, but that I could not act otherwise. Then, at length he said, he believed I could not; and when he left me, told a friend, as he very well might, that he took me to be really mad. This friend hearing from my tutor what had happened, came to me urging the command of Scripture, to be subject to the higher powers. I answered, "Yes; but I had a new revelation." Lord, what is man?

As I daily got strength, by continued, though almost silent, prayer, in my study, my temptations grew stronger also, particularly for two or three days before deliverance came.

Near five or six weeks I had now spent in my study, except when I was obliged to go out. During this time I was fighting with my corruptions, and did little else besides kneeling down by my bedside, feeling, as it were, a heavy pressure upon my body, as well as an unspeakable oppression of mind, yet offering up my soul to God, to do with me as it pleased Him. It was now suggested to me, that Jesus Christ was amongst the wild beasts when He was tempted, and that I ought to follow His example; and being willing, as I thought, to imitate Jesus Christ, after supper I went into Christ Church Walk, near our College, and continued in silent prayer under one of the trees for near two hours, sometimes lying flat on my face, sometimes kneeling upon my knees, all the while filled with fear and concern lest some of my brethren should be overwhelmed with pride. The night being stormy, it gave me awful thoughts of the Day of Judgment. I continued, I think till the great bell rung for retirement to the college, not without finding some reluctance in the natural man against staying so long in the cold.

The next night I repeated the same exercise at the same place. But the hour of extremity being now come, God was pleased to make an open show of those diabolical devices by which I had been deceived.

By this time, I had left off keeping my diary, using my forms, or scarce my voice in prayer, visiting the prisoners, &c. Nothing remained for me to leave, unless I forsook public worship, but my religious friends. Now it was suggested that I must leave them also for Christ's sake. This was a sore trial; but rather than not be, as I fancied, Christ's disciple, I resolved to renounce them, though as dear to me as my own soul. Accordingly, the next day being Wednesday, whereon we kept one of our weekly fasts, instead of meeting with my brethren as usual, I went out into the fields, and prayed silently by myself. Our evening meeting I neglected also, and went not to breakfast, according to appointment, with Mr. Charles Wesley the day following. This, with many other concurring circumstances, made my honored friend, Mr. Charles Wesley, suspect something more than ordinary was the matter. He came to my room, soon found out my case, apprised me of my danger if I would not take advice, and recommended me to his brother John, Fellow of Lincoln College, as more experienced in the spiritual life. God gave me — blessed be His Holy Name — a teachable temper, I waited upon his brother, with whom from that time I had the honor of growing intimate. He advised me to resume all my externals, though not to depend on them in the least. From time to time he gave me directions as my various and pitiable state required; and, at length, by his excellent advice and management of me, under God, I was delivered from those wiles of Satan. Praise the Lord, O my soul, and all that is within me praise His Holy Name!

During this and all other seasons of temptation my soul was inwardly supported with great courage and resolution from above. Every day God made me willing to renew the combat, and though my soul, when quite empty of God, was very prone to seek satisfaction in the creature, and sometimes I fell into sensuality, yet I was generally enabled to wait in silence for the salvation of God, or to persist in prayer, till some beams of spiritual light and comfort were vouchsafed me from on high. Thomas a Kempis, since translated and published by Mr. John Wesley; Castaniza's *Combat*; and the Greek Testament, every reading of which I endeavored to turn into a prayer, were of great help and furtherance to me. On receiving the holy Sacrament, especially before trials, I have found grace in a very affecting manner, and in abundant measure, sometimes imparted to my soul, — an irrefragable proof to me of the miserable delusion of the author of that work called, *The Plain Account of the Sacrament*, which sinks that holy ordinance into a bare memorial, who, if he obstinately refuse the instruction of the Most High, will doubtless, without repentance, bear his punishment, whosoever he be.

To proceed — I had now taken up my externals again and though Satan for some weeks had been biting my heel, God was pleased to show me that I should soon bruise his head. A few days after, as I was walking along, I met with a poor woman, whose husband was then in Bocardo, or Oxford Town-Jail, which I constantly visited. Seeing her much discomposed, I enquired the cause. She told me, not being able to bear the crying of her children, ready to perish for hunger, and having nothing to relieve them, she had been to drown herself, but was mercifully prevented, and said she was coming to my room to inform me of it. I gave her some immediate relief, and desired her to meet me at the prison with her husband in the afternoon. She came, and there God visited them both by His free grace. She was powerfully quickened from above; and when I had done reading, he also came to me like the trembling jailer, and, grasping my hand, cried out, "I am upon the brink of hell!" From this time forward, both of them grew in grace. God, by His providence, soon delivered him from his confinement. Though notorious offenders against God and one another before, yet now they became help-meet for each other in the great work of their salvation. They are both now living, and, I trust, will be my joy and crown of rejoicing in the great day of our Lord Jesus.

Soon after this, the holy season of Lent came on, which our friends kept very strictly, eating no flesh during the six weeks, except on Saturdays also, and ate nothing on the other days, except on Sunday, but sage-tea without sugar, and coarse bread. I constantly walked out in the cold mornings till part of one of my hands was quite black. This, with my continued abstinence, and inward conflicts, at length so emaciated my body, that, at Passion-week, finding I could scarce creep upstairs, I was obliged to inform my kind tutor of my condition, who immediately sent for a physician to me.

This caused no small triumph amongst the collegians, who began to cry out, "What is his fasting come to now?" But I rejoiced in this reproach, knowing that, though I had been imprudent, and lost much of my flesh, yet, I had nevertheless increased in the Spirit.

This fit of sickness continued upon me for seven weeks, and a glorious visitation it was. The blessed Spirit was all this time purifying my soul. All my former gross and notorious, and even my heart sins also, were now set home upon me, of which I wrote down some remembrance immediately, and confessed them before God morning and evening. Though weak, I often spent two hours in my evening retirements, and prayed over my Greek Testament and Bishop Hall's most excellent *Contemplations*, every hour that my health would permit. About the end of the seven weeks, and after I had been groaning under an unspeakable pressure both of body and mind for above a year, God was pleased to set me free in the following manner. One day, perceiving an uncommon drought and a disagreeable clamminess in my mouth and using things to allay my thirst, but in vain, it was suggested to me, that when Jesus Christ cried out, "I thirst," His sufferings were near at an end. Upon which I cast myself down on the bed, crying out, "I thirst! I thirst!" Soon after this, I found and felt in myself that I was delivered from the burden that has so heavily oppressed me. The spirit of mourning was taken from me, and I knew what it was truly to rejoice in God my Savior; and, for some time, could not avoid singing psalms wherever I was; but my joy gradually became more settled, and, blessed be God, has abode and increased in my soul, saving a few casual intermissions, ever since.

Thus were the days of my mourning ended. After a long night of desertion and temptation, the Star, which I had seen at a distance before, began to appear again, and the Day Star arose in my heart. Now did the Spirit of God take possession of my soul, and, as I humbly hope, seal me unto the day of redemption.

III. From the Time of My First Leaving the University to go to Gloucester, till the time of my Ordination

As fast as I got strength after my sickness, my tutor, physician, and some others were still urging me to go into the country, hoping thereby to divert me, as they thought, from a too intense application to religion. I had for some time been aware of their design, and wrote letters beseeching my mother, if she valued my soul, not to lay her commands on me to come down. She was pleased to leave me to my choice; but, finding at last it was necessary for my health, and many other providential circumstances pointing out my way, after earnest prayer for support, by the advice of my friends, I left my sweet retirement at Oxford, and went to Gloucester, the place of my nativity.

Having now obtained mercy from God, and received the Spirit of Adoption in my heart, my friends were surprised to see me look and behave so cheerfully, after the many reports they had heard concerning me. However, I soon found myself to be as a sheep sent forth amongst wolves in sheep's clothing; for they immediately endeavored to dissuade me, as they had lately done a friend that began with me, from a constant use of the means of grace, especially from weekly abstinence, and receiving the blessed Sacrament. But God enabled me to resist them steadfast in the faith; and, by keeping close to Him in His holy ordinances, I was made to triumph over all.

Being unaccustomed for some time to live without spiritual companions, and finding none who would join heartily with me — no, not one, — I watched unto prayer all the day long, beseeching God to raise me some religious associates in His own way and time.

"I will endeavor either to find or make a friend," had been my resolution now for some time; and therefore, after importunate prayer one day, I resolved to go to the house of one Mrs. W......., to whom I had formerly read Plays, *Spectators*, Pope's *Homer*, and such-like trifling books — hoping the alteration she would now find in my sentiments might, under God, influence her soul. God was pleased to bless the visit with the desired effect. She received the Word gladly. She wanted to be taught the way of God more perfectly, and soon became a fool for Christ's sake. Not long after, God made me instrumental to awaken several young persons, who soon formed themselves into a little Society, and had quickly the honor of being despised at Gloucester, as we had been before them at Oxford. Thus, *all* that will live godly in Christ Jesus, must suffer persecution.

My mind being now more open and enlarged, I began to read the Holy Scriptures upon my knees, laying aside all other books, and praying over, if possible, every line and word. This proved meat indeed, and drink indeed, to my soul. I daily received fresh life, light, and power from above. I got more true knowledge from reading the Book of God in one month, than I could *ever* have acquired from *all* the writings of men. In one word, I found it profitable for reproof, for correction, for instruction in righteousness, every way sufficient to make the man of God perfect, throughly furnished unto every good word and work.

During my absence from Oxford I spent three weeks at Bristol, whither I went to see some relations, but could not do them much good, because of the prejudices they had conceived against me. However, I daily walked with God, and going to visit an aunt then in an almshouse there, God brought in my way a young woman who was hungering and thirsting after righteousness. She received the Word into an honest and good heart, and since has proved a true follower of Jesus Christ. So gracious was the Lord, even in these my very early days, not to leave Himself without witness, in that He *thus* vouchsafed to bless my poor endeavors in *every* place whereto His providence now sent me.

According to His abundant mercy, He also raised me up some temporal supplies. For some considerable time, I had followed the example of Professor Frank, and whenever I wanted any worldly assistance, pleaded the Scripture promises for the things of this life, as well as that which is to come, in the Name of Jesus Christ. This is still my practice, and I never yet failed of success. When I came from Oxford, on account of my sickness, and other extraordinary and unavoidable expenses, I owed, I think, about 12 or 13 pounds; and when I went to Bristol, I was so poor that I was obliged to borrow money of my kind hostess, Mrs. H....., with whom I lodged at Gloucester, — and whose husband and family I pray God eternally to bless, — to bear my charges on the road. This, I bless God, did not dishearten me; but I continued pleading the promises in the Name of Christ; and soon after my coming to Bristol, I received an answer. For, a brother of mine coming from the sea, God inclined him to give me four guineas and some other necessaries. And when I returned to Gloucester, as I did after I had continued a short time at Bristol, those I expected should assist me, did not; but persons I never spoke to, and who, I thought, were my enemies, were raised up to supply my wants, and fulfill that promise which I always pleaded, "Seek first the Kingdom of God and His Righteousness, and all these things shall be added unto you."

Oh, what sweet communion had I daily vouchsafed with God in prayer after my coming again to Gloucester! How often have I been carried out beyond myself when sweetly meditating in the fields! How assuredly have I felt that Christ dwelt in me, and I in Him! and how did I daily walk in the comforts of the Holy Ghost, and was edified and refreshed in the multitude of peace! Not that I was always upon the mount; sometimes a cloud would overshadow me; but the Sun of Righteousness quickly arose and dispelled it, and I knew it was Jesus Christ that revealed Himself to my soul.

I always observed, as my inward strength increased, so my outward sphere of action increased proportionably. In a short time, therefore, I began to read to some poor people twice or thrice a week. I likewise visited two other little Societies besides my own; and almost every day, both then and since, have found the benefit of being tempted myself, because that alone taught me how to give proper advice to those that came to me when tempted.

Occasionally, as business and opportunity permitted, I generally visited one or two sick persons every day; and though silver and gold I had little of my own, yet, in imitation of my Lord's disciples, who entreated in the behalf of the fainting multitude, I used to pray unto Him, and He, from time to time, inclined several that were rich in this world to give me money, so that I generally had a little stock for the poor always in my hand. One of the poor whom I visited in this manner was called effectually by God as at the eleventh hour. She was a woman above three score years old, and, I really believe, died in the true faith of Jesus Christ.

About this time God was pleased to enlighten my soul, and bring me into the knowledge of His free grace, and the necessity of being justified in His sight by *faith only*. This was more extraordinary, because my friends at Oxford had rather inclined to the mystic divinity; and one of them, a dear servant of the Lord, lately confessed he did not like me so well at Oxford, as the rest of his brethren, because I held justification by faith *only*. And yet, he observed, I had most success. But, blessed be God! most of us have now been taught this doctrine of Christ, and, I hope, shall be willing to die in the defense of it. It is the good old doctrine of the Church of England. It is what the holy martyrs in Queen Mary's time sealed with their blood, and which I pray God, if need be, that I and my brethren may seal with ours.

Burkitt's and Henry's *Expositions* were of admirable use to lead me into this, and all other Gospel truths. For many months have I been almost always upon my knees, to study and pray over these books. The Holy Spirit, from time to time, has led me into the knowledge of Divine things, and I have been directed, by watching and reading the Scripture in this manner, even in the minutest circumstances, as plainly as the Jews were, when consulting the Urim and Thummin at the High Priest's breast.

Alleine's *Alarm*, Baxter's *Call to the Unconverted*, and Janeway's *Life*, which I read at leisure hours, much benefited me. I bless God, the partition wall of bigotry and sect-religion was soon broken down in my heart; for, as soon as the love of God was shed abroad in my soul, I loved all of whatsoever denomination, who loved the Lord Jesus in sincerity of heart.

During my stay here, God enabled me to give a public testimony of my repentance as to seeing and acting plays. For, hearing the Strollers were coming to town, and knowing what an egregious offender I had been, I wrestled with God in prayer to put me in a way to manifest my abhorrence of my former sin and folly. In answer to this, I was stirred up to extract Mr. Law's excellent treatise, entitled *The Absolute Unlawfulness of the Stage Entertainment*. God gave me favor in the printer's sight; and, at my request, he put a little of it in the *News* for six weeks successively, and God was pleased to give it His blessing.

Having been absent for about six months from the University, I thought it time to think of returning thither; but before I came to a resolution, was convinced of the contrary.

At my first coming to Gloucester, being used to visit the prisoners at Oxford, I prayed most earnestly that God would open a door for me to visit the prisoners here also. Quickly after, I dreamed that one of the prisoners came to be instructed by me; and it was impressed much upon my heart. In the morning I went to the door of the County Jail. I knocked, but nobody came to open it. I thought the hour was not yet come. I waited still upon God in prayer, and in some months after came a letter from a friend at Oxford, desiring me to go to one Pebworth, who had broken out of Oxford Jail, and was retaken at Gloucester. As soon as I read this letter, it appeared to me that my prayer was now answered. Immediately I went to the prison, assuredly gathering that the Lord called me thither. I met with the person, and finding him and some others willing to hear the Word of God, and having gained leave of the keeper and two ordinaries, I constantly read to and prayed with them every day I was in town. I also begged money for them, whereby I was enabled to release some of them, and cause provision to be distributed weekly amongst them, as also to put such books into their hands as I judged most proper. I cannot say any one of the prisoners was effectually wrought upon; however, much evil was prevented, many were convinced, and my own soul was much edified and strengthened in the love of God and man.

Thus employed, I continued in my own city three months longer — despised indeed by man, but highly blessed by the grace of God. My understanding was enlightened, my will broken, and my affections more and more enlivened with a zeal for Christ. Many such, I believe, were added to our little Society as shall be saved. Fresh supplies came from unexpected hands to defray my expenses at the University; and, at the end of nine months I returned thither, to the mutual joy and comfort of my friends, till I was called to enter into Holy Orders — the particular circumstances of which I shall relate in the following section.

IV. MY PREPARATION FOR HOLY ORDERS

From the time I first entered at the University, especially from the time I knew what was true and undefiled Christianity, I entertained high thoughts of the importance of the ministerial office, and was not solicitous what place should be prepared for me, but how I should be prepared for a place. The saying of the Apostle, "Not a novice, lest being puffed up with pride, he fall into the condemnation of the Devil"; and that first question of our excellent Ordination Office, "Do you trust that you are *inwardly* moved by the Holy Ghost to take upon you this office and administration?" used even to make me tremble whenever I thought of entering into the ministry. The shyness that Moses and some other prophets expressed, when God sent them out in a public capacity, I thought was sufficient to teach me not to run till I was called. He Who knoweth the hearts of men, is witness that I never prayed more earnestly against anything than I did against entering into the service of the Church *so soon*. Oftentimes I have been in an agony in prayer, when under convictions of my insufficiency for so great a work. With strong cryings and tears I have often said, "Lord, I am a youth of uncircumcised lips; Lord, send me not into Thy vineyard yet!" And sometimes I had reason to think God was angry with me for resisting His will. However, I was resolved to pray *thus* as long as I could. If God did not grant my request in keeping me out of it, I knew His grace would be sufficient to support and strengthen me whenever He sent me into the ministry.

To my prayers I added my endeavors, and wrote letters to my friends at Oxford, beseeching them to pray God to disappoint the designs of my country friends, who were for my taking Orders as soon as possible. Their answer was, "Pray we the Lord of the harvest to send thee and many more laborers into His harvest." Another old and worthy minister of Christ, when I wrote to him about the meaning of the word *novice*, answered, it meant a novice in grace, and not in years; and he was pleased to add, if St. Paul were then at Gloucester, he believed St. Paul would ordain me. All this did not satisfy me. I still continued instant in prayer against going into Holy Orders, and was not thoroughly convinced it was the Divine will, till God, by His providence, brought me acquainted with the present Bishop of Gloucester.

Before I conversed with his lordship, God was pleased to give me previous notice of it. Long ere I had the least prospect of being called before the bishop, I dreamed, one night, I was talking with him in his palace, and that he gave me some gold, which seemed to sound again in my hand. Afterwards this dream would often come into my mind; and whenever I saw the bishop at church, a strong persuasion would arise in my mind that I should very shortly go to him. I always checked it, and prayed to God to preserve me from ever desiring that honor which cometh of man. One afternoon it happened that the bishop took a solitary walk, as I was told afterwards, to Lady Selwyn's, near Gloucester, who, not long before, had made me a present of a piece of gold. She, I found, recommended me to the bishop; and, a few days after, as I was coming from the cathedral prayers, thinking of no such thing, one of the vergers called after me, and said, the bishop desired to speak with me. I, forgetful at that time of my dream immediately turned back, considering within myself what I had done to deserve his lordship's displeasure. When I came to the top of the palace stairs, the bishop took me by the hand, told me he was glad to see me, and bid me to wait a little till he had put off his habit, and he would return to me again. This gave me an opportunity of praying to God for His assistance, and adoring Him for His providence over me.

At his coming again into the room, the bishop told me he had heard of my character, liked my behavior at church, and enquired my age. "Notwithstanding," said he, "I have declared I would not ordain anyone under three-and-twenty, yet I shall think it my duty to ordain you whenever you come for Holy Orders." He then made me a present of five guineas to buy me a book, which, sounding again in my hand, put me in mind of my dream, whereupon my heart was filled with a sense of God's love.

Before I came home, this news [of the bishop's sending for me. — Edit. 1756] had reached my friends; who, being fond of my having such a great man's favor, were very solicitous to know the event of my visit. Many things I hid from them; but when they pressed me hard, I was obliged to tell them how the bishop, of his own accord, had offered to give me Holy Orders whenever I would; on which they, knowing how I had depended on the declaration his lordship had made some time ago, that he would ordain none under three-and-twenty, said, — and I then began to think myself, — "That if I held out any longer, I should fight against God." At length I came to a resolution, by God's leave, to offer myself for Holy Orders the next Ember Days.

The only thing now in dispute was into what part of my Lord's vineyard I should be sent to labor first. God had given me much success in Gloucester; and, my friends being desirous of having me near them, I had thoughts of settling among them. But, when I came to Oxford, my friends urged several reasons for my continuing at the University. "The Mr. Wesleys had not long been gone abroad, and now no one was left to take care of the prison affairs, &c." They further urged, "That God had blessed my endeavors *there* as well as at Gloucester; that the University was the fountain-head; that every gownsman's name was Legion; and that if I should be made instrumental in converting one of *them*, it would be as much as converting a whole parish." At the same time, unknown to me, some of them sent to that great and good man, the late Sir John Philips, who was a great encourager of the Oxford Methodists; and, though he had never seen, but only heard of me, yet he sent word he would allow me 30 pounds a year, if I would continue at the University. Upon this, finding the care of the prisoners would be no more than, under God, I could undertake with pleasure, and knowing the University was the best place to prosecute my studies, I resolved, God willing, to wait at Oxford a blessing on the first-fruits of my ministerial labors.

In the meanwhile, having before made some observations upon the thirty-nine Articles, and proved them by Scripture, I strictly examined myself by the qualifications required for a minister in St. Paul's *Epistle to Timothy*, and also by every question that I knew was to be publicly put to me at the time of my ordination. This latter I drew out in writing at large, and sealed my approbation of it every Sunday at the blessed Sacrament. At length, Trinity Sunday being near at hand, and having my testimonials from the College, I went, a fortnight beforehand to Gloucester, intending to compose some sermons, and to give myself more particularly to prayer.

But God's thoughts are not as our thoughts. When I came to Gloucester, notwithstanding I strove and prayed for several days, and had matter enough in my heart, yet I was so restrained that I could not compose anything at all. I mentioned my case to one clergyman. He said, "I was an enthusiast." I wrote to another who was experienced in the Divine life. He gave me some reasons why God might deal with me in that manner, and withal promised me his prayers. I joined with him in importunate supplication to know whether this restraint was of God or not. At last, in reading Mr. Henry upon the Acts of the Apostles, this passage was much pressed upon my heart, "We assayed to go into Bithynia, but the Spirit suffered us not." Looking a little farther, I found a quotation out of Ezekiel, wherein God said to that young prophet, just after He had given him a Divine and public commission, "Thou shalt be dumb; but when I speak unto thee, then thou shalt speak." This made me quite easy. The remainder of the fortnight I spent in reading the several missions of the Prophets and Apostles, and wrestled with God to give me grace to follow their good examples.

About three days before the time appointed for ordination, the bishop came to town. The next evening, I sent his lordship an abstract of my private examination upon these two questions. "Do you trust that you are inwardly moved by the Holy Ghost to take upon you this office and administration?" And, "Are you called according to the will of our Lord Jesus Christ, and the laws of this realm?" The next morning, I waited on the bishop. He received me with much love, telling me "he was glad I was come; that he was satisfied with the preparation I had made, and with the allowance given me by Sir John Philips. I had myself," said he, "made provision for you of two little parishes; but since you choose to be at Oxford, I am very well pleased. I doubt not but you will do much good." Upon this, I took my leave, abashed with God's goodness to such a wretch, but withal exceedingly rejoiced that, in every circumstance He made my way into the ministry so very plain before my face!

This, I think, was on Friday. The day following I continued in abstinence and prayer. In the evening, I retired to a hill near the town, and prayed fervently for about two hours, on behalf of myself and those who were to be ordained with me.

On Sunday morning, I rose early, and prayed over St. Paul's *Epistle to Timothy*, and more particularly over that precept, "Let no one despise thy youth." "When I went up to the altar, I could think of nothing but Samuel's standing a little child before the Lord with a linen ephod. When the bishop laid his hands upon my head, my heart was melted down, and I offered up my whole spirit, soul and body, to the service of God's sanctuary. I read the Gospel, at the bishop's command, with power, and afterwards sealed the good confession I had made before many witnesses, by partaking of the Holy Sacrament of our Lord's most blessed Body and Blood.

Being restrained from writing, as was before observed, I could not preach in the afternoon, though much solicited thereto; but I read prayers to the poor prisoners, being willing to let the first act of my ministerial office be an act of charity.

The next morning, waiting upon God in prayer to know what He would have me to do, these words, "Speak out, Paul," came with great power to my soul. Immediately my heart was enlarged. God spake to me by His Spirit, and I was no longer dumb. I finished a sermon I had in hand some time before, and began another; and preached the Sunday following to a very crowded audience, with as much freedom as though I had been a preacher for some years.

Oh, the unspeakable benefit of reading to the poor, and exercising our talents while students at the University! Such previous acts are very proper to prepare us for the work of our Lord, and make us not unapt to teach in a more public manner. It is remarkable that our Lord sent out His disciples on short missions before they were so solomnly authorized at the day of Pentecost. Would the Heads and Tutors of our Universities but follow His example, and, instead of discouraging their pupils from doing anything of this nature, send them to visit the sick and the prisoners, and to pray with, and read practical books of religion to the poor, they would find such exercises of more service to them, and to the Church of God, than all their private and public lectures put together.

Thus God dealt with my soul. At the same time, by His gracious providence, He supplied me with all things needful for my body also. For He inclined the bishop's heart to give me five guineas more; and, by this time, a quarter's allowance was due to me from Sir John Philips, both which sums put together fully served to defray the expenses of my ordination, and taking my bachelor's degree, which was conferred on me at Oxford the week after my being ordained, when I was about one-and-twenty years of age.

These changes from a servitor to a Bachelor of Arts — from a common drawer to a clergyman — were no doubt temptations to think more highly of myself than I ought to think and some were therefore jealous of me, as I trust they always will be, with a godly jealousy. God, who is rich in mercy, thereby forewarned me of my danger, stirred up my heart to pray against spiritual pride, and kept me, as I hope He will to the end, in some measure always humbled before Him.

Thus did God, by a variety of unforeseen acts of providence and grace, train me up for, and at length introduce me into, the service of His Church.

What has happened to me since that time, especially for these two last years, is so well-known as to need no repetition. However, as I find freedom in myself, and leisure from my ministerial employ, I shall hereafter relate God's further dealings with my soul, and how He led me into my present way of acting.

In the meanwhile, my dear reader, whosoever thou art, I pray God what I have now written may not prove a savor of death unto death, but a savor of life unto life unto thy soul. Many, I fear, through ignorance, prejudice, and unbelief, when they read this, will contradict and blaspheme. Be not thou of this number; but if thou art yet uninfected with the contagion of the world, I pray God to keep thee so; for, believe me, innocence is better than repentance; and though sin may afford thee some brutish present pleasure, yet the remembrance of it afterwards is exceedingly bitter. If thou art immersed in sin as I was, take no encouragement from me to continue in it on the one hand, nor despair of mercy on the other. Let God's goodness to me lead thee also to repentance. The same Lord is rich unto all who call upon Him through faith in Christ Jesus. If through Divine grace I have done anything praise-worthy, not unto me, but unto God give all the glory! If thou art awakened to a sense of the Divine life, and art hungering and thirsting after that righteousness which is by faith only in Jesus Christ, and the indwelling of His blessed Spirit in thy heart, think it not absolutely necessary to pass through all the temptations that have beset me round about on every side. It is in the spiritual as in the natural life — some feel more, others less, but all experience some pangs and travails of soul, ere the Man Christ Jesus is formed within them, and brought forth and arrived unto the measure of His fullness Who filleth all in all. If God deals with thee in a more gentle way, yet so that a thorough work of conversion is effected in thy heart, thou oughtest to be exceeding thankful. Or, if He should lead thee through a longer wilderness that I have passed through, thou needest not complain. The more thou art humbled now, the more thou shalt be exalted hereafter. One taste of Christ's love in the heart will make amends for all. And, if thou hast felt the powers of the world to come, and been made a partaker of the Holy Ghost, I know thou wilt rejoice, and give thanks for what God has done for my soul.

To conclude, — may all who peruse these few sheets be as much affected alternately with grief and joy in reading, as I have been in writing them; they will then have the desired effect, and cause many thanks-givings to be offered in my behalf to that God Who has called me out of darkness into His marvelous light! And that thou, O reader, whoever thou art, mayest experience the like and greater blessings, is the hearty prayer of thy soul's friend and servant.

George Whitefield.

A HYMN

I.   When all Thy mercies, O my God,
        My rising soul surveys,
      Why my cold heart, art thou not lost
        In wonder, love, and praise!

II.   Thy providence my life sustain'd,
        And all my wants redrest,
      While in the silent womb I lay,
        And hung upon the breast.

III.   To all my weak complaints and cries!
        Thy mercy lent an ear;
      E'er yet my feeble thoughts had learn'd
        To form themselves in prayer.

IV.   Unnumber'd comforts on my soul,
        Thy tender care bestow'd,
      Before my infant heart conceiv'd,
        From Whom those comforts flow'd.

V.   When in the slippery paths of youth
        With heedless steps I ran,
      Thine arm unseen convey'd me safe,
        And led me up to man.

VI.   Through hidden dangers, toils and deaths,
        It gently clear'd my way,
      And through the pleasing snares of vice,
        More to be fear'd than they.

VII. Ten thousand thousand precious gifts
    My daily thanks employ;
Nor is the least a cheerful heart,
    That tastes those gifts with joy.

VIII. Through every period of my life
    Thy goodness I'll pursue,
And after death in distant worlds
    The pleasing theme renew.

IX. Through all eternity to Thee
    A grateful song I'll raise:
But O! eternity's too short
    To utter all Thy praise.

A
FURTHER
ACCOUNT

OF

GOD'S DEALINGS

With the Reverend
Mr. GEORGE WHITEFIELD

from

The Time of His Ordination to His
Embarking for Georgia
(June, 1736 — December, 1737)

Genesis 32:10. *I am not worthy of the least of all the mercies, and of all the truth, which Thou hast showed unto Thy servant.*

THE PREFACE

The Royal Psalmist, filled no doubt with a deep sense of the Divine goodness in general, and of the many mercies conferred upon himself in particular, breaks out into this moving language, "Come all ye who fear God, and I will tell you what He hath done for my soul." And great reason he had for so doing. Experience daily convinces devout souls, that nothing has a more immediate tendency to affect themselves, and recommend their glorious and bountiful Benefactor to the choice and adoration of others, than an artless, humble narration of the many favors, spiritual or temporal, which they have received from Him, in Whom they live, and move, and have their being. This and such like considerations, if I know anything of my heart, led me some years ago to publish "A Short Account of God's Dealings with me, from the Time of my Birth, to my Entering into Holy Orders"; and as it has pleased a Sovereign God to bless that little tract in a manner I durst not expect, both at home and abroad, I now sit down, in His fear, to fulfill a promise made at the end of it, viz., to give a further account of the Lord's dealing with me from that time to my embarking for America.

WHITEFIELD'S FURTHER ACCOUNT

Having been ordained at Gloucester, on Trinity Sunday, 1736, and preached my sermon on the *Necessity and Benefit of Religious Society*, to a very crowded auditory, in the church in which I was baptized, the Lord's Day following, I set out the next Wednesday to Oxford, where I was received with great joy by my religious friends. For about a week I continued in my servitor's habit, and then took my degree of Bachelor of Arts, after having been at the University three years and three quarters, and going on towards the 22nd year of my age. My dear and honored friends the Reverend Messrs. John and Charles Wesley, being now for some time embarked for Georgia, and one or two more having taken Orders, the interest of Methodism, as it was then and is now termed, had visibly declined, and very few of this reputed mad way were left at the University. This somewhat discouraged me at times, but the Lord Jesus supported my soul, and made me easy by giving me a strong conviction that I was where He would have me to be. My degree, I soon found, was of service to me, as it gave me access to those I could not be free with when in an inferior station; and, as opportunity offered, I was enabled to converse with them about the things which belonged to the Kingdom of God. The subscriptions for the poor prisoners, which amounted to about 40 pounds per annum, were soon put into my hands. Two or three small charity schools, maintained by the Methodists, were under my more immediate inspection; which, with the time I spent in following my studies, private retirement, and religious converse, sweetly filled up the whole of my day, and kept me from that unaccountable, but too common, complaint of having any time hang upon my hands. The distributing money and books amongst the poor prisoners, and employing such as could work, I found was of admirable service. For hereby they were kept from that worst of jail diseases — idleness; and were not only convinced that we bore a good will towards them, but also led them, as it were, under an obligation to hear the instructions we gave them from time to time. This practice was first taken up by the Messrs. Wesley; and would to God all Ordinaries of prisons would copy after their good example! They would deserve well of the Commonwealth, and if actuated by the love of God, would receive a glorious reward from Him, Who hath said, "I was sick and in prison, and ye came unto Me."

In a short time I began to be more than content in my present state of life, had thoughts of abiding at the University, at least for some years, to finish my studies, and do what good I could amongst the poor despised Methodists. But "God's thoughts are not as man's thoughts, neither are our ways as His ways." By a series of unforeseen, unexpected, and unsought-for providences, I was called in a short time from my beloved retirement to take a journey to the Metropolis of England. Whilst I was an undergraduate, amongst other religious friends, I was very intimate with one Mr. Broughton, a professed Methodist, who had lately taken Orders, and was curate at the Tower of London. With him, when absent, I frequently corresponded; and, when present, took sweet counsel together, and walked to the house of God as friends. He mentioned me to that late good and great man, Sir John Philips. Being called down, for a while, into Hampshire, he wrote to me to be of good courage, and bid me hasten to town to officiate in his absence, and be refreshed with the sight and conversation of many who loved me for Christ's sake, and had for a long time desired to see me.

Accordingly, on Wednesday, August 4th, (the prisoners being provided for by the coming of Mr. Hervey, another young worthy Methodist, who had lately taken Deacon's Orders), with fear and trembling, I obeyed the summons, and went in the stage coach to London. There being no other passenger, I employed myself a good part of the way in earnest supplication to the God of all grace to be my Guide and my Comforter; at the same time I could not help praising Him for changing my heart, and calling me to preach the Gospel at a place to which, not many years ago, I would have given much money, would my circumstances have permitted, to have gone up and seen a play. In the evening, I reached the Tower, and was kindly received by my dear friend. The remainder of the week was spent in visiting Sir John Philips, and others who were glad to see me. But God sent me something to ballast it; for, as I passed along the streets, many came out of their shops to see so young a person in a gown and cassock. One I remember in particular, cried out, "There's a boy parson," which served to mortify my pride, and put me also upon turning that apostolical exhortation into prayer, "Let no man despise thy youth."

On Sunday, August 8th, in the afternoon, I preached at Bishopsgate Church, the largeness of which, and the congregation together, at first a little dazed me; but, by adverting to God, and considering in Whose Name I was about to speak, my mind was calmed, and I was enabled to preach with power. The effect was immediate and visible to all; for as I went up the stairs almost all seemed to sneer at me on account of my youth; but they soon grew serious and exceedingly attentive, and, after I came down, showed me great tokens of respect, blessed me as I passed along, and made great enquiry who I was. The question no one could answer, for I was quite a stranger. I speedily slipped through the crowd, and came to the Tower, blessing God for His goodness to me the unworthiest of the sons of men.

Here I continued for the space of two months, reading prayers twice a week, catechizing and preaching once, besides visiting the soldiers in the infirmary and barracks daily. I also read prayers every evening at Wapping Chapel, and preached at Ludgate Prison every Tuesday. God was pleased to give me favor in the eyes of the inhabitants of the Tower. The Chapel was crowded on Lord's Days. Religious friends from divers parts of the town attended the Word, and several young men came on Lord's Day morning, under serious impressions, to hear me discourse about the new birth, and the necessity of renouncing all in affection in order to follow Jesus Christ.

After I had been about a month in town, letters came from the Messrs. Wesley, and the Rev. Mr. Ingham, their fellow-laborer, an Israelite indeed, from Georgia. Their accounts fired my soul, and made me even long to go abroad for God too; but having no outward call, and being, as I then thought, too weak in body ever to undertake a voyage to sea, I endeavored to lay aside all thoughts of going abroad. But my endeavors were all in vain; for I felt at times such a strong attraction in my soul towards Georgia, that I thought it almost irresistible. I strove against it with all my power, begged again and again with many cries and tears, that the Lord would not suffer me to be deluded, and at length opened my mind to several dear friends. All agreed that laborers were wanted at home; that I had as yet no visible call abroad; and that it was my duty not to be rash, but wait and see what providence might point out to me. To this I consented with my whole heart, and having stayed in London till Mr. Broughton came out of the country, I returned to my little charge at Oxford, and waited upon my deaconship according to the measure of grace imparted to me.

But, oh what a delightful life did I lead there! What communion did I daily enjoy with God! How sweetly did my hours in private glide away in reading and praying over Mr. Henry's *Comment upon the Scriptures*! Whilst I am musing on and writing about it, the fire I then felt again kindles in my soul. Nor was I alone happy; for several dear youths were quickened greatly, and met daily at my room to build up each other in their most holy faith. God raised up friends for our temporal support. The late Honorable Betty Hastings, that elect lady, allowed some of them two or three small Exhibitions. I also partook of her ladyship's bounty; and a gentleman, whose heart was in an especial manner knit to me when last at London, was stirred up, without being solicited, to send me not only money for the poor, but also a sufficiency to discharge debts I had contracted for books before I took my degree. Upon his recommendation I was chosen a corresponding member of the Society for Promoting Christian Knowledge, which I rejoiced in, as it gave me an opportunity of procuring books at a cheap and easy rate for the poor people. May the great High Priest and Apostle of our profession continue to bless that Society, and prosper all their pious undertakings, to the advancement of His own glory, and His people's eternal good!

About the middle of November 1736 I was once more called from my beloved, though little, scene of action. The Rev. Mr. Kinchin, now with God, had lately been awakened, and accordingly resolved to associate with the despised Methodists, determining to know nothing but Jesus Christ and Him Crucified. He was then minister of Dummer, in Hampshire; and being likely to be chosen Dean of Corpus Christi College, he desired me to come and officiate for him, till that affair should be decided. By the advice of friends I went, and he came to supply my place at Oxford. His parish consisting chiefly of poor and illiterate people, my proud heart at first could not well brook it. I would have given all the world for one of my Oxford friends, and mourned for lack of them as a dove that has lost her mate. But upon giving myself to prayer, and reading Mr. Law's excellent character of *Ouranious*, in his *Serious Call to a Devout Life*, my mind was reconciled to such conversation as the place afforded me. Before I came to Dummer, Mr. Kinchin had used his people, according to the Rubric, to have public prayers twice a day, viz., in the morning, it being the winter season, before it was light; and in the evening after the people returned from their work. He also catechized the lambs of the flock daily, and visited from house to house. He loved his people, and was beloved by them. I prosecuted his plan, and generally divided the day into three parts — eight hours for study and retirement, eight hours for sleep and meals, and eight hours for reading prayers, catechizing, and visiting the parish. The profit I reaped by these exercises, and conversing with the poor country people, was unspeakable. I frequently learnt as much by an afternoon's visit, as in a week's study. During my stay here, an invitation was sent me to a very profitable curacy in London; but I had no inclination to accept it.

The thoughts of going to Georgia still crowded continually in upon me, and at length Providence seemed to point my way thither. About the middle of December, came a letter from Mr. Broughton, informing me that Mr. Charles Wesley was arrived at London. Soon after came a letter from Mr. Charles himself, wherein he informed me that he had come over to procure laborers; but, added he, "I dare not prevent God's nomination." In a few days after this came another letter from Mr. John Wesley, wherein were these words — "Only Mr. Delamott is with me, till God shall stir up the hearts of some of His servants, who, putting their lives in His hands, shall come over and help us, where the harvest is so great, and the laborers so few. What if thou art the man, Mr. Whitefield?" In another letter were these words — "Do you ask me what you shall have? Food to eat, and raiment to put on; a house to lay your head in, such as your Lord had not; and a crown of glory that fadeth not away." Upon reading this, my heart leaped within me, and, as it were, echoed to the call. Many things concurred to make my way clear. Mr. Kinchin was now elected Dean of Corpus Christi College, and being thereby obliged to reside at Oxford, he willingly took upon him the charge of the prisoners. Mr. Hervey was ready to serve the cure of Dummer. Mr. Wesley was my dear friend, and I thought it would be a great advantage to me to be under his tuition. Georgia was an infant, and likely to be an increasing colony; and the Government seemed to have its welfare much at heart. I had heard many Indians were near it, and had thought it a matter of great importance that serious clergymen should be sent there. Retirement and privacy were what my soul delighted in. A voyage to sea would, in all probability, not do my constitution much hurt; nay, I had heard the sea was sometimes beneficial to weakly people. And supposing the worst, as I must necessarily return to take priest's Orders, it would then be left to my choice whether I would fix in my native country or go abroad any more. These things being thoroughly weighed, I at length resolved within myself to embark for Georgia; and knowing that I should never put my resolution into practice if I conferred with flesh and blood, wrote to my relations to inform them of my design, and withal told them, "if they would promise not to dissuade me from my intended voyage, I would come and take a personal leave of them; if otherwise, knowing my own weakness, I was determined to embark without visiting them at all." A few days after, Mr. Kinchin came to Dummer, and introduced Mr. Hervey into the cure. I apprised them of my intention. They gave me some friendly counsel, and having spent the beginning of Christmas sweetly together, and taken an affectionate leave of the Dummer people, I returned once more to Oxford, to bid adieu to my friends, who were as dear to me as my own soul. My resolution at first a little shocked them; but having reason to think, from my relation of circumstances, that I had a call from Providence, most of them said, "The will of the Lord be done!"

On New Year's Day, 1737, I went to Gloucester to hear the bishop's opinion, and to take my leave of my mother and other relations. His lordship received me, as he always did, like a father, approved of my design, wished me much success, and said "he did not boubt but God would bless me, and that I should do much good abroad." My own relations, at first, were not so passive. My aged mother wept sore; and others urged what pretty preferment I might have, if I would stay at home. But, at length, they grew more quiet, and, finding me so fixed, gain said no longer.

During my stay, here, I began to grow a little popular. God gave me honor for a while, even in my own country. I preached twice on the Sabbaths. Congregations were very large, and the power of God attended the Word; and some I have reason to believe were truly converted, who will be my joy and crown of rejoicing in the day of the Lord Jesus.

In about three weeks, I went to Bristol, to take leave of some more of my relations who lived there. As it was my constant practice, go where I would, to attend on the daily public offices of the Church, I went, the Thursday after my coming, to hear a sermon at St. John's Church. Whilst the Psalm was being sung, after prayers, the minister came to my seat, and asked me to give the congregation a sermon. Having my notes about me, I complied. The hearers seemed startled, and after sermon, enquiry was made who I was. The next day there was another lecture at St. Stephen's. Many crowded thither in expectation of hearing me again. The lecturer asked me to preach, as the other did the day before. I again complied; and the alarm given here was so general, that, on the following Lord's Day, many of all denominations were obliged to return from the churches, where I preached, for want of room. Afterwards, I was called by the Mayor to preach before him and the Corporation. And for some time following, I preached all the lectures on week-days, and twice on Sundays besides visiting the Religious Societies. The Word, through the mighty Power of God, was sharper than a two-edged sword. The doctrine of the New Birth and Justification by Faith in Jesus Christ (though I was not so clear in it as afterwards) made its way like lightning into the hearers' consciences. The arrows of conviction stuck fast; and my whole time, between one lecture and another, except what was spent in necessary refreshment, was wholly occupied in talking with people under religious concern. Large offers were made me, if I would stay at Bristol. All wondered that I would go to Georgia, who might be so well provided for at home; and some urged that, if I had a mind to convert Indians, I might go amongst the Kingswood colliers, and find Indians enough there. But none of these things moved me. Having put my hand to the plough, I was determined, through Divine grace, not to look back. And therefore, at length, I took my leave, but with what mutual affection and concern cannot easily be expressed.

During my stay at Bristol, I made a little elopement to Bath, where I was kindly received by a dear friend, the Rev. Mr. Chapman, and some elect and honorable women who befriended the Oxford Methodists. I preached at the Abbey Church twice. The late Dr. Cockman was pleased to thank me for my sermon; and application was made to me by several to print both my discourses.

It was now about the middle of February. Lent was at hand, and I was obliged to be at Oxford to perform the remainder of my College exercise, which they call "determining." I went through Gloucester, as it lay in my way, and abode there a week, visiting the prisoners, and encouraging the awakened souls. Having stayed about ten days at the University, I took, as I thought, my last farewell of my dear friends, and came up to London in the beginning of March, in order to wait upon James Oglethorpe, Esq., and the Honorable Trustees. I was kindly received by both. The former introduced me to his Grace the present Archbishop of Canterbury; and the Rev. Mr. Arthur Bedford at the desire of the latter (with whom I dined at their public anniversary), went with me to the present Lord Bishop of London. Both approved of my going abroad; the former was pleased to say, "He would take particular notice of such as went to Georgia, if they did not go out of any sinister view." This put me upon enquiry what were my motives in going? And, after the strictest examination, my conscience answered, "Not to please any man living upon earth, nor out of any sinister view, but simply to comply with what I believe to be Thy will, O God, and to promote Thy glory, Thou great Shepherd and Bishop of souls."

I continued in London about three weeks, waiting for Mr. Oglethorpe, who expected to sail every day. In this season I preached more frequently than when there before. Many more came to hear me; and the last Sunday I was in town I read prayers twice, and preached four times. But, finding Mr. Oglethorpe was not likely to go for some time, and having lain under particular obligation to the Rev. Mr. Sampson Harris, minister of Stonehouse, in Gloucestershire, I went down thither, at his request, to supply his place, whilst he came up to dispatch some affairs in town.

Hither I had reason to think God sent me in answer to prayer: for there was a little sweet Society of seeking souls, who had heard me preach at an adjacent town, and wrestled with God, if it was His will, to send me amongst them. They received me with joy, and most of the parishioners were very civil, when I came to visit them from house to house. Upon examination I found them more knowing than I expected. Their pastor had catechized the little ones in the summer season, and expounded the four Lessons every Lord's Day in the church. I followed his good example, and found great freedom and assistance given me both in my public and private administrations. Having the use of the parsonage house, I expounded every night. Many who were not parishioners came to hear, and were edified. On Sundays, besides expounding the Lessons, catechizing and preaching, I repeated my sermons to the Society. Neither church nor house could contain the people that came. I found uncommon manifestations granted me from above. Early in the morning, at noonday, evening, and midnight, nay, all the day long, did the blessed Jesus visit and refresh my heart. Could the trees of a certain wood near Stonehouse speak, they would tell what sweet communion I and some others enjoyed with the ever blessed God there. Sometimes, as I was walking, my soul would make such sallies as though it would go out of the body. At other times, I would be so overpowered with a sense of God's Infinite Majesty, that I would be constrained to throw myself on the ground, and offer my soul as a blank in His hands, to write on it what He pleased. One night, was a time never to be forgotten. It happened to lighten exceedingly. I had been expounding to many people, and some being afraid to go home, I thought it my duty to accompany them, and improve the occasion, to stir them up to prepare for the coming of the Son of Man. In my return to the parsonage house, whilst others were rising from their beds, frightened almost to death, I and another, a poor, but pious countryman, were in the field, exulting in our God, and longing for that time, when Jesus should be revealed from heaven in a flame of fire! Oh that my soul may be in a like frame, when He shall actually come to call me! For I think I never had been happier than that night, or, all things considered, more blessed than during my abode at Stonehouse. Every week the congregations increased; and on Ascension Day, when I took my leave, the concern they showed at my departure was inexpressible. Their sighs and tears almost broke my heart. Many cried out with Ruth, "Whither thou goest I will go, where thou lodgest I will lodge." But I only took one with me, who proved a good servant, and is, I believe, a true follower of our ever blessed Jesus.

The Incumbent having returned from London, and the people of Bristol having given me repeated invitations, nay, having insisted upon my coming again, since the time of my embarking was deferred; on May 23rd, I paid them a second visit. Multitudes came on foot, and many in coaches a mile without the city, to meet me; and almost all saluted and blessed me as I went along the street.

Upon my coming here, I received letters from London, informing me, that Mr. Oglethorpe would not embark these two months. This gladdened many hearts, though I cannot say it did mine; for I counted the hours, as it were, till I went abroad. I preached, as usual, about five times a week; but the congregations grew, if possible, larger and larger, It was wonderful to see how the people hung upon the rails of the organ loft, climbed upon the leads of the church, and made the church itself so hot with their breath, that the steam would fall from the pillars like drops of rain. Sometimes, almost as many would go away, for want of room, as came in; and it was with great difficulty that I got into the desk, to read prayers or preach. Persons of all denominations flocked to hear. Persons of all ranks, not only publicly attended my ministry, but gave me private invitations to their houses. A private Society or two were erected. I preached and collected for the poor prisoners in Newgate twice or thrice a week; and many made me large offers if I would not go abroad.

During my stay here I paid another visit to Bath, and preached three times in the Abbey Church, and once in Queen's Chapel. People crowded, and were affected as at Bristol; and God stirred up some elect ladies to give upwards of 160 pounds for the poor of Georgia.

June 21st, I took my last farewell at Bristol; but when I came to tell them, it might be, that they would *"see my face no more,"* high and low, young and old burst into such a flood of tears, as I had never seen before. Multitudes, after sermon, followed me home weeping; and, the next day, I was employed from seven in the morning till midnight, in talking and giving spiritual advice to awakened souls.

About three the next morning, having thrown myself on the bed for an hour or two, I set out for Gloucester, because I heard that a great company on horseback, and in coaches, intended to see me out of town. Some, finding themselves disappointed, followed me thither, where I stayed a few days, and preached to a very crowded auditory. Then I went on to Oxford, where we had, as it were, a general *rendezvous* of the Methodists; and, finding their interests flourishing, and being impatient to go abroad, I hastened away, after taking a most affectionate leave, and came to London about the end of August.

Every hour now seemed a week, and every week a year, till I embarked. I knew there was no minister at Frederica, for which place I was then appointed, and I did not care to be absent longer from my proper charge. Mr. Oglethorpe's going was still retarded, and I had thought it my duty to go immediately without him, had not he and my other friends urged that the soldiers would shortly embark, and that I had best go over with them. This somewhat pacified me; and having now taken a final farewell of all my friends in the country, I was resolved to abide at London, and give myself wholly to prayer, the study of the Scriptures, and my own heart, till the soldiers should embark.

The house I lodged at was good old Mr. Hutton's in College Street, Westminster, where I had the pleasure of seeing my dear friend, Mr. Ingham, lately returned from Georgia; and perceiving him, as I thought, remarkably grown in grace, I longed still more to be sent to the same school, hoping to catch some of that holy flame with which his soul was fired. We freely and solemnly conversed together about my call abroad; and, it seemed to both quite clear. Our hearts were knit to each other, like the hearts of David and Jonathan. At midnight, we would rise to sing praises to God, and to intercede for the whole state of Christ's militant Church here on earth.

With this dear friend, I, one day paid a visit to a worthy Doctor of Divinity, near London, who introduced us to some Honorable ladies, who delighted in doing good. It being my constant practice to improve my acquaintance with the rich for the benefit of the poor, I recommended two poor clergymen, and another pious person, to their charity. They said little, but, between them, gave, I think, thirty-six guineas. When we came to the Doctor's house, and he saw the ladies' liberality, he said, "If you had not spoken for others, you would have had a good deal of that yourself." God gave me to rejoice that I had nothing, and the poor all. The next day, upon my return to London, in the first letter that I opened, was a Bank Note of 10 pounds, sent from an unexpected hand as a present for myself. This encouraged me to go on doing good to others, with a full assurance, that the Lord would not let me want. Blessed be His Name! I have had many such instances of His tender concern for my temporal, as well as my eternal welfare.

About this time, through the importunity of friends, and aspersions of enemies, I was prevailed upon to print my sermon *On the Nature and Necessity of our Regeneration or New Birth in Christ Jesus*, which under God began the awakening at London, Bristol, Gloucester, and Gloucestershire. The Dissenters, I found, were surprised to see a sermon on such a subject from a clergyman of the Church of England; and finding the author came from Oxford, were ready to say "Can any good come out of Nazareth?" This sermon sold well to persons of all denominations, and was dispersed very much both at home and abroad. A second impression was soon called for; and finding another of my sermons was printed without my leave, and in a very incorrect manner at Bristol, I was obliged to publish in my own defense; and afterwards, thought I had a clear call to print any other discourses, though in themselves mean, that I found blessed to the good of souls.

But to return to my public administrations. Being determined to abide in London till the time of my departure, I followed my usual practice of reading and praying over the Word of God upon my knees. Sweet was this retirement to my soul, but it was not of long continuance. I was invited to preach at Cripplegate, St. Ann's and Forster Lane churches, at six on the Lord's Day morning, and to assist in administering the Holy Sacrament. I embraced the invitations, and so many came, that sometimes we were obliged to consecrate fresh elements two or three times; and stewards found it somewhat difficult to carry the offerings to the communion table. I also preached at Wapping Chapel, the Tower, Ludgate, Newgate, and many of the churches where weekly lectures were kept up. The congregations continually increased, and generally, on a Lord's Day, I used to preach four times to very large and very affected auditories, besides reading prayers twice or thrice, and walking, perhaps, twelve miles in going backwards and forwards from one church to the other. But God made my feet like hind's feet, and filled me with joy unspeakable at the end of my day's work. This made me look upon my friends' kind advice which they gave me, to spare myself, as a temptation. For I found by daily experience, the more I did, the more I might do for God.

About the latter end of August, finding there were many young men belonging to the Religious Societies that attended my administrations, I entered into one of their singing societies, hoping to have greater opportunities of doing them good. It answered my design. Our Lord gave me to spiritualize their singing. And after they had taught me the gamut, they would gladly hear me teach them some of the mysteries of the new birth, and the necessity of living to God. Many sweet nights we spent together in this way; and many of these youths afterwards, to all appearance, walked with God, and will, I trust, join the heavenly choir in singing praises to the Lamb, and Him Who sitteth upon the throne forever.

About the middle of September my name was first put into the public newspapers. The Sunday before, I was prevailed upon to preach a charity sermon at Wapping Chapel. [From the text "Almost thou persuadest me to be a Christian."] The congregation was very large, and more was collected than had been for many years upon a like occasion. My friends entreated me to preach another charity sermon, at Sir George Wheeler's Chapel; and through the importunity of Mr. Habersham, (since my faithful assistant in the Orphan House), I agreed to do it. I discoursed upon the widow's giving her two mites. God bowed the hearts of the hearers as the heart of one man. Almost all, as I was told by the collectors, offered most willingly. This still drew on fresh applications. The Sunday following, I preached in the evening at St. Swithin's, where 8 pounds was collected instead of ten shillings. The next morning, as I was at breakfast with a friend at the Tower, I read in one of the newspapers, "that there was a young gentleman going volunteer to Georgia; that he had preached at St. Swithin's, and collected 8 pounds instead of ten shillings, 3 pounds of which were in half-pence; and that he was to preach next Wednesday before the Societies, at their general quarterly meeting." This advertisement chagrined me. I immediately sent to the printer, desiring he would put me in his paper no more. His answer was, that "he was paid for doing it, and that he would not lose two shillings for anybody." By this means, people's curiosity was stirred up more and more. On the Wednesday evening, Bow Church, in Cheapside, was crowded exceedingly. I preached my sermon on "Early Piety," and, at the request of the Societies, printed it.

Henceforward, for near three months successively, there was no end of the people flocking to hear the Word of God. The churchwardens and managers of charity schools, were continually applying to me to preach for the benefit of the children; and, as I was to embark shortly, they procured the liberty of the churches on weekdays, − a thing never known before. I sometimes had more than a dozen names of different churches, at which I had promised to preach, upon my slate-book at once; and, when I preached, constables were obliged to be placed at the door, to keep the people in order. The sight of the congregations was awful. One might, as it were, walk upon the people's heads; and thousands went away from the largest churches for want of room. They were all attention, and heard like people hearing for eternity.

I now preached generally nine times a week. The early sacraments were exceeding awful. At Cripplegate, St. Ann's and Forster Lane, how often have we seen Jesus Christ crucified, and evidently set forth before us! On Sunday mornings, long before day, you might see streets filled with people going to church, with their lanthorns in their hands, and hear them conversing about the things of God. Other Lecture Churches near at hand would be filled with persons who could not come where I was preaching; and those who did come, were so deeply affected, that they were like persons struck with pointed arrows, or mourning for a firstborn child. People gave so liberally to the charity schools, that this season near 1,000 pounds sterling was collected at the several churches, besides many private contributions and subscriptions sent in afterwards. I always preached *gratis*, and gave myself.

The Blue Coat boys and girls looked upon me as their great

benefactor; and, I believe frequently sent up their infant cries in my behalf. Worthy Mr. Seward, afterwards my dear fellow-traveler, was their hearty friend and advocate. He was concerned in above twenty charity schools, and, as I found some months afterwards, inserted the paragraph that so chagrined me.

The tide of popularity now began to run very high. In a short time, I could no longer walk on foot as usual, but was constrained to go in a coach, from place to place, to avoid the hosannas of the multitude. They grew quite extravagant in their applauses; and, had it not been for my compassionate High Priest, popularity would have destroyed me. I used to plead with Him, to take me by the hand and lead me unhurt through this fiery furnace. He heard my request, and gave me to see the vanity of all commendations but His own.

Not that all spoke well of me. No; as my popularity increased, opposition increased also. At first, many of the clergy were my hearers and admirers; but some soon grew angry, and complaints were made that the churches were so crowded that there was no room for the parishioners, and that the pews were spoiled. Some called me a spiritual pick-pocket, and others thought I made use of a kind of charm to get the people's money. A report was spread abroad, that the Bishop of London, upon the complaint of the clergy, intended to *silence* me. I immediately waited upon his lordship, and enquired whether any complaint of this nature had been lodged against me? He answered, "No." I asked his lordship whether any objection could be made against my doctrine? He said, "No; for he knew a clergyman who had heard me preach a plain spiritual sermon." I asked his lordship, whether he would grant me a license? He said, "I needed none, since I was going to Georgia." I replied, "then your lordship would not forbid me?" He gave me a satisfactory answer, and I took my leave. Soon after this, two clergymen sent for me, and told me they would not let me preach in their pulpits any more, unless I renounced that part of my sermon on regeneration, wherein I wished, "that my brethren would entertain their auditories oftener with discourses upon the new birth." This I had no freedom to do, and so they continued my opposers.

What, I believe, irritated some of my enemies the more, was my free conversation with many of the serious Dissenters, who invited me to their houses, and repeatedly told me, "that, if the doctrine of the new birth and justification by faith was preached powerfully in the Church, there would be but few Dissenters in England." My practice in visiting and associating with them, I thought, was quite agreeable to the Word of God. Their conversation was savory, and I imagined the best way to bring them over was not by bigotry and railing, but by moderation and love, and undissembled holiness of life. But these reasons were of no avail. One minister called me a *pragmatical rascal*, and vehemently inveighed against the whole body of Dissenters. This stirred up the people's corruptions; and, having an overweening fondness for me, whenever they came to church and found that I did not preach, some of them would go out again. This spirit I always endeavored to quell, and made a sermon on purpose from those words, "Take heed how ye hear." One time, upon hearing that a churchwarden intended to take 8 pounds a year from his parish minister, because he refused to let me preach his lecture, I composed a sermon upon "Love your enemies," and delivered it where I knew the churchwarden would be. It had its desired effect. He came after sermon, and told me he was convinced by my discourse, that he should not resent the injury the Doctor had done me, and then thanked me for my care.

Nor was I without opposition from friends, who were jealous over me with a godly jealousy. Thousands and thousands came to hear. My sermons were everywhere called for. News came from time to time of the springing up and increase of the seed sown in Bristol, Gloucester, and elsewhere. Large offers were made me, if I would stay in England. And all the opposition I met with, joined with the consciousness of my daily infirmities, was but ballast little enough to keep me from oversetting.

However, the Lord (oh infinite condescension!) was pleased to be with and bless me day by day. I had a sweet knot of religious friends, with whom I at first attempted to pray *extempore*. Some time, I think in October, we began to set apart an hour every evening, to intercede with the Great Head of the Church to carry on the work begun, and for the circle of our acquaintance, according as we knew their circumstances required. I was their mouth unto God, and He only knows what enlargement I felt in that Divine employ. Once we spent a whole night in prayer and praise; and many a time, at midnight and at one in the morning, after I have been wearied almost to death in preaching, writing, and conversation, and going from place to place, God imparted new life to my soul, and enabled me to intercede with Him for an hour-and-a-half and two hours together. The sweetness of this exercise made me compose my sermon upon *Intercession*, and I cannot think it presumption to suppose that partly, at least, in answer to prayers then put up by His dear children, the Word, for some years past, has run and been glorified, not only in England, but in many other parts of the world.

It was now, I think, that I was prevailed on to sit for my picture. The occasion was this. Some ill-minded persons had painted me leaning on a cushion, with a bishop looking very enviously over my shoulder. At the bottom were six lines, in one of which the bishops were styled "Mitred Drones." The same person published in the papers that I had sat for it. This I looked upon as a snare of the Devil to incense the clergy against me. I consulted friends what to do. They told me I must sit for my picture in my own defense. At the same time, my aged mother laid her commands upon me to do so in a letter, urging, "that if I would not let her have the substance, I would leave her at least the shadow." She also mentioned the painter, and meeting with him one night, accidentally, I, with great reluctance complied, and endeavored, whilst the painter was drawing my face, to employ my time in beseeching the great God, by His Holy Spirit, to paint His blessed image upon his and my heart.

Christmas now drew near. Notice was given me, that the soldiers were almost ready to embark for Georgia; but Mr. Oglethorpe being yet detained, I resolved to throw myself into the hands of God, and go with the soldiers. The nearer the time of my departure approached, the more affectionate and eager the people grew. There was no end of persons coming to me under soul concern. I preached, and God blessed me more and more, and supported me for some time with but very little sleep.

At the beginning of Christmas week, I took my leave; but, oh, what groans and sighs were to be heard, when I said, "Finally, brethren, farewell!" At Great St. Helen's, the cry was amazing. I was nearly half-an-hour going out to the door. All ranks gave vent to their passions. Thousands and thousands of prayers were put up for me. They would run and stop me in the alleys, hug me in their arms, and follow me with wishful looks. Once in the Christmas before my departure, with many others, I spent a night in prayer and praise, and, in the morning, helped to administer the Sacrament at St. Dunstan's, as I used to do on Saints' Days. But such a Sacrament I never before saw. The tears of the communicants mingled with the cup, and had not Jesus comforted our hearts, our parting would have almost been insupportable.

At length, on December 28, I left London, and went on board the *Whitaker*, after having preached in a good part of the London churches, collected about 1,000 pounds for the charity schools, and got upwards of 300 pounds for the poor of Georgia among my friends, for which I have since publicly accounted. At the same time God raised me a sufficiency to supply my own temporal necessities; and gave me repeated proofs, that if we *seek first the Kingdom of God and His Righteousness, all other things* (I mean food and raiment, which is all a Christian should desire) *shall be added unto us.* For which, and all His other unmerited mercies, I desire to praise Him in time, and magnify His holy Name, through the boundless ages of eternity.

Some particulars that befell me whilst abroad, and how this tide of popularity rose still higher at my return home: how I came to commence a field-preacher, and part with my friends, who were as dear to me as my own soul: how they who would now have plucked out their eyes, and have given them unto me, afterwards accounted me their enemy because I told them the truth: by what means the seed now sown sprang up, and grew into a great tree, in England, Scotland, and America: how divisions arose among God's people, and what were the effects and consequences of them, all this I say must be reserved for another tract, if God should continue my life and strength, and give me leasure and freedom to prosecute and finish it.

In the meanwhile, let me exhort thee, O reader, if serious and a child of God, to bless Him for what He has done for my soul: or, if thou art yet in the gall of bitterness, and through prejudice, thinkest that I have either not told truth, or written out of a vain-glorious view, let me only entreat thee to suspend thy judgment for a little while, and Jesus shall decide the question. At His tribunal we shall meet, and there thou shalt know what is in my heart, and what were the motives which led me out into such a scene of life. At present I will trouble thee no more; but beg thee, whether serious or not, to endeavor to calm thy spirit, by singing or reading over the following lines, translated by that sweet singer of Israel, and my worthy and honored friend Doctor Watts.

Poem Based on Psalm 71:5-9

I.   My God, my everlasting Hope,
        I live upon Thy truth;
    Thine hands have held my childhood up,
        And strengthened all my youth.

II.   My flesh was fashioned by Thy power,
        With all these limbs of mine;
    And from my mother's painful hour,
        I've been entirely Thine.

III.   Still has my life new wonders seen,
        Repeated every year;
    Behold my days that yet remain,
        I trust them to Thy care.

IV.   Cast me not off should health decline,
        Or hoary hairs arise;
    And round me let Thy glory shine,
        Whene'er Thy servant dies.

V.   Then in the history of my age,
        When men review my days,
    They'll read Thy love in every page,
        In every line Thy praise.

THE FIRST JOURNAL

A VOYAGE

FROM

LONDON TO SAVANNAH
IN GEORGIA

December, 1737 — May 1738)

IN TWO PARTS

Part I. From London to Gibraltar
Part II. From Gibraltar to Savannah

By GEORGE WHITEFIELD, A.B.,
of Pembroke College, Oxford

I. From London to Gibraltar

My dear Friends,

According to your request, I have herewith sent you an account of what God has done for my soul since I left England. The sole motive (if my heart doth not deceive me) which induced me to leave my native country was a full conviction that it was the Divine Will. What reasons I can urge for this persuasion, is needless to mention, because few in this case would judge impartially; and what seems a reason to me, may not be deemed so by another. Let it suffice to inform you, that after earnest prayer for a year-and-a-half that if the design was not of God, it might come to naught, though strongly solicited to act in a contrary manner, I found myself as eagerly bent on going abroad as ever.

Accordingly, Wednesday, December 28, 1737, after having continued instant in prayer with my friends at Mr. James Hutton's, and afterwards receiving the Holy Sacrament at St. Dunstan's, being recommended to the grace of God by a great number of weeping Christian brethren at the Rev. Mr. H's, I set out at night for Deptford in a coach, accompanied by four friends, and got there safe at ten. Here a widow woman gladly received us into her house; and many of my friends gave me the meeting, who came on foot from London, with intent to accompany me to the ship; and with them I took a little bodily refreshment; spent two or three hours in particular intercession for our friends and enemies, and all mankind; sung psalms and hymns and spiritual songs, and then betook ourselves to rest, and the Lord made us to dwell in safety. Oh who can express the unspeakable joy of religious friends!

Thursday, December 29. Rose early in the morning, and continued instant in intercession, chanting, and singing of psalms with my friends until nine, at which our hearts were much rejoiced. After this we went in quest of our ship, but finding she was fallen down to Purfleet, and was not to remove to Gravesend for some time, we returned to Deptford praising God, and praying for a blessing on our intended voyage. The Lord perform our petitions!

Being returned to Deptford with my friends, we dined comfortably together, joined in a psalm, read the Lessons for the day, and concluded with prayer. Some were then obliged to depart for London. After they were gone, I continued with the rest in particular intercession for near two hours, and then God was pleased to comfort my heart. If parting from a few earthly friends for a season be so grievous, how will the wicked bear to be parted from God and good men for all eternity!

It happened providentially that a lecture was to be preached that evening at Deptford, and several importuned me to preach it; at first I was fearful (O me of little faith), having no notes. But afterwards (having got the consent of the minister), I went up, depending on the promise, "Lo! I am with you always even unto the end of the world," and was enabled to preach to a large congregation without the least hesitation. Did anyone yet ever trust in the Lord and be forsaken? What gave me great comfort, and made me more thankful was, that the opportunity, I believe, was granted in answer to prayer.

Friday, December 30. Went with our baggage and nine or ten friends in a Gravesend boat to Purfleet, where the *Whitaker* was fallen down. Spent the time we were on the water in singing psalms and particular intercession, and came on board about ten in the morning.

I spoke some few things to my new charge; and spent the remainder of the day on shore with my friends, in singing psalms, prayer, and exhorting one another to love and good works. Returned at night to our ship, and lay with my friend Habersham upon the ground on a mattress, in the great cabin, and God was pleased to give me a proof that He was with me in the ship.

Saturday, Dec. 31. Began this morning to have public prayers on open deck, at which the officer and soldiers attended with decency and reverence. After prayer, I enlarged a little on those words of St. Paul, "I am determined to know nothing among you save Jesus Christ and Him crucified"; told them what my future conduct would be; made some professions of my hearty love and sincere affection for their souls; and then dismissed them, I believe somewhat moved. Oh! that I may have grace to act suitably to this profession.

Today, also, I began to visit the sick, and took that opportunity of discoursing on the uncertainty of life and the certainty of a future judgment, to those around me; and God was pleased not to let my words fall to the ground.

About twelve, I went and paid my friends a visit who were on shore, and spent two or three delightful hours in praising and blessing God.

Soon after came another friend with two honest men from Gravesend, desiring me in the name of the minister to come and preach to them the following Lord's Day. At first, I was unwilling to leave my own flock in the ship; but my friends' reasonings overbalanced mine, and I went on board, read public prayers, visited the sick, gave the soldiers an exhortation (at which the soldiers were much affected), and then took boat with them for Gravesend. My heart was much enlarged in intercession. The evening was exceedingly calm, the sky clear, and all things conspired to praise that glorious and lofty One Who inhabits eternity, who stretcheth forth the heavens like a curtain, and holdeth the waters in the hollow of His hand.

About seven at night, God brought us safe to Gravesend, where Mr. Hutton received both me and my friends most courteously, and loaded us with many benefits.

We spent the evening very agreeably in prayer, and singing; and then betook ourselves to sleep, having before exhorted one another to prepare our spices and ointments of praise and thanksgiving, and to rest on the approaching Sabbath.

Sunday, January 1, 1738. Blessed be God for the happy beginning of a new year; for it has been a day of fat things. We rose in the morning, and retired to an adjacent hill with my friends, to prayer; and, afterwards, were most agreeably surprised with the coming of several more London friends who came all night on the water to see me.

About ten, we went to church, where I preached; and the curate was so kind, at our request, as to give us the Sacrament. In the afternoon I preached again to a more numerous congregation than in the morning; and as we were to stay there but one Lord's Day, I was pressed to preach and read prayers a third time, — at six in the evening. It was a thing I found entirely new; but upon the curate's readily complying to lend the pulpit, and my friends' and the people's importunity, I looked upon it as a call of Providence, and accordingly read prayers and preached to a very thronged auditory; and this I did without notes, having brought but two written sermons with me. Oh! who can express the loving kindness of the Lord, or show forth all His praise!

Monday, January 2. Sat up till twelve at night, to take leave of some of my friends, whose business obliged them to be at London the next morning; and then, after three or four hours; rest, rose and walked to Greenhithe with the remainder of my friends, intending to take a boat there, and so return to my charge at Purfleet. But just as we were entering the boat, providentially came a boy, telling us the *Whitaker* was fallen down to Gravesend, and ready to sail, if not actually under sail. We immediately hastened back from whence we came, and went on our way rejoicing.

About eleven, we reached Gravesend, and found the ship was not to sail till the morrow. This put gladness into my heart, as it gave me an opportunity of settling some affairs of consequence, and conversing a little longer with my dear friends.

About twelve o'clock I went on board, leaving my friends to dine on shore, and as I went along God was pleased to show me He had given a blessing to my discourses. The people seemed greatly alarmed, and wished me heartily a good voyage; and the very sailors were surprisingly affectionate. Blessed be God for setting His seal to my unworthy ministry! Spent the remainder of the day in settling things on board, visiting the sick, teaching the children, and reading prayers, and preaching. All love, all glory be to God through Christ!

In the evening, I went on shore again to my friends, prayed, sung psalms, and expounded a chapter out of the Holy Scriptures to them, and was not a little comforted. Praise the Lord, O my soul!

Tuesday, January 3. Went on board, read prayers, and preached, visited the sick; and then took a final leave, as I thought, of my friends. Spent the afternoon in writing letters, and putting things in order.

This evening began to read prayers between decks, judging it would be too cold above.

At night I went, according to custom, on shore to Gravesend, where I was agreeably surprised by seeing my friends. I took leave of them in the morning once more, the weather preventing their going to London. Here also Mr. C.W. and Mr. W.H. gave me the meeting; with whom we prayed, sung psalms, commended one another to God, and parted the next morning, like Christian brethren.

Wednesday, January 4. Came on board at ten in the morning; but I could not have public prayers, because the soldiers were engaged with their officer. But I visited the sick, and perceived the soldiers were attentive to hear me, when I applied myself to those around the sick persons. I also distributed presents amongst the sick of my London friends, to convince them I had a love for, and to gain an access to, their souls. I visited the sick, read prayers, and preached *extempore* (as I constantly do morning and evening); and went with Mr. H. in the evening on shore to Gravesend, where we interceded for friends, expounded a chapter, and went to bed, with that peace of mind which passeth all understanding. Oh that the sensual, careless, half-Christian could but know the comforts of religion!

Thursday, January 5. This day, I was refreshed in spirit, by hearing from some London friends, and receiving some kind presents from persons I could never have thought of; was assisted much in writing letters; came on board, read prayers, and preached; visited the sick, and had God with me all the day long. Began to catechize six or seven of the young soldiers on open deck. I was surprised they would submit to it; but God has the hearts of all men in His hands.

Great civility was shown me on board by the officers; and Captain Whiting sent his boat to fetch me to Gravesend, whither I went, having first visited the sick, read prayers, and preached on deck. When on shore, I wrote several letters, and expounded a chapter to a room full of people. I catechized the children of the house and three of my own companions; and then went to bed, full of peace and joy in the Holy Ghost.

My health of body, I could perceive, increased, and my soul was much refreshed. I now began, once more, to feel the comforts of a retired life, and blessed God from my heart, that He had called me whither I was going.

Friday, January 6. About nine, I came on board, read prayers, and preached between decks; and Mr. H. sung a psalm, as he generally does. In the meanwhile, the ship loosed from Gravesend, and sailed by twelve o'clock to the Nore. We had a very brisk gale of wind. God gave me great comfort, and I went between decks, and sat down on the ground, and read Arndt's *True Christianity*. Part of the time I stood upon deck, and admired the wonders of God in the deep.

Three or four were added today to my catechumens, some of whom I have great hopes. I read prayers, preached upon deck, and catechized my own companions; interceded upon deck near the stern, having no place for retirement; talked to the sailors on the forecastle; wrote my journal; and climbed up into my cabin to bed, where my friend Habersham and I lay as comfortably as on a bed of state. Some of the passengers, amongst whom was Mr. Habersham, began now to be sick, but I felt very little of it; on the contrary, God enabled me to rejoice with exceeding great joy. My heart was warmed by talking to the sailors, and I was lifted even above myself. I found that above a hundred, exclusive of the ship's company, were on board. God grant that not one of them may perish through my neglect!

Saturday, January 7. Breakfasted with some of the gentlemen in the great cabin, who were very civil, and let me put in a word for God.

Read public prayers, and began to expound the Lord's Prayer to the soldiers, by way of sermon; and God enabled me to do it with power. After that, I instructed my catechumens, who now amounted to twelve or thirteen. God make them soldiers of Christ as well as of the King.

Had an hour's conversation with a gentlemen on board, on our fall in Adam, and the necessity of our new birth in Christ Jesus; and hope it was not unpleasant to him.

Today I obtained what I prayed for, viz., a place to retire into; for Capt. Whiting, on my bare mentioning my want of such a thing, offered me the free use of his own cabin, — a place very commodious for that purpose.

Catechized those that went with me on open deck, for example to others; and found they improved. Capt. Whiting, the two cadets and sergeants, sat very serious and attentive. But when the Captain of the soldiers came, my heart sank a little, though without reason; however, I did not leave off. O corruption, thou art my sister!

Read public prayers, and finished my exposition of the Lord's prayer to the soldiers, at which they attended very orderly. At night, I and my five companions went upon deck, and interceded and sung psalms, by which my heart was much enlarged. The weather was very cold, and the wind magnified that God at Whose word the stormy wind ariseth.

Now I fulfilled my promise to the Lord's people; and while the winds and storms were blowing over me, I made earnest supplication to God for them.

The ship continued at the Nore all this day, but I hope we made some advances towards eternity.

In the evening the wind blew very fresh indeed; and had our ship been in the Downs, we should have been in great danger. How wisely doth God provide for us! Most people began now to be seasick, particularly J.D., one of my companions, was grievously afflicted.

Sunday, January 8. My friend Habersham and I have great reason to be thankful to God; for we slept as well as we could desire, though the wind blew very hard, and the sailors were very busy in taking care of the ship, which by the morning had dragged her anchor two miles.

I went early and visited the seasick soldiers and their families between decks; gave them some sage tea and sugar, etc., and excited them all to thankfulness and repentance, out of gratitude for their preseveration from the last night's storm, and returned public thanks at morning prayers.

Thought much of my dear London friends; though absent in body, was present in spirit in sacred ordinances; and interceded for them and all mankind. Read public prayers, and preached twice to the soldiers; and read prayers once in the great cabin to the officers, at their request, which I liked very well. Catechized my own companions, but had not time to catechize the soldiers, on account of attending the sick.

Today being the first Lord's Day I have spent this long time in so private a manner, I could not avoid reflecting on the following lines:

> I.   I sigh whene'er my musing thoughts
>   Those happy days present,
> When I with troops of pious friends
>   Thy temple did frequent;
>
> II.   When I advanc'd with songs of praise,
>   My solemn vows to pay,
> And led the joyful sacred throng
>   That kept the festal day.

But I considered it was the Divine will that placed me here, and therefore I rejoiced. He is unworthy the name of a Christian, who is not as willing to hide himself when God commands, as to act in a public capacity.

I began now to live a little by rule, and to examine into the interiors of those who came with me; which I found a most useful exercise, both for them and me. Continued all this day at the Nore, being quite becalmed, and at night had a most comfortable intercession for all friends, etc.

Monday, Jan. 9. Mr. Habersham began to learn Latin. I had near twenty catechumens with my own companions, who I believe made some advances.

Weighed from the Nore, and sailed before the wind in company with several others, which carried us on so briskly that we anchored before Margate about one. Here I enjoyed a wished-for opportunity of writing to some of my London friends, and found my heart greatly enlarged towards them.

After dinner, having some necessaries to buy, Mr. H. and I went on shore to Margate. The wind blew very fresh, and the sea raged horribly; but He Who dwelleth on high was mightier, and kept us from the least fright, and filled me with great joy and brought us safe on shore.

We had the most abandoned man with us I ever saw, who came out of an East India ship. He had so much of the Devil in him, that the very boatmen, profane as they were, abhorred him; from whence I infer, that were the Devil himself to appear as he is, the wickedest sinners could not but detest him.

This afternoon I began to feel the power of faith more than ever I did before; and to find that, as the day, so will our strength be. When I went into the boat the sea ran dangerously high; but I could boldly say: —

> God is our Refuge in distress,
> A present Help when dangers press;
>   In Him undaunted we'll confide,
> Though earth were from her centre toss'd,
> And Mountains in the ocean lost,
>   Torn piecemeal by the roaring tide.

About five we got safe to Margate, where having received a little bodily refreshment, and recommended ourselves to God in prayer, we went about the town to buy the things we came for. The generality of the people we met with were civilized and teachable.

After we had done our secular business, we paid the curate a visit, the minister being at Canterbury. He received us most courteously. Our conversation ran chiefly upon the great importance of the ministerial function, the necessity of preaching the doctrine of the new birth, and the necessity and benefit of visiting from house to house.

About ten we left him, greatly refreshed in spirit, and thankful to God for exciting persons everywhere to entertain us. On the morrow I sent him Mr. Law's *Serious Call* and *Christian Perfection*, with some other books; and also a few catechisms and sermons to some other serious people, whom Providence put in our way. Now "thanks be to God," saith the Apostle, "Who always causeth us to triumph in Christ, and maketh manifest the savor of His knowledge by us in every place!"

Tuesday, Jan. 10. About four this morning, Mr. H. and I arose, intending to go on board immediately; but the wind blew so violently, that by the advise of the boatmen we deferred going on board till daylight; and therefore, after we had kneeled on the shore, and prayed for ourselves and others, we went back to the inn, and took that opportunity of writing to a friend or two.

About seven, we took boat and praised and blessed God to see the floods clap their hands. About eight we came on board, and found we had great reason to be thankful that we were on shore last night. The sailors told us that the lightning shone on the sea all night; that the storm was very great, and the ship's long boat was lost.

I read public prayers, returned public thanks for our deliverance, and expounded by way of sermon the second article of the Creed, which I began yesterday, and did the same after evening prayers. Spent the remainder of the day in writing letters; and have not enjoyed a more calm delightful frame of mind a long time.

The sick increased on my hands, but were very thankful for furnishing them with sage-tea, sugar, broth, etc. At the sight of so many objects of pity, I was sensibly touched with a fellow-feeling of their miseries. I could not but transverse the prodigal's complain, *How many of my Father's children are ready to perish with hunger, whilst I have enough and to spare?*

I had a most comfortable sense of the Divine Presence with me in many particulars; and in the evening joined in intercession with my other companions on deck, in behalf of absent friends and all mankind.

Wednesday, January 11. Weighed from Margate road, and cast anchor in the Downs, the ship sailing most pleasantly before the wind. Wrote several letters whilst the ship was under sail. Had my spirits refreshed upon our arrival in the Downs, by hearing from two or three Christian brethren at London, and was desirous to bless God for an opportunity that was offered of sending a whole packet to them and some other friends, to acquaint them how lovingly the Lord had dealt with me.

Had no public prayers this morning, being much hurried in writing letters to go by post; and when I went to read, the soldiers were engaged in their military affairs upon deck, so that I did nothing but visit the sick. I fear I did foolishly.

Went on in explaining the Creed after evening prayers, and was enabled to talk of the crucifixion of our Lord. I believe it pricked them to the heart. O that I could hear them cry out, "What shall we do to be saved?"

Had the comfort to hear good was done among the soldiers; and the Captain was pleased to express his approbation of my conduct. God grant I may with a single eye seek to please the Captain of my salvation!

After evening prayers and visiting the sick, went ashore with Mr. Habersham to Deal, and were so delighted with a prospect of the Downs, that we expressed our thankfulness in singing of psalms all the way. The boatmen, I believe, wondered at it at first; but they were not ashamed to blaspheme, and I thought I had no reason to be ashamed to praise God. I had the satisfaction before we got to Deal, to hear one of them join seriously with us; and perceived a surprising alteration in their behavior always after. Blessed be God!

About five we got to Deal, and not knowing a single person, went, as at Margate, to pay my respects to the two ministers of the place; but finding neither of them at home, spent the remainder of the evening with my friend H. very comfortably in religious talk, family prayer, interceding for absent friends and all mankind, and writing to Christian brethren. And even here God did not leave my ministry without a witness; for He was pleased to impress something I said on a poor woman's heart, who providentially came in, and joined with us in family prayer; for which we endeavored to thank Him. Behold how great a fire this little spark kindled before we left Deal!

Thursday, January 12. Spent most of the morning in writing letters. Went about eleven on board; and was highly delighted with the prospect on the Downs, which was exceedingly calm. A great many beautiful ships which were riding here added to the prospect. O that men who occupy their business in the great waters would (since they cannot but see) admire God's wonders in the deep!

Read prayers and went on explaining the Creed to the soldiers; visited and prayed with the sick, and began this afternoon to explain the Catechism to the women by themselves. I find they are in number about sixteen. Blessed be God! they were much affected. Prosper Thou, O Lord, this work of my hands upon me!

Had some religious talk with the surgeon of the soldiers, who seems very well disposed. I seldom, if ever, see him idle, and find he has many good qualities. God grant Christianity may be grafted in him!

After evening prayers and expounding the Creed, went again to Deal with Mr. H. to buy some necessaries for our companions. Spent the remainder of the evening in writing letters, and reading and praying with eight or nine poor people, who came, I suppose, at the report of the other poor women to hear me.

Friday, January 13. Remained all day on shore, the weather being too rough to go on board. Was in care about leaving my flock so long; but hope this short absence will make our meeting more agreeable tomorrow. Had the pleasure of joining in public worship at Deal, in a pretty chapel, which was more pleasant on account of our being confined for some time within the narrow limits of a ship.

Set apart this day as a day of humiliation, abstinence, and intercession for friends and all mankind; and found my heart greatly enlarged in that Divine exercise. Intercession is a glorious means to sweeten the heart.

Spent the remainder of the day, and sat up till one in the morning, in writing to friends. Had two or three added to my company at night, who seemed very attentive, and prayed for me most heartily. The poor receive the Gospel. I dispersed some books among them, as I saw proper; I hope God will give them His blessing.

Expected letters tonight from London, but was disappointed. God enable me in everything to give thanks!

Fancied myself all this day in my little cell at Oxford; for I have not spent so many hours in sweet retirement since I left the University.

Saturday, Jan. 14. Spent the morning in writing letters, and was much pleased with the pious conversation of a poor woman, who was one of my auditors last night, and who, I believe, has passed through the pangs of the new birth.

Hastened on board about eleven, the wind promising fair to take us out of the channel, and was affectionately received by the people. I was greatly delighted to see all the ships sail together from the Downs. Nature, indeed, would have been glad to have stayed till the morrow, that I might have received letters from my London friends; but God, I considered, ordereth all things for the good of those that love Him, and therefore I gave thanks from my heart. Examined into the state of my little ones, (my friend H's charge), and had reason to hope well of them.

Was enlarged in preaching after prayers to the soldiers; and spent two most pleasant hours in reading God's Holy Word. At night, though it was piercingly cold, we continued instant in intercession on deck; and the prospect of a clear sky, the stars glittering, and the moon shining bright, warmed my heart, and made me greatly rejoice in spirit. I now began to be more reconciled to a ship life; for God gave me health of body, and, — without which all is nothing, content of mind. Had near an hour's conversation with one who, I hope, will become an altogether Christian. Oh! that that blessed time would come!

Sunday, January 15. God gave me and Mr. H. sweet sleep. Had near two hours' retirement in the Captain's round house; and was much delighted with singing psalms on deck with my companions. Read public prayers in the cabin this morning; and was much enlarged in preaching to the soldiers on this Article, *I believe in the Holy Ghost*, — in treating of which, I took occasion to show the nature and necessity of the new birth, a subject on which I delight to dwell.

Catechized the soldiers, and, blessed be God! I find some of them improved. Was enlarged again in my evening sermon to the soldiers, and had prayers a second time in the great cabin, which gave me no small satisfaction; the officers and others willingly complied as soon as I imposed it. God be praised!

Had great delight in reading the Holy Scriptures, enjoyed an unspeakable peace of mind, and was much comforted in interceding for friends, etc. on deck. The weather was cold, and the wind blew very hard; but when the heart is full of God, outward things affect it little. Surely my friends in England pray for me; methinks I feel they do.

All the day the sea was entirely becalmed; and everything about us seemed hushed and quiet, as though it would remind us of that sacred rest the day was set apart to commemorate. In the evening the wind blew very fresh, but being full against us, we were obliged to sail back to the Downs (though we had got near fifty miles) where we arrived about twelve o'clock.

Monday, January 16. After private prayer, was most agreeably entertained with some letters from my London friends, which filled my soul with unspeakable pleasure. If the correspondence of good people is so transporting here, O, how unspeakably ravishing must the personal communion of saints be hereafter! Hasten, O Lord, that blessed time, and let Thy Kingdom come.

Was a little affected by seeing a poor soldier tied neck and heels, for several mutinous words he had spoken. The captain related the case to me, and said if I could make him sensible of his crime, I might beg him off. I endeavored to do it, but alas, in vain; he continued obstinate, and thereby hindered my design taking effect. After this, the captain ordered him to be tied down between decks; from whence I took occasion, in my morning sermon, to exhort the soldiers to obey them that had the rule over them, and to avoid those sins, that would provoke God to command them to be tied hand and foot, and to be cast into outer darkness, where would be weeping and gnashing of teeth.

About twelve, a Deal boat coming alongside, I was minded to go on shore to answer my letters. The sea was very boisterous, but God brought us to shore rejoicing. O wherefore did I in the least fear? What am I, when left to myself!

It being the 16th day of the month, Mr. H. and I joined in an hour's intercession and abstinence, with all those who meet together to bewail their own and the sins of the nation. About four, took some bodily refreshment, and from thence till one in the morning, continued answering my correspondents.

Tuesday, January 17. Was awakened with an alarm, that the ship was ready to sail, but found it soon contradicted. Spent an hour in particular intercession, and the rest of the morning in writing letters, and teaching Mr. H. Latin. Oh, that I may be made an instrument of breeding him up for God!

Came on board about two in the afternoon, and found all things quiet in the ship; I was most kindly received, and the women were very attentive when I proceeded to explain the Catechism to them. May God open their hearts as He did that of Lydia, that these may give diligent heed to the things that are spoken.

Was much enlarged in my evening discourse, and hope the Word entered into their hearts. Was kindly invited by the Postmaster of Deal, to lie at his house. Gained an opportunity, by walking at night on deck, after intercession, to talk closely to the chief mate and one of the sergeants of the regiment; and hope my words were not altogether spoken in vain. O that all men would come to the knowledge of the truth, and be saved!

Wednesday, January 18. Spent all the morning in retirement, reading the Scriptures, public prayer, and preaching, the weather being extremely pleasant. Began to live by rule more than ever, for nothing I find is to be done without it. All who had been sick, being recovered, came to prayers, for whom I gave thanks; at the end of my sermon exhorting them with the utmost earnestness, to sin no more, lest a worse evil should befall them, and to show forth their thankfulness, not only with their lips, but in their lives. O that there may be always in them such a mind!

Finished my exposition on the Creed. Read public prayers, and preached as usual in the afternoon. Catechized both my own companions and the soldiers, and was pleased to see many others were attentive to hear. Had great comfort in reading the Scriptures. Was afterwards a little inclined to heaviness, but drove it off by a long intercession. Prayer is an antidote against every evil.

Upon examination had reason to hope my companions grew in grace. Blessed be God for it! About eleven at night, went and sat down among the sailors in the steerage, and reasoned with them about righteousness, temperance, and a judgment to come.

Thursday, January 19. Was much comforted by hearing from my friends. Began, after prayers this morning, to explain the Catechism to the soldiers, and drew proper inferences by way of sermon. I find it is much approved of, and, for them, by far the fittest way of instruction.

Spent the afternoon in answering correspondents. Was much assisted in my evening exposition on the Catechism, and had great hopes of two soldiers becoming Christians indeed. Would to God all the King's soldiers were such!

We had now such a calm and smooth sea, that all the people expressed their admiration of it. God grant we may in a calm provide for a storm, and, like the primitive Christians, when the churches had rest, walk in the comforts of the Holy Ghost, and be edified!

Friday, January 20. Spent all the morning in composing a sermon. Happily composed a difference between a soldier and his wife, who were one of the four couples I married when first I came on board. The man had resolved to leave her, but upon my reminding him of his marriage vow, and entreating him with love, he immediately took to her again. What may not a minister do through Christ, when his flock love him? Almost finished the sermon I began yesterday.

Went on in expounding the Catechism after evening prayer, and now began to read the first Lesson, which I purposely omitted before, not knowing whether they would bear it.

Proposed to the Captain to read a few prayers in the great cabin every night, which he readily consented to, and withal said, he should be glad to hear me preach, whenever I should think proper.

Was surprised in the midst of my evening's discourse by the chief mate, who came and told me, that the minister of Upper Deal had sent a boat for me, desiring me immediately to come on shore. Accordingly, after I had concluded, Mr. H. and I went and found the minister who was left to officiate, who desired me, at the request of the inhabitants, to preach the Sunday following. After this, we retired to our lodging in Deal, and after a sermon, and long intercession, was comforted by the reception of several letters from persons, who, I believe, sincerely fear God.

Found the number of my hearers greatly increased tonight, and very joyful to see me once more on shore. I sat up till one in the morning, answering my correspondents, and then laid down, filled with such joy as no man could take from me, nor a stranger intermeddle with. Oh that all men knew the comforts of religion!

Saturday, January 21. Spent all the day in writing letters, and delightful conversation with Mr. Habersham. At night, the number of my hearers was so increased, that the stairs were full, as well as my room. I expounded to them the 25th of St. Matthew; at which they were much affected, and seemed to love and pray for me most earnestly. I desire to have no greater portion than the prayers of the poor.

Sunday, January 22. About nine, went on board with Captain Whiting, who is always extremely civil. Visited the sick, and read prayers in the great cabin. Read prayers, and preached my sermon on early piety on open deck to the soldiers; the officers and other gentlemen attending seriously. The weather was very cold, but preaching warmed my heart.

About noon went on shore with Capt. Whiting and Mr. Habersham. Dined at the Postmaster's, who received us hospitably. In the afternoon, preached at Upper Deal on Acts 28:26. Many seemed pricked to the heart, and some so quickened, that they expressed a desire to follow me wherever I should go. O free grace in Christ Jesus! I have scarce known a time I have preached anywhere, but I have seen some effect of my doctrine. From the hearts of the mighty the Word of the Lord hath not turned back, the Sword of the Spirit returned not empty. A proof this, I hope, that the words are not my own, and that God is with me of a truth. May I never by pride and vainglory provoke Him to depart from me.

Stayed all night on shore to expound the Lord's Prayer, and had a large company to hear me; and should have had seven hundred, as my hostess told me, would the house have held them — so swiftly ran the Word of God and prevailed.

Was again refreshed by receiving five letters. Sat up till past ten to answer some of them, and then went to rest, with comfortable reflections of God's unmerited loving kindness to me.

> I. Ten thousand, thousand precious gifts,
> My pious thanks employ:
> Nor is the least a thankful heart
> That tastes those gifts with joy.

> II. Through all eternity, to God
> My grateful song I'll raise:
> But oh! eternity's too short
> To set forth all His praise.

Monday, January 23. Was much comforted by receiving five more letters; answered some of them, and about eleven in the morning went on board the *Amy*, to pay my respects to Col. C., and to visit the soldiers, whom I looked upon as part of my charge. I was received very civilly by the officers and went among the soldiers and inquired into the state of their souls; gave them a word or two of exhortation, promised to bring them some books (I saw their wants), and, at the officers' request, to come and preach to them, if opportunity should offer, before we left the Downs.

After this, I visited the *Lightfoot*, our other transport ship, in which were about twelve soldiers and a sergeant; they received me kindly. I sat down and conversed with them, promised to send them some books, and to come and preach to them also, if Providence should permit. The Downs being exceedingly calm, and the weather clear, going from ship to ship was very pleasant. Mine are but little flocks. O that it may be my Heavenly Father's good pleasure to give them the Kingdom.

About two, went again on board the *Amy*, to dine with the officers; being kindly invited by them when I was before on board. They all treated me with great kindness, and in the midst of our meal was most agreeably surprised by the coming of two London friends, who made a journey from thence on purpose to see me. Dinner being ended, I went and dispersed some books among the soldiers; took my leave and hasted on board my own ship; read prayers and preached, and then went on shore with my friends, being not a little rejoiced to see them. This night God let me see greater things than before, for so many came to hear me that the poor landlady who owned the house where I lodged sent to her tenants, beseeching them to let no more come in for fear the floor should break under them; and indeed there were such numbers that I first expounded the Creed to about eighty, and then the Second Lesson to as many more, among whom I observed there were many of the chief inhabitants.

About eleven, they went, and I then rejoiced with my friends for what God had done for my soul; interceded for absent friends and all mankind, and went to bed about two in the morning. Oh what shall I render unto the Lord for all the mercies He pours down upon me!

Tuesday, January 24. Spent all the morning in writing letters, walking, singing psalms, and intercession all along the seashore, from whence we had a most delightful prospect of the Downs, which afforded me and my friends most noble matter for praise and thanksgiving. Met with a little opposition today; but I should have wondered indeed, if such an effectual door had been opened for preaching Christ, and there had been no adversaries. Nothing has done more harm to the Christian Church than thinking the examples recorded in Holy Scriptures, were written only to be read and not imitated by us.

More people came to hear me tonight than ever, so that I divided them into two companies again, and providentially from the Second Lesson for the morning, had a glorious opportunity for showing the absolute unlawfulness of running or buying smuggled goods, a sin that does most easily beset the Deal people.

After exposition, paid Mr. E. a visit, who most kindly entertained us, and offered me his boat to go or come on shore when I pleased, which would save me much expense. After we returned from his house, we kneeled down on the seashore; and prayed for them who opposed themselves; and then went to bed, blessing and praising God.

Wednesday, January 25. Went on board in the morning with my friends intending to read prayers and preach to the soldiers; but they were engaged about their own affairs, and I could not stay long. Had great civilities shown us by the officers, etc., who treated my friends respectfully; and the Captain, upon my request, pardoned a woman who otherwise was to have been sent on shore.

After breakfast, returned on shore with my friends; and read prayers, and preached at Upper Deal to a large congregation. I was surprised to see such a number of people, but all Deal seems to be in a holy flame, and was I prepared for it, I should see still greater things than these.

Dined at Mr. R's, a grocer in Deal, with my friends. We were most hospitably entertained, and what was far better, had an excellent opportunity given me of discoursing for a considerable time on our fall in Adam, and the necessity of our new birth in Jesus Christ.

Expounded to two companies again at night the Epistle for the morning, and the two Lessons for the evening, as most suitable for the day. More people came tonight than before, so that they now did actually put a prop under the floor of the room. Was agreeably entertained with more letters, and though the duty of the day had a little fatigued me, yet God strengthened me to sit up till three in the morning, answering my Christian correspondents.

Thursday, January 26. I had a visit paid me by an Anabaptist teacher, who came to discourse with me about the things that belong to the Kingdom of God. By what I could find out he was a spiritual man. I asked him several questions about taking the ministerial function, without being called as was Aaron; but he did not answer to my satisfaction. However, we both agreed in this, that unless a man be born again, he cannot enter into the Kingdom of God.

I was much comforted by the coming of two more friends from London, with whom I took sweet comfort, and could not but fancy myself once more at London, being surrounded with religious intimates.

> I. How sweet must their advantage be,
>   How great their pleasure prove,
> Who live like brethren and consent
>   In offices of love.

> II. 'Tis like refreshing dew, which does
>   On Hermon's top distil,
> Or like the early drops that fall
>   On Zion's fruitful hill.

In the afternoon I took my friends on board, and read prayers and preached to the soldiers. After this, I went on shore, sung psalms with my friends, and then expounded to the people, who now increased so much that I was obliged to divide them into three companies; and God enabled me to continue expounding three hours without any intermission, or the least weariness. Thanks be to God for His strengthening grace! As our day is, so shall our strength be.

Received three more letters, and sat up till one in the morning to answer some sent before; and then went to bed rejoicing and blessing God for the great things He had done for me, but, withal, desirous to say with the divine Herbert, "Less than the least of God's mercies shall be my motto still."

Friday, January 27. Spent the beginning of the morning in writing letters; then breakfasted with all my friends at one Mrs. H's, a widow gentlewoman, who kindly invited, and as kindly entertained us.

About twelve, I came on board, being unwilling to be absent from my proper charge long together. I was received kindly, visited the sick and catechized the soldiers, some of whom answered most aptly, for which I distributed amongst them all something I knew would be agreeable. Oh! that I may catch them by a holy guile! But that power belongeth only unto God.

About two, came a clergyman on board, from a neighboring village to pay me a visit, with whom I spent an hour or two agreeably; had prayers on open deck, and enforced the duty of keeping holy the sabbath day, which then came in course to be explained, but was afraid to sing a psalm, Mr. H. being at Deal with friends. Where was my courage then? Lord what am I when left to myself!

At five, returned ashore with the clergyman, to whom I promised some books for his parishioners. Expounded three hours to three companies as before. Glad tidings of great joy sent me by four or five correspondents; sat up till one in the morning answering them, and then went to bed and had a feeling possession of my God. And will God in very deed, dwell in this heart of mine? O free grace in Christ! Praise the Lord, O my soul, and all that is within me praise His Holy Name!

Spent the morning most agreeably in conversation, intercession for all friends and all mankind, walking on the seashore.

Dined with Mrs. St. L., who hospitably entertained us. Went, about three in the afternoon intending to go on board, but could not, which gave me a little uneasiness, thinking it by no means right to leave my flock so long. At night I expounded to three companies more numerous than before. Received letters, and sat up till one in the morning answering them.

Sunday, January 29. Went on board early in the morning, read prayers, preached to the soldiers, and visited the sick; then returned on shore, and, accompanied with a troop of pious friends hasted to Shroulden Church, about a mile-and-a-half distant from Deal, where I preached to a weeping and thronged congregation, at the request of the minister, who at my request, gave me and my friends the blessed Sacrament. Others stayed also, to the number of sixteen, and, which I never observed before, the Clerk pronounced a loud Amen to every person who received either bread or wine. An excellent custom, and worthy in my opinion to be imitated in all churches. After this, I and my friends went on our way rejoicing; dined at Mr. R's, and in the afternoon preached at Upper Deal. The Church was quite crowded, and many went away for want of room; some stood on the leads of the Church outside, and looked in at the top windows, and all seemed eager to hear the Word of God. I preached against worldly-mindedness, and had great reason to think God gave it His blessing.

The weather was exceedingly pleasant, and seeing the people go in such flocks over the fields, put me in mind of our blessed Lord's words, when He saw the people coming in companies from Samaria, "The fields are white already to harvest." I then prayed that He would be pleased to enable me to gather wheat into His heavenly garner.

In the evening, such numbers came to hear me, that I was obliged to divide them into four companies, and God enabled me to expound to them from six till ten. Some would have persuaded me to have dismissed the last company without expounding, but I could not bear to let so many go empty away. I find the more we do for God, the more we may. My strength held out surprisingly, and I was but little, if at all fatigued. Afterwards, I gave thanks with my friends for the blessings of the day, and we went to our respective beds about twelve at night. Oh! who can express the loving kindness of the Lord, or show forth all His praise?

Monday, January 30. At the request of the inhabitants, and the leave of Mr. R. (who sent from Canterbury a most obliging message), I preached again at Upper Deal, to as crowded and attentive an audience as I had yesterday; and afterwards, I with Mr. H. waited upon the Rev. Mr. W., who read prayers, and most courteously invited me to come and see him. Our conversation ran chiefly on the expediency of baptizing infants at church. I continued with him about an hour, and then at his request visited a poor woman of the parish, who was grievously troubled in mind; and God was pleased to bless my ministry to her comfort. To Him be all the glory!

> I. So poor, so frail an instrument
>   If Thou my God vouchsafe to use,
>   'Tis praise enough to be employ'd,
>   Reward enough if Thou excuse.
>
> II. If Thou excuse, then work Thy will
>   By so unfit an instrument;
>   It will at once Thy goodness show,
>   And prove Thy power omnipotent!

Soon after this we went to Mr. R's, where our friends expected us. But we had not been long there before the wind shifted about on a sudden, and a cry came, "the wind is fair, prepare yourselves for sailing." I received the news with joy; but sorrow filled the hearts of my dear friends who came from London to see me. We immediately retired, intending to intercede for all mankind before we parted; but the people were in such a hurry, for fear the sea should grow too tempestuous to go off, that we were obliged to be very brief. Having therefore recommended ourselves to God, I took my leave. But oh, what affection did the Deal people express to my unworthy person! For no sooner were they apprized of the wind being fair, but they came running in droves after me to the seashore, wishing me good luck in the name of the Lord, and with tears and other expressions of kindness praying for my success and safe return. I was confounded with a sense of God's mercies to me.

The sea was very boisterous indeed, and the waves rose mountains high; but God was pleased to give Mr. H. and me an unusual degree of faith, and we went on singing psalms and praising God, the water dashing in our faces all the way.

About five, we came on board, and were received with joy, for the ship was under sail, and the people were afraid I should be left behind. As I was going into the great cabin, I fell down the steerage stairs, but received little or no hurt. After we had sailed for a short time, the man-of-war not moving, we cast anchor again. Mr. H. was so sick by the ship's motion after we came on board, that he was obliged to go to bed.

Tuesday, January 31. Spent the morning in writing letters, visiting the sick, reading prayers and preaching to the soldiers. About twelve, was pleasingly surprised with another sight of my London friends, who stayed at Deal all night, and finding the ship did not sail, came with some more Deal friends to take me on shore, that I might bid them once more farewell. I was a little unwilling at first; but by their importunity and affectionate entreaties they compelled me. I accordingly went with them, singing psalms and praising God all the way.

I had scarce been on shore an hour before the man-of-war gave a signal for sailing, and so we were obliged to hasten back on board. The people expressed much joy at seeing me come to Deal again, and accompanied me to the seashore, as before. The weather being fair, we went on board with pleasure; the ship was under sail, but we met with it. I hope that these frequent and sudden removes will put me in mind that I have here no continuing city.

Another thing I could not but reflect on yesterday, when I saw Deal all in a confusion at the time the wind shifted about so suddenly, some crying for one thing, some another, but all anxious lest their ship should sail without them. Alas! what confusion, thought I, will the inhabitants of the world be in, when in a moment, in the twinkling of an eye, they shall hear the voice of the Archangel and trump of God, crying aloud, "Arise, ye dead, and come to judgment!"

After I was on board, I preached, read prayers to the soldiers, visited the sick, wrote some letters, and interceded for all mankind on deck; and retired to bed about twelve. Our ship sailed briskly for a few hours; but the wind shifting again, was obliged to return back once more, and we cast anchor in the Downs about nine at night. After this I went cheerfully about my ministerial business, visited the sick, read prayers and preached to the soldiers, and answered some letters I had received in the morning.

Wednesday, February 1. Sent some books for the soldiers on board the *Lightfoot* and at night went on shore at Deal with Mr. H., where we were kindly entertained and lodged at Mr. R's. Did nothing that night, it being late, save that I visited a sick person at her earnest desire and the minister's consent, and talked about half-an-hour on the benefit of afflictions.

Answered two or three letters I received after I came on shore, prayed with some well-disposed people who were at Mr. R's, and about twelve went to bed.

Thursday, February 2. Rose early in the morning, went on board in Mr. E's boat, intending to read prayers and preach to the soldiers, and then return to Upper Deal to preach there, being asked to do so by the inhabitants and the minister.

About ten o'clock there sprang up a pleasant fair gale, which carried us from the Downs near forty miles that day, during which time I read prayers, preached to and catechized my soldiers, wrote some letters, and had an opportunity of sending them as we sailed by Dover.

Anyone must needs think I should have been glad to have heard from Mr. Wesley, as he went by Deal; but I considered God ordered all things for the best, and therefore I now joyfully went, but not knowing whither I went, and doubted not but He Who strengthened David when he went out against Goliath, would also strengthen me against all my spiritual adversaries, and send His Holy Ghost to guide, assist, and comfort me in all emergencies. The good Lord keep me always thus minded!

Friday, February 3. Let this day be noted in my book, for God wrought for us a wonderful deliverance! About seven in the morning, the men upon decks not keeping a good look-out, one of the East India ships in shifting to the wind ran near us so very briskly, that had not Captain Whiting providentially been on deck, and beseeched them for God's sake to tack about, both the ships must inevitably have split one against another. They were within four yards of each other. The Captain said he never was in so great danger in his life. Mr. Habersham and I knew nothing of it till it was over; but when I was apprised of it, I endeavored to excite all to thankfulness, and returned public thanks at prayers. Too many seemed to be unsensible of the mercy received. But,

> Since God does thus His wondrous love
> Through all our lives extend;
> Those lives to Him let us devote,
> And in His service spend.

Read public prayers and preached to the soldiers as usual; explained the Catechism to the women, and exhorted them particularly to be obedient to their own husbands, which they had lately been wanting in; and was pleased to hear the Captain, as I came on deck, remind me of the motion I made to him some time ago, about having prayers daily in the great cabin, and withal desired that from henceforward I would read prayers morning and evening to them. This I most readily consented to, it being what I had long desired and prayed for, and what I was just then about to propose to him again. Accordingly, I went immediately and acquainted the lieutenant, etc. of the Captain's desire, and we began this night to have full public prayers; and at the request of Captain Whiting, expounded the Second Lesson, and a glorious Lesson it was. Blessed be God! I hope we shall now begin to live like Christians, and call upon the Name of the Lord daily. The very thought of God's granting me this petition filled me with joy.

Saturday, February 4. Began to have prayers in the great cabin in the morning, read prayers and preached twice to the soldiers as usual, and expounded the Second Lesson in the evening to the gentlemen after prayers in the great cabin, which from henceforward I intended, God willing, to continue. Unspeakable will be the benefit of it, for it gives me an opportunity of saying many salutary truths, and affords us matter for serious table-talk afterwards.

I was much pleased to see our ship sail directly before the wind; furnished three soldiers with books, who began today to learn to read. God enable them not only to read, but to do their duty! Mr. Habersham's scholars increase. The Lord increase his strength!

Sunday, February 5. Joined in spirit with absent friends in holy ordinances; spent some time most delightfully in reading the Word of God; read prayers, and made some observations on both the Lessons to the soldiers. O that the Lord would open our understandings! for they are but a dead letter without the illumination of His Holy Spirit.

Read prayers and preached my sermon on *Justification* in the afternoon to the officers, etc. in the great cabin.

Began tonight to turn the observations made on the Lessons in the morning into catechistical questions; and was pleased to hear some of the soldiers and my companions make such apt answers. I find this an excellent way of instruction; it makes them bring their Bible, and give diligent heed to the things that are spoken; it teaches them the Scriptures practically, and consequently, will, by the Divine blessing make them wise unto salvation.

Monday, February 6. Had no prayers in the morning between decks; but read prayers in the cabin. Did the same in the evening, and expounded the 6th chapter of St. Mark, the Second Lesson, which containing an account of John's reproving Herod, gave me an opportunity of telling them, that great men should not be angry if ministers should reprove them out of love. They seemed to assent to it.

Read prayers and preached to the soldiers as usual; interceded warmly for absent friends and all mankind, and went to bed full of peace and joy. Thanks be to God for His unspeakable Gift!

Was pleased to see Mr. Habersham so active in teaching the children. He has now many scholars. May God prosper the works of his hands!

Tuesday, February 7. Read prayers and expounded the Lessons as usual to the soldiers and in the great cabin; and after dinner sung psalms with Mr. Habersham and a gentleman on board, on open deck. Being now in the Bay of Biscay, the ship rocked very much, though there was a great calm.

Wednesday, February 8. Had public worship and expounded as usual to both my congregations. Was pleased to hear a gentlemen discourse for some time of the utter inability of anything to make us happy but God.

In the afternoon I preached and read prayers on open deck, at the Captain's desire, who ordered chairs to be brought and boards put across them for the soldiers to sit upon. My subject was, the eternity of hell torments, and I was earnest in delivering it, being desirous that none of my dear hearers should experience them. Praying and singing psalms on open deck enlarged my heart.

Was enabled to make good part of a sermon this evening, and lay down to sleep. God grant that I may die daily!

Thursday, February 9. Read prayers, expounded and catechized as usual. Had delightful sailing, and very thankful that God called me abroad to see and admire His wonders in the deep. O, who can serve a better Master than Jesus Christ?

Friday, February 10. Read prayers, and according to custom, went on in explaining the Catechism to the women; and after evening prayer expounded the 49th Psalm instead of the Lesson. Had still greater reason to bless God for bringing me to sea. O what shall I render unto the Lord?

Saturday, February 11. Catechized, visited the sick, expounded and read prayers as usual, and met with some soldiers who could sing by note, with whom I propose to join in Divine psalmody every day.

> A psalm may win him who a sermon flies,
> And turn delight into a sacrifice.

In the evening gave thanks for the blessings, and examined into the actions of the past week. It is well I have a Savior to satisfy for my performances as well as my person; for if otherwise, how should I stand before thee, O Holy Lord God? God be merciful to me a sinner.

Sunday, February 12. Did as usual, and preached my sermon on *Glorification* to the gentlemen in the great cabin. Oh that God may make us partakers of it!

Honest Joseph, my servant, returned thanks after morning prayer for his recovery from a late severe fit of sickness. I hope now Christ has touched him by the right hand of His healing power, he will arise and minister unto Him. He tells me he can say with David, "It is good for me that I have been afflicted." God be praised! for sanctified afflictions are signs of special love.

Monday, February 13. Did as usual, only instead of the Second Lesson, expounded the 22nd chapter of St. Matthew, at the Captain's request, who takes all opportunities to express his kindness to me. May the God Whom I serve sanctify and save him!

Tuesday, February 14. May I never forget this day's mercies, since the Lord was pleased to deal so lovingly with me! About twelve at night a fresh gale arose, which increased so much by four in the morning, that the waves broke in like a great river on many of the poor soldiers, who lay near the main hatchway. Friend Habersham and I knew nothing of it, but perceived ourselves restless, and could not sleep at all. He complained of a grievous headache. I arose and called upon God for myself and those who sailed with me, absent friends, and all mankind. After this I went on deck; but surely a more noble, awful sight my eyes never yet beheld! For the waves rose mountain high, and sometimes came on the quarter-deck. I endeavored all the while to magnify God, for thus making His power to be known. Then, creeping on my knees (for I knew not how to go otherwise), I followed my friend H. between decks, and sang psalms and comforted the poor wet people. After this, I read prayers in the great cabin, but we were obliged to sit all the while. Though things were tumbling, the ship rocking, and persons falling down unable to stand, and sick about me, I never was more cheerful in my life, and was enabled, though in the midst of company, to finish a sermon before I went to bed, which I had begun a few days before. Praise the Lord, O my soul, and all that is within me praise His Holy Name!

Thursday, February 16. Did as usual in the ship, only instead of catechizing, examined into the proficiency of my friend Habersham's scholars; gave them proper encouragement, as I saw they wanted, and had hopes that some of them would become living members of Jesus Christ.

Joined with those at night, who set apart this day as a day of fasting and humiliation, to deprecate the judgments our national sins deserve. Lord, hear our prayers, and let our cry come unto Thee.

Friday, February 17. Read prayers, expounded the Lessons, and proceeded in my explanation of the Catechism to the women. Expounded part of the Lord's prayer, after evening prayer, in the great cabin, and intend, after this is done, to go on with the Creed and Ten Commandments. God give us all praying, believing, obedient hearts.

Found honest Mr. D. particularly useful to me, I being a little sick by the late shaking of the ship, and the heat and smell of the people between decks, who, as yet, have scarce had time to recover themselves since the storm. O how soon are these frail tabernacles of ours put out of order! Happy the man who serves God in his health, and has nothing to do when sickness seizes him, but quietly to lie down and die.

Saturday, February 18. Performed the usual duty, and finished the Lord's Prayer. Perceived my bodily disorders to go off, and was enabled to preach to the soldiers. The Captain observed me a little disordered, and gave Mr. H. a cordial for me.

After dinner, I grew better, and was exceedingly delighted by sitting on deck, praising God for the pleasantness of the weather, and reading Archbishop Cranmer's *Life*. Surely he was a righteous man. The account of his fall made my heart tremble within me. But why shouldest thou be cast down. O my soul? Still trust in God. He Who has begun will carry on and finish the good work. Even so, Lord Jesus.

Though the weather was exceedingly pleasant all the day, yet it grew more and more so in the evening, and our ship sailed at the rate of nine miles an hour, and as steady as though we were sitting on shore. The night was unusually clear, and the moon and stars appeared in their greatest lustre; so that not having patience to stay below, I went upon deck with friend Habersham, and praised God for His wonderful loving-kindness, in singing psalms, and gave thanks for the blessings, and asked pardon for the offenses of the week; and then had a long intercession. God grant I may learn a lesson from this good Providence of God; and the nearer I come to my journey's end, the quicker may my pace be.

It is worth coming from England, to see what we have beheld this day. God be praised for all His mercies!

Sunday, February 19. Slept better tonight than I have for a long while, blessed be the Keeper of Israel! Read prayers in the great cabin; was enlarged in expounding both the Lessons to the soldiers; and had prayers, and preached one of the sermons God enabled me to make since I came on board, on open deck in the afternoon. All the gentlemen attended, benches were laid for the people, and the ship sailed smoothly, and the weather was finer than I can express; so that I know not where I have performed the service more comfortably. I have been so delighted these two days, with our pleasant sailing, and the promontories all around us, that I could not avoid thanking God for calling me abroad, and stirring up all to praise Him, Who by His strength setteth fast the mountains, and is girded about with power.

For these two days our ship has sailed at the rate of a hundred-and-sixty miles in twenty-four hours, and rode in triumph directly before the wind, and cast anchor about two in the morning, until which time I sat up on purpose to give thanks in Gibraltar Haven. Oh! that my friends would therefore praise the Lord for His goodness, and extol Him for the wonderful works He doth for me, the least of the sons of men.

How Providence will be pleased to dispose of me here, I cannot yet know, but I thought proper to send you this account of my short voyage already, to show you how God has heard your prayers, to provoke you to thankfulness, and to encourage you to persevere in praying on my behalf.

I cannot help transcribing the verses that follow, as a conclusion to what I have now sent you.

I.   How are Thy servants bless'd, O Lord!
        How sure is their Defence!
    Eternal Wisdom is their Guard;
        Their Help Omnipotence.

II.   Think, O my soul, devoutly think,
        How with affrighted eyes
    Thou saw'st the wide extended deep
        In all its horrors rise!

III.   Confusion dwelt in ev'ry face,
        And fear in ev'ry heart;
    When waves on waves, and gulf on gulf,
        O'ercame the pilot's art.

IV.   Yet then from all my griefs, O Lord!
        Thy mercy set me free;
    Whilst in the confidence of prayer,
        My soul took hold on Thee.

V.   For though in dreadful whirls we hung
        High on the broken wave;
    I knew Thou wert not slow to hear,
        Nor impotent to save.

VI.   The storms were laid, the winds retir'd,
        Obedient to Thy will:
    The sea that roar'd at Thy command.
        At Thy command was still.

VII.   In midst of dangers, fears, and death,
        Thy goodness I'll adore;
    And praise Thee for Thy mercies past,
        And humbly hope for more.

VIII.   My life, if Thou preserv'st my life,
        Thy sacrifice shall be:
    And death, if death shall be my doom,
        Shall join my soul to Thee.

II. From Gibraltar to Georgia

My Dear Friends,

Though I know no reason why you should be solicitous about anything that happens to such an one as I am, yet, as your love abounds exceedingly towards me, I am positive you will give thanks unto our good God for all the mercies He hath conferred upon me; therefore I have sent you as full and particular an account of the remainder of my voyage, as the little leisure I have had from my ministerial offices would permit me to give.

Monday, February 20, 1738. Spent the morning on board, in writing letters to my dear friends in England, to acquaint them of my safe arrival. Went in the afternoon on shore to Gibraltar, and was delighted with the prospect of the place. My friend Habersham and I dined at an inn, and went afterwards with Capt. Whiting and some other company, to view one side of the fort, which to us seemed impregnable, and at the sight of it I could scarce avoid crying out, "Who is so great a God as our God?"

Seeing persons of all nations and languages gave me great pleasure; and the difference of the value of their money and ours gave me occasion to reflect on the stupidity of those who place their happiness in that which has no intrinsic worth in itself, but only so much as we arbitrarily put upon it.

Went into a Romish Chapel, wherein were the relics of a vast deal of pageantry, and several images of the Virgin Mary, dressed up, not like a poor Galilean, but in her silks and damasks. Oh! thought I, who hath bewitched this people, that they should thus depart from the simplicity of Christ, and go a whoring after their own inventions? Surely, were the great St. Paul to rise from the dead, and come and view the Romish Church, his spirit would be stirred up within him, as it was at Athens, to see them thus wholly given to idolatry.

Tuesday, February 21. After having read prayers, and written some more letters to my friends in England, I went again to Gibraltar, to pay my respects to Governor Sabine, being told by Capt. M. that he expected to see me. The worthy old gentlemen, like Sergius Paulus, received me with the utmost candour, and gave me a general invitation to come and dine with him every day, during my stay at Gibraltar. I thanked him for his kindness, had a quarter-of-an-hour's conversation with him, and took my leave for that time.

At one o'clock, I returned to dine with him, according to his appointment; and was well pleased with the regular behavior of the officers at table. We had what an Epicurean would call *coena dubia*. At three I took my leave, and walked about with Capt. Whiting and other friends, to take a second view of the fort; went on board about five, read prayers, and began expounding the Creed in the cabin; wrote some more letters, and went to bed, very thankful to God for sending me abroad.

Wednesday, February 22. This day I went again on shore, and paid both the ministers of Gibraltar a visit, who received me very affectionately, and offered me the use of the pulpit. Oh what a blessed thing it is for the clergy to dwell together in unity!

At eleven, went to public prayers, and was much pleased to see many officers and soldiers attend General Columbine to church. Methinks religion looks doubly amiable in a soldier.

After prayers, dined again with the General, who gave me another particular invitation, as I went out of the church. He treated me with uncommon civility, and desired me to preach the following Sunday.

Had an opportunity of sending a packet of letters with my Journal to my dear friends in England.

Went in the afternoon to visit a deserter, who had sent me a letter, desiring me to intercede for him with the Governor. He being apprehensive he should die for desertion, I intended to answer his request; but the Governor was so merciful that he ordered him to be whipped only, which I thought punishment little enough. O sin, what mischief dost thou make in the world!

In the evening I returned as usual on board; read prayers and expounded in the great cabin; buried a child and made an exhortation to the soldiers proper for the occasion; wrote to some friends at Deal, and went to bed with unusual thoughts and convictions that God would do some great things at Gibraltar. Oh that I was a pure vessel fit for my Master's use!

Thursday, February 23. Continued all this day on board; did my usual duty in the ship, and put my dear friend B's sermon into the hands of two officers at Gibraltar, who came to dine on board with Lieutenant D. They behaved like gentlemen, and seemed pleased with serious conversation. May the God whom I serve, add the Christian to the gentlemen!

Friday, February 24. Blessed be God! Who this day hath shown me that He hath heard my prayer, and not taken His loving-kindness from me. Long before I reached Gibraltar, I prayed that God would open an effectual door at the place whither we were going, and direct me where I should lodge, and lo! this day He has answered me. About ten in the morning came Capt. Mackay on board, telling me that one Major S. (a person I never saw), had provided me a convenient lodging at one merchant B's, and desired that I should come on shore. I looking upon this as a call from Providence, received it with all thankfulness and went with friend Habersham on shore, first praying that God would direct us how to behave.

About the middle of the town, Major S. gave us the meeting, conducted us to our new lodgings, which were very commodious, and engaged us to dine with him and Capt. Mackay. "When I sent you without scrip or shoes, lacked ye anything?" And they said, "Nothing, Lord!"

About eleven I was introduced by Doctor C. to General Columbine, who was desirous of seeing me. He received me exceeding kindly; and after a little serious conversation, we went to Governor Sabine's, and from thence to public prayers. I was highly pleased to see so many officers attending on the Generals to church. Doctor C. told me he had not known Governor Sabine absent himself from prayers once these several years, except when he was hindered by sickness. Oh that all others would let their light so shine before men!

Retired in the evening to our lodgings. Had family prayer, wrote some few religious letters, and spent near half-an-hour in serious conversation with the people of the house, and was soon convinced that God had sent me to that particular lodging of a truth. Be careful for nothing; but in every (even the minutest) thing, make your wants known unto God. For He careth for you.

Saturday, February 25. About six this morning went with friend Habersham to the church to pray with some devout soldiers, who I heard used to meet there at that time, and with whom my soul was knit immediately. After we had finished our devotion, I made an inquiry into their state, and found that their Society had been subsisting about twelve years and that one Sergeant B., (a devout soldier indeed) now amongst them, was the first beginner of it. At first, they told me they used to meet in dens and mountains, and caves, in the rocks; but, afterwards, upon their applying for leave to build a little place to retire in, Doctor C. and Governor Sabine gave them the free use of the Church, where they constantly meet three times in a day to pray, read, and sing psalms, and at any other season when they pleased. They have met with contempt, and are now, in derision, called *The New Lights*. A glorious light they are indeed; for I conversed closely with several of them, and they made me quite ashamed of my little proficiency in the School of Christ. Many have joined with them for a time, but a servile fear of man — that bane of Christianity — made them draw back. However, some continue steadfast and immovable, though despised by the world. Governor Sabine countenances them much, and has spoken of them often to me with respect. Blessed be God! even the Father of our Lord Jesus Christ, Who hath not left Himself without witness in any place, but hath some everywhere, who serve Him and work righteousness.

The Sunday before we came hither, I was telling my friend Habersham that I had reason to think by what had happened to me, that God had some work for me to do at Gibraltar. He answered that there could not be much good expected from among soldiers. I replied — No doubt God has some secret ones in all places, who tremble at His Word. And lo! He hath this day brought me to them.

There is also another Society of the Scotch Church, who in contempt are called *Dark Lanthorns*. It has subsisted about a year, and is made up of many serious Christians, I was informed. I did not think it agreeable to visit them; but I sent them, as well as the other Society, some proper books. I had religious talk with several of them, and endeavored to unite both Societies together. Oh, when will that time come, when all differences about externals shall be taken away, and we all with one heart, and one mouth glorify our Lord Jesus Christ!

About eight I returned to my lodgings, and after having written some letters, went on board the *Amy* to marry a couple who sent to me yesterday to come and celebrate their nuptials. I took that opportunity of exhorting them all to take heed to the things that belong to their peace. Some, I believe, were affected, but the generality of them behaved so careless, that I could not but see a difference between those who have a minister and those who have not.

About twelve, went on board my own ship, dined, did some necessary business, read prayers, gave my flock a warm exhortation, and returned about five on shore, where I spent near two hours with the devout soldiers in the church. Many of them conversed most spiritually, and seemed well acquainted with the pangs of the new birth. May God perfect the good work begun in their hearts! O how amiable are Thy servants, O Lord of hosts! But Satan does now as formerly dress them in bears' skins, in order to have them baited.

Sunday, February 26. Between five and six in the morning went with Mr. Habersham (which I did all the while I was at Gibraltar) and sung psalms, prayed, and expounded the Lessons to the devout soldiers in the church, and was much enlarged. Thanks be unto Thee, O Lord!

Intended to go and preach to my people, but was prevented by the violence of the wind. I was pleased to hear from some Gibraltar officers, who dined that day on board the *Whitaker*, that some of my flock had the courage to read prayers and sing psalms themselves, and (as I found afterwards) continued so to do, during my absence from them. Blessed be God! I hope I shall have some who dare be singularly good, and will not be kept out by the press.

Preached in the morning at Gibraltar, before such a congregation of officers and soldiers as I never before saw. The church, though very large, was quite thronged; and God was pleased to show me, that He had given extraordinary success to my sermon. O how is the Divine strength magnified in my weakness! O grant I may, like a pure crystal, transmit all the light Thou pourest over me, and never claim as my own what is Thy sole property!

Dined with friend Habersham at Governor Sabine's, who sent most kindly to invite us. The law at his table was the same with that of Ahasuerus, "No one was compelled"; and all the officers behaved in such a decent manner every time I dined there, that they pleased me very much. After evening prayers (for there is no sermon in the afternoon), I went and expounded, prayed, and sung psalms with the Society, and had near thirty hearers.

At night, I had some devout conversation with my host and hostess, who seemed to love me as their own son, prayed for absent friends, and went to bed ashamed I had done so little for God on a Sabbath day.

Monday, February 27. Went to the church, and did as yesterday; and was visited afterwards by two of the Nonconforming Society, who seemed to be Israelites indeed. I exhorted them to love and unity, and not to let a little difference about a few externals occasion any narrow-spiritedness to arise in their hearts. I advised them to come and hear me expound in the church, which they did; and providentially the Lesson was the 4th of the Ephesians, from whence I took occasion to urge on them the necessity of loving one another with a catholic disinterested love, to be of one heart and one mind, and to join without respect of persons in hastening the Kingdom of our Lord Jesus Christ. I hope God gave a blessing to what was said, for I observed they came constantly afterwards, and was told there was a perfect harmony between them. What infinite mischief have needless divisions occasioned in the Christian world! *Divide et impera*, is the Devil's motto.

Dined and supped at General C's with Mr. Habersham, and was received most courteously. The officers seemed studious to oblige me, and to be solicitous for my stay at Gibraltar; but my face was set to go towards Georgia. The Lord direct my going in His way!

Tuesday, Feb. 28. Expounded in the church as usual; went on board, read prayers and expounded to my own flock; dined with friend Habersham at Governor Sabine's, who sent to invite us; and expounded to a large number of soldiers in the evening at church.

Was asked by Dr. C. in the name of the Governor and Colonel C. to preach every Prayer Day whilst I stayed at Gibraltar, which I promised to do. Many of the inhabitants pressed me to stay with them, and were exceeding kind to those who were with me. Blessed be God! for thus giving me favor in His people's sight. Lord, what am I, that Thou shouldest thus so highly honor me? Grant, O Lord, the more Thou exaltest me, the more I may abase myself, and look to the rock from whence I was hewn!

Conversed with one of the devout soldiers, who was under strong spiritual trials; and God was pleased to give him comfort. I find it necessary more and more every day, that ministers should be tempted in all things, that they may be able experimentally to succour those that are tempted.

Wednesday, March 1. Expounded in the morning, and was pleased at my entrance into the church, to see several soldiers kneeling in several parts of the House of God at their private devotions. O happy Gibraltar, that thou hast such a set of praying men! Some, I hear, often come in by two o'clock in the morning, to pour out their hearts before God. The Lord perform all their petitions!

Preached, according to my promise, to a numerous and affected audience of officers, soldiers, etc. Dined, at his invitation, at Governor Sabine's; and expounded at night to near 200 people, amongst whom were many of the officers, and of the honorable women, not a few. Oh that they may with meekness receive the engrafted Word, and that it may be a means of saving their souls!

Thursday, March 2. Spent part of the day in writing letters. Dined and supped at Mr. Argat's, chief civil magistrate in Gibraltar. Expounded twice in the church, as usual; and at night had above 300 hearers, amongst whom were many officers, ladies, and Dr. C., the minister of the church himself, who would have had me go up into the reading desk, that I might have the greater command of the people, but I declined it that night. God be praised for sending me abroad, and prospering the work of His hands upon me!

> When all Thy mercies, O my God!
> My rising soul surveys;
> Transported with Thy love, I'm lost
> In wonder, joy, and praise!

Friday, March 3. Still God lets me see greater things than before. Oh that my thanks may increase proportionably! This morning, besides a great number of the soldiers, near, if not more, than a dozen of the townspeople came to church to hear me expound. Afterwards, we breakfasted with a gentlewoman, who sent by Major S. to invite us, and most gladly received us into her house. About ten I preached my sermon against *Swearing*, and made a farewell application to the soldiers who were going over to Georgia out of that garrison. The Governor had that morning reviewed them; and as I could not be in the same ship with them, I desired they might be ordered to come to church, that I might have an opportunity of telling them how to behave in that land which they were going over the sea to protect. The Colonel and Governor most readily consented; there was a most thronged audience, and God was pleased to set His seal to my sermon. Many officers and soldiers wept sorely, and a visible alteration was observed in the garrison for some days after. Oh that their convictions may end in their conversion, and that they may bring forth the fruits of the Spirit!

Bought some wine out of the money which I had collected for the use of the sick poor in Georgia. The parsonage-house ought to be the poor's storehouse.

Had about 500 to hear me expound this evening, and went up into the desk, by the advice of Dr. C., who now constantly makes one of my hearers. After this, we supped at Mr. B's, of the Victualling Office, and returned home with joy and great gladness of heart. Who can express the loving-kindness of the Lord, or show forth all His praise?

Saturday, March 4. Expounded in the morning to more hearers than ever, some of whom wept. Dined and supped with General C., who sent last night to invite me and my friend, and treated us with particular respect.

Went in the afternoon to the Jewish synagogue, and was surprised to see one of the head of them come from the farthest end, and put me in one of their chiefest seats. But afterwards he told me he had heard my sermon yesterday against swearing, and thanked me for it. I continued with them their whole service, and spent most of my time there in secret prayer to God that the veil might be taken from their hearts, and that blessed time might come when His chosen people should again be engrafted into their own Olive Tree, and all Israel be saved.

Visited an unhappy man in prison, who last night, in a drunken fit, murdered a fellow-soldier. I providentially met him just as he was apprehended, and laid before him the terrors of the Lord. At first he seemed unconcerned; but in a short time he was pricked to the heart, desired me to come and see him, and today trembled, and wept bitterly. Oh Drunkenness, what mischief hast thou done! Thy name is legion, for behold a troop of sins come along with thee.

In the evening, I had near, if not more than a thousand hearers; and I took occasion, from the poor man's example before mentioned, to warn the soldiery not to be drunk with wine, wherein is excess, — a sin that most easily besets the men of Gibraltar. May they hear and fear, and sin no more presumptiously. I had a great hoarseness upon me; but notwithstanding, God enabled me to speak with power. When we are weak, then are we strong. What mercies has God shown me this last week! Oh that my friends, when they hear of it, may praise Him! for surely God has hearkened to their prayer.

Sunday, March 5. After morning exposition in the church, went and saw the Roman Catholics at their High Mass; and shall only make this remark: That there needs no other argument against Popery, than to see the pageantry, superstition, and idolatry of their worship.

About ten, went to the church belonging to the garrison; preached to a most thronged audience, and received (what my soul longed after), the Sacrament of Christ's Most Blessed Body and Blood. Both the Generals were there, and near fifty more communicants. The weekly collection for the poor was larger than was ever known; and ... was so affected, that he wished himself a despised Methodist.

Dined at Governor Sabine's, and, at the request of the inhabitants and gentlemen of the garrison, preached in the afternoon. Expounded, in the evening, to above a thousand hearers of all denominations; supped with General Columbine; and went home betimes, full of unspeakable comfort. I am never better than when I am on the full stretch for God. God grant I may not, like Jehu, drive furiously at first, and afterwards fall back; but "forgetting those things which are behind, may I reach out to those things that are before, and press forwards towards the mark, for the prize of my high calling in Christ Jesus.

Monday, March 6. Had near, if not more than, a hundred at morning exposition; and it being the last day of my sojourning at Gibraltar, many came to me weeping, telling me what God had done for their souls, desiring my prayers, and promising me theirs in return. Others both gave and sent me tokens of their love, as cake, figs, wine, eggs, and other necessaries for my voyage, and seemed to want words to express their affection. The good Lord note their kindnesses in His book, and reward them a thousandfold!

About twelve, went to the church, according to appointment, and made a farewell exhortation, as God gave me utterance, to a great number of weeping soldiers, women, etc. After which, we kneeled down, and having recommended each other to the care of God, I left them, and went and took my leave of the two Generals; visited the confined prisoner; dined at a gentlewoman's house of the town; left near fifty letters to be sent to England; and, about four, went on board, accompanied to the seaside with near two hundred soldiers, women, officers, etc., who sorrowed at my departure, and wished me good luck in the Name of the Lord. Surely I may now expect greater success abroad, having such an addition of intercessors in my behalf. O Lord put their tears into Thy bottle, and let their cry come unto Thee!

Samson's riddle has been fulfilled at Gibraltar. *Out of the eater came forth meat; out of the strong came forth sweetness.* Who more unlikely to be wrought upon than soldiers? And yet, amongst any set of people, I have not been where God has made His power more to be known. Many who were quite blind, have received their sight; many who had fallen back, have repented, and turned unto the Lord again; many who were ashamed to own

Christ openly, have waxen bold; and many who were saints have had their hearts filled with joy unspeakable, and full of glory. This is the Lord's doing, and it is marvelous in our eyes. May He give a blessing to the books dispersed amongst them, and perfect the good work begun in their hearts, till the day of our Lord Jesus! May they be my joy and crown of rejoicing at the last day, and may God's mercies to me in every place make me more humble, more zealous, more thankful, and more steady to do or suffer whatever my dear Redeemer hath allotted for me.

About five, came on board, and was gladly received by my flock, whom I hope to love better for being a little absent from them. Interceded and gave thanks, as usual, at night on deck; and was pleased that I was again retired from the world. It rained much. Water us, O Lord, we beseech Thee, with the dew of Thy heavenly benediction.

Tuesday, March 7. Went and conversed with, and dispersed some books amongst the soldiers whom we took from Gibraltar. Three of them belonged to one of the Societies, and desired, with some others, to come with me in our ship. God sanctify my ministry unto them. Most of the rest are of the Scots Church, but seem very willing to conform. What a pity it is, Christ's seamless coat should be rent in pieces on account of things in themselves purely indifferent!

At dinner we were likely to be struck against by the man-of-war, but God had mercy on us, commanded the wind to shift about, and delivered us out of so great a danger. Oh, that we may show forth our thankfulness, not only with our lips, but in our lives! How ought creatures to live, who are every moment liable to be hurried away by death to judgment!

This day we set sail from Gibraltar. At first the wind was fair, but afterwards blew contrary, which made both me and many others sick. I should have wondered if God had not sent me a thorn in the flesh, after such abundant success. May I learn to suffer, as well as do Thy will, O God!

Wednesday, March 8. Had a useful conference with one who was an instrument, under God, of introducing me at Gibraltar, and who, I trust, will make a devout centurion.

Finished my exposition on the Creed in the great cabin, and did my other duty in the ship, as usual. The wind blew hard, and God sent abroad His lightning great part of the day. J.D., friend Habersham and myself also, were sick, but not so as to prevent our intercession for absent friends. Whatever befalls me, O God, may I never forget their works and labor of love.

Gave myself, as much as my indisposition of body would give me leave, to the Word of God and prayer; and was much affected with what is said of Hezekiah, 2 Chron. 32:25, that because he rendered not again, was not thankful enough for the great things God had done for him, he was permitted to fall through the pride of his heart. Alas! what danger am I in of sharing the same fate! O my friends, cry mightily unto God, that no such evil come upon me.

Thursday, March 9. Married a couple on deck. I endeavored to give them a suitable exhortation after the solemnity was over, and hope this couple did call Christ to their marriage. It is through a neglect of this, that we have so few happy matches.

The contrary wind still continuing, my sea-sickness increased, so that I was obliged to omit reading prayers to the soldiers, and go to bed sooner than usual. I find this sickness will purge my body.

Friday, March 10. My bodily indisposition still increased; there was a great storm without, but, blessed be God, a calm within. Sometimes, indeed, my will would inwardly rebel; but I hope, through inward and outward sufferings, I shall at length be able to say in all things, "Father, not my will, but Thine be done."

Did my usual duty in the great cabin, and began expounding the Ten Commandments; interceded for friends on deck, and went to bed full of a sense of my own unworthiness. Oh, that I could always see myself in my proper colors! I believe I should have little reason to fall down and worship myself. God be merciful to me a sinner!

Saturday, March 11. Blessed be God, this morning the storm began to blow over, and light broke in upon my soul. Was enabled to read prayers and expound both in the cabin and to the soldiers, with more vigour than I have done since we left Gibraltar. Had reason to think my late indisposition had been sanctified to me. Suffering times are a Christian's best improving times; for they break the will, wean us from the creature, prove the heart, and by them God teaches His children, as Gideon by thorns and briars taught the men of Succoth.

Sunday, March 12. Expounded with more enlargement than usual, and gave my people notice that I intended speaking to them one by one; to see what account they could give of their faith. "I have not ceased warning every one of you," says the Apostle. May I follow his steps!

Preached the sermon God enabled me to make in the storm before we came to Gibraltar, in the great cabin; and God was pleased to set His seal to it. Had some close conversation with my companions about their interior; interceded for absent friends, and had reason to hope my weak efforts to promote His glory had not been in vain in the Lord. May God give me a thankful heart!

Monday, March 13. Blessed be God, this is the most comfortable day I have had since I came last aboard; slept better than usual; was enabled to compose freely; perceived my appetite to return; was enlarged much in intercession, and found I had reason to give thanks for my late indisposition. O how gently does my gracious Master deal with me! Though sorrow may endure for a night, yet joy cometh in the morning. Lord, grant that I may spend that health Thou hast now restored to me to Thy honor and service! It is good for me that I have been a little chastised; for who knows but I might otherwise have perished by being lifted up above measure with my last success? Lord give me humility, though it be through sufferings! So shall Thy blessings never prove my ruin.

Tuesday, March 14. Began to put in execution what I promised on Sunday, i.e., inquired into the faith of those committed to my charge; and though all of them were not so great proficients as I could wish, yet I find they know enough to save them, if they put what they know in practice, so that they cannot charge God, if they miscarry. Oh! that the Lord may give them His blessing!

Had much of the presence of God with me, and felt such a fervent love for my Christian friends, that I feared how I should behave, was God to call any of them from me. But I trust sufficient for such an hour will be the strength thereof.

Wednesday, March 15. Was much pleased with my present situation, and had reason to bless God for some further visible effects of my ministry. Was highly delighted in seeing friend Habersham active in teaching the lambs of my flock. He has now got a regular school, and the children began today to come at regular set hours. Several also of the soldiers learn to write and read, so that my friend is likely to make a useful man.

Thursday, March 16. Preached this afternoon my sermon against *Swearing*, at which several of the soldiers wept. Blessed be God! that sin is much abated amongst us; and I think visible alteration may be perceived through the whole ship.

Was much strengthened in my present undertaking, by reading the story of Ezra, and joined an intercession with those who set apart this day as a day of fasting and prayer for the sins of the nation to which we belong. May they prove as effectual as those which Moses put up for the children of Israel!

The sick increased today. I visited near a dozen. May I by this frequent visiting sick beds, learn to improve my time of health; for, alas! what can be done in time of sickness? I find but few who are able with any tolerable patience to sustain their bodily infirmities: but to have a wounded spirit at the same time, good God, who can bear it?

Friday, March 17. Last night God sent us a fair wind, and we began to sail pleasantly. I was comforted on every side, and enabled to intercede fervently for all mankind. Oh, that the love of God and man was shed abroad in my heart!

Saturday, March 18. The weather being exceeding fair, and the sea calm, I went with Capt. Whiting on board the *Lightfoot*; dined with the gentlemen belonging to the ship and Colonel C., who came on board to pay them a visit; married a couple; dispersed Bibles, Testaments, Soldiers' Monitors amongst the men; exchanged some books for some cards, which I threw overboard; preached a sermon against drunkenness, which God enabled me to finish yesterday; and returned in the evening, delighted with seeing the porpoises roll about the great deep. O Lord, the sea is full of Thy riches! marvelous are Thy works, and that my soul knoweth right well. O that I may live to praise Thee for them! What mercies have I received this week! they are more in number than the hairs of my head.

Sunday, March 19. Went with Captain Whiting on board the *Amy*; read prayers and preached to above two hundred and twenty hearers, and married a couple, who did not behave so well as I could wish. The bridegroom laughed several times in the midst of the solemnity, upon which I shut up my prayer book. He began to weep; and I then proceeded, and gave him and the bride a Bible, as the best present I could make them, and exhorted all to holiness of life. God give them a hearing ear, and an obedient heart!

Dined with Colonel Cochrane, who treated me with the utmost civility, and took care to dispose of some books I brought with me to proper persons. About three, we returned to the *Whitaker*, read prayers and preached my sermon against drunkenness; after which, Captain Mackay made a useful speech to the men, and exhorted them to give heed to the things that had been spoken. Religion is likely to go on well, when both the civil and ecclesiastical powers are engaged in keeping up the purity of it. But, Lord, unless Thou assist us, all our endeavors are but in vain. Vouchsafe then, we beseech Thee, to give us Thy blessing!

Had above an hour's close conversation with my companions concerning their interior; and walked with friend Habersham on deck until twelve at night, admiring God's wonders in the deep.

Monday, March 20. Today Colonel Cochrane came to dine with us, and in the midst of our meal we were entertained with a most agreeable sight. It was a shark about the length of a man, which followed our ship, attended with five little fishes called the Pilot Fish, much like a mackerel, but larger. These, I am told, always keep the shark company, and what is most surprising, though the shark is so ravenous a creature, yet let it be never so hungry, it never touches one of them. Nor are they less faithful to him; for if at any time the shark is hooked, these little creatures will not forsake him, but cleave close to his fins, and are often taken up with him. Go to the pilot fish, thou that forsakest a friend in adversity, consider his ways and be abashed. This simple sight one would think sufficient to confute any atheist (if there be such a fool as a speculative atheist) in the world.

After dinner I read prayers and expounded to my own people, and then went aboard the *Amy* with Colonel Cochrane, and married a couple; and came back to the *Whitaker*, rejoicing to see the works of the Lord, and the beauty of the great deep.

Tuesday, March 21. The weather growing warmer, friend Habersham had some cloths hung over to cover his school. His children come very regularly both to learn and say their prayers at night. Captain Whiting takes great delight in them, and Captain Mackay much encourages the soldiers to learn to read and write, so that we begin to live as regularly now as we could wish to do on shore.

Though God gives me so much comfort, yet my dear England friends are seldom out of my mind; though absent in body, I am present with them in spirit. The Lord direct my way unto them, and grant if ever I return it may be in the fullness of the blessing of the Gospel of peace!

Wednesday, March 22. Saw a large grampus rolling and spouting out water for a long while, at a short distance from our ship. It put me in mind of the behemoth spoken of by Job, and of the leviathan mentioned by the Royal Psalmist. O God, who is like unto Thee?

Thursday, March 23. This morning we began to have prayers at six o'clock, and the drum beat to call the people. We grow more and more regular every day. God be praised!

Was fervent in intercession for absent friends and all mankind. Oh, intercession is a most delightful exercise! How does it sweeten and purify the heart!

Visited near twelve or fourteen sick persons, and yet such is God's mercy to me, that though the place where they lie is much confined, and they catch the fever of one another, yet God keeps me from infection. The way of duty is the way of safety. Now God has sent His visitations abroad amongst us, I hope we shall learn righteousness.

Friday, March 24. Today the sick still increased, and friend Habersham was very ready to assist and carry things to them. Nothing more useful than visiting sick beds! How are those to be pitied, who purposely shun such improving sights!

We begin now to live so happy on shipboard, that I believe we shall part with each other with regret. By this may all men know we are Christ's disciples, that we love one another.

Sailed a hundred and fifty-four miles the last twenty-four hours, and was much delighted in seeing many porpoises playing about the ship, one of which Captain Whiting caught, and part of its liver we had dressed for dinner. It had a head much like a pig, and was about six feet long. The works of the Lord are exceeding great, and to be admired of all them who have a delight therein.

Churched a woman who lately was delivered of a dead child, and afterwards gave her an exhortation applicable to her circumstances. God grant she may apply it to her heart!

Sunday, March 26. This day, God, I trust, magnified His power in the conversion of a young gentleman on board, whom He has been pleased to visit with a fever. His convictions were strong, and as far as I could find, a thorough renovation begun in his heart. The Lord perfect it till the day of his dissolution. Now God begins to show me wherefore He hath sent me. O that I was humble! that I might be fit for the High and Lofty One, Who inhabiteth eternity, to work by.

Preached a sermon in the afternoon, on Luke 3:14. *And the soldiers likewise came unto Him, and demanded, saying, "And what must we do?" and He said unto them, "Do violence to no man, neither accuse any falsely, and be content with your wages."* I made it at the request of Capt. Mackay who seems in earnest about the great work of his salvation. He has read Arndt's *True Christianity*, and is now reading Law's *Christian Perfection*, — books worth their weight in gold, and which God has blessed to the conversion of many. But what are books without Thy Spirit, O Lord? Do Thou bless them unto him, and they shall be blessed.

Exchanged some bad books that were on board (which I threw immediately into the sea), for some good ones. All that I have found with them, as yet, have been ready to surrender them up; and I find by daily experience more and more, that people who are truly awakened to a sense of the Divine life, cannot bear to read anything trifling, but throw away their useless books, as those did the books of divination and curious arts, whose conversion we read in the Acts, Chapter 19.

Monday, March 27. Last night God was pleased to take away a black boy of Captain Whiting's, after he had been ill of a violent fever for some days. He was never baptized; but I had a commission from his master, who seemed much affected at his death, to instruct, and baptize him, if it had pleased the Most High that he should recover; but God saw fit to order it otherwise. His holy will be done. About ten in the morning he was wrapped up in a hammock and thrown into the sea. I could not read the Office over him being unbaptized, but Capt. Mackay ordered the drum to be beaten, and I exhorted all the soldiers, sailors, etc., as God gave me utterance, to remember their Creator in the days of their youth, and to prepare for that time, when the sea should give up its dead, and all nations be called together to appear before the Son of God. Oh that they may be made wise by it, that they may lay to heart what has been said, and practically consider their latter end!

Had our blessed Lord been here, I believe He would have wept to see what havoc sin had made amongst us. Do Thou, Lord, teach us so to number our days, that we may apply our hearts unto wisdom.

Tuesday, March 28. This day Capt. Mackay began to come at six in the morning and join in prayers on deck, instead of having prayers in the great cabin. Surely our soldiers will be without excuse since their Captain leads so good an example. I have no reason to complain of them, for they come very regularly twice a day to prayer, and an oath seems to be a strange thing amongst most of them. Many marks of a sound conversion appear in several on board, and we live in perfect harmony and peace, loving and beloved by one another. Surely, my friends, your prayers are heard. Continue instant in them, and you shall see greater things than these, for God delights in the prosperity of His servants.

Wednesday, March 29. Sailed nearly one hundred and sixty miles every twenty-four hours, for several days; had most delightful weather, and much of God's presence amongst us.

> Heaven is, dear Lord, where'er Thou art,
> Oh never then from us depart;
> For to my soul 'tis hell to be
> But for one moment void of Thee.

Thursday, March 30. Had still more proofs of a thorough conversion being wrought in some in the ship. I hope many of us shall have reason to bless God for coming on board the *Whitaker*. God grant, while I preach to others, I myself may not be a castaway! But God is Love, and He will not, if my eye be single, let His blessings destroy me. O let Thy power be exerted in preserving me, even me always, O my Savior.

> I.   Renew Thy likeness, Lord, in me,
>   Lowly and gentle may I be,
>   No charms but these to Thee are dear;
>   No anger mayst Thou ever find,
>   No pride in my unruffled mind,
>   But faith and heaven-born peace be there.

II.   A patient, a victorious mind,
A life that all things casts behind,
Springs forth obedient to Thy call;
A heart that no desire can move;
But still t'adore, and praise, and love,
Give me, my Lord, my Life, my All.

Friday, March 31. This being the crucifixion of our blessed Lord, I preached a sermon on the penitent thief; and I hope God gave it His blessing. We began prayers later than usual, so that before I had done, darkness came upon us, which put me in mind of that darkness which overwhelmed the world, when the God of Nature suffered. Oh that our hearts may rend like the rocks, and our souls arise from the death of sin, as the bodies of those did from their graves, who appeared to many in the Holy City, after our Lord's resurrection.

Had a good instance of the benefit of breaking children's wills betimes. Last night going between decks (as I do every night) to visit the sick and to examine my people, I asked one of the women to bid her little boy who stood by her, say his prayers; she answered his elder sister would, but she could not make him. Upon this, I bid the child kneel down before me, but he would not till I took hold of his two feet and forced him down. I then bid him say the Lord's Prayer (being informed by his mother he could say it if he would); but he obstinately refused, till at last, after I had given him several blows, he said his prayer as well as could be expected, and I gave him some figs for a reward. And this same child, though not above four years of age, came tonight on deck, and when the other children came to say their prayers to my friend Habersham, he burst out into tears, and would not go away till he had said his too. I mention this as a proof of the necessity of early correction. Children are sensible of it sooner than parents imagine. And if they would but have resolution to break their wills thoroughly when young, the work of conversion would be much easier, and they would not be so troubled with perverse children when they are old.

Saturday, April 1. Wonderfully pleasant sailing still, and what was infinitely better, had reason to think several went forward in the great work of their salvation. Oh that we may be buried with Christ in baptism, and rise with Him to newness of life.

Sunday, April 2. Rose early this morning, and joined in spirit with my dear absent friends, who were receiving the Holy Eucharist, and celebrating our blessed Lord's resurrection. I find my not being in Priest's Orders is a great hindrance to my ministry, which will oblige me to return to England as soon as possible. The good Lord prepare me for that second imposition of hands.

Preached a sermon in the afternoon on Phil. 3:10. *That I may know Him and the power of His resurrection.* Oh that we may all experience it in our hearts! For without it, Christ as to us is dead in vain.

Monday, April 3. Had some further conversation with the young gentleman whose conversion I mentioned before, and who I hope is really quickened from above. He told me he used to wonder to hear me talk that all our thoughts, words, and actions ought to be dedicated unto God; but now he perceived what I said to be true. How does the new nature give us new notions! It seems a difficult task to the natural man to turn his whole life into one continued sacrifice, but the spiritual man does it with ease. He feels a Divine attraction in his soul, which as sensibly draws his heart towards God, as the loadstone attracts the needle. Draw us then, O God, and our affections will ascend up after Thee.

About eleven, went on board the *Lightfoot*, prayed with a sick man, and preached my sermon on the penitent thief. Afterwards, went on board the *Amy*, catechized the children, dined on a dolphin, had some useful conversation, preached to the soldiers, returned home about six, read prayers, visited the sick, interceded for friends, and went to bed praising and blessing God.

Friday, April 7. Great enlargement of heart has been given me for these four days last past, particularly today, in which God hath vouchsafed me much of His presence, and assisting grace. Observed still stronger signs of a thorough conversion being wrought in some on board; had most delightful sailing, and everything as pleasant as this vain world can afford. These are preparatives for future trials. Welcome in the Name of God. He will uphold me. If it were not for the corruptions of my own heart, which are continually stirring, what Have I to disturb my peace? But as long as those Amalekites remain in my soul, I shall never be perfectly at ease. Lord keep me but striving, and I shall at last be more than conqueror through Jesus Christ Who loved me.

Saturday, April 8. Went on board the *Lightfoot* and *Amy*, and preached to the soldiers of each ship; dined with Colonel Cochrane, and, at my return found the sick increase upon my hands. But few in the ship escape. The good Lord make all their beds in their sickness.

Had much of the presence of God with me today. The heat is uncommonly temperate, as it has been for some time, and the ship sailed all day as though she were carried on the wings of the wind. Preached two sermons, besides my exposition at six in the morning; and I hope God set His seal to them. Was well pleased to hear by my friend H. (who is very active in carrying things to the sick), that the poor people between decks prayed heartily for me.

And now, indeed, we live more comfortably in the great cabin than can easily be imagined. We talk of little else but God and Christ. God has greatly blessed the *Country Parson's Advice to his Parishioners*, that excellent book, and scarce a word is to be heard amongst us when together, but what has reference to our fall in the first, and our new birth in the Second Adam, the Lord from Heaven; so that we all, I trust, are resolved to put my afternoon's text into practice, and are determined not to know anything save Jesus Christ, and Him crucified. Grant this, O Father, for Thy dear Son's sake. Oh that I knew how to be thankful! Oh that Heaven and earch would join with me in praising God! For

> I would not, Lord, alone,
> Thy praises celebrate,
> I'd call the blessed angels down,
> I'd move the world's united state,
> Till they in fervent songs, Thy gracious acts relate.

Monday and Tuesday, April 10,11. Spent good part of these two days in mending my nets. Had exceedingly pleasant weather. Some more of the sailors were convicted of sin, and others send notes to be prayed for, and give thanks as regularly as in any parish.

Wednesday and Thursday, April 12 and 13. Today Captain Whiting caught a dolphin which was most beautiful when drawn out of the water, but its color soon changed. Just so is man; he flourishes for a little while, but when once death cometh how quickly is his beauty gone! A Christian may learn a lesson of instruction from everything he meets with.

Friday, April 14. Today, I could have wished for some young prodigals aboard the *Whitaker*, to see one of our soldiers dying. Alas! how did his breast heave, his heart pant, and great drops of sweat trickle down his face! His eyes looked ghastly, and the whole man was in a bitter agony. Captain Whiting went down between decks with me once or twice to see him. I used the last Prayer several times. About nine at night he expired, I fear without hope, for he killed himself by drinking. Oh that all drunkards would learn from him to be wise in time, and practically consider their latter end!

Saturday, April 15. This morning I buried the dead soldier in time of public prayers, chose Proper Lessons, and gave the soldier a suitable exhortation; but I was so affected with a sense of the misery of fallen man, that I could not speak with my usual vigor.

Today I was called in a hurry to pray by one of the devout soldiers who came from Gibraltar, and who was supposed to be expiring. I came, I saw, and rejoiced in spirit, for his soul seemed full of God. Instead of being affrighted at the approach of the King of Terrors, he welcomed it, and said he was going to his dear Redeemer; then he fell as it were into a trance, and poured out his heart in repeating some very applicable verses out of the Psalms. Upon which, we thought he would have died; but lo! God brought him from the nethermost hell. From that instant the fever left him, and he recovered. Oh, what difference is there between him that feareth God, and him that feareth Him not, in their last hours! Lord, let me die the death of the righteous, and let my future stake be like his.

Exercised a little discipline this evening on a boy, whom Captain Mackay took notice of above a week ago for behaving ill at church, and said he would deliver him up to me. I therefore, by the advice of his master, ordered him to be tied till he could say the 51st Psalm, which he repeated tonight very solemnly in the midst of the congregation. May it be a warning to him for the future!

Sunday, April 16. Read prayers and expounded at six in the morning, and preached to my own people. I then went and preached on board the *Lightfoot*, and afterwards dined, read prayers, and preached on board the *Amy*. Returned about five in the evening to the *Whitaker*; read prayers and preached, visited the sick, and went to bed blessing God for the strength of the day. All the officers continue extremely kind, and seem studious to oblige me all they can.

This evening, I was sent for by a sailor, who has been the most remarkable swearer on board, and whom I in an especial manner warned about two days ago, telling him, I believed God would remarkably visit him. He laughed, and said he hoped not. But tonight he sent for me trembling and burning with a fever; he told me what grievous sins he had been guilty of, and prayed most fervently for repentance. Two or three of the same stamp have been taken in the same manner. God grant they may flee from the wrath to come! Sinners must either bend or break.

Tuesday, April 18. Was greatly delighted in seeing two waterspouts, which ran along for several miles, and by the especial Providence of God escaped us. We saw one of them coming, and were surprised to observe a sudden calm for about six minutes round the *Whitaker*, when the other parts of the sea boiled like a pot. Surely the Everlasting I AM said to the sea at that instant, *Let there be a calm in that place*; for our ship was immediately stopped in her course, and so the waterspout passed by before we came up to it; otherwise, it would have torn our sails in pieces. God's hand was so visible in this, that several said, they never beheld the like before. Oh, how does Providence watch over us, when we think nothing of it! Who would but live well to be under the immediate protection of such an overruling Power? After this, several squalls came upon us, which afforded me glorious matter for adoring that great and good God, Whom winds and storms obey. The sailors were in great hurry and confusion; but to my comfort, not one single oath was heard all the while — a proof this, that sailors may pull their ropes without swearing, and that the words spoken to them have not altogether fallen to the ground. Blessed be God!

Saturday, April 22. Fled as it were, on the wings of the wind for three days past, sailing sometimes a hundred-and-seventy, sometimes a hundred-and-eighty miles in twenty-four hours. I find that God generally sends us strongest winds when nearest our port. May I learn from hence a lesson of instruction, and the nearer I come to my Haven of Eternal Rest, the quicker may I move!

Spent most of these days in writing to my dear friends in England, and in particular supplication for direction how to act in the land whither I am going. The thoughts of my own weakness, and the greatness of those trials which I must necessarily meet with, fill me with a holy fear. But wherefore do I fear? The Eternal Almighty I AM hath and will no doubt protect me.

Sunday, April 23. Preached twice to my people today, and spent most of the rest of the day in earnest prayer for the Divine assistance in my present undertaking, being as we imagined near the haven where we would be. The morning Lessons were exceedingly applicable, so that we could not help taking notice of it.

Monday, May 1. This morning went out upon deck, after being confined to my bed for a week by a violent fever, with which all except three or four in the ship have been visited. I was blooded thrice, and blistered and vomited once, and, blessed be God! can say, *It is good for me that I have been afflicted*; for as afflictions abounded, consolations much more abounded, and God enabled me to rejoice with joy unspeakable. Satan desired to have me to sift me as wheat; but Jesus Christ prayed for me, and my faith failed not. I had all the conveniences I could have on shore: Capt. Whiting resigned his own bed to me; J.D. and friend H. sat up with me every night, and nothing was wanting to make my sickness comfortable and easy. Blessed be God for these abundant mercies in Christ Jesus!

I hope I shall now experimentally sympathize with those who are sick, and learn to be more tender-hearted to my fellow Christians. I am now made whole. May I sin no more, be more fervent in spirit, serving the Lord lest a worse thing befall me!

Friday, May 5. About ten o'clock this morning I buried the cook of the ship, who expired last night. I could have wished for a hundred tongues to have sounded a loud alarm to the people; but the sight of the corpse, and the weakness of my body, would but just permit me to read out the Office. Lord, what is man? Oh why are others taken and I left, but that God's longsuffering should lead me to repentance? Grant it, O Lord, for Thy dear Son's sake!

In the afternoon I privately baptized a new-born infant. Thus it is, some coming into the world, others going out of it continually. Good God! Who can desire to live here always?

This afternoon, after having lain about a week on this coast, we saw Savannah River, and sent off for a pilot. Oh what joy appeared in everyone's countenance! How infinitely more joyful will the children of God be, when having passed through the waves of this troublesome world, they arrive at the haven of everlasting rest? Hasten, O Lord, that blessed time, and let Thy Kingdom come!

Sunday, May 7. Last night, by the blessing of God, we cast anchor near Tybee Island, about fourteen miles off Savannah, and today God gave me strength to preach my farewell sermon (which I have sent you), at which many wept.

After this, I took boat with my friend Habersham, and arrived safe at Savannah, about seven in the evening, having a most pleasant passage. How God is pleased to deal with me there, I will endeavor to inform you hereafter.

Though we have had a long, yet it has been an exceedingly pleasant voyage. God, in compassion to my weakness, has set me but few trials, and sanctified those He hath sent me. He who protected Abraham when he went out not knowing whither he went, will also guide and protect me; and therefore I cannot close this part of my *Journal* better than with Mr. Addison's translation of the 23rd Psalm:

I.   The Lord my pasture shall prepare,
And feed me with a Shepherd's care;
His Presence shall my wants supply,
And guard me with a watchful eye;
My noonday walks He shall attend,
And all my midnight hours defend.

II.   When in the sultry glebe I faint,
Or on the thirsty mountain pant,
To fertile vales and dewy meads
My weary wand'ring steps He leads;
Where peaceful rivers soft and slow,
Amidst the verdant landscapes flow.

III.   Though in the paths of death I tread,
With gloomy horrors overspread,
My steadfast heart shall fear no ill,
For Thou, O Lord, art with me still;
Thy friendly crook shall give me aid,
And guide me through the dreadful shade.

IV.   Though in a bare and rugged way,
Through devious lonely wilds I stray,
Thy bounty shall my pains beguile;
The barren wilderness shall smile,
With sudden greens and herbage crown'd,
And streams shall murmur all around.

THE SECOND JOURNAL

FROM WHITEFIELD'S ARRIVAL AT SAVANNAH TO HIS RETURN TO LONDON

(May 1738 – December 1738)

Though the Journals already published were printed without my knowledge, yet as God has been pleased to let me see, by letters sent to me, that He has greatly blessed them, I now, upon the importunity of friends, consent to the publishing a Continuation of them, that those pious persons who have interceded in my behalf, may see what God, in answer to their prayers, has done for my soul.

I am sensible that this, as well as everything else of such a nature, must necessarily meet with great contempt from natural men, who are strangers to the influences of the Holy Ghost upon the heart. If any of God's children receive the least consolation from my experiences, let almost, formal Christians be offended, and the scoffers of these last days mock on. I rejoice, yea, and will rejoice.

Sunday, May 7. Arrived at Savannah Town about seven this evening, and joined in prayer, and a psalm of thanksgiving with Mr. Delamotte, and some pious souls who were rejoiced at my arrival. The good Lord sanctify our meeting to His glory, and His people's welfare. Spent the remainder of the evening in taking sweet counsel with Mr. Delamotte, who seems providentially left behind at Savannah against my coming. How sweetly does Providence order things for us! Oh may I constantly follow it as the Wise Men did the star in the East.

Monday, May 8. Began to read public prayers, and expound the Second Lesson at five in the morning, to seventeen adults and twenty-five children. May God open their hearts that they may attend to the things that were spoken. In the afternoon, Mr. Causton sent word, that he and the magistrates would wait upon me; but I chose rather to wait upon them. I was received with great civility, and our chief conversation ran upon the place of my settlement; at last it was resolved that I should have a house and tabernacle built at Frederica, and serve at Savannah, when, and as long as, I pleased. I find there are many divisions amongst the inhabitants; but God, I hope, will make me an instrument of composing them. Grant this, O Lord, for Thy dear Son's sake!

Sunday, May 14. After another week's confinement, by the return of my fever, under which God showed me great mercies, and which went off with a fit of the ague, I attempted to read prayers; but was so exceedingly faint and weak, that I was obliged to leave off before I began the second service.

Tuesday, May 16. Having by the blessing of God gotten a little strength, I went to see Tomo Chachi, who, I heard, was near expiring at a neighbor's house. He lay on a blanket, thin and meagre, and little else but skin and bones. Senauki, his wife, sat by, fanning him with some Indian feathers. There was nobody who could talk English, so I could only shake hands and leave him.

Friday, May 19. God still strengthening me more and more, I went this morning to two little villages, Hampstead and Highgate, about five miles off Savannah: the former consists of three families, making in all eleven souls, one man a Jew, two men, one woman and seven children Swissers. I was much delighted with seeing the improvements a few pairs of hands had made in their respective plantations, and was surprised to see what industry will do. Surely they speak not truth, who say that the Georgia people have been idle; for I never saw more laborious people than are in these villages. They live exceedingly hard, but with a little assistance may do very well. I was at a loss, because I could not speak French, but I resolved, under God, to follow my worthy predecessor's [John Wesley] example, and to visit them once a week, and read prayers to as many as could understand me. I also inquired into the state of their children, and found there were many who might prove useful members of the Colony, if there was a proper place provided for their maintenance and education. Nothing can effect this but an Orphan House, which might easily be erected at Savannah, would some of those who are rich in this world's goods contribute towards it. May God in His due time, stir up the wills of His faithful people, to be ready to distribute, and willing to communicate on this commendable occasion.

Saturday, May 20. Went once more to see Tomo Chachi, hearing his nephew Tooanoowee was there, who could talk English. I desired him to inquire of his uncle, whether he thought he should die; who answered, He could not tell. I then asked, Where he thought he should go after death? He replied, "to Heaven." But alas, how can a drunkard enter there! I then exhorted Tooanoowee (who is a tall proper youth) not to get drunk, telling him he understood English, and therefore would be punished the more, if he did not live better. I then asked him, "Whether he believed in Heaven?" He answered, "Yes." I then asked, "Whether he believed in a Hell?" and described it by pointing to the fire; he replied, "No," from whence we may easily gather, how natural it is to all mankind to believe there is a place of happiness, because they wish it may be so, and on the contrary, how averse they are to believe in a place of torment, because they wish it may not be so. But God is true and just, and as surely as the good shall go into everlasting happiness, so the wicked shall go into everlasting punishment.

Wednesday, May 24. Went today to Thunderbolt, a village about six miles off Savannah, situated very pleasantly near the river, and consisting of three families, — four men and two women, and ten servants. I was kindly received, expounded a chapter, used a few collects, called on a family or two that lay near our way, and returned home to Savannah very comfortably, with my friend Delamotte, about six o'clock in the evening. Blessed be God for strengthening my weak body.

Friday, June 2. This evening, parted with kind Captain Whiting and my dear friend Delamotte, who embarked for England about seven at night. The poor people lamented the loss of him, and went to the waterside to take a last farewell. And good reason had they to do so, for he has been indefatigable in feeding Christ's lambs with the sincere milk of the Word, and many of them (blessed be God) have grown thereby. Surely, I must labor most heartily, since I come after such worthy predecessors. The good, Mr. John Wesley has done in America, under God, is inexpressible. His name is very precious among the people; and he has laid such a foundation, that I hope neither men nor devils will ever be able to shake. Oh, that I may follow him, as he has Christ!

Monday, June 5. Had a conference with a certain person of the parish, who, I heard last night, had been broaching many heretical doctrines to one of my friends, particularly in denying the eternity of hell torments. I therefore invited him this morning to breakfast, and after imploring God's assistance, in the spirit of meekness, I asked him, "Whether he believed in the eternity of hell torments?" He answered frankly, "No." I replied, "What do you mean, sir, when you repeat the twelfth Article of our Creed?" He said, "he believed wicked men were to be annihilated." I then read Pearson's exposition of the last Article, but he denied it all, said he thought himself in the right, and believed it his duty to inform mankind, that they were to be annihilated. Upon which, I repeated to him that passage out of the *Revelation*, "If any man shall take away from, or add unto the words that are written in this book, God shall take away his name out of the Book of Life, and add unto him all the plagues that are written in this book." This, he said, he believed. Afterwards we discoursed afresh, but finding him resolute to propagate his principles, I then told him with the utmost calmness that I was sorry I gave him the cup yesterday at the Sacrament; but for the future, he must pardon me, if I refused ever to give it him again. This staggered him a little, but he bore it pretty patiently, yet thought me uncharitable.

Saturday, June 10. Placed one who came with me, at Highgate, to teach the children English that belong to that village and Hampstead. There are about twenty in all, of French extraction, but some few of them are able to speak a little in our vulgar tongue. I thought, placing a master there would be of great consequence. First, because I cannot think children will ever be naturalized to the colony till they can talk our language. Secondly, because the present generation will soon wear off, and these children being well instructed in ours, will make them forget their own tongue, and should they marry and have children, they would naturally teach their children the same; so that at length we shall all be of one speech. Thirdly, as they are but few in number, and no likelihood of any French minister coming amongst them, I or my successors will be unable to catechize or bring them to hear the Word of God at our church, unless they are acquainted with the English tongue.

Monday, June 12. Opened a school today for the girls of Savannah, a friend, whose heart God was pleased to touch on board the ship, having at my request undertaken to teach them. The work is for my Master, and therefore I doubt not of being supplied some way or another with a sufficient fund for the support of it. May God enable him who is set over them to feed them with the sincere milk of the Word, and give them grace to grow thereby!

Thursday, June 22. Was taken (as all about me thought for death) with a violent purging and vomiting, which in the space of five hours quite exhausted my spirits, and brought me in appearance almost to the point of death. But God supported me by His inward comforts, caused me to rejoice in it, and cast me into a deep sleep, out of which I awoke perfectly well, to the surprise of all about me. O who can express the loving kindness of the Lord, or show forth all His praise! My parishioners in general showed they loved me, for they seemed most solicitious for my welfare. For their sake, as well as for my own, I hope God has so suddenly restored me. God grant I may now begin to be active in my Master's service, that whensoever He shall call, I may be found so doing.

Friday, June 23. To the great surprise of myself and people, was enabled to read prayers and preach with power before the Freemasons, with whom I afterwards dined, and was used with the utmost civility. May God make them servants of Christ, and then and not till then will they be free indeed.

Friday, July 7. Being the anniversary for opening the Court, I preached in the morning, at the magistrate's request, and endeavored with all plainness and humility to show both them and the people what they ought to do to promote their temporal and eternal welfare. O God do Thou bless it, and it shall be blessed through Jesus Christ.

Tuesday, July 11. Returned this evening from Ebenezer (where I went yesterday) the place where the Saltzburghers are settled; and was wonderfully pleased with their order and industry. Their lands are improved surprisingly for the time they have been there, and I believe they have far the best crop of any in the colony. They are blest with two such pious ministers as I have not often seen. They have no Courts of Judicature, but all little differences are immediately and implicitly decided by their ministers, whom they look upon and love as their fathers. They have likewise an Orphan House, in which are seventeen children and one widow, and I was much delighted to see the regularity wherewith it is managed. Oh that God may stir up the hearts of His servants to contribute towards that and another which we hope to have erected at Savannah. Mr. Boltzius, one of the ministers, being with me on Saturday, I gave him some of my poor's store for his orphans, and when I came to Ebenezer, he called them all before him, catechized and exhorted them to give God thanks for His good Providence towards them; then prayed with them, and made them pray after him; then sang a psalm, and afterwards the little lambs came and shook me by the hand, one by one, and so we parted, and I scarce was ever better pleased in my life. Surely, whoever contributes to the relief of the Saltzburghers, will perform an acceptable sacrifice to our blessed Master. They are very poor; but with a little assistance might live comfortably and well. They want a place for public worship, and money to buy cattle, and other necessaries for the Orphan House and people. May the great God raise up instruments to assist and relieve them, for surely they are worthy.

Tuesday, July 18. About ten o'clock this evening, returned to Savannah, having set out from thence yesterday to visit four or five families that live at some of the outward settlements, about twelve miles off. Their beginnings as yet are but small; but I cannot help thinking there are foundations being laid for great temporal and spiritual blessings in Georgia, when the inhabitants are found worthy. Blessed be God, in Savannah they hear the Word gladly, and people everywhere receive me with the utmost civility, and are not angry when I reprove them. May God keep them always thus minded, and prepare me for whatever sufferings He shall permit to fall upon me for doing my duty.

Tuesday, July 25. I am now waiting for the scout-boat which Mr. Horton has sent to take me to Frederica, to preach the Gospel there also. For therefore am I sent. I should part with regret from the people of Savannah, did I not know God called me from them. For they seem to have a sincere affection for me, and flock (especially every evening) to hear the Word of God. I have endeavored to let my gentleness be known amongst them, because they consist of different nations and opinions; and I have striven to draw them by the cords of love, because the obedience resulting from that principle I take to be most genuine and lasting. My ordinary way of dividing ministerial labors has been as follows, —

On Sunday morning, at five o'clock, I publicly expound the Second Lesson for the Morning or Evening Service as I see most suited to the people's edification; at ten I preach and read prayers; at three in the afternoon I do the same; and at seven expound part of the Church Catechism, at which great numbers are usually present. I visit from house to house, read public prayers, and expound twice, and catechize (unless something extraordinary happens), visit the sick every day, and read to as many of my parishioners as will come thrice a week. And blessed be God, my labors have not been altogether vain in the Lord. For He has been pleased to set His seal to my ministry, in a manner I could not, I dared not in America, expect. Not unto me, O Lord, not unto me, but unto Thy Name be the glory!

AT FREDERICA: Thusday, August 8. After a pleasant passage of five or six days, I arrived at Frederica, a town situated southwardly above a hundred miles from Savannah, and consisting of about a hundred-and-twenty inhabitants. The people received me most gladly, having had a famine of the Word for a long season. May God give a blessing to my coming amongst them.

In the evening we had public prayers, and expounding of the Second Lesson under a large tree, and many more present than could be expected.

Wednesday, August 9. Began today visiting from house to house, and found the people in appearance desirous of being fed with the sincere milk of the Word, and solicitous for my continuance amongst them. Poor creatures! my heart ached for them, because I saw them and their children scattered abroad as sheep having no shepherd. Lord, in Thy due time send forth some laborer into this part of Thy vineyard.

This evening, had prayers in a house which Mr. Horton hired for us during my stay, and most of the inhabitants, I believe, were present. Blessed be God, timber is sawing for the erecting a more commodious place for public worship, till a church can be built. God grant we may always worship Him in spirit and in truth, and then we may be assured that at all times and in all places He will hear us.

Friday, August 11. Went in the morning to, and returned in the evening from the Darien, a settlement about twenty miles off from Frederica, where I went to see Mr. MacLeod, a worthy minister of the Scotch Church; and God gave me a most pleasant passage.

Saturday, August 12. This afternoon was alarmed with the news of a family disaster. My dear friend H's brother going to find a horse that was lost in the woods, got lost himself, and many guns shot after him for several days, but in vain. I endeavored to give thanks to God for this and everything that befalls me, because it is His will, and resolved to set out for Savannah immediately, knowing what concern my dear friend H. must be in at so sudden a loss.

In the evening, because I was to go about midnight, I gave notice I would preach as well as expound, at which almost all the inhabitants were present; for many were obliged to stand without the door. The Lesson was very applicable to my circumstances. It was the First of St. James wherein the Apostle bids us rejoice when we fall into divers temptations. God enabled me to enlarge on it pretty much. I told the people that God called me and I must away, at which some wept. Oh God, how dost Thou follow me with Thy blessings wherever Thou sendest me! I looked for persecution, but lo! I am received as an angel of God.

Sunday, August 13. Being disappointed of going by the boat last night, I read prayers and preached to my dear little flock twice, which caused great joy among them. Mr. Horton was extremely civil, and did everything he could to oblige me. This afternoon after sermon, I intended to go with him to preach to the soldiers at the Fort of St. Simon's, and then the next day to go to St. Andrew's, but Lord Thou callest me elsewhere. Oh grant I may have no will of my own, but whenever or wherever Thou shalt be pleased to call me, may I without the least reluctance say, Lo I come! Had an alarm brought to Frederica that the Spaniards had taken possession of Fort St. George, and fired at one of our boats; but this was quickly found to be entirely groundless.

About two in the afternoon, having first read prayers, and preached, most of the inhabitants accompanied me to the Bluff or river side and took their leave of me in an affectionate manner, and laded me with things convenient for my journey. The good Lord reward them ten thousandfold, and make me thankful for His unmerited mercies!

AT SAVANNAH: Wednesday, August 16. Arrived this day at Savannah, and had the pleasure of meeting my friend who had been lost; he was from Tuesday till Friday roving about the woods, during which time the great guns were fired according to custom, and the people showed what a great respect they had for me and my friends, many of them going out all day and night after him. As soon as I had refreshed myself, I went and visited my parishioners from house to house to return them thanks for their kindness to my friends. An unusual joy appeared in their faces at my unexpected return, and they were ready to say, "How beautiful are the feet of him that bringeth the glad tidings of salvation." At evening prayers (and a very large congregation was present), I returned my dear hearers' hearty thanks for the late instance of their sincere affection; I publicly exhorted my friend who was lost to show forth his thankfulness, not only with his lips but with his life, and desired their prayers to God for me that I might now more devote myself to my blessed Master's service, and study daily to purify my corrupt nature, that I might be made an instrument under Him of winning their souls to God.

Wednesday, August 23. A necessity was laid on me today to express my resentment against infidelity, by refusing to read the Burial Office over the most professed unbeliever I ever yet met with. God was pleased to visit him with a lingering illness, in which time I went to see him frequently. Particularly about five weeks ago, I asked what religion he was of; he answered, "Religion was divided into so many sects he knew not which to choose." Another time, I offered to pray with him, but he would not accept it, upon which I resolved to go and see him no more; but being told two days before he died, that he had an inclination to see me, I went to him again, and after a little conversation, I put to him the following questions. "Do you believe Jesus Christ to be God, the one Mediator between God and Man?" He said, "I believe Christ was a good man." "Do you believe the Holy Scriptures?" "I believe," replied he, "something of the Old Testament, the New I do not believe at all." "Do you believe, sir, a judgment to come?" He turned himself about, and replied, "I know not what to say to that." "Alas," said I, "Sir, if all these things should be true" — which words, I believe gave him concern, for he seemed after to be very uneasy, grew delirious, and departed in a day or two. Unhappy man, how quickly was he convinced that all I said was true! Now he and I are of one mind. The day after his decease, he was carried to the ground, and I refused to read the office over him, but went to the grave and told the people what had passed between him and me, warned them against infidelity, and asked them whether I could safely say, "as our hope is this our brother doth." Upon which I believe they were thoroughly satisfied that I had done right. God grant this may be a warning to surviving unbelievers.

Thursday, August 24. This day I went to Highgate with a friend or two, and read prayers, preached and baptized a child, and catechized in a house lately erected by the inhabitants. For upon my sending a master to teach their children, one offered to give me a part of his lot, and the rest to give their labor. Accordingly, I accepted it, found materials, and today it was fit to preach in, and be made a school house of. The children, though foreigners, answered admirably well, which gave me great hopes that the other foreign children of the colony may also learn our English tongue when a proper master is provided. After service, we refreshed ourselves together, thanked our good God, and ate our bread with gladness of heart.

Sunday, August 27. God having now shown both me and my friends that it was His will I should return for awhile to England, this afternoon I preached my farewell sermon, to the great grief of my dear parishioners; for their hearts, I found, were very full as well as mine. But a sensible alteration appeared in their countenances, when I promised them solemnly before God to return as soon as possible. May God enable me to perform my promise, and prepare my way before me.

The weather was exceedingly hot, and the greatness of the congregation made it still hotter; but God enabled me to preach with power. Thanks be to God for the strength He gives me through Jesus Christ!

Monday, August 28. This being the day of my departure, it was mostly spent in taking leave of my flock, who expressed their affection now more than ever. They came to me from the morning to the time I left them with tears in their eyes, wishing me a prosperous voyage and safe return, and gave me other tokens of their love, for they brought me wine, ale, cake, coffee, tea, and other things proper for my passage, and their love seemed without dissimulation.

About four in the afternoon, I went into the boat provided for me by Mr. Causton, who with the Recorder came to my house and took their leave. A great number of people came to the Bluff and wished me a good voyage with all their souls, and a speedy return. I thanked them, and having desired their prayers, blessed them in the name of God, and took my leave.

My heart was full, and I took the first opportunity of venting it by prayers and tears. I think I never parted from a place with more regret; for America in my opinion is an excellent school to learn Christ in, and I have great hopes some good will come out of Savannah because the longer I continued there, the larger the congregations grew. And I scarce knew a night, though we had Divine service twice a day, when the Church House has not been nearly full — a proof, this, I hope, that God has yet spiritual and temporal blessings in store for them. Hasten, O Lord, that blessed time!

CHARLESTON: Arrived last night here, and preached twice today, I hope with some good effect. The Bishop of London's Commissary, the Rev. Mr. Garden, a good soldier of Jesus Christ, received me in a most Christian manner. He and several others offered me a lodging, and were more than civil to me. How does God raise me up friends wherever I go! Who is so good a God as our God?

Was much pleased with the neatness of the buildings, and the largeness of the place. The church is very beautiful, and the inhabitants seem to be excellently well settled. God's judgments have been lately abroad amongst them by the spreading of the small-pox. I hope they will learn righteousness.

Monday, September 4. Was much delighted with a packet of letters I received from Savannah friends, and was soon hurried on board, the wind being fair for sailing. Great kindness has been shown me at Charleston, some presents made me, and there was a general and earnest expectation of my preaching on Sunday. But God seeth not as man seeth.

ON BOARD THE *MARY*, CAPTAIN COC, COMMANDER, BOUND FROM CHARLESTON TO ENGLAND: Saturday, September 9. About noon, came on board with great composure of mind, and thought of my absent friends, settled my things, wrote my journal, and finished some other matters. The wind being fair, weighed anchor, and set sail about five in the evening. The Lord send us a prosperous voyage, and bring us in His appointed time to the haven where we would be.

Saturday, September 16. Had contrary winds all the week, and got but a few leagues from Charleston, yet God showed me great mercies, for He enabled me to write several things, and correct others. I have been but a little sea-sick; and though I have not had my clothes off, and lay upon deck or on a chest every night, yet the goodness of God keeps me healthy and strong, and gives me a feeling possession of His Holy Spirit. My sphere of action is now contracted into a very narrow compass. There are but few souls on board, and all that I can do is to read public prayers, and add a word of exhortation twice every day, and catechize those I brought with me. The Captain and all are very civil. My Christian friends have been much upon my heart, and caused me some dejections, but God was my comforter. Had I my own will, I could wish myself a speedy passage, that I may return the sooner to those few sheep I have left at Savannah; but God knows best, and this retirement, I hope, may break my will, purify my heart, and fit me for the great work that lies before me. Even so Lord Jesus, Amen, and Amen.

Saturday, September 23. God is pleased to send us contrary winds, except one night about the middle of the week. However, He enables me to give thanks, and great reason have I to do so, for the Holy Spirit has been with me of a truth.

I have observed, that before God calls me to a public work, He always sends me into some retirement, but never to so great a one as now. A sign this, I hope, that a greater work is yet before. Lord, fit and prepare me for it.

My mind has been composed and easy. Only the absence of my friends now and then struck a damp upon my spirits. But the Friend of all is with and in me, and He by His Spirit, I trust, will supply the want of their dear company. Amen, Lord Jesus, Amen.

Sunday 24. Monday, September 25. Was oppressed much in spirit these two days. The wind was contrary, and the sea wrought and was tempestuous; but blessed be God, He enabled me to be resigned to His will, this outward and inward trial being only what was to be expected after my late assistances. We must not always be upon the Mount in this life.

Ever since Monday evening, God has been pleased to send us fair winds, particularly today, when our ship has sailed seven miles an hour.

I have been chiefly busied about writing letters, to engage more laborers, and to get contributions for my poor flock.

Blessed be God! He has made me frequently rejoice in spirit, and now quite reconciles me to my present retirement. When shall I have no will but God's!

Sunday, October 1. Had very little sleep all night, and was like to fall off the chest whereon I lay several times, the sea being very rough, and the wind turning in an instant directly contrary. Oh that I could learn from winds and storms to obey my Master!

Buried a young man who came from Georgia, and died this morning. Lord, what is man? He solaced himself with the thoughts of seeing his friends in England; but God saw fit to prevent it by shortening his days. Lord, Thy judgments are like the great deep!

When I buried him, I could not say much, because of the rolling of the ship; but at evening prayer I took occasion from the Lesson, which was the 15th Chapter of the First of Corinthians, to exhort all my shipmates to consider, so as to prepare for their latter end. I believe my words came with power. God grant they may have a due effect. Amen, Lord Jesus, Amen!

Friday, October 6. Before I left Savannah, the Lesson appointed for the morning, was St. Paul's shipwreck, out of the Acts, and before I left Charleston, the Lesson was the First of Jonah, both of which made such a deep impression upon me, that I wrote to my friend Habersham, to acquaint him I was apprehensive we should have a dangerous voyage. Since I have been on board, what St. Paul said to his companions, "That he perceived their voyage would be with much damage," has frequently been pressed upon my heart; and God has now shown me wherefore He gave these previous notices. For on Tuesday night last, after we had sailed 150 miles, the last twenty hours, about eleven o'clock, arose a sudden violent east wind, which continued till about four in the morning, and put all the sailors to their wits' end. Most of them declared they had never seen the like before. The mainsail was slit in several pieces, and several of the other sails, and much of the tackling all to tatters. Not a dry place was to be found in all the ship. The Captain's hammock, in the great cabin, was half filled with water; and though I lay in the most dry part of the ship, yet the waves broke in upon me twice or thrice. In short, all was terror and confusion, men's hearts failing them for fear, and the wind and the sea raging horribly. But God (for ever be adored His unmerited goodness) was exceeding gracious unto me. I felt a sweet complacency in my will, in submission to His. Many particular promises God has made me from His Word, that I should return in peace, flowed in upon my heart; and He enabled me greatly to rejoice. This is the first day we have ventured to pull down any of our dead lights, which put me in mind of the long night the Egyptians once saw. But I spent my time in reading, and fervent intercession for absent friends, and comforted myself much with the remembrance of them. Most of our fresh provisions are washed overboard, and our tackling much out of order, so that we have a prospect but of an indifferent voyage; but, blessed be God, the prospect pleases me, for now I shall learn, I trust, how to want as well as how to abound, and how to endure hardship like a good soldier of Jesus Christ. O Lord, let Thy strength be magnified in my weakness, say unto my soul, "It is I, be not afraid," and then let storms and tempests do their worst.

Saturday, October 7. Today, adored be the Divine goodness, the weather has cleared up more and more, and our ship has sailed directly before the wind, at the rate of four or five miles an hour. A desire to see my friends in England, to dispatch my business, and to return to my poor flock, prompts me secretly to wish for a continuance of this prosperous gale. But Lord, I know not what to pray for as I ought. Do with me as seemeth good in Thy sight. Only I beseech Thee to sanctify my present retirement, that the longer I am upon the sea, the more zealous I may be in Thy service, when I come upon dry land.

Saw a Jamaica ship, Captain Philips, who has been out nine weeks. What reason have we to be thankful!

Having had no opportunity before, since the storm, of getting the people together, gave a word or two of exhortation to my ship-mates, to bless God for our late deliverance, and to sin no more lest a worse storm should befall us.

Saturday, October 14. Sailed this week about 600 miles; but yesterday God was pleased to send us a contrary wind, which still continues. A few days ago I flattered myself we should soon be at our desired port, but God is pleased to defer the accomplishment of my hopes. However, blessed be His Name! He enables me to give thanks. Most of this week has been spent in searching the Scriptures, and in retirements for direction and assistance in the work before me. My fresh provisions are gone, and the people are put to the allowance of a quart of water each man for a day. I hope now the spiritual man will grow, having so little for the natural man to feed on. Amen, Lord Jesus! Blessed be God! I can by His grace, say that I rejoice in necessities, and in everything give thanks. Had this sentence out of Henry much pressed upon my heart to comfort me in my retirement. "The mower loses no time whilst he is whetting his scythe."

Sunday, October 15. The weather being calm, and I being invited yesterday, went on board the *Constant*, Captain Philips, bound from Jamaica, which now sails in company with us, and was kindly received both by the Captain and his passengers, and not only so, but they spared me what they could of their provisions. A most providential supply, for ours was quite out. But our extremity is God's opportunity. Blessed be His Name for thus strengthening our faith! May this be looked upon as a pledge that He will never leave or forsake us.

Our chief discourse was about Georgia; and staying a little longer than was thought, my shipmates were very suspicious I should be detained on board. Though there was provision for the flesh, yet I like my own situation best, because here are greater opportunities of denying myself, and consequently of making further improvement in the Spirit. Oh that I may always walk by this rule!

Saturday, October 21. Made but slow advances in our voyage, having had but one or two days of fair wind. But notwithstanding, I believe we shall now soon reach shore; for God has been pleased to visit me all the week with a variety of inward trials, which is a sign to me that I shall experience yet more and more of His mercies. How good is God thus to prepare me by sufferings, that so His blessings may not be my ruin. These things to the natural man are not joyous, but grievous; but God enables me to take comfort in Him, to thank Him sincerely for His loving correction, and therefore when I am sufficiently exercised thereby, I hope it will bring forth in me the peaceable fruits of righteousness. Amen.

Sunday, October 22. At the desire of the Captain, preached my sermon on rash anger, having hitherto been used to expound only. In the Lesson were these remarkable words, "Return to thy own house, and show how great things God has done unto thee." And again, "It came to pass that when Jesus was returned, the people gladly received Him, for they were all waiting for Him." These last words were remarkably pressed upon me at Savannah, when I was consulting God by prayer, whether it was His will that I should go to England. Thus God's Word is in particular cases as well as in general, a light unto our feet, and a lanthorn unto our paths.

Thursday, October 26. Was much comforted this evening in reading the 33rd and 34th chapters of Ezekiel, wherein I could not but observe many circumstances of God's dealing with him corresponding with what I have experienced in myself. The following verses in particular were set home to my heart, "Also, thou son of man, the children of thy people are still talking against thee by the walls, and in the doors of the houses, and speak one to another, saying, Come, I pray you, and hear what word cometh from the Lord. And they come unto thee as the people cometh, and they hear thy words, but they will not do them, for with their mouth they show much love, but their heart goeth after covetousness. And lo, thou art unto them as a very lovely song of one who hath a pleasant voice, and can play well on an instrument: for they hear thy words, but do them not." Who that knows how God has dealt with me since I have been in the ministry, sees not that this passage answers to my circumstances, as face answers to face in the water? However, this I know, what I have spoken from God will come to pass, and then shall these scoffers and despisers know that a minister of Christ has been amongst them. O that I may never be brought forth as a swift witness against any; but we must all appear before the judgment seat of Christ.

Saturday, October 28. Sailed about 300 miles the first four days of this week. Had a little storm on Wednesday night, and a great calm ever since. We are now within 150 leagues of land, and our provisions and water very scanty, and our ship very weak; but the hour of our arrival is not yet come. Lord, teach me to be resigned and thankful.

God has this week enlarged my heart, and filled me with great comfort, after great inward conflicts. Is not all this to prepare me for further trials we are yet to endure ere we get to England? Lord, Thy grace, I know, will be sufficient for me, and therefore I rejoice in the prospect of enduring tribulation.

Had reason to believe one on board was offended at my enlarging one night on the sin of drunkenness. I always endeavor to speak with the meekness and gentleness of Christ; but if people will account me their enemy, because, out of love, I tell them the truth, I cannot help that.

Monday, October 30. Still God is pleased that the wind, what there is of it, should be contrary, and our ship's company are now brought into great straits. Their allowance of water is a quart a day, and our constant food for some time has been salt beef and water dumplings, which do not agree with the stomachs of some amongst us. But God enables me to rejoice in that and all our other necessities. When we are destitute of outward comforts, then does God more comfort our souls. This morning, when I awoke, the faith of Abraham was greatly pressed upon me; and the example of Daniel, and the Three Children, who were fat and well favored, notwithstanding they were fed with pulse and pease, is continually before my eyes. Some say we are within a hundred leagues of land; but what does that signify, if God says, "Hitherto shall you go, and no further." Lord, in Thy due time, let that which now letteth be taken away, but not before this trial has done what it was sent for, though it make us smart.

This afternoon we joined in solemn prayers suitable to our present circumstances. Lord, let our cry come unto Thee. I know it will, and that we shall be answered, if it be best. But great blessings await me on shore, and great trials must precede.

Tuesday, October 31. Was comforted tonight in my present circumstances, by these verses out of this evening's Lesson — "I have learnt in whatsoever state I am, therewith to be content. I know both how to be abased, and I know how to abound and to suffer need. I can do all through Christ Who strengtheneth me." "Even so come, Lord Jesus." Amen, and Amen.

Reading afterwards in the Book of Maccabees, and thinking of my present situation, this verse was pressed with unspeakable comfort upon my soul: "After this, they went home, and sung a song of thanksgiving, and praised the Lord in Heaven; because it is good, because His mercy endureth forever." I hope my friends will take care to fulfill this when we meet together on shore.

Wednesday, November 1. This afternoon, about 4 o'clock, as I was in secret, humbling myself before God, interceding for my friends, and had been praying for a fair wind, and assistance in the great work lying before me, news was brought that the wind was fair; which put me in mind of the angel's being sent to Daniel, to tell him his prayer was heard, when he was humbling his soul with fasting, and praying for the peace and restoration of Jerusalem. Indeed I cannot say, I have purposely, for these three weeks, eaten no pleasant food, or fasted as he did; but our food is so salt, that I dare eat but little, so that I am now literally in fastings often. Oh, that I may improve this blessed season for humiliation, and extraordinary acts of devotion, that I may be duly prepared to approve myself a faithful minister of Jesus Christ, whether by honor or dishonor, by evil report or good report.

As soon as we found the wind fair, we joined in thanksgiving, and in singing the first part of the 34th Psalm (new version), which was very applicable to our circumstances. For they tell me they have not above three days' water on board, allowing a quart to each man a day. But He, who at one time, at the request of His disciples, considered the multitude, and worked a miracle for their relief, and at another time, at the intercession of Moses, gave water to the wandering Israelites, I trust now has heard our prayers, and sent this wind with a commission to bring us where He will supply all our wants. If not, O blessed Jesus, Thy will be done, Give me grace, I most humbly beseech Thee, to hold out my three watches, and at the fourth watch I know Thou wilt come. Even so, come Lord Jesus.

Thursday, November 2. For these two days last past, God has been pleased greatly to humble my soul, and bring me low by spiritual desertions. And today He has thought proper again to send us a contrary wind. Our allowance of water now is but a pint a day, so that we dare not eat much beef. Our sails are exceedingly thin, some more of them were split last night, and no one knows where we are; but God does, and that is sufficient.

Last night He lifted up the light of His blessed countenance upon me, and today fills me with joy unspeakable and full of glory; so that, though I have little to eat, yet I inwardly possess all things. I am sometimes afraid lest continued abstinence may occasion a bodily sickness. But wherefore do I fear? If it does, that and everything else I know will work for my good. What I most dread, is lest any on board should charge God foolishly; but I check the first notions I discern arising in any one's heart, and endeavor to justify our good God in all the evil that He hath brought upon us. I put before them the example of the widow of Sarepta, and caution them against murmuring like the Israelites at the waters of Meribah. Thus I endeavor to comfort and support them with the comforts wherewith I myself am comforted of God.

This is now the eighth week I have been aboard. If my friends ask me why I arrived no sooner, I may truly answer, Satan hindered us. For I believe it is he who is permitted to do this; but this still gives me greater hopes, that a more effectual door than ever will be opened in England for preaching the everlasting Gospel. O Satan, thou mayest toss me up and down, and bring me into jeopardy on every side, but Jesus Christ is praying for me on the Mount. And when the time appointed by the Father is come, and my soul hereby prepared, He Whom winds and storms obey, will speak the word, and then I shall have a happy meeting with my dear friends!

Sunday, November 5. This day, we rejoiced with trembling; for though we thereon commemorated our deliverance from the Gunpowder Plot, yet as our circumstances called for acts of humiliation, I used part of the Office of Commination (besides solemn prayer and psalms three times), and enlarged on these words of St. James: "My brethren, count it all joy when ye fall into divers temptations, knowing this that the trying of your faith worketh patience. But let patience have her perfect work." I hope this had a good effect upon my hearers' hearts, and calmed their spirits; for indeed we are brought very low. But I can say with the penitent thief "that I suffer justly," and do not receive the ten thousandth part of the reward due to my crimes. Lord, remember me now Thou art in Thy kingdom.

Monday, November 6. Last night, about seven o'clock, God was pleased to suffer a violent wind to arise, which would not permit me to rise till this afternoon, about which time it began in some measure to abate. Blessed be God, through the precaution used by our shipmates, we shipped but little water, only we were driven some leagues back. The weather was pretty cold, and a little cake or two baked on the coals, and a very little salt beef was all my provision for the day; but thus Elijah lived for a long while, and why not I? Nay, he fasted forty days and forty nights; and though I dare not presume to do so, yet if God still brings me into greater wants, I doubt not, but that I shall find that man liveth not by bread alone, but by every word that proceedeth out of the mouth of God. Lord, I desire not to be exempted from sufferings, but to be supported under them.

Wednesday, November 8. Preached myself, yesterday and this morning, inwardly weak and fainting, and unable to read scarce anything; but, blessed be God, though He slay me, yet will I put my trust in Him.

When my spirits are gone, I then find my faith, as it were, less lively: but I trust that is only owing to the frame of my body. At all other times I have great confidence in God, and was He now to put it to my choice, whether this trial should continue, or He should send us a fair wind, I should humbly refer it to Him again, for I know not what is best for me.

Most in the great cabin now begin to be weak, and look hollow-eyed; yet a little while, and we shall come to extremities, and then God's arm will bring us salvation. May we patiently tarry the Lord's leisure. Amen, Amen.

Great part of this day I lay down, being weak and much oppressed in my head; but at night when some doubted what the end of this visitation would be, the following verses were with great comfort pressed upon my soul: "For I am in a strait between two, having a desire to be dissolved, and to be with Christ, which is far better. Nevertheless, to abide in the flesh is more needful for you. And having this confidence, I know that I shall abide and continue with you all, for your furtherance and joy of faith, that your rejoicing may be more abundant in Jesus Christ for me, by my coming to you again." Thus Christians have meat to eat, which the world knoweth not. In confidence of this, and such-like texts, that have been from time to time applied to my soul, I still (as often as my strength will permit), continue to write letters ready to send when I come on shore, which reminds me of Jeremiah's being commanded to buy land, when his whole country was about to be carried into captivity. Blessed are they who walk by faith, and not by sight.

Though one in his haste the other day cried out, "What Jonah have we here on board?" and I answered, "I am he;" yet many now, I believe, bless God, that I am with them. For, say they, "How should we have been blaming and cursing one another, had not Mr. Whitefield been amongst us?" Blessed be God, if my ministry or presence can be instrumental to prevent sin against Thee, O Lord, toss me on the ocean as long as it pleaseth Thee.

Thursday, November 9. Enjoyed great peace of mind today, and was stronger in body than usual. We are now making for Ireland, and are advancing some leagues towards it. Whether we shall arrive there or not, God only knows. I find all uneasiness arises from having a will of my own. And therefore I simply desire to will what God willeth. Oh! when will this once be?

Friday, November 10. Was much strengthened in our present distress by the Second Lesson for the day. It was our Savior's turning the water into wine at the marriage at Cana. We have applied to Him as the holy Virgin did, and told Him in prayer, that, "We have but very little water." At present, He seems to turn away His face, and to say, "What have I to do with you?" But this is only because the hour of extremity is not yet come. When it is, I doubt not but He will now as richly supply our wants as He did theirs then. May we in patience possess our souls.

Saturday, November 11. Still we are floating about, not knowing where we are; but our people seem yet to have hopes of seeing Ireland. I know not whether I am out in my conjecture, but I imagine some of those ships we have seen, have arrived at England before us. Upon which, perhaps, my friends will expect me, pray for me, and at last give me up for lost. And then God will retore me to them.

The weather now begins to be cold, so that I can say, with the Apostle, I am "in hunger and thirst, cold and fastings often." Hereafter, perhaps, I may add, moreover in bonds and imprisonments. But I trust the sufferings of this life will not move me, for they are not worthy to be compared with the glory that shall be revealed in us.

My outward man sensibly decayeth, but the spiritual man, I trust, is renewed day by day. I have besought the Lord many times to send us a fair wind; but now I see He does not think fit to answer me. I am wholly resigned, knowing that His grace will be sufficient for me, and that His time is best.

Our ship is much out of repair, and our food by no means enough to support nature in an ordinary way, being of the most indifferent kind, too — an ounce or two of salt-beef, a pint of muddy water, and a cake made of flour and skimmings of the pot. I think often on Him who preserved Moses in the ark of the bulrushes. So long as I look upwards my faith will not fail.

It pities me often to see my brethren lying in the dust, as they have done these many weeks, and exposed to such straits; for God knows both their souls and bodies are dear unto me. But thanks be to God, they bear up well, and I hope we shall all now learn to endure hardships, like good soldiers of Jesus Christ.

Sunday, November 12. This morning, the doctor of our ship took up the Common Prayer Book, and observed that he opened upon these words, "Blessed be the Lord God of Israel, for He hath visited and redeemed His people." And so, indeed, He has, for about 8 o'clock this morning news was brought that our men saw land, and I went and was a joyful spectator of it myself. The air was clear, and the sun arising in full strength, so that it is the most pleasant day I have seen these many weeks. Now know I that the Lord will not always be chiding, neither keepeth He His anger forever. For these two or three days last past, I have enjoyed uncommon serenity of soul, and given up my will to God. And now He hath brought us deliverance — from whence I infer, that a calmness of mind, and entire resignation to the Divine Will, is the best preparative for receiving Divine mercies. Lord evermore make me thus minded.

As soon as I had taken a view of the land, we joined together in a prayer and psalm of thanksgiving, and already began to reflect with pleasure on our late straits. Thus it will be hereafter, the storms and tempests of this troublesome world will serve to render our haven of eternal rest doubly agreeable. I fear now nothing so much as the treachery of my heart, lest like the ungrateful lepers, I should not turn to God and give thanks by leading a holy life. But all things are possible with God, on Whose rich mercies and free grace in Jesus Christ, I alone depend for Wisdom, Righteousness, Sanctification and Redemption.

Spent a good part of this afternoon in walking upon deck, and blessing God for the prospect I saw all around me. His good Providence has been pleased to bring us into a fine large bay, surrounded on each side with high lands and hummocks, much like those near Gibraltar, and a large lighthouse on the foreland, from which, in the evening, was shown a light. It lies on the north-west of Ireland, and most suppose we are near Limerick, but are not certain, only one of our men having been here before. There are no soundings till you come very near the land. The wind being against us (the little that was of it), we could not get much forward. But God in His due time will bring us on shore. The weather is exceedingly clear, and this is the most comfortable day I have seen for a long time. Lord make me mindful of these Thy mercies all the days of my life.

Tuesday, November 14. Let this day, my soul, be noted in thy book, for God has visited thee with His salvation. On Monday midnight, as I was lying on my bed, my sleep departed from me, and I had no rest in my spirit, because although the weather was so exceeding calm, and we in so great distress, yet no boat was sent to fetch us provisions. Upon this, I spoke to the Captain, and he to the mate, who, in the morning went with a boat, and about noon this day returned loaded with provisions and water, and not only so, but told us, he was kindly entreated by the people he met with, expecially by a great country gentleman, who came from his seat at midnight, on purpose to relieve him and his companions; furnished them with a fresh boat and other necessaries, most kindly invited me, though unknown to his house, to stay as long as I please, and has ordered horses to wait ready to take me thither.

Who is so great, so good a God, as our God? Our hour of extremity was indeed come, for we had but half a pint of water left, and my stomach was exceedingly weak through my long abstinence, but now His Almighty Arm has brought us salvation.

> Through all the changing scenes of life,
>   In trouble and in joy,
> The praises of my God shall still
>   My heart and tongue employ.
>
> Of His deliverance I will boast,
>   'Till all that are distrest
> From my example comfort take
>   And charm their grief to rest.
>
> Fear Him ye saints, and you will then
>   Have nothing else to fear;
> Make you His service your delight,
>   Your wants shall be His care.

As soon as the provisions came, we kneeled down and returned hearty thanks to our good God, Who has heard our prayers, and sent His angel before us, to prepare our way.

> Therefore my life's remaining years,
>   Which God to me shall lend,
> Will I in praises to His Name,
>   And in His service spend.

A little before our provision came, I had been noting in my dairy, that I believed deliverance was at hand; for last night and this morning, I had the most violent conflict within myself that I have had at all. Thus God always prepares me for His mercies. Oh that this may strengthen my faith, and make me willing to follow the Lamb wheresoever He shall be pleased to lead me. Amen, Lord Jesus, Amen.

Still greater mercies God confers on His unworthy servant. For after our provisions were brought aboard, the wind still continued fair, and by six at night blew us to a little place on Carrigaholt Island, before which we cast anchor. Praise the Lord, O my soul, and all that is within me praise His holy Name.

Ever since I have been on board the *Mary*, these words, "Howbeit we must be cast upon a certain island" (which were part of the Lesson I read last at Savannah), have been continually pressed upon my heart, so that I have often mentioned it to one of my companions. Behold they are now fulfilled. Oh how unsearchable are Thy doings, O Lord, and Thy ways past finding out!

Why God dealeth thus with me, I know not now, but I shall know hereafter. However, this I know, that this voyage has been greatly for my good; for I have had a glorious opportunity of searching the Scriptures, composing discourses, writing letters, and communing with my own heart. We have been on board just nine weeks and three days, — a long and perilous, but profitable voyage to my soul; for I hope, it has taught me, in some measure, to endure hardships as becometh a minister of Christ. My clothes have not been off (except to change me) all the passage. Part of the time I lay on open deck; part on a chest; and the remainder on a bedstead covered with my buffalo's skin. These things, though little in themselves, are great in their consequences; and, whosoever despiseth small acts of bodily discipline, it is to be feared, will insensibly lose his spiritual life by little and little. Many inward trials also God has been pleased to send me, which I believe, He has sanctified to my great good. I am now going on shore, to the house of a wealthy gentleman, whom God has commanded to receive me. I may yet be exposed to many perils by land ere I see my dear friends; but His grace Who has preserved me from so many perils by water, will also be sufficient for me on dry land. Whilst I continue on this side Eternity, I never expect to be free from trials, only to change them. For it is necessary to heal the pride of my heart, that such should come. With a particular fear and trembling, I think of going to London; but He Who preserved Daniel in the den of lions, and the Three Children in the fiery furnace, will, I hope, preserve me from the fiery trial of popularity, and from the misguided zeal of those, who without cause, are my enemies.

As for the success of my ministry whilst on board, I shall only say, much sin has been prevented, and one I hope effectually converted, who is to be my fellow-traveler to England. Lord, if I can but be made instrumental to save one soul, I care not if I am tossed on the ocean through my whole life. Glory be to God on high.

Just as we had cast anchor, a violent wind arose, which (had it happened sooner) must have greatly hurt us. Marvelous are Thy works, and that my soul knoweth right well. About seven at night I dressed myself and went on shore, and was received in a strong castle belonging to Mr. MacMahon, the gentleman who sent me an invitation. He himself was not at home, having gone some miles to meet me; but his maidservant kindly received us. I asked for water, and she gave me milk, and brought forth butter in a lordly dish, and never did I eat a more comfortable meal. About ten, the gentleman (having missed me at the place appointed) came throught the rain, and entertained us most hospitably, and about one we went to bed — I hope with hearts full of a sense of the Divine Love. My song shall henceforward be always of the loving-kindness of the Lord. I will make mention of His Righteousness and Truth, in the assemblies of His saints. Now our water is turned into wine.

KILRUSH IN IRELAND: This morning about 11 o'clock, after being most hospitably entertained by Mr. MacMahon, and furnished with three horses, I and my servant and my new convert set out for Dublin and reached Kilrush, a little town, eight Irish miles from Carrigaholt, about two in the afternoon, where we were refreshed and tarried the remainder of the day with Captain Coc, who last night, with his whole crew was like to be shipwrecked; but this morning by the good Providence of God, was brought hither on shore. Surely my shipmates will, of all men be most miserable if they continue impenitent, having such loud and repeated calls from God.

As I rode along, and observed the meanness of the poor people's living in these parts, I said, if my parishioners at Georgia complain to me of hardships, I must tell them how the Irish live; for their habitations are far more despicable, and their living as hard, I believe, as to food; and yet, no doubt, content dwells in many of these low huts.

At my first coming into our inn, we kneeled down and prayed, and again at night sang psalms, and prayed with the Captain and several of my shipmates — the first time, I believe, the room was ever put to such a use by a ship's crew and their chaplain.

FOURTHFARGUS: Friday, November 17. Had a very pleasant ride, over a fine fruitful open country to Fourthfargus, a village that was reckoned only ten, but at a moderate computation, thirty English miles from Kilrush. But this is not the first piece of Irish I have met with — their innocent blunders often extort smiles from one.

As I stopped to have my horses shoed I went into one of the poor people's cabins, as they call them; but it may as well be called a sty, a barn, or a poultry-coop. It was about twenty feet long, and twelve broad, the walls built with turf and mud. In it was a man threshing corn, two swine feeding, two dogs, several geese; a man, his wife, three children, and a great fire. Georgia huts are a palace to it. Indeed, the people live very poorly in this part, some walk barefoot with their shoes in their hands to save them from wearing out, others out of necessity. I observed many of their feet to be much swollen, and ready to gush out with blood, through extremity of cold.

Whilst I was in the cabin, as they call their little Irish huts, I talked with the woman in the house, and found she was a Roman Catholic; and, indeed, the whole commonalty almost, are of the Romish Profession, and seem to be so very ignorant, that they may well be termed the wild Irish. No wonder, when the key of knowledge is taken from them. Woe unto their blind guides. I can think of no likelier means to convert them from their erroneous principles, than to get the Bible translated into their own native language, to have it put in their houses, and charity schools erected for their children, as Mr. Jones has done in Wales, which would insensibly weaken the Romish interest; for when once they could be convinced they were imposed upon, they would no longer suffer themselves to be misled. Oh that some man, in whom is the Spirit of the Holy God, would undertake this!

LIMERICK: Saturday, November 18. Presuming the people where I lay last night were Roman Catholics, I neglected to call them in to join in prayer; but to my great grief found afterwards that some were Protestants, and expected prayers from me. Oh base ingratitude! Is this my zeal for my late signal deliverance? Oh treacherous heart! Fie upon thee, fie upon thee. God be merciful to me a sinner.

About two this afternoon we reached Limerick, a large garrison town, with a cathedral in it, about twenty-one English miles from Fourthfargus. The roads, as we came along, grew better, but the people much more subtle and designing. Here are also many beggars, which I impute to the want of parish provisions for them. At Evening Prayer we went to the Cathedral, and returned public thanks for our safe arrival. The remainder of the night was spent in necessary business, refreshing our bodies, religious conversation, and in writing some things I stood in need of.

Where was I last Saturday? In hunger, cold and thirsting; but now I enjoy fullness of bread, and all things convenient for me. God grant, I may not, Jeshurun-like, wax fat and kick. Perhaps it is more difficult to know how to abound, than how to want. I endeavor to receive both with thanksgiving.

Sunday, November 19. Having sent last night to inform Dr. Burscough, Bishop of Limerick, that I had lately arrived, at his lordship's appointment, I waited on him this morning, and was received with the utmost candour and civility. At his lordship's request, I preached this morning at the Cathedral to a very numerous audience, who seemed universally affected, and full of expectation that I would preach in the afternoon; but Providence did not seem to open a door. But why should not a strange minister always offer his service? I think it is a wrong piece of modesty not to do it. For a sermon from a stranger may do more good than many from those the people are constantly used to.

After sermon, the Mayor sent twice to invite me; but I was pre-engaged to the Bishop, who kindly invited both me and my friend, thanked me for my sermon, and offered me the free use of his palace, and would have insisted of my accepting of it, had I not told his lordship I was to leave Limerick in the morning. Oh into what a wealthy place has my good God brought me? How does He everywhere command some or other to receive me? As I was eating at dinner, I was meditating on the Divine goodness in spreading such a table for me, when last Sunday I was in danger almost of perishing with hunger. But I thought at the same time, if this was so great a blessing, what an infinitely greater one will it be, after the troubles of this life, to sit down and eat bread in the Kingdom of God. O that I may be accounted worthy of that heavenly banquet!

TULLER-BRIDGE: Monday, November 20. Went about Limerick town this morning, to dispatch some necessary business, and found the good seed sown yesterday had received a blessing from above. All the inhabitants seemed alarmed, and looked most wishfully at me, as I passed along. One substantial tradesman, in particular, even compelled me to come in, and showed me and my friend uncommon civilities, and told me how solicitous the people were for my staying longer. Another came to my inn, and begged me to come and see him which I did, and the good Bishop, when I went to take leave of his lordship, kissed me, and said, "Mr. Whitefield, God bless you! I wish you success abroad. Had you stayed in town, this house should have been your home."

About four in the afternoon, against much persuasion to the contrary, we left Limerick, and reached Tuller-Bridge, six miles distant from thence, by six o'clock, where I and my friend were agreeably refreshed, and spent the remainder of the evening in writing to some at Limerick, and strengthening one another, and blessing God for these fresh instances of His unmerited mercies. Who knows what a great matter this little fire may kindle? This I am assured of, God did not send me to Ireland for nothing.

BURRASS AND OSSORY: Tuesday, November 21. Went on journeying before day, and came about five in the evening to Burrass and Ossory, twenty-five miles from Tuller-Bridge.

In my way I had a short conference with a Roman Catholic, who seemed more knowing than the generality of those of that persuasion, but sadly misguided. My main drift was to convince him he was imposed upon. "Am I?" says he, with great earnestness; "did I know that, I would follow him (i.e. the priest) no longer."

As far as I can find by all I converse with, they place religion in being of the Protestant or Roman Catholic communion, and are quite ignorant of the nature of inward purity and holiness of heart. Lord, the Christian world is cast into a deep sleep; send forth, I beseech Thee, some faithful and true pastors to awaken them out of it.

Thursday, November 23. Came forwards last night, to a place called Neas, thirty-three miles from Burrass and Ossory, and reached Dublin about noon, without the least fatigue or weariness. Blessed be God, He causes me to renew my strength, or otherwise it would not be thus with me.

Two things I can remark much for the credit of Ireland — that the roads, especially to Dublin, are surprisingly good, and provisions exceedingly cheap. A person may travel without much expense.

DUBLIN: Friday, November 24. Went today with Mr. Bradford, brother to Mr. Bradford of Georgia, to visit Dr. Delany, who most kindly received me, and invited me to dine with him on Sunday. Some other part of the day I was necessarily obliged to go and see the busy part of Dublin; but the more I see of the world, the more I grow sick of it every day.

Sunday, November 26. Preached twice today at the churches of St. Werburgh's and St. Andrew's: I believe with success, for God enabled me to speak with power. And the people, as it were, not only hung upon me to hear me in the morning, but also flocked to the church where I preached in the afternoon, so that it was like a London congregation. Great good might be done in Dublin, by preaching charity sermons for the establishing of Protestant Schools.

Tuesday, November 28. By the advice, and through the introduction of Mr. Delany, I waited on Dr. Rundle, Bishop of London-derry, and on his Grace the Archbishop of Armagh, Lord Primate of all Ireland. The former engaged me to dine with him on the morrow, if I stayed in town, the latter to dine with him at three in the afternoon, at which time I waited on his Grace, and was courteously received both by him and his clergy, having heard of me, as the Bishop of Derry told me, from some friend at Gibraltar.

ENGLAND

PARKGATE: Thursday, November 30. After near twelve months' absence from London, three months from Georgia, and a pleasant passage from Dublin, to my inexpressible comfort, God brought me to Parkgate, and so fulfilled a promise which was pressed upon my heart last Innocents' Day, in Hampshire, when I was under a great concern what my mother would say to the resolution I had then made to go to Georgia.

NANTWICH: Friday, December 1. Rode from Park Gate to Nantwich, in hopes of seeing my old friend Mr. Salmon, but God was pleased to disappoint me. However, He enlarged my heart, and enabled me to write several letters to friends at Dublin; and I now, as I have often done before, make this remark, "That God never disappoints us one way, but He opens a door to do good in another."

MANCHESTER: Saturday, December 2. Reached Manchester, by four this afternoon, and was much edified by dear Mr. Clayton's judicious conversation, for the benefit of which I came so far out of my way.

Sunday, December 3. Preached twice at Mr. Clayton's Chapel to a thronged and very attentive audience, especially in the afternoon, and assisted with six more ministers in administering the blessed Sacrament to three hundred communicants. Never did I see a table more richly spread, nor a greater order and decency observed. Blessed be God for my coming to Manchester; I hope it has greatly benefited and strengthened my soul. This has been a sabbath indeed. May it prepare me for that eternal rest which awaits the children of God.

STONE: Monday, December 4. Set out at daybreak and got to Stone, thirty-four miles from Manchester, by five in the evening; was a little fatigued, but quite refreshed by the morning. Oh, that I may always look upon myself as a stranger and a sojourner upon earth.

Friday, December 8. After having ridden thirty-six miles on Tuesday, and twenty-four on Wednesday, on Thursday, about three in the afternoon, I reached St. Albans. In the morning I set out for London, and was agreeably surprised with the sight of some of my Christian friends on the road, who were coming to meet me, which put me in mind of St. Paul's friends, meeting him at the Three Taverns, and I, like him, was not a little comforted. Oh, that I may, like him also, be willing to follow my Master wheresoever He shall be pleased to call me, not counting my life dear unto myself, so that I may finish my course with joy.

THE THIRD JOURNAL

FROM HIS ARRIVAL AT LONDON TO HIS DEPARTURE TO GEORGIA

(December, 1738 — June, 1739)

LONDON: Friday, December 8, 1738. About noon, I reached London; was received with much joy by my Christian friends, and joined with them in psalms and thanksgiving for my safe arrival. My heart was greatly enlarged hereby. In the evening went to a truly Christian Society in Fetter Lane, and perceived God had greatly watered the seed sown by my ministry when last in London. The Lord increase it more and more.

Saturday, December 9. Waited this morning on the Archbishop of Canterbury, and the Bishop of London, and met with a favorable reception.

Sunday, December 10. When I was on board the *Mary*, those particular parts of the Book of Jeremiah, which relate to the opposition he met with from the false prophets, were deeply impressed upon my soul. Now I begin to see the wisdom of God in it; for five churches have been already denied me, and some of the clergy, if possible, would oblige me to depart out of these coasts. But I rejoice in this opposition, it being a certain sign that a more effectual door will be opened, since there are so many adversaries.

However, I had an opportunity of preaching in the morning at St. Helen's, and at Islington in the afternoon, to large congregations indeed, with great demonstration of the Spirit, and with power. Here seems to be a great pouring out of the Spirit, and many who were awakened by my preaching a year ago, are now grown strong men in Christ, by the ministrations of my dear friends and fellow-laborers, John and Charles Wesley. Blessed be God, I rejoice in the coming of the Kingdom of His dear Son.

The old doctrine about Justification by Faith only, I found much revived, and many letters had been sent concerning it to me, all which I providentially missed; for now I come unprejudiced, and can the more easily see who is right. And who dare assert that we are not justified in the sight of God merely by an act of faith in Jesus Christ, without any regard to works past, present, or to come?

In the evening, I went to Fetter Lane Society, where we had (what might not improperly be called) a love-feast — eating a little bread and water, and spending about two hours in singing and prayers. I found my heart greatly united with the brethren. Surely a primitive spirit is reviving amongst us. May God knit my heart to theirs more and more.

Sunday, December 24. Preached twice, and went in the evening to Crooked Lane Society, where God enabled me to withstand several persons, who cavilled against the doctrine of the new birth. But the passion wherewith they oppose is a demonstration that they themselves have not experienced it. Lord make them partakers of it, for Thy dear Son's sake.

After I left Crooked Lane, I went and expounded to a company at Mr. B . . .'s, in Little Britain; then I went to another love-feast at Fetter Lane, and, it being Christmas Eve, continued till near four in the morning in prayer, psalms, and thanksgiving, with many truly Christian brethren, and my heart was much enlarged and full of love. God gave me a great spirit of supplication. Adored be His free grace in Christ Jesus. Amen and Amen.

Monday, December 25. About four this morning, went and prayed, and expounded to another Society in Redcross Street, consisting of near two or three hundred people, and the room was exceedingly hot. I had been watching unto prayer all night, yet God vouchsafed so to fill me with His blessed Spirit that I spoke with as great power as ever I did in my life. My body was weak, but I found a supernatural strength, and the truth of that saying, "When I am weak, then I am strong."

At six I went to Crutched Friars' Society, and expounded as well as I could, but perceived myself a little oppressed with drowsiness. How does the corruptible body weigh down the soul? When shall I be delivered from the burden of this flesh?

Preached thrice, and assisted in administering the Sacrament the same day. This day 24 years ago I was baptized. Lord, to what little purpose have I lived? However, I sealed my baptismal covenant with my dear Savior's most blessed Body and Blood, and trust in His strength I shall keep and perform it. Amen, Amen.

Saturday, December 30. Preached nine times this week, and expounded near eighteen times, with great power and enlargement. I am every moment employed from morning till midnight. There is no end of people coming and sending to me, and they seem more and more desirous, like new-born babes, to be fed with the sincere milk of the Word. What a great work has been wrought in the hearts of many within this twelvemonth! Now know I, that though thousands might come at first out of curiosity, yet God has prevented and quickened them by His free grace. Oh that I could be humble and thankful!

Glory be to God that He fills me continually, not only with peace, but also joy in the Holy Ghost. Before my arrival, I thought I should envy my brethren's success in the ministry, but blessed be God, I rejoice in it, and am glad to see Christ's Kingdom come, whatsoever instruments God shall make use of to bring it about. Sometimes I perceive myself deserted for a little while, and much oppressed, especially before preaching, but comfort soon after flows in. The Kingdom of God is within me. Oh! free grace in Christ!

Sunday, December 31. Preached twice to large congregations, especially in the afternoon, at Spitalfields. I had a great hoarseness upon me, and was deserted before I went up into the pulpit; but God strengthened me to speak, so as to be heard by all.

After I left Spitalfields, my cold being very great, I despaired of speaking much more that night; but God enabled me to expound to two companies in Southwark, and I was never more enlarged in prayer in my life. These words, "And the power of the Lord was present to heal them," were much pressed upon my soul, and indeed I believe it was, for many were pricked to the heart, and felt themselves to be sinners. Oh that all the world knew and felt that!

Monday, January 1, 1739. Received the Holy Sacrament, preached twice, and expounded twice, and found this to be the happiest New Year's Day that I ever yet saw. Oh! what mercies has the Lord shown me since this time twelvemonth! And yet I shall see greater things than these. Oh that my heart may be prepared to see them! Oh that my old things may pass away, and all things become new!

Had a love-feast with our brethren at Fetter Lane, and spent the whole night in close prayer, psalms, and thanksgivings. God supported me without sleep. Oh, that our despisers were partakers of our joys!

Tuesday, January 2. Stayed at home on purpose to receive those who wanted to consult me. From seven in the morning till three in the afternoon, people came, some telling me what God had done for their souls, and others crying out, "What shall we do to be saved?" Being obliged to go out after this, I deferred several till Thursday. God enabled me to give them answers of peace. How does God work by my unworthy hands! His mercies melt me down.

Thursday, January 4. Though my cold continued, and I feared it would prevent my speaking, yet God enabled me to expound with power in a private Society, and then to preach at Wapping Chapel, so that the Word pierced the hearers' souls. Afterwards I expounded and prayed for an hour and a half with power and demonstration of the Spirit, and my heart was full of God. How immediately does Jesus Christ reward me for my poor services! As soon as my daily work is done, He says, "Enter thou into the joy of Thy Lord."

Friday, January 5. Held a conference at Islington, concerning several things of very great importance, with seven true ministers of Jesus Christ, despised Methodists, whom God has brought together from the East and the West, the North and the South. What we were in doubt about, after prayer, we determined by lot, and everything else was carried on with great love, meekness, and devotion. We continued in fasting and prayer till three o'clock, and then parted with a full conviction that God was going to do great things among us. Oh that we may be in any way instrumental to His glory! That He would make us vessels pure and holy, meet for our Master's use!

Expounded twice afterwards in London with power, and then was much enlarged for near an hour in prayer, in Fetter Lane Society. The spirit of supplication increases in my heart daily. May it increase more and more.

Did not find the pity I ought, upon seeing a brother full of self-love. Lord, enlarge my narrow heart, and give me that charity which rejoices not in iniquity, but in the truth. Perceived something a little bordering on envy towards my brother H. I find more and more that true humility consists in being submissive to those who are a little above, or a little below us. Oh when shall I come to rejoice in others' gifts and graces as much as in my own. I am resolved to wrestle with Jesus Christ by faith and prayer till He thus blesses me.

Saturday, January 6. Preached six times this week, and should have preached a seventh time, but one minister would not permit me, which caused me to pray for him most earnestly. Blessed be God, I can say, "I love mine enemies."

Expounded twice or thrice every night this week. The Holy Ghost so powerfully worked upon my hearers, pricking their hearts, and melting them into such floods of tears, that a spiritual man said, "he never saw the like before." God is with me of a truth. Adored be His unmerited goodness; I find His grace quickening me more and more every day. My understanding is more enlightened, my affections more inflamed, and my heart full of love towards God and man.

Sunday, January 7. Preached twice today, and expounded to three Societies, one of which I never visited before. God grant I may pursue the method of expounding and praying extempore. I find God blesses it more and more.

Had another love-feast, and spent the whole night in prayer and thanksgiving at Fetter Lane. There was a great pouring out of the Spirit amongst the brethren; but I cannot say I was so full of joy as the last night we spent together.

Monday, January 8. Though I sat up all night, yet God carried me through the work of the day with about an hour's sleep. Expounded in the evening, and confuted a virulent opposer of the doctrine of the New Birth, and Justification by Faith only. But what can be said to those who will not be convinced? Lord open Thou their hearts and eyes. Spent the remainder of the evening with our bands, which are little combinations of six or more Christians meeting together to compare their experiences. Build ye up one another, even as also ye do. Confess your faults one to another, and pray for one another, that ye may be healed.

Tuesday, January 9. Stayed at home again today to talk with those who came to consult me, and found that God has awakened several, and excited in them a hunger and thirst after righteousness by my sermon on the *Power of Christ's Resurrection, and Have ye received the Holy Ghost?* Every day I hear of somebody or another quickened to a sense of the Divine life. Oh what abundant reason have I to be thankful!

This evening I preached a sermon at Great St. Helen's, for erecting a church for the Saltzburghers of Georgia, and collected 33 pounds. The people gave most readily, many wishing they had more to give.

OXFORD: Wednesday, January 10. Slept about three hours, rose at five, set out at ten, and reached Oxford by five in the evening. As I entered the city, I called to mind the mercies I had received since I left it. They are more than I am able to express. Oh that my heart may be melted down by a sense of them. Amen, Lord Jesus. Spent the remainder of the evening very agreeable with several Christian friends. May God sanctify our meeting.

Friday, January 12. Breakfasted with sixteen or seventeen Christian brethren; expounded and read prayers at the Castle to many devout souls. Afterwards, I waited on the Bishop of Gloucester, who received me very kindly. Waited on the Master of Pembroke; afterwards on the Archdeacon. Went to public worship at Pembroke. Supped, prayed, and sung psalms with a room full of brethren at Mr. F . . .'s, then adjourned to Corpus Christi College, where God assisted me to talk clearly of the New Birth, and Justification by Faith alone, with one who opposed it. Lord, open Thou our eyes that we may prove what is that acceptable and perfect Will of God.

Saturday, January 13. Received the Holy Sacrament at St. Mary's; expounded with great power at Mr. F . . .'s, went with the other candidates for Holy Orders to subscribe to the Articles, and secretly prayed that we all might have our names written in the Book of Life. Drank tea with a well-disposed Gentleman Commoner, and had close conversation with many others at Corpus Christi College. I enjoyed great tranquillity of soul, and had much reason to bless God for sending me to the University. Oh, that I may be prepared for receiving the Holy Ghost tomorrow by the imposition of hands. Amen, Lord Jesus, Amen.

Sunday, January 14. This, blessed be God, has been a day of fat things. Rose in the morning, and prayed and sang psalms lustily, and with a good courage, and afterwards was ordained priest at Christ Church. Before I was a little dissipated, but at imposition of hands, my mind was in a humble frame, and I received grace in the Holy Sacrament. That I might begin to make proof of my ministry, I preached and administered the Sacrament at the Castle; and preached in the afternoon at St. Alban's to a crowded congregation. The church was surrounded with Gownsmen of all Degrees, who, contrary to their custom, stood attentive at the windows during my sermon. God enabled me to preach with the demonstration of the Spirit, and with power, and quite took away my hoarseness, so that I could lift up my voice like a trumpet. After sermon, I joined in giving thanks to our good God for all the mercies He had conferred upon me. Then I read prayers at Carfax; expounded to a large and devout company both of men and women at a private house; and spent the remainder of the evening with thirteen more, where God gave me great cheerfulness of spirit.

LONDON: Monday, January 15. Took a most affectionate leave of my dear Oxon. brethren; set out at seven, reached London by five, and spent the evening in answering some letters, especially one from Howell Harris, an instrument, under God, of doing much good in Wales. Read a pamphlet written against me by a clergyman, I bless God, without any emotion; prayed most heartily for the author; opened my heart to my brethren in bands, and left great peace consequent thereupon.

Tuesday, January 16. After much opposition, read prayers, and preached to a thronged and affected audience at St. Helen's. After this, I expounded twice to two companies, and prayed by name for the author of the pamphlet; left my auditors in tears, and went home full of love and joy and peace which passeth all understanding. Oh, that he felt what I do! Happy, unspeakably happy, would he then be.

Wednesday, January 17. Dined with and convinced several who were prejudiced against extempore prayer. Waited on the Trustees, and was most kindly received. Afterwards much assisted in expounding twice at Mr. C . . .'s. The more I am opposed, the more God enlightens my understanding. So it was formerly, so it is now. Spent the remainder of the evening at Fetter Lane Society, and God enabled me to tell of some experiences, which I hope comforted their hearts.

Thursday, January 18. Perceived myself much disordered, so that I was obliged to lie down to sleep; but afterwards God greatly enlarged my heart, and enabled me to expound to two Societies. I made a collection for two poor housekeepers. I find action is the best way to take all oppression off the spirits. God will meet and bless us when doing His work.

Friday, January 19. Did some necessary business for Georgia, and spent the afternoon in visiting some Dissenting brethren, who are Christians indeed. But, as such, I acknowledge all who love our Lord Jesus in sincerity and truth.

Saturday, January 20. Preached three times this week, and expounded to about sixteen thronged companies, wherein God gave me great power and success. Had many contributions sent me for the Orphan House.

Sunday, January 21. Went this morning and received the Sacrament at the hands of the minister who wrote against me. Blessed be God, I do not feel the least remonstrance against, but a love for him; for I believe he has a zeal for God, though, in my opinion, not according to knowledge. Oh that I could do him any good.

Preached twice with great power and clearness in my voice to two thronged congregations, especially in the afternoon, when I believe near a thousand people were in the churchyard, and hundreds more returned home that could not come in. Thus God magnifies His power most when most opposed.

Expounded twice afterwards, where the people pressed most vehemently to hear the Word. God enabled me to speak with the demonstration of the Spirit, and with power; and the remainder of the evening, filled me with a humble sense of His infinite mercies. I think I am never more humble than when exalted.

Monday, January 22. Spent all the day in necessary business for my poor flock, and in going about doing good. In the evening I expounded to three several Societies, one of which was the most polite I ever yet saw;

but God enabled me to speak upon the doctrine of the New Birth, and however some might mock, yet others, I believe, were affected, especially three Quakers, who afterwards came and paid me a visit, and glorified God on my behalf. Oh how thankful, how humble ought I to be. God fills me with love, peace, and joy in the Holy Ghost. Such is His free grace in Christ Jesus.

Tuesday, January 23. Stayed at home today as usual, to receive people, and still had the comfort of having many come to me, who have been awakened to a sense of the new birth. What reason have I to bless God for sending me to England! How does He daily set His seal to my ministry! Praise ye Him, all His hosts; let everything that hath breath praise the Lord!

Received a packet of letters from my dear friend Habersham, by which I find the Infinite Wisdom of God, more and more, in sending me to England. The poor people of Savannah love me still most affectionately, but the colony seems to be at a low ebb. Poor Georgia! When thou art universally despised, and quite despairest of human help, then will God manifest His mighty arm in thy salvation.

Read prayers and preached at St. Helen's with power to a crowded and attentive audience. Was enabled to expound to two companies, and collected above forty shillings for the Orphan House of Georgia. I could wish to have it built with mites. Oh how does the Holy Ghost cause me to joy in God! How does He bring me acquainted with His faithful servants!

Wednesday, January 24. Preached a charity sermon. Went to Newington, to see Dr. Watts, who received me most cordially, and returned in the evening and expounded with power to two companies. Wrote several letters to my friends at Savannah, and was filled with the Holy Ghost. Oh, that all who deny the promise of the Father might thus receive it themselves!

Thursday, January 25. Received the Sacrament at Bow, where four of my opposers administered, one of whom was the person who wrote the self-answering pamphlet against me. At first a thought darted into my mind that they were of a persecuting spirit, but I soon checked it, and was filled with love towards them. God grant that they may be like-minded towards me.

At two in the afternoon read prayers and preached at Christ Church, Spitalfields, for the Orphan House. The congregation was not so large as might be expected, and that of the poorest sort, so that I began to doubt. But wherefore did I fear? For God enabled me to preach with power, and 25 pounds was collected, to our great surprise, and to the glory of our great and good God; for which we kneeled down and gave most hearty thanks.

This done, I went and gave a word or two of exhortation, and prayed to a company that waited for me. Then I expounded to another Society in Leadenhall Street, and collected very near 5 pounds for the Orphan House. About eight, I went to another Society; after nine, to a third, at both of which I spoke with the demonstration of the Spirit, and made collections for the Orphan House. The strength God gives me would surprise me, did I not know what a gracious Master I serve.

Received a letter from Edinburgh, from a truly pious gentleman, who tells me his heart was knit to me most strongly, upon the reading of my Journal. How many are there, whom I know not, praying for me in secret! Surely God intends to bring mighty things to pass. Is not His strength made perfect in weakness?

Friday, January 26. Waited upon an opposing clergyman, and had a conference with him of near two hours. His grand objection was against our private Societies, and using extempore prayer, which he grounded on the authority of the Canons, and the Act of Charles II. In answer, I showed that that Act was entirely leveled against seditious schismatical meetings, contrary to the Church of England, which confines us to a Form in public worship only. He replied, that ours was public worship, but this I deny. For ours were Societies never intended to be set up in opposition to the public worship, by law established; but only in imitation of the primitive Christians, who continued daily with one accord in the Temple, and yet in fellowship building up one another, and exhorting one another from house to house. Went with Mr. Seward to Bexley, about ten miles from London, where I preached to a large congregation, and afterwards spent the evening most delightfully in religious conversation, and in singing psalms and hymns and spiritual songs with Mr. Delamotte's family, who seem almost with one accord ready to receive Jesus Christ. A happier household have I seldom found, or one that more resembles that of Martha, Mary, and their brother Lazarus.

Saturday, January 27. Slept but little tonight, as well as the night before; but was much strenghtened by the Holy Spirit. Rose about five, spent above an hour most agreeably in prayer, singing and reading the Scriptures with the church in Mr. Delamotte's house; some of whom, after the example of their Lord, passed the whole night in the same delightful employment.

Came to London about nine in the morning, and expounded twice in Beech Lane, where I believe near seven hundred people were present. Collected 5 pounds for the Orphan House.

Had extraordinary comforts this week; heard much of what God has done abroad for me in other places, where I am not known in the flesh, and desired greatly to be humble and thankful.

Sunday, January 28. Received the Sacrament at Crooked Lane, but was a little dissipated; however, I found I received Christ, and fed on Him in my heart by faith with thanksgiving. Went and preached at Ironmongers Almshouses at St. Catherine's, in the afternoon; afterwards expounded to two large companies in the Minories, with such demonstration of the Spirit as I never spoke with before. I offered Jesus Christ freely to sinners, and many, I believe, were truly pricked to the heart. Now, my friends, your prayers are heard, God has given me a double portion of His Spirit indeed. Oh free grace in Christ Jesus. With what love, peace, and joy does God fill this soul of mine! Lord I am not worthy, but Thy mercies in Christ Jesus are infinite.

Monday, January 29. Expounded twice, and sat up till near one in the morning, with my honored brother and fellow-laborer, John Wesley, in conference with two clergymen of the Church of England, and some other strong opposers of the doctrine of the New Birth. God enabled me, with great simplicity, to declare what He had done for my soul, which made them look upon me as a madman. We speak what we do know, and testify that we have seen, and they receive not our witness. Now, therefore, I am fully convinced there is a fundamental difference between us and them. They believe only an outward Christ, we further believe that He must be inwardly formed in our hearts also. But the natural man receiveth not the things of the Spirit of God, for they are foolishness unto him: neither can he know them, because they are spiritually discerned.

Tuesday, January 30. Preached at Duke's Place and St. Helen's, to crowded audiences, and afterwards expounded twice on Dowgate Hill, where the people pressed mightily to come in. The minister of the parish threatens the master of the house with a prosecution, though it will be hard for him to prove such Societies any ways contrary to the laws either of God or man.

GRAVESEND: Wednesday, January 31. Slept about two hours; rose at three in the morning, and went with some Christian friends in a boat to Gravesend, where I have been long expected. God inclined the ministers' hearts to let me have the use of both the pulpits, and I preached and read prayers at three in the afternoon at the church without the town; and did the same at the church in the town, and the people, as elsewhere, hung upon me to hear the Word of God. God is with me wherever I go.

Thursday, February 1. Read prayers and expounded on the Third of St. John; expounded at a private house in the afternoon, and read prayers and expounded a third time on the conversion of St. Paul in the evening. I had great freedom of speech, and was filled with exceeding great joy at the consideration of what great things God yet continues to do for my soul; and yet I shall see greater things than these. I spent the remainder of the evening in singing hymns, and religious conversation; took boat about eleven; spoke warmly to the passengers, and came to London rejoicing, about five in the morning. The Lord preserve my going out, and my coming in, from this time forth forevermore.

LONDON: Friday, February 2. Slept about two hours; went and preached at Islington, and collected for my Orphan House.

Had a great number of communicants. This is the first time I have preached without notes (for when I preached at Deptford and Gravesend, I only repeated a written sermon); but I find myself now, as it were, constrained to do it.

Expounded in the evening, and collected 3 pounds for the Orphan House, at Mr. Abbot's; preached extempore with great freedom at Wapping Chapel; then expounded to another Society, and returned home without fatigue or weariness. How does God deal with me! He gives me a heaven upon earth, and makes my heart leap for joy almost continually. Oh that all who now oppose it, were partakers of this joy!

Saturday, February 3. Stayed at home this day on purpose to settle my private affairs; and did it to my satisfaction. Began a new Society at the house of Mr. M . . . n, and was much assisted in expounding twice at Beech Lane to two companies, making in all near a thousand people. Visited a sick brother, and came home full of peace, and love, and joy in the Holy Ghost.

Near nime times has God enabled me to preach this week, and to expound 12 or 14 times; near 40 pounds, I believe has been collected for the Orphan House. I find I gain greater light and knowledge by preaching extempore, so that I fear I should quench the Spirit, did I not go on to speak as He gives me utterance.

Sunday, February 4. Was warmed much by talking to an almost Christian, who came to ask me certain questions. Preached in the morning at St. George's in the East; collected 18 pounds for the Orphan House; and had, I believe, 600 communicants, which highly offended the officiating curate. Poor man, I pitied and prayed for him sincerely.

Preached again at Christ Church, Spitalfields; and gave thanks, and sang psalms at a private house. Went thence to St. Margaret's, Westminster; but something breaking belonging to the coach, could not get there till the middle of prayers. Went through the people to the minister's pew, but, finding it locked, I returned to the vestry till the sexton could be found. Being there informed that another minister intended to preach, I desired several times that I might go home. My friends would by no means consent, telling me I was appointed by the Trustees to preach, and that if I did not, the people would go out of the church. At my request, some went to the Trustees, church-wardens, and minister; and, whilst I was waiting for an answer, and the last psalm being sung, a man came with a wand in his hand, whom I took for the proper church officer, and told me I was to preach. I, not doubting that the minister was satisfied, followed him to the pulpit, and God enabled me to preach with greater power than I had done all the day before.

After this, I prayed with and gave a word or two of exhortation to a company that waited for me. Then I went to a love-feast in Fetter Lane, where I spent the whole night in watching unto prayer, and discussing several important points with many truly Christian friends. About four in the morning, we went all together, and broke bread at a poor sick sister's room; and so we parted, I hope, in a spirit not unlike that of the primitive Christians.

This has been a sabbath indeed! How has God owned me before near twelve thousand people this day! How has He strengthened my body! How has He filled and satisfied my soul! Now know I, that I did receive the Holy Ghost at imposition of hands, for I feel it as much as Elisha did when Elijah dropped his mantle. Nay, others see it also, and my opposers, would they but speak, cannot but confess that God is with me of a truth. Wherefore then do they fight against God?

Monday, February 5. Went about gathering for my poor flock; had a little time to write my journal; was somewhat weak part of the day; but grew strong by expounding to four companies at night. I always get strength by working. What great things has God done for my soul. Oh, that I could praise Him with my whole heart!

Tuesday, February 6. Was refreshed much this morning, and found that the sleep of a laboring man was sweet. Waited on the Bishop of Gloucester with brother John Wesley, and received his lordship's liberal benefaction for Georgia.

Went to St. Helen's, where Satan withstood me greatly — for on a sudden I was deserted, and my strength went from me. But I thought it was the Devil's doing, and therefore was resolved to resist him steadfast in the faith. Accordingly, though I was exceedingly sick in reading the prayers, and almost unable to speak when I entered the pulpit, yet God gave me courage to begin, and before I had done, I waxed warm and strong in the Spirit, and offered Jesus Christ freely to all who would lay hold on Him by faith. Many, I believe, were touched to the quick, for they seemed to feel what was spoken, and said hearty and loud Amens to my sentences. The church was greatly thronged, and after I had done, prayers were put up on all sides for my safe journey and return. Surely these are not curious hearers. If they are, why do they follow more and more for such a continuance? No; many conversions have been wrought in their hearts. God has set His seal to my ministry, and I trust they will be my joy and crown of rejoicing in the Day of the Lord Jesus. Oh the riches of God's free grace in Christ to the chief of sinners! Oh that I fully felt the sense of these words!

After this, the people waited in great companies to see and follow me; but I got away from them by going out at a back door. Perhaps, hereafter, I may be let out in the same manner to escape the fury of mine enemies.

In coming along I perceived myself more and more strengthened, and was much comforted in reading a letter sent me by an excellent saint, who loves me in the bowels of Jesus Christ. About nine at night, I expounded with great enlargement at Dowgate Hill to a most crowded audience. Tongue cannot express what power God gave me, or how the hearts of the poor people were affected. They signed and mourned, and wept sorely, when I mentioned my departure from them, though but for a season. I exhorted them particularly not to forsake the assembling themselves together, notwithstanding the people of the house had been threatened with a prosecution. But so far as our opposers are permitted to go, shall they go, but no farther. I never was more opposed and never met with so great success. My dear Christian friends waited at my coming home, to salute me. God filled me with love and joy, and I waxed stronger and stronger in spirit, to their and my own unspeakable comfort in Jesus Christ our Lord. All love, all glory be to the ever Blessed Trinity, now and forevermore. Amen.

Wednesday, February 7. Spent the morning in providing things for my journey, and taking leave of my dear Christian friends. Had several presents made me by such as God had worked upon by my ministry; and after having prayed and sung psalms in several Christian houses, about two I set out for Windsor, desiring to be thankful for those marvelous great kindnesses God had shown me in this city. I perceived my heart so nearly knit to my dear friends, that was it the Divine Will, I should gladly continue here. But I must go into every place and city where I have been already. Lord, send Thy angel before me to prepare my way. But wherefore should I doubt, since so many thousands are continually praying for me? The good Lord pour down upon them the choicest of His blessings.

WINDSOR: Got here about six in the evening, and was joyfully received by several Christian friends, who were waiting for me. About seven I was taken very ill indeed, but God strengthened me to go out, and I expounded with freedom and power in the schoolhouse to a great number of people, who were apprised of my coming, and, I believe, felt what I spoke; for some wept, and many expressed their thankfulness for my exposition.

Being much refreshed by talking for God, I spent the remainder of the evening in writing to some dear Christian friends, and in singing, praying, and conversing with others, as likewise with the people of the inn where we lodged.

Thursday, February 8. Breakfasted, prayed, and sung a hymn at the house of Mr. D . . .'s, who kindly invited both me and my friends. Some other persons sent for me to their houses, and I believe, much good might be done here. Lord open an effectual door for preaching Thy gospel, wheresoever Thou shalt send me. Amen.

I find much service might be done to religion on journeys, if we had but courage to show ourselves Christians in all places. Other sing songs in public houses, why should not we sing psalms? And when we give the servants money, why may we not with that give them a little Book, and some good advice? I know by experience it is very beneficial. God grant this may be always my practice.

BASINGSTOKE: Left Windsor about ten in the morning, dined at Bagshot, and reached Basingstoke at five in the evening. Not meeting with our friends, who were to come from Dummer, I wrote to some Christian brethren I had left behind me, and afterwards was agreeably surprised by several who came uninvited to see me. After a little conversation, I perceived they were desirous to hear the Word of God, and being in a large dining room in the public house, I gave notice I would expound to as many as would come. In a short time, I had above a hundred very attentive hearers, to whom I expounded for above an hour, for which they were very thankful. Blessed be God for this opportunity! I hope I shall learn more and more every day, that no place is amiss for preaching the Gospel. God forbid, that the Word of God should be bound, because some out of a misguided zeal deny the use of their churches. Though they bid me no more speak to the people in this way, yet I cannot but speak the things that I have seen and felt in my own soul. The more I am bidden to hold my peace, the more earnestly will I lift up my voice like a trumpet, and tell the people what must be done in them before they can be finally saved by Jesus Christ.

Friday, February 9. After breakfast and prayer with the family where we lodged, I set out for Dummer (a parish once for a little while under my care), and met with near a dozen Christian brethren, with whom we took exceeding sweet counsel, prayed, and sang psalms, and ate our bread with gladness and singleness of heart. I wish all knew how cheerful we, that are beginning to be Christians, live. And if the beginning be so sweet, what must the end of believing be? Oh the goodness of God in thus bringing me back to the places where I have been already! Lord melt down my frozen heart with a sense of Thy unmerited love. Amen, Amen.

After having written several letters, I returned with my friends to Basingstoke, where I had appointed to expound. Accordingly, in the evening I went to a large room prepared for that purpose, and expounded for an hour. The place was very much thronged, many were very noisy, and others did us the honor of throwing up stones at the windows. But I spoke so much the louder, being convinced some good must come out from a place where opposition is. I should doubt whether I was a true minister of Christ, was I not opposed. And I find it does me much good; for it drives me nearer to my Lord and Master, Jesus Christ, with Whom I long to dwell.

After exposition, near twenty friends came to visit me, and two young men in particular (once leaders of the Religious Society, but since fallen back). They came, I believe, with a design to puzzle me about the doctrine of regeneration; but alas, they soon showed what strangers they were to it. One was so full of zeal that he could not keep his seat, and both were entirely ignorant of the indwelling of the Spirit. One thing they took care to show as much as possible, viz., that they had read the Fathers (I suppose the English translations), but, at the same time, denied experience in religion. Poor men! I pitied and told them, how they rested in learning, falsely so called, while they were strangers to the power of godliness in their hearts. At last, finding no probability of convincing them, and being called away to supper, I and my friends took our leave in love, with true concern to see what an unhappy spirit our opposers are of. Afterwards, we prayed for them, and endeavored to bless God for making us to triumph, through His dear Son, in every place.

Saturday, February 10. Breakfasted with some friends, and after family prayer went with my dear brethren, Mr. Kinchin and Mr. Hutchings, to Dummer, where I spent most of the day in visiting that poor flock from house to house, who rejoiced exceedingly at the sight of me, and had not forgotten their former love. Their simplicity delighted me and my friend Seward much, and God enlarged my heart greatly to praise Him, and to pray for my dear absent brethren. Indeed, I love them in the bowels of Jesus Christ.

About four in the afternoon we returned to Basingstoke, in order to expound. And near three large rooms were filled. We expected ill treatment ere we returned home, and some did begin to interrupt me; but God enabled me to speak with such irresistible power, that they were quite struck dumb and confounded. Many said, "We will never oppose again"; others said, they would follow me wheresoever I should go, and the hearts of God's children, as well as my own, were filled with joy unspeakable. This night I hope salvation is come to this place.

After exposition, many Christian friends came to see me, and about nine at night we set out for Dummer. But no one can tell what enlargement of heart God gave me. My soul was full of ineffable comfort and joy in the Holy Ghost. I poured out my heart before the throne of grace as I rode by the way, and felt the Spirit of God working in me, and enabling me to intercede most earnestly for my dear friends. Lord hear my prayers, and let my cry come unto Thee. In a short time we reached Dummer, and after having taken a little refreshment, I went to bed full of love, and rejoicing for the great things God had done for my soul.

Sunday, February 11. Rose full of love and joy, but afterwards, on a sudden was deserted, and then taken very ill in body. I struggled just like one in his last agonies, and longed to stretch myself into God. After having vomited several times, I was obliged to go to bed. Oh, how did I long to be dissolved, and be with Jesus Christ! How did I wish for the wings of an eagle, that I might fly away to Heaven! But that happy hour is not yet come. There are many promises to be fulfilled in me, many souls to be called, many sufferings to be endured, before I go hence.

After having fallen asleep for a short time, I arose and went to public worship, and preached and administered the Sacrament, but without any life or power.

My sickness still continuing, after service I went to bed again full of peace, but weak in body, oppressed much in my head, and quite shut up till near five at night, at which time, by the advice of my brother Seward, I took courage, and though it rained hard, rode with my dear friends to Basingstoke, where above five hundred were waiting to hear me expound; but my indisposition continuing, brother Kinchin expounded in my stead. After this, my spirits revived, my body was strengthened, and God gave me utterance, so that I spoke freely to near twenty people who came to converse with me, and to hear the Word of God. How thankful ought I to be to my dear Master for sending me here. A most beneficial and comfortable meeting have I had with my dear Christian friends, and many, I hope, will have reason to bless God for what they have seen and heard. A vestry, I find, was called to stop my proceedings, and I hear I am to be presented to the Diocesan. Several lies have been told in the *News* about my preaching at St. Margaret's last Sunday. Blessed be God! that I can rejoice in these lower marks of my discipleship. Wherever I go, God causeth me to triumph, knits the hearts of His people most closely to me, and makes me more than conqueror through His love. The comforts I enjoy within are inexpressible, — they have a great effect upon my outward man, and make me of a cheerful countenance, which recommends my Master's service much. Oh, free grace in Christ Jesus!

SALISBURY: Monday, February 12. Perceived myself perfectly recovered, and was much refreshed by the coming of many dear friends, with whom after I had breakfasted and prayed, I took a most affectionate leave. Called at Dummer, sang a hymn, prayed, and gave a word of exhortation to certain disciples who were there, and reached Salisbury with my companion in travel, Mr. Seward, about six in the evening. Here I wrote several letters to my London and Basingstoke friends, and sent for Mr. Chubb, in order to have a conference with him concerning his late book, but he happened not to be at home. Oh that that unhappy man were turned from his erroneous principles! For I fear, like Simon Magus, he has bewitched many about Salisbury with his false doctrines. Lord, suffer not Thy people to believe a lie, though they have held the truth in unrighteousness. Raise up some true pastors amongst them, who may acquaint them with the nature and necessity of the new birth, and point out to them the blessed Spirit, whereby they may have that repentance wrought in their souls, which the self-righteous Mr. Chubb falsely asserts may be wrought in them by a moral persuasion.

STAPLEASHWIN, WILTS: Tuesday, February 13. Thought when I rose, to abide at Salisbury a few days, but finding it quite inconsistent with my other business, I left that place (after public worship, and paying a visit to an old disciple, my brother Wesley's mother), and reached Stapleashwin about six at night. After having refreshed ourselves, we intended to set forward towards Bath, but finding the people, at whose house we put up, were worthy, we altered our resolution. Our hostess having called in many of her neighbors, I prayed, conversed, and sang psalms with them for a considerable time; wrote some letters, and went to bed, not doubting but the Lord would cause me to dwell in safety. Who knows but some good may have been done here this night? I am to follow my Lord, Who, wheresoever He came, talked of the one thing needful.

BATH AND BRISTOL: Wednesday, February 14. After family prayer, and giving a word of exhortation, I set out for Bath, and was greatly comforted there with some Christian brethren. I then waited on Doctor C . . . y, desiring I might have the use of the Abbey Church to preach for the Orphan House, the Trustees having obtained leave of the Bishop before I went to Georgia. But he was pleased to give me an absolute refusal to preach either on that, or any other occasion, without a positive order from the King or Bishop. I asked him his reasons. He said, he was not obliged to give me any. Upon which, I took my leave, and retired with my friends, and prayed for him most fervently.

After dinner, other circumstances concurring, we thought God called us to Bristol. With cheerfulness of heart, we reached that place about seven in the evening. But who can express the joy with which I was received? To add to my comfort, many letters came to my hands from London friends, which rejoiced me exceedingly; and what was the chiefest pleasure, somebody or other thought me considerable enough to write a letter in the *Weekly Miscellany* against me, and with several untruths, about my preaching at St. Margaret's, Westminster. Thou shalt answer for me, my Lord and my God. A little while and we shall appear at the judgment seat of Christ. Then shall my innocence be made clear as the light, and my dealings as the noonday.

BRISTOL: Thursday, February 15. Sat up till past one in the morning answering my friends' letters, having no time otherwise. Received a letter from a dear Christian brother, wherein were these words, "I was told that Mr. B . . . n said to Mr. C . . . h, 'I believe the Devil in hell is in you all. Whitefield has set the town on fire, and now he is gone to kindle a flame in the country.' Shocking language for one who calls himself a minister of the gospel. But, my dear friend, I trust this will not move you, unless it is to pity him, and pray the more earnestly that he may experience the power of those truths he is now opposing, and have the same fire kindled in his breast, against which he is so much enraged. For I trust I am persuaded, it is not a fire of the Devil's kindling, but a holy fire that has proceeded from the Holy and Blessed Spirit. Oh, that such a fire may not only be kindled, but blow up into a flame all England, and all the world over!"

After having breakfasted and prayed with some religious friends, I went with Mr. Seward to public worship; from thence to the Rev. Mr. Gibbs, minister of St. Mary Redcliffe, who, I was informed, had promised to lend me his church to preach in for the Orphan House. But he, in effect, gave me a refusal, telling me, that he could not lend his church without a special order from the Chancellor. Upon this, I immediately waited upon the Chancellor, to whom I had sent the night before. But he told me frankly, that "he would not give any positive leave, neither would he prohibit any one who should lend me a church; but he would advise me to withdraw to some other place, till he had heard from the Bishop, and not preach on that or any other occasion." I asked him his reasons. He answered, "Why will you press so hard upon me? The thing has given a general dislike." I replied, "Not the design of the Orhpan House: even those who disagree with me in other particulars, approve of that. And as for the gospel, when was it preached without dislike?" Soon after this, I took my leave, and waited upon the Reverend the Dean, who received me with great civility. When I had shown him my Georgia accounts, and answered him a question or two about the colony, I asked him, "Whether there could be any just objection against my preaching in churches for the Orphan House?" After a pause for a considerable time, he answered he "could not tell." But, somebody knocking at the door, he replied, "Mr. Whitefield, I will give you an answer some other time; now I expect company." "Will you be pleased to fix any, Sir?" said I. "I will send to you," said the Dean, O Christian simplicity, where art thou fled! Why do not the clergy speak the truth — that it is not against the Orphan House, but against me and my doctrine, that their enmity is leveled.

About three in the afternoon, God having given me great favor in the jailer's eyes, I preached a sermon on the Penitent Thief to the poor prisoners in Newgate, and collected fifteen shillings for them. Many seemed much affected, and I hope the power of the Lord was present to awaken them.

At seven, I expounded for an hour with very great power to a young Society, which God has caused to be established since I was in Bristol last; and many, I heard afterwards, were pricked to the heart. Blessed be God! the good seed sown by my ministry, though but as a grain of mustard seed, is now, being watered by the dew of Heaven, beginning to grow into a great tree. Lord, this is Thy doing, and it is marvelous in our eyes.

The Lessons were very remarkable, and the people made an application for me. The First was the opposition made against Aaron's priesthood, and God's determining who was in the right, by causing his rod to blossom when the other rods produced nothing. The Second was the eleventh chapter of St. Paul's 2nd Epistle to the Corinthians, where the Apostle recounted his sufferings for Christ, against the insinuations of the false apostles. Blessed be God, in most of the things there recorded, I have, in some small degree, had fellowship with the Apostle, and before I die, I doubt not but I shall sympathize with him in most other articles. Suffering is the best preferment.

Friday, February 16. Began this morning to settle a daily exposition, and reading prayers to the prisoners in Newgate. I opened it by enlarging on the conversion of the jailer, and I trust the same good work will be experienced in this prison before I leave it.

Dined with a religious family; spent a considerable time in singing hymns, and prayer; visited and prayed with two choice servants of our Blessed Lord, and expounded from five till near nine, to two thronged Societies, one of which chiefly consisted of young men whom God seems to have called to shine as lights in the world, in a crooked and perverse generation. Oh how thankful ought I to be, for seeing these fruits of my poor labors!

Saturday, February 17. Read prayers and expounded the parable of the Prodigal Son at Newgate to a great number of people; and afterwards was much refreshed by the coming of a dear London friend, and the receipt of several letters. One thing affected me much in these letters, viz., the news of a great opposer's being given over by the physicians. Alas poor man! We all prayed most heartily for him, knowing how shortly he must give an account of what he had most unjustly said and written against me and many true servants of Jesus Christ.

About one in the afternoon, I went with my brother Seward, and another friend, to Kingswood, and was most delightfully entertained by an old disciple of the Lord. My bowels have long since yearned toward the poor colliers, who are very numerous, and as sheep having no shepherd. After dinner, therefore, I went upon a mount, and spake to as many people as came unto me. They were upwards of two hundred. Blessed be God that I have now broken the ice! I believe I never was more acceptable to my Master than when I was standing to teach those hearers in the open fields. Some may censure me; but if I thus pleased men, I should not be the servant of Christ.

About five, we returned full of joy; and I wrote to the Bishop of Bristol (as I had done before to the Bishop of Bath and Wells) for leave to preach in his lordship's churches, for the benefit of the Orphan House. May God incline him to send me an answer of peace. At seven I went to expound to a Society of young men for near two hours, and then came home with my friends, blessing and praising God.

Sunday, February 18. Arose this morning about six, being called up by near fifty young persons, whom I appointed to meet me at my sister's house, and with whom I spent above an hour in prayer, psalm-singing and a warm exhortation. Soon after this, I read prayers, and preached at St. Werburgh's to a large audience. I thought yesterday I should not have the use of any pulpit; but God, Who has the hearts of all men in His hands, disposed the Rev. Mr. Penrose to lend me his, who thanked me for my sermon; and the Rev. Mr. Gibbs sent to me and offered me the use both of St. Thomas's and St. Mary Redcliffe. The latter of these I accepted, and preached to such a congregation as my eyes never yet saw, with great liberty and demonstration of the Spirit. Many went away for want of room, and Mr. Gibbs and his lady were exceedingly civil both to me and Mr. Seward.

After sermon, and taking a little refreshment, I hastened to a Society in Baldwin Street, where many hundreds were assembled to hear me, so that the stairs and court below, besides the room itself, were crowded. Here I continued expounding for near two hours, and then expounded for as long a time at another Society in Nicholas Street, equally thronged. Surely, that same Jesus Who came to His disciples, the doors being shut, when they assembled together, was with us of a truth; for great numbers were quite melted down, and God so caused me to renew my strength, that I was better when I returned home than when I began to exhort my young fellow-soldiers at six in the morning. I could not do this, except Jesus Christ did strengthen me. By His free grace alone, I am what I am. Not unto me, but unto Thy Name, O Lord, alone be all the glory.

Monday, February 19. Read prayers and expounded as usual at Newgate, and preached in the afternoon to a great multitude at the parish church of St. Philip and Jacob, and collected 18 pounds for the Orphan House. Thousands went away, because there was no room for them within; and God enabled me to read prayers and preach with great boldness. See ye not, ye opposers, how you prevail nothing? Why do you not believe that it would not be thus, unless God was with me? Lord, open Thou their eyes, that they may see that this is Thy doing.

About six in the evening I went to a new Society greatly thronged, and was enabled, notwithstanding I had exerted myself so much at St. Philip's, to expound with great freedom of spirit for above an hour. Thence I went and expounded for near the space of two hours to another Society in Baldwin Street, and much power from above was amongst us. This done, I returned home full of joy, which was kept up by conversing, singing, and praying with many Christian brethren. We parted, rejoicing that God caused us to go on conquering and to conquer.

Amongst the letters I received from religious correspondents, one writes to me thus: "Mr. . . ., who wrote that letter in the *Miscellany*, died yesterday." He is now gone to give an account of the many hard speeches contained therein, and is convinced that orthodoxy in notions is not the whole of religion. In another part of his letter he writes thus: "We had such a remarkable and sensible presence of God with us at Beech Lane this evening, as my eyes and ears were never such witnesses of before. In the midst of Mr. John Wesley's exposition, a woman present had such convictions of her lost estate by nature, and such a sense of sin, that she could not forbear crying out aloud; upon which Mr. Wesley, breaking off, went to her, who earnestly desired him to pray for her, which he did in the presence of two or three hundred people, hardly one of whom, I think, could forbear tears; upon which she had comfort." Blessed be God, the more we are despised, the more He shows that we are teachers sent by Him: for no one could do these things, except God was with him.

Tuesday, February 20. This day my Master honored me more than ever He did yet. About ten in the morning, in compliance with a summons received from the Apparitor yesterday, I waited upon the Rev. Mr. R ... l, the Chancellor of Bristol, who now plainly told me he intended to stop my proceedings. "I have sent for the Registrar here, Sir," said he, "to take down your answer." Upon which, he asked me "by what authority I preached in the diocese of Bristol without a license?" I answered, "I thought that custom had grown obsolete." "And why, pray, Sir," replied I, "did you not ask the Irish clergyman this question, who preached for you last Thursday?" He said "that was nothing to me." He then read over part of the Ordination Office, and those Canons that forbid any minister preaching in a private house, etc., and then asked me what I said to them. I answered, that "I apprehended those Canons did not belong to professed ministers of the Church of England." "But," he said, "they do." "There is also a Canon," said I, "forbidding all clergyman to frequent taverns and play at cards. Why is not that put in execution?" "Why does not somebody complain of them?" said he, "and then it would." When I asked him why I was thus taken particular notice of (referring to my printed discourses for my principles), he said, "You preach false doctrine:" upon which I answered him not a word, but told him, notwithstanding those Canons, "I could not but speak the things that I knew, and was resolved to proceed as usual." "Observe his answer, Mr. Registrar," said he, — and turning to me, added, "I am resolved, Sir, if you preach or expound anywhere in this diocese till you have a license, I will first suspend, and then excommunicate you." I then took my leave — he waited upon me very civilly to the door, and told me, what he did was in the name of the clergy and laity of the city of Bristol; and so we parted.

Being taken ill, just before I went to the Chancellor, on my return home I found I had not so much joy as peace. But however, I did not perceive the least motion of resentment to arise in my heart; and to show how little I regarded such threatenings, after I had joined in prayer for the Chancellor, I immediately went and expounded at Newgate as usual, where God gave me great joy, and wondrously pricked many to the heart, as though He would say, "This is the way, walk in it." After this we dined with several Christian friends with the kind Keeper of the prison, and rejoiced exceedingly at the thought, that we should one day or other sing together in such a place as Paul and Silas did. God prepare us for that hour; for I believe it will come. I shall be exalted, I must be humbled.

At four there was a general expectation of my preaching at St. Nicholas. Thousands went to hear me, but the Lecturer sent word, that orders were given by Mr. B ... r, that I should not preach in his church, which rejoiced me greatly. Lord, why dost Thou thus honor me?

At five, I went and expounded on the First of St. James, to a Christian assembly, who were much affected; and afterwards I hastened to Nicholas Street, where was a great crowd waiting for me upon the stairs, yard, and entry of the house, as well as in the room itself. I expounded the Ninth of St. John, and exhorted all to imitate the poor beggar, and not to fear the face of men. God was pleased to fill me with unspeakable.joy and power. All were wondrously touched, and when, after my exposition, I prayed particularly for the Chancellor, the whole company was in tears, and said most earnest Amens to all the petitions I put up for him. It is remarkable we have not had such a continued presence of God amongst us since I was threatened to be excommunicated. But thus it was formerly, so it will be now. When we are cast out, Christ will more clearly reveal Himself to us.

Wednesday, February 21. Had several come to me this morning to inquire about the state of their souls, amongst whom was a little girl of thirteen years of age, who told me in great simplicity, "She was pricked through and through with the power of the Word." And, indeed, a good work, I believe, has been wrought in her heart. Out of the mouths of babes and sucklings hast Thou perfected praise.

Preached at Newgate with uncommon freedom and power, and observed the audience to be quite melted down. After this I made a collection for the poor prisoners, and on my return home was much comforted by another gracious soul, whom God brought unto me, and who was willing to follow me not only to Georgia, but also to prison and to death.

At three in the afternoon, according to my appointment, I went to Kingswood amongst the colliers. God highly favored us in sending a fine day, and nearly two thousand people were assembled on that occasion. I preached on John, Chapter 3, verse 3, and enlarged for near an hour — I hope to the comfort and edification of those who heard me. God grant the seed sown may not fall on stony or thorny, but on good ground.

About six in the evening I expounded to a Society without Lawford's Gate, and afterwards to another in Baldwin Street; both were exceedingly crowded and attentive. At first I could not speak so strongly, because I had exerted myself so much upon the mount; but afterwards God gave me a fresh supply of grace, and I was enabled to go through my work cheerfully. Lo, I am with you always, even unto the end of the world.

BATH: Thursday, February 22. This morning I went with some Christian friends to Bath, where I was much comforted by meeting with several who love our Lord Jesus in sincerity. More especially, I was edified by the pious conversation of the Rev. Mr. Griffith Jones, whom I have desired to see of a long season. His words came with power, and the account he gave me of the many obstructions he had met with in his ministry, convinced me that I was but a young soldier, just entering the field. Good God, prepare me manfully to fight whatsoever battles Thou hast appointed for me. I can do all things through Thee strengthening me.

BRISTOL: Friday, February 23. Returned here about ten this morning. At eleven, went as usual, and preached a written sermon at Newgate, and collected 2 pounds 5 shillings for the prisoners. Many, I believe, were much affected. "To God be all the glory!"

After dinner, I was taken very ill, so that I was obliged to lie upon the bed; but, looking upon it as a thorn in the flesh, at three I went, according to appointment, and preached to near four or five thousand people from a mount in Kingswood. The sun shone very bright, and the people standing in such an awful manner round the mount, in the profoundest silence, filled me with a holy admiration. Blessed be God for such a plentiful harvest. Lord, do Thou send forth more laborers into Thy harvest.

This done, God strengthened me to expound to a Society without Lawford's Gate, and afterwards to another in the city, and afterwards to a third. I spoke with more freedom the last time than at the first. When I am weak, then am I strong.

Saturday, February 24. About ten in the morning I waited on the Chancellor, and showed a letter I had received from the Lord Bishop of Bristol. My Master gave me great boldness of speech, and I asked the Chancellor why he did not write to the Bishop according to his promise? I think, he answered, he was to blame. I then insisted on his proving I had preached false doctrine, and reminded him of this threatening to excommunicate me in the name of the clergy and laity of the City of Bristol. But he would have me think that he had said no such thing; and confessed, at this time, that he had neither heard me preach, nor read any of my writings. I asked him his reasons for prohibiting my collecting for the Orphan House. He answered, "It would hinder the people's benefactions to the Bristol clergy." I replied, "It would by no means hinder their contributions, and the clergy ought first to subscribe themselves for example's sake." After much conversation on this subject, I, with meekness, told him, I was resolved to go on preaching, and that if collections were not made here for the poor Georgians, I would lay it entirely upon him; adding, withal, I would not be one who should hinder such a design for the universe.

After I left the Chancellor, I went and preached at Newgate; and at three in the afternoon, went to a Poor-house without Lawford's Gate, but the room and yard being full, I stood upon the steps going up to the house, and preached to them from thence. Many who were passing along the road on horseback stood still to hear me, and I hope, many were bettered by what was spoken.

This evening I declined going to any Society, that I might have a little time to write letters; amongst which I wrote the following one to the Bishop of Bristol.

"Bristol, February 24, 1739.

"My Lord, — I humbly thank your Lordship for the favor of your Lordship's letter. It gave abundant satisfaction to me, and many others, who have not failed to pray in a particular manner for your Lordship's temporal and eternal welfare. Today, I showed your Lordship's letter to the Chancellor, who (notwithstanding he promised not to prohibit my preaching for the Orphan House, if your Lordship was only neutral in the affair) has influenced most of the clergy to deny me their pulpits, either on that or any other occasion. Last week, he was pleased to charge me with false doctrine. Today, he has forgotten that he said so. He also threatened to excommunicate me for preaching in your Lordship's diocese. I offered to take a license, but was denied.

"If your Lordship should ask, What evil I have done? I answer, None, save that I visit the Religious Societies, preach to the prisoners in Newgate, and to the poor colliers in Kingswood, who, they tell me, are little better than heathens. I am charged with being a Dissenter; though many are brought to the Church by my preaching, not one taken from it. The Chancellor is pleased to tell me my conduct is contrary to the Canons; but I told him those Canons which he produced were not intended against such meetings as mine are, where his Majesty is constantly prayed for, and every one is free to see what is done.

"I am sorry to give your Lordship this trouble; but I thought it proper to mention these particulars, that I might know of your Lordship wherein my conduct is exceptionable.

"I heartily thank your Lordship for your intended benefaction. I think the design is truly good, and will meet with success, because so much opposed.

"God knows my heart, I desire only to promote His glory. If I am spoken evil of for His sake, I rejoice in it. My Master was long since spoken evil of before me. But I intrude on your Lordship's patience.

"I am with all possible thanks, my Lord, your Lordship's dutiful son and servant,

"George Whitefield."

Sunday, February 25. What mercies has my good God shown me this day! When I arose in the morning, I thought I should be able to do nothing; but the Divine strength was greatly magnified in my weakness. About six in the morning I prayed, sung with, and exhorted my young morning visitors, as I did last Lord's Day. At eight I read prayers, and preached to a very thronged congregation at Newgate, and from thence I rode to Brislington, a village about two miles from Bristol, where was such a vast congregation, that after I had read prayers in the church, I thought proper to go and preach in the churchyard, that none might be sent empty away. The people were exceedingly attentive, and God gave me utterance, and what was best of all, by the leave of the minister, who invited me thither, we had a Sacrament; and, I hope, it was a communion of saints indeed. All things, I find, happen to the furtherance of the Gospel; why then should I fear what man can do unto me?

At four I hastened to Kingswood. At a moderate computation, there were about ten thousand people to hear me. The trees and hedges were full. All was hush when I began; the sun shone bright, and God enabled me to preach for an hour with great power, and so loudly, that all, I was told, could hear me. Mr. B . . . n spoke right. The fire is kindled in the country; and, I know, all the devils in hell shall not be able to quench it.

Finding myself strengthened from above, I went and expounded at Baldwin Street Society, when above 5 pounds was collected for the Orphan House. Afterwards, I went to another, and about nine at night came home, rejoicing at the great things God had done for my soul. This day I have been exalted, I must expect now to be humbled. Anything is welcome to me that God sends.

Monday, February 26. Preached at Newgage; was refreshed by the conversation of some whom God had wrought upon by my ministry; answering my religious friends' letters, and expounded twice in the evening to two large Societies. I find myself much refreshed in spirit, and a new supply of strength given me. Thus shall it be done to the man whom God delighteth to honor. Oh, free grace in Christ Jesus!

Tuesday, February 27. Expounded at Newgate with more power than ever; had success in my collections for the Orphan House, and expounded twice, as usual, and was greatly strengthened with might in the inner man. This is to prepare me for some fresh opposition. I wonder I meet with so little; but God will lay upon me no more than I am able to bear. For ever adored be his unmerited love, through Christ.

Wednesday, February 28. Preached at Newgate, and expounded to the Societies, as usual, and intended to go and preach upon the mount in Kingswood; but was dissuaded from it, by a report that the waters were out. However, many, as I was told afterwards, came from far to hear me, so that it repented me that I went not. When people are willing to hear, it is a pity that any minister should be slow to preach.

Thursday, March 1. Amongst my other letters by this day's post, I received the following one from the Rev. Mr. John Wesley: —

"February 20, 1739.

"My dear Brother, — Our Lord's Hand is not shortened amongst us. Yesterday I preached at St. Katherine's, and at Islington, where the church was almost as hot as some of the Society rooms used to be. I think I never was so much strengthened before. The fields, after service, were white with people praising God. About three hundred were present at Mr. S . . . s; thence I went to Mr. B . . . s, then to Fetter Lane, and at nine to Mr. B . . . s, where also we only wanted room. Today, I expound in the Minories at four, at Mrs. W . . . s at six, and to a large company of poor sinners in Gravel Lane (Bishopsgate) at eight. The Society at Mr. Crouch's does not meet till eight, so that I expound before I go to him near St. James's Square, where one young woman has been lately filled with the Holy Ghost, and overflows with joy and love.

"On Wednesday at six, we have a noble company of women, not adorned with gold or costly apparel, but with a meek and quiet spirit, and good works. At the Savoy, on Thursday evening, we have usually two or three hundred, most of them at least, thoroughly awakened. Mr. A . . .s parlor is more than filled on Friday, as is Mr. P . . .'s room twice over, where, I think, I have commonly had more power given me than at any other place. A week or two ago a note was given me there, as near as I can remember in these words: 'Your prayers are desired for a sick child that is lunatic, and sore vexed day and night, that our Lord should heal him, as He did those in the days of His flesh; and that He should give his parents faith and patience till his time is come.'

"On Saturday a week a middle-aged, well-dressed woman at Beech Lane (where I expounded usually to five or six hundred before I go to Mr. E . . .s Society) was seized, as it appeared to several about her, with little less than the agonies of death. We prayed that God Who had brought her to the birth, would give her strength to bring forth, and that He would work speedily, that all might see it and fear, and put their trust in the Lord. Five days she travailed and groaned, being in bondage. On Thursday evening our Lord got Himself the victory, and from that moment, she has been full of love and joy, which she openly declared at the same on Saturday last; so that thanksgiving also were given to God by many on her account. It is to be observed, her friends have accounted her mad for these three years, and accordingly bled, blistered her, and what not. Come and let us praise the Lord, and magnify His Name together."

The following paragraph was likewise in a letter I received from my dear brother Kinchin of Oxon: —

"God has greatly blessed us at Oxford of late. We have reason to think that four within this fortnight have been born of God. The people crowd to the Societies on Sunday nights, several gownsmen among the rest. God has much assisted me. Last night we had a thronged Society, and about forty gownsmen."

Blessed be God, I hope the Kingdom of Jesus Christ will now come with power, and that a remnant of despised Methodists will still be left at Oxford, which shall take root downwards, and bear fruit upwards.

The weather being fair, after I had preached, and collected thirty-seven shillings at Newgate I went on the mount at Kingswood, where about fifteen hundred colliers and country people were gathered together, and were very attentive to hear me. I have reason to believe, by what I have heard, that my words have not altogether fallen to the ground. Some of the colliers, I find, have been much affected.

BATH: Friday, March 2. Went to Bath this morning to see the Rev. Mr. Thompson, who came from Cornwall to see me. In the afternoon, I read prayers at the hospital; the Lessons were exceedingly applicable, and gave us comfort. I spent the evening in taking sweet counsel with some pious, honorable women, Mr. Griffith Jones, and other good soldiers of Jesus Christ.

BRISTOL: Saturday, March 3. Returned before ten to Bristol, and was greatly refreshed by a packet of letters from London. Expounded at

Newgate, and preached in the afternoon on the steps before the Poor-house without Lawford's Gate, and perceived my audience much increased since last Saturday. Many went affected away.

Sunday, March 4. Rose much refreshed in spirit, and gave my early attendants a warm exhortation as usual. Went to Newgate, and preached with power to an exceedingly thronged congregation. Then hastened to Hannam Mount, three miles from the city, where the colliers live altogether. God favored us in the weather. Above four thousand were ready to hear me, and God enabled me to preach with the demonstration of the Spirit. The ground not being high enough, I stood upon a table, and the sight of the people covering the green fields, and their deep attention, pleased me much. I hope that same Lord, Who fed so many thousands with bodily bread, will feed all their souls with that Bread Which cometh down from Heaven: for many came from far.

At four in the afternoon, I went to the mount on Rose Green, and preached to above fourteen thousand souls, and so good was my God, that all could hear. I think it was worth while to come many miles to see such a sight. I spoke, with great freedom, but thought all the while, as I do continually, when I ascent the mount, that hereafter I shall suffer as well as speak for my Master's sake. Lord, strengthen me against that hour. Lord, I believe (O help my unbelief!) that Thy grace will be more than sufficient for me.

In the evening I expounded at Balwin Street Society, but could not get up to the room without the utmost difficulty, the entry and court were so much thronged. Blessed be God! the number of hearers much increases, and as my day is, so is my strength. Tonight I returned home much more refreshed in my spirits than in the morning when I went out. I was full of joy, and longed to be dissolved, and to be with Jesus Christ. This has been a sabbath indeed to my soul!

Monday, March 5. Had the pleasure of having many whom God has touched by my ministry, come to me, inquiring about the new birth. At eleven, I preached at Newgate and collected thirty-nine shillings for the poor prisoners; and, being invited by many colliers, at three in the afternoon I went to a place called the Fishponds, on another side of Kingswood, where about two thousand were gathered together. The sight pleased me much, and having no better place to stand upon, the wall was my pulpit; and, I think, I never spoke with greater power. My preaching in the fields may displease some timorous, bigoted men, but I am thoroughly persuaded it pleases God, and why should I fear anything else?

At my return home, I was much refreshed with the sight of two pious friends. After some conversation, they went with me to a Society, where I prayed and expounded for above an hour, and then spent the remainder of the evening with them and many other Christian brethren, in warming one another's hearts by mutual exhortation, and singing of psalms.

NEW PASSAGE: Tuesday, March 6. Having left my dear brother Hutchins, whom I sent to for the purpose of supplying my place during my absence, after many kind salutations, psalms, and prayers on both sides, Mr. Seward, myself, and another brother, took leave of our Bristol friends, and got to New Passage in a short time. Here we stayed and refreshed ourselves and endeavored to go off in the boat about noon; but the wind not permitting us, we took this opportunity of writing to many of our Christian friends, and exhorting them to lay hold of Jesus Christ by faith.

At the inn where we put up there was an unhappy clergyman, who would not go over in the passage boat because I went in it. Alas! thought I, this very temper would make Heaven itself unpleasant to that man, if he saw me there. I was likewise told, that in the public kitchen, he charged me with being a Dissenter. A little after, as I passed by, I saw him shaking his elbows over a gaming table. I heartily wish those who charge me causelessly with schism, and being righteous overmuch, would consider that the Canon of our Church forbids our clergy to frequent taverns, to play at cards or dice, or any other unlawful games. Their indulging themselves in these things is a stumbling-block to thousands.

After supper, in the evening, I called the family of the inn together, and was pleased to see near twenty come to hear the Word. God enabled me to speak and pray, and having dispersed some extracts from our Church Homilies among them, I and my friends went early to bed, being apprised that we were to be called up betimes. Blessed be God, for any opportunity of doing good.

CARDIFF: Wednesday, March 7. Arose before twelve at night, sang psalms, and prayed, and the wind being fair, we had a speedy passage over to the Welsh shore. Our business requiring haste, God having, of His good Providence, sent one to guide us, we rode all night, stopped at Newport to refresh us, where we met with two friends, and reached Cardiff about eleven in the morning.

The town, I soon found, was apprehensive of my coming, and therefore, whilst I was giving a word of exhortation to some poor people at the inn, Mr. Seward went to ask for the pulpit; being denied, we pitched on the Town Hall, which Mr. Seward got by his interest, and at four in the afternoon, I preached from the Judge's seat to about a hundred hearers. Most were very attentive; but some mocked. However, I offered Jesus Christ freely even to them, and should have rejoiced if they would have accepted Him; but their foolish hearts were hardened. Lord, make them monuments of Thy free grace!

After I came from the seat, I was much refreshed with the sight of my dear brother Howell Harris, whom, though I knew not in person, I have long since loved in the bowels of Jesus Christ, and have often felt my soul drawn out in prayer in his behalf. A burning and shining light has he been in those parts, a barrier against profaneness and immorality, and an indefatigable promoter of the true Gospel of Jesus Christ. About three or four years God has inclined him to go about doing good. He is now about twenty-five years of age. Twice he has applied (being every way qualified) for Holy Orders, but was refused, under a false pretence that he was not of age, though he was then twenty-two years and six months. About a month ago he offered himself again, but was put off. Upon this, he was, and is still resolved to go on in his work; and indefatigable zeal has he shown in his Master's service. For these three years (as he told me from his own mouth) he has discoursed almost twice every day for three or four hours together, not authoritatively, as a minister, but as a private person, exhorting his Christian brethren. He has been, I think, in seven counties, and has made it his business to go to wakes, etc., to turn people from such lying vanities. Many alehouse people, fiddlers, harpers, etc., (Demetrius-like) sadly cry out against him for spoiling their business. He has been made the subject of numbers of sermons, has been threatened with public prosecutions, and had constables sent to apprehend him. But God has blessed him with inflexible courage — instantaneous strength has been communicated to him from above, and he still continued to go on from conquering to conquer. He is of a most catholic spirit, loves all who love our Lord Jesus Christ, and therefore he is styled by bigots, a Dissenter. He is contemned by all who are lovers of pleasure more than lovers of God; but God has greatly blessed his pious endeavors. Many call and own him as their spiritual father, and, I believe, would lay down their lives for his sake. He discourses generally in a field, but at other times in a house, from a wall, a table, or any thing else. He has established nearly thirty Societies in South Wales, and still his sphere of action is enlarged daily. He is full of faith, and the Holy Ghost.

When I first saw him, my heart was knit closely to him. I wanted to catch some of his fire, and gave him the right hand of fellowship with my whole heart. After I had saluted him, and given a warm exhortation to a great number of people who followed me to the inn, we spent the remainder of the evening in taking sweet counsel together, and telling one another what God had done for our souls. My heart was still drawn out towards him more and more. A divine and strong sympathy seemed to be between us, and I was resolved to promote his interest with all my might. Accordingly, we took an account of the several Societies, and agreed on such measures as seemed most conducive to promote the common interest of our Lord. Blessed be God, there seems to be a noble spirit gone out into Wales, and I believe, ere long, there will be more visible fruits of it. What inclines me strongly to think so is, that the partition wall of bigotry and party-zeal is broken down, and ministers and teachers of different communions, join with one heart and one mind to carry on the Kingdom of Jesus Christ. The Lord make all the Christian world thus minded! For till this is done, I fear, we must despair of any great reformation in the Church of God. After much comfortable and encouraging discourse with each other, we knelt down and prayed, and great enlargement of heart God was pleased to give me in that duty.

This done, we ate a little supper, and then, after singing a hymn, we went to bed, praising and blessing God, for bringing us face to face. I doubt not but Satan envied our happiness, but I hope, by the help of God, we shall make his kingdom shake. God loves to do great things by weak instruments, that the power may be of God, and not of man.

Thursday, March 8. Was much refreshed by last night's rest, and spent the beginning of the morning in prayer and private discourse with the members of the Religious Society. About ten, according to appointment, I went to the Town Hall, and preached for about an hour and a half to a large assembly of people. My dear brother, Howell Harris, sat close by me. I did not observe any scoffers within; but without some were pleased to honor me so far, as to trail a dead fox, and hunt it about the Hall — but, blessed be God! my voice prevailed. God gave me great strength, and I could have heartily wished all such scoffers had been present, that I might have offered them salvation through Jesus Christ. This being done, I went with many of my hearers, amongst whom were two worthy Dissenting ministers and my brother Howell Harris, to public worship: and in the Second Lesson were these remarkable words: "But the chief priest, and the scribes, and the chief of the people sought to destroy Him; and could not find what they might do, for all the people were very attentive to hear Him."

In the afternoon, about four of the clock, I preached again to the people without any scoffing or disturbance, and at six in the evening, I talked for above an hour and a half, and prayed with the Religious Society, whose room was quite thronged. God was with us of a truth. I think I never spoke with greater freedom and power, and never saw a congregation more melted down. The Love of Jesus Christ touched them to the quick; most of them were dissolved into tears, and seemed to have their hearts perfectly knit towards me. Afterwards they came to me weeping, bidding me farewell, and wishing I was to continue with them longer. Indeed, their love and undissembled simplicity affected me much. My bowels yearned towards them; I wrestled with God in prayer for them, and blessed His holy Name for sending me into Wales. I hope these are the first-fruits of a greater harvest, if ever it should please God to bring me back from Georgia.

NEWPORT IN WALES: Friday, March 9. Left Cardiff about six in the morning, and reached Newport about ten, where many came from Pontypool, and other parts, on purpose to hear me. The minister being asked and readily granting us the pulpit, I preached to about a thousand people, and then, with my brother Howell Harris, Seward, etc., we went rejoicing, and blessing God for opening an effectual door by the way. I think Wales is excellently well prepared for the Gospel of Christ. They have many burning and shining lights among both the Dissenting and Church ministers, amongst whom Mr. Griffith Jones shines in particular. No less than fifty Charity Schools have been erected by his means, without any settled visible fund, and fresh ones are setting up every day. People make nothing of coming twenty miles to hear a sermon, and great numbers there are who have not only been hearers, but doers also of the Word; so that there is a most comfortable prospect of the spreading of the Gospel in Wales.

BRISTOL: Saturday, March 10. Got safe to Bristol, with my dear fellow-travelers about eleven at night. Preached in the morning at Newgate, and in the afternoon on the Poor-house steps. The hearers were much affected, and melted into tears.

Sunday, March 11. Had a whole room full of people come to hear me at six in the morning, with whom I prayed and sang psalms for near an hour. Then I read prayers, and preached at Newgate. Afterwards, went to Hannam Mount, where was near a third part as many as last Sunday, and at four in the afternoon, preached, as usual, on the mount at Rose Green. The congregation was not quite so large as before, on account of the coldness of the weather; but God was pleased to withhold the rain and hail while I was speaking, and we collected 10 pounds for the Orphan House. Satan has been very quiet this week past, and God has poured much comfort into my soul, so that I must prepare for fresh trials. O my dear Redeemer, grant that I may put on the whole armour of God, that I may withstand all the fiery darts of the Devil.

BATH: Monday, March 12. Went, in company with seven more dear friends to Bath, and had the comfort of meeting with some true followers of Jesus Christ, whom I knew not before. Received news of the wonderful progress of the Gospel in Yorkshire, under the ministry of my dear brother Ingham. Had the pleasure of hearing that the Mayor and Sheriffs of Bristol had absolutely forbidden the Keeper of Newgate letting me preach there any longer, because I insisted upon the necessity of the new birth. The Keeper was much concerned, and told them I preached agreeably to Scripture; but they were offended at him. "They answered and said unto him, Thou wast altogether born in sins, and dost thou teach us?" John 9:34.

Finding many in Bath were desirous to hear me, having given a short notice, about five in the evening I preached out on the town common, to a much larger audience than could reasonably be expected. It snowed good part of the time, but the people stayed very contentedly. Indeed some said (as I heard afterwards) that I spoke blasphemy; but the people of God were much rejoiced, and some, I hope, effectually wrought upon. Praised be God for opening such an effectual door here. Many adversaries must be expected in so polite a place as Bath. But God is with me, and I fear neither men nor devils.

After sermon I returned to our inn, and spent the remainder of the evening in sweet conversation with a great number of experienced Christians. My heart was much enlarged in prayer, and I can say, the Love of God was shed abroad abundantly therein. For ever adored be the riches of His free mercy!

Tuesday, March 13. Preached again at the Fishponds, and observed all to behave exceedingly orderly. Had extraordinary power given me at the Society in Nicholas Street, and exhorted them with all possible earnestness, not to let bigotry, or party-zeal be so much as mentioned among them; for I despair of seeing Christ's Kingdom come, till we are all thus minded.

Wednesday, March 14. Being forbidden to preach in the prison, and, being resolved not to give place to my adversaries, I preached at Baptist Mills, a place very near the city, to three or four thousand people, from these words, "What think ye of Christ?" Blessed be God, all things happen for the furtherance of the Gospel. I now preach to ten times more people than I should, if I had been confined to the churches. Surely the Devil is blind, and so are his emissaries, or otherwise they would not thus confound themselves. Every day I am invited to fresh places. I will, by the Divine assistance, go to as many as I can; the rest I must leave unvisited, till it shall please God to bring me back from Georgia.

Thursday, March 15. It snowing all day, I could not go to Sison to preach, as I proposed, but spent the day in religious discourse, writing letters, and expounding, in which God was pleased to give me unspeakable comfort. Received a strong invitation to come to Cardiff once more, and to preach at Llandaff; but business will not permit. Blessed be God, that people are ready to hear His Word! Surely the Lord will fulfill the desires of them that fear Him.

Friday, March 16. Being much entreated by the people, and horses being sent for me, I went and preached at Elberton, a village about nine miles off Bristol. The clergyman denied me the pulpit, so I preached on a little ascent on which the Maypole was fixed. The weather being cold, and the adjacent villages having but little notice, I had not above two hundred hearers. But after dinner, I hastened to Thornbury, where I was invited also, and preached to a great part of my morning congregation, and many hundreds besides. Mr. Willis, the incumbent, lent me the church, and used me with great civility, as did two other clergymen who were there present. The people were very desirous to have me stay; but I had promised to lie at Winterbourne, at a Quaker's house, where three more Friends met us, and with whom we had agreeable conversation. But I cannot say their arguments for omitting the outward call to the ministry were at all convincing; however, they wished me good luck in the Name of the Lord, and we parted from each other lovingly. God grant I may be always of a catholic spirit.

BRISTOL: Saturday, March 17. Returned to Bristol about eight in the morning, and had the pleasure of hearing that Mr. Mayor, etc., had engaged a clergyman to preach to the poor prisoners at Newgage, rather than agree to a petition they had presented to have me. "Some preach Christ out of contention, supposing to add afflictions to my bonds, and others of good will: however, Christ is preached, and I therein rejoice, yea, and will rejoice."

Had the honor of seeing another letter, intended against me, put in print; and God rewarded me for it, by giving me such extraordinary power at the Poor-house this afternoon, that great numbers were quite melted, and dissolved into tears. The enemies of God's Church undesignedly do God's work. I never am so much assisted, as when persons endeavor to blacken me, and I find the number of my hearers so increase by opposition, as well as my own inward peace, and love, and joy, that I only fear a calm. But the enmity that is in the heart of all natural men against God, will not suffer them to be quiet long. I only say, I would send my adversaries to school to Gamaliel. "If this work be not of God," says he, "it will come to nought; but if it be, ye cannot overthrow it, lest haply ye be found to fight against God."

Sunday, March 18. Had the pleasure of seeing my morning audience so much increased, that above a hundred were obliged to stand without in the street. Was taken ill for about two hours, but, notwithstanding, was enabled to go and preach at Hannam to many more than were there last Sunday; and in the afternoon, I really believe no less than twenty thousand were present at Rose Green. Blessed are the eyes which see the things which we see. Surely God is with us of a truth. To behold such crowds stand about us in such an awful silence, and to hear the echo of their singing run from one end of them to the other, is very solemn and surprising. My discourse continued for near an hour and a half, and at both places, above 14 pounds were collected for the Orphan House; and it pleased me to see with what cheerfulness the colliers and poor people threw in their mites. Contrary to my expectation, having a cold upon me, God enabled me afterwards to expound for above an hour to a crowded Society with great freedom and plainness of speech. I came home full of peace and joy in the Holy Ghost. What a mystery is the Divine life! Oh that all were partakers of it!

BATH: Monday, March 19. After having refreshed myself and friends by reading a packet of letters from London, and dispatched some other business, according to appointment, I set out for Bath, and got there about three in the afternoon. Dinner being ended, through great weakness of body, and sickness in my stomach, I was obliged to lie down upon the bed; but the hour being come for my preaching, I went, weak and languid as I was, depending on the Divine Strength, and, I think, scarce ever preached with greater power. There were about four or five thousand of high and low, rich and poor, to hear. As I went along, I observed many scoffers, and when I got upon the table to preach, many laughed; but before I had finished my prayer, all was hushed and silent, and ere I had concluded my discourse, God, by His Word, seemed to impress a great awe upon their minds; for all were deeply attentive, and seemed much affected with what had been spoken. Men may scoff for a little while, but there is something in this foolishness of preaching which will make the most stubborn heart to bend or break. "Is not My Word like fire," saith the Lord, "and like a hammer that breaketh the rock in pieces?"

Tuesday, March 20. Had the pleasure of hearing of the success of my discourse yesterday upon many souls, especially upon two little children, who were observed to come home crying, and to retire to prayers. Spent the morning in writing letters, and visiting some few righteous souls who live in this Sodom. God has a remnant everywhere. At eleven o'clock I read prayers at the hospital, and was greatly comforted by the Second Lesson, which was the 7th of St. John. After dinner I was taken ill again, but, notwithstanding, God strengthened me to preach to about as great a congregation as yesterday, and, I believe, with great success, for some wept, and all seemed much affected, and were very silent. The remainder of the evening I spent with many gracious souls, who came to my lodgings, with whom I took sweet counsel, and went to bed full of comfort and unspeakable joy. Blessed be God! I can say, "The life which I now live in the flesh, I live by the faith of the Son of God, Who loved me, and gave

Himself for me."

Wednesday, March 24. Breakfasted this morning with one Mr. M . . . r, who kindly invited me and my friends. Afterwards, went to a private house, where many were assembled to hear the Word. But God only can tell how their hearts were melted down. Oh, how did the poor souls weep over me! How did they pray that I would come amongst them again! Surely I might have said with St. Paul on another occasion, "What mean you to weep, and to break my heart?" But I could do no more than pray that God would send them some faithful laborers. Having dispersed among them some of my sermons *On the Marks of the New Birth*, I at length took my leave, and retired to my lodgings. Every time I look upon the Bath, I think on the Pool of Bethesda. O blessed Jesus, look down with compassion upon it, and as Thou hast cured many impotent persons by these healing waters, heal, I beseech Thee, the diseases of their sin-sick souls by the power of Thy all-quickening, strengthening grace. Even so, Lord Jesus. Amen.

KEYNSHAM: Dined with one Mr. M . . . , an eminent Quaker in Bath, who entertained me and my friends in a most Christian manner. About three, we left Bath, and though it was a wet day, were agreeably surprised by meeting great numbers of horsemen, etc. from Bristol, besides several thousands from the neighboring villages, who came to hear me, according to appointment. The church being refused, I preached on a mount. Our Master being with us, I preached with power. We came on our way rejoicing, and reached Bristol about seven at night, and went immediately and expounded the 7th of St. John to Baldwin Street Society, where we also gave thanks for the great things we had seen and heard since we met together last.

Thursday, March 22. Received unspeakable pleasure from a letter of this day's post, which brought me word of the flourishing of the Gospel at Oxford. Had many come to consult me in spiritual cases, and could not but rejoice to see how secretly and irresistibly the Kingdom of Jesus Christ is carried on, in spite of all opposition. In the afternoon, I preached again at Baptist Mills, where somebody was so kind as to put some turf together for me to stand upon. I had a great freedom of speech, and insisted much on original sin, because there are many in this city who, I fear, have imbibed the principles of that polite preacher, Mr. F . . . . But woe be to them who deny that they are born in sin. Woe be to them who deny the Lord Who bought them: for it saps the very foundation of the Christian Religion. And as for my own part, did I not firmly believe that Jesus Christ was truly and properly God, I never would preach the Gospel again. Had great power among us at the Society in the evening. The people throng more and more — a good sign that all do not come out of curiosity, but with a desire to know and do their duty.

Friday, March 23. Dined with many Quakers at Frenchay, who entertained me and my friends with much Christian love; but we could by no means agree about the disuse of the two outward signs in the Sacrament, nor of their absolute refusing to pay tithes. But I think their notions about walking and being led by the Spirit are right and good. I should rejoice to find all Quakers thus minded. Much sincerity and simplicity seems to be among them, but I think at the same time, they insist so much upon the inward life, that they place too much religion in their not using externals.

After dinner, I went and preached at Fishponds, as usual, where were many coaches, and about as great a number of people as before. Many, I believe, were affected. After I came home, I visited two Societies, where God was pleased to give us great tokins of His presence, and the way up to the last room was so exceedingly thronged that I was obliged to go up by a ladder through the window.

Saturday, March 24. Received glad tidings of great joy from my religious correspondents. Spent the morning in answering their kind letters, and preached in the afternoon at the Poor-house, where both the number of the people and my strength were greatly increased. After sermon, I collected for the Orphan House, and the poor people so loaded my hat with their mites, that I wanted somebody to hold up my hands. The cheerfulness with which they gave is inexpressible, and the many prayers they joined with their alms, I hope, will lay a good foundation for the house intended to be built. After this, God brought me to some more of His own dear children, and I spent the remainder of the evening in expounding to a Society, where almost all were drowned in tears, when I mentioned my departure to them. The good Lord send somebody among them to water what His own right hand hath planted.

Sunday, March 25. God will work, and who shall hinder? I am shut out of the prison, and my sister's room was not large enough to contain a fourth part of the people who come to me on a Sunday morning. But God put it into the hearts of some gentlemen to lend me a large bowling-green, where I preached to about five thousand people, and made a collection for my poor orphans, till my hands were quite weary. Blessed be God, that the bowling-green is turned into a preaching place! This, I hope, is a token that assembly rooms and playhouses will soon be put to the same use. O may the Word of God be mighty to the pulling down of these strongholds of the Devil!

Preached at Hannam to a larger congregation than ever, and again in the afternoon to upwards (as was computed) of 23,000 people. I was afterwards told, that those who stood farthest off could hear me very plainly. Oh may God speak to them by His Spirit, at the same time that He enables me to lift up my voice like a trumpet!

About eight I went to the Society in Nicholas Street, and with great difficulty at last got up into the room, which was extremely hot. At the close of my exhortation, I recommended a charity-school, which was opened by this Society today. I collected at the door myself, and few passed by without throwing in their mites. Yet a little while, and I hope Bristol will be as famous for charity-schools as London. We must not despise the day of small things. The Lord make me humbly thankful.

Monday, March 26. Still God has pleased to give me fresh tokens of His love. Letters are sent me, and people come to me continually, telling me what God hath done for their souls by my unworthy ministry. At four in the afternoon, I preached again at the bowling-green, to, I believe, seven or eight thousand people. The sun shone bright, and the windows and balconies of the adjoining houses were filled with hearers. I was uncommonly enlarged in prayer, and carried out beyond myself in preaching, especially when I came to talk of the Love and Free Grace of Jesus Christ. The concern the people were in is inexpressible; and I am sure that thousands come not out of curiosity, but a sincere desire of being fed with the milk of the Word. Afterwards, I again collected for the Orphan House, and it was near an hour and a half before the people could go out. Many were very faint because of the throng, which was so great that they trod one upon another.

At eight I hastened to Weaver's Hall, in Temple Street, which was procured me, because the Society rooms were too little. I was almost faint before I could get in through the crowd, but God enabled me to speak with freedom, and was with us of a truth. I believe there might be a thousand hearers. Well may the Devil and his servants rage horribly; their kingdom is in danger.

After I had done, I went to a Christian house, where many waited for me. At my return home, my Master paid me my wages: for my soul was filled with an intenseness of love, and I knew what it is not only to have righteousness and peace, but joy in the Holy Ghost. This is my continual food.

Tuesday, March 27. At four this afternoon, being invited several times, I preached in a yard belonging to the Glass Houses, where many dwell, who I was informed neither feared God, nor regarded man. The congregation consisted of thousands, and God enabled me to lay before them His threatenings and promises, so that none might either despair or presume. Oh that I may be taught of God rightly to divide the Word of truth!

While I was preaching, I heard many people behind me, holloing, and making a noise, and supposed they were set on by somebody on purpose to disturb me. I was not in the least moved, but rather increased the more in strength; but when I had done, and inquired the cause of that noise, I was informed that a gentlemen (being drunk) had taken the liberty to call me *dog*, and say, "That I ought to be whipped at the cart's tail," and had offered money to any who would pelt me. Instead of that, the boys and people near began to cast stones and dirt at him. I knew nothing of it till afterwards, when I expressed my dislike of their behavior, but could not help observing what sorry wages the Devil gives his servants.

In the evening I expounded again in Weaver's Hall, to a most crowded and attentive assembly. People follow more and more; there is a Divine attraction in the Word of God. Still draw us, O Lord, and we shall still come after Thee.

Wednesday, March 28. Had the pleasure of hearing that above a hundred people set apart a day for prayer in behalf of me and my dear brother Howell Harris, etc. While our friends thus continue to hold up their hands, our spiritual Amalek will never prevail against us.

Preached in the afternoon at Publow, a village about five miles from Bristol, to several thousands of people. The church was offered, but not being sufficient to contain a third part of the audience, by the advise of friends I preached in the fields, which put me in mind of our Lord's saying, "Go out into the highways and hedges, and compel them to come in."

Found out some more of God's secret ones; received some temporal mercies; expounded to the Society in Baldwin Street and went to a Friend's house, where we ate our bread with gladness and singleness of heart. Oh the comforts of a spiritual life!

Thursday, March 29. Blessed be God, I hope a good work is begun today. Having had several notices that the colliers of Kingswood were willing to subscribe, I went to dinner with them near a place called Two Mile Hill, and collected above twenty pounds in money, and got above forty pounds in subscriptions towards building them a charity school. It was surprising to see with what cheerfulness they parted with their money on this occasion. Were I to continue here, I would endeavor to settle schools all over the wood, as also in other places, as Mr. Griffith Jones has done in Wales; but I have only just time to set it on foot. I hope God will bless the ministry of my honored friend Mr. John Wesley, and enable him to bring it to good effect. It is a pity that so many little ones, as there are in Kingswood, should perish for lack of knowledge.

After dinner I preached a farewell sermon, and recommended the charity school to their consideration; and they all seemed willing to assist, either by their money or their labor, and to offer such things as they had. I doubt not but the Lord will prosper this work of my hands.

As soon as I came to town, I took my leave of a Society in Castle Street, but tongue cannot express the sorrow they were in at the mention of my departure. After this, I did the same at a Society in Nicholas Street, and, I believe, for near an hour, they wept aloud and sorely all over the room. Oh, how close are their hearts knit to me! Blessed be God, there is One coming after me, who, I hope, will cherish the spark of Divine love now kindled in their hearts, till it grows into a flame. Amen, Lord Jesus.

Friday, March 30. Preached this afternoon near Coal-Pit Heath, seven miles from Bristol, a place to which I was earnestly invited, and where great numbers of colliers live. I believe there were above two thousand people assembled on this occasion. The weather was exceedingly fair, the hearers behaved very well, and the place where I preached being near the maypole, I took occasion to warn them of misspending their time in revelling and dancing. Oh, that all such entertainments were put a stop to. I see no other way to effect it, but by going boldly, and calling people from such lying vanities in the Name of Jesus Christ. That reformation which is brought about by a coercive power, will be only outward and superficial; but that which is done by the force of God's Word, will be inward and lasting. Lord, make me fit by Thy grace for such a work, and then send me.

About seven, I returned to Bristol, and took leave of the Society without Lawford's Gate, but there were so many people, that I was obliged to stand and expound at the window, that those in the yard (which was full) might hear also. Their hearts were ready to burst with grief, but I hope my dear Master will come and comfort them.

Saturday, March 31. Went this morning and visited the poor man who was misused at the Glass House. He seemed much concerned for what he had done, and confessed he knew not what he did; upon which, I took occasion to dissuade him from the sin of drunkenness, and parted from him very friendly.

At eleven, I went and gave the prisoners a farewell exhortation, and left orders concerning the distribution of the money that had been collected for them. At four, I preached as usual, at the Poor-house, where was a greater congregation than ever, and where very near 9 pounds was gathered for the Orphan House. The longer I stay, the more my hearers increase. At my return home, I was much refreshed with the sight of my honored friend, Mr. John Wesley, whom God's Providence has sent to Bristol.

Sunday, April 1. Preached at the Bowling Green, Hannam, and Rose Green; at all of which places, the congregations were much enlarged, especially at the latter. There were twenty-four coaches, and an exceedingly great number of other people, both on foot and horseback. The wind was not so well set to carry the voice as usual; but however, I was strengthened to cry aloud, and take my last farewell. As I was returning home, it comforted me exceedingly, to hear almost every one blessing me, and wishing me a good voyage in the Name of the Lord, and indeed, my heart is so knit to Bristol people, that I could not with so much submission leave them, did I not know dear Mr. Wesley was left behind to teach them the way of God more perfectly. Prosper, O Lord, the works of his hands upon him.

At seven, I went and took my leave of Baldwin Street Society, but the yard, and entry leading to it was so exceedingly crowded, that I was obliged to climb up a ladder, and go over the tiling of another house adjoining before I could get to the door.

Monday, April 2. Spent a good part of the morning in talking with those who came to take their leave; and tongue cannot express what a sorrowful parting we had. Floods of tears flowed plentifully, and my heart was so melted, that I prayed for them with strong cryings — and many tears. The scene was very affecting. About one, I was obliged to force myself away. Crowds were waiting at the door to give me a last farewell, and near twenty friends accompanied me on horseback. Blessed be God for the marvelous great kindness He hath shown me in this city! Many sinners, I believe, have been effectually converted; numbers have come to me under convictions; and all the children of God have been exceedingly comforted. Various presents were sent me as tokens of their love. Several thousands of little books have been dispersed among the people, about 200 pounds collected for the Orphan House; and many poor families relieved by the bounty of my friend Mr. Seward. What gives me the greater comfort is the consideration that my dear and honored friend, Mr. Wesley, is left behind to confirm those who are awakened, so that, when I return from Georgia, I hope to see many bold soldiers of Jesus Christ.

KINGSWOOD: Having taken my leave, and passed through the people of Bristol, who poured out many blessings upon me, I came about two to

Kingswood, where the colliers, unknown to me, had prepared a hospitable entertainment, and were very forward for me to lay the first stone of their school. At length, I complied, and a man giving me a piece of ground, (in case Mr. C... should refuse to grant them any), I laid a stone, and then kneeled down and prayed God that the gates of hell might not prevail against our design. The colliers said a hearty Amen, and after I had given them a word of exhortation, I took my leave, promising that I would come among them again, if ever God should bring me back to England. I hope a reformation will be carried on amongst them. For my own part, I had rather preach the Gospel to the unprejudiced, ignorant colliers, than to the bigoted, self-righteous, formal Christians. The colliers will enter into the Kingdom of God before them.

THORNBURY: About five, I and my friends got safe to Thornbury, where I had appointed to preach on this day, when I was there last. The minister, I find, was offended at my doctrine, and therefore would not lend me the pulput again. However, there being above a thousand people waiting to hear the Word, I stood upon a table, and taught in the street. All was solemn and awful around us; every one behaved with gravity, and God gave me freedom of speech. The remainder of the evening was spent delightfully in singing psalms and hymns with my dear companions; and had not the parting with my Bristol friends cast a little damp upon my heart, no one could have laid down his head to sleep with greater pleasure than I did. I find I never undertake a new thing for my Master, but He gives me new manifestations of joy and comfort. Who would but work for Jesus Christ?

OLD PASSAGE, CHEPSTOW: Tuesday, April 3. Came to the Old Passage by nine in the morning, and, according to appointment, preached from some steps to many people who came to hear me. Then I exhorted, and sang with as many as the room above, in the inn would contain; and providentially lost our passage. About three in the afternoon I preached a second time from the steps, at which many were much affected. The remainder of the day I spent in writing and praying with my friends, and having taken a last farewell, we passed over to Beechly about seven, and got so far as Chepstow, where the people, I find, expected to hear me; but it being late, I could only sing, and pray, and preach to about forty who came to the inn, and gave a promise, if possible, that I would come and preach in their church before I left Wales. Every day do I see the benefit more and more of this public way of acting.

USK AND PONTYPOOL: Wednesday, April 4. Came hither before ten, and was much refreshed with the sight of my dear brother Howell Harris, and several Christian friends, who came from Cardiff and other places, to give me the meeting. The pulpit being denied, I preached upon a table under a large tree to some hundreds, and God was with us of a truth. After dinner, with near forty on horseback, I set out for Pontypool, five Welsh miles from Usk, and in the way was informed, by a man who heard it, that Mr. C...H...ry did me the honor, at the last Monmouth Assizes, to make a public motion to Judge P . . . d, to stop me and brother Howell Harris from going about teaching the people. Poor man! he put me in mind of Tertullus in the Acts; but the hour is not yet come; I have scarce begun my testimony; for my finishing it, my enemies may have power over me from above. Lord, prepare me for that hour. About five we got to Pontypool, and several thousands were ready to hear me. The curate being very solicitous for it, I preached first, (he having read prayers) in the church; but there being great numbers that could not come in, I went afterwards and preached to all the people in the field. My own heart was much enlarged, and the Divine presence was much among us; and indeed, I always find I have most power when I speak in the open air. A proof this to me, that God is pleased with this way of preaching. After sermon, we went and joined in prayer at the gentlewoman's house who owned the field, and then we returned to the house of Mr. G . . . s of Pontypool, where, after taking a little supper, and expounding the third chapter of Genesis to two rooms full of people, I prayed, and betook myself to rest. God be praised for my coming here. Here are many gracious souls, and their hearts are knit to me in Christian love.

ABERGAVENNY AND COMIHOY: Thursday, April 5. Spent some time very comfortably with my dear friends at Pontypool, in singing, praying, and religious conferences, and then in company with about thirty on horseback, I came to Abergavenny, ten miles from Pontypool, by eleven in the morning. All the way as we journeyed, God strengthened me mightily in the inner man, and I could think of nothing so much as Joshua going from city to city, and subduing the devoted nations. Here I expected much opposition, having been informed that many intended to disturb me.

But God impressed a Divine awe upon all, so that though there were many opposers present when I preached, yet not any dared to utter a word. God caused me to speak with extraordinary authority, and I did not spare the polite scoffers in the least. Oh that they may come to the knowledge of the truth, and be saved. The place I preached from was the backside of a garden, belonging to one Mr. W . . . s, who invited me to Abergavenny, and erected a place very commodious for my standing upon, so that the people (in number about two thousand), could all hear very well. Afterwards we retired, and sang a hymn; and some ladies having the curiosity to come and hear us, I took that opportunity of dissuading them against balls and assemblies, and all other polite entertainments. I hope God intended them good: for afterwards I heard they were the chief mistresses of the assembly in Abergavenny. Oh the polite world! How are they led away by lying vanities!

After dinner, I went according to appointment with about forty on horseback, to Comihoy, five miles from Abergavenny, and found the minister of the church to be a hearty friend, and two or three others like-minded with him. This rejoiced me exceedingly; and to see how loving the poor people were to me, much increased my joy. The church not being quite large enough to hold half the congregation, I preached from the cross in the churchyard. The Word came with power. Did not God call me elsewhere, I could spend some months in Wales very profitably. The longer I am in it, the more I like it. To me they seem a people sweetly disposed to receive the Gospel. They are simple and artless. They have left bigotry more than the generality of our Englishmen, and, through the exhortations of Howell Harris, and the ministry of others, they are hungering and thirsting after the righteousness of Jesus Christ. When I had done, I hastened back with my friends to Abergavenny, where we were kindly entertained, and, after having written a letter or two, and expounded to three rooms full of people, I went to bed, rejoicing that my eyes every day saw the salvation of God.

CAERLEON AND TRELECK: Friday, April 6. Set out about eight in the morning from Abergavenny, with near a dozen friends on horseback, and soon after, near fifty or sixty more joined us, most of whom, I hope, had been effectually called by the grace of God. About noon we reached Caerleon, fifteen miles from Abergavenny, a town famous for having thirty British kings buried in it, and producing three noble Christian martyrs. I chose particularly to go there, because when my brother Howell Harris was there last, some of the baser sort beat a drum, and huzzaed around him, on purpose to disturb him. But God suffered them not to move a tongue now, though I preached from the very same place, and prayed for him by name, as I have in every place where I have preached in Wales. God forbid I should be ashamed either of my Master or His servants. Many thousands were there from all parts to hear me, and God gave me such extraordinary assistance, that I was carried out beyond myself; and I believe the scoffers felt me to some purpose. Oh that the love of Christ may melt them down!

After dinner, we parted with some of our friends, who were obliged to return home, because they came from far. It gave me great pleasure to see how affectionately the poor people came, with tears in their eyes, blessing God for my speedy return among them. Surely godliness has the promise of the life that now is, as well as that which is to come. The numbers of my enemies are inconsiderable, but my friends cannot be numbered; and what gives me more satisfaction is, that they are friends of God's making, not of the world's, who follow only for interest, but such as love me for the sake of Jesus Christ, and who, I believe, would go with me to prison or to death.

At three in the afternoon we set out for Treleck, ten Welsh miles from Caerleon; but the miles being very long, we could not reach there till it was almost dark, so that most of the people who had been waiting for me, had returned home. However, the church being denied, I stood upon the horse-block before the inn, and preached from there for about three quarters of an hour to those that were left behind; but I could not speak with such power as usual, for, though the spirit was willing, the flesh was weak through the fatigue of the past day. Lord, when shall I be delivered from the burden of this flesh?

CHEPSTOW: Saturday, April 7. Found myself but weak in body when I rose in the morning, and it being a very rainy day, I resolved to stay at

Chepstow (which we reached by eleven o'clock). Great numbers that came from the country round about, were ready to hear, but the minister being unwilling to lend the pulpit on a week day, I only exhorted the people in the dining room where I lodged. Oh, how swiftly has this week passed off! To me it has been but as one day. How do I pity those polite ones who complain that time hangs heavy upon their hands. Let them but love Christ, and spend their whole time in His service, and they will find no dull melancholy hours. Want of the love of God I take to be the chief cause of indolence and vapors. Oh that our gentry would be up and doing for Jesus Christ. They would not complain then for the want of spirits.

Sunday, April 8. Arose much refreshed, and highly pleased with the last afternoon's retirement; read prayers, and preached twice at Chepstow church to very attentive congregations, many of whom came from far. After sermon I gave a word of exhortation, and prayed with several who came to the inn, and God was pleased to give it His blessing. About five, I set out with my friends to Coleford, eight miles from Chepstow, and went and visited the Religious Society, which has met with much opposition. Wherever I go, people are ready to perish for lack of knowledge, and are as ignorant of Jesus Christ as the Papists. My heart within me is broken because of the prophets. Jeremiah 23.

At night, I was pleased with the company of several friends, who came from Pontypool to see me once more. We spent the evening very agreeably in singing psalms, prayer, and conversation.

COLEFORD AND GLOUCESTER: Monday, April 9. Preached this morning in the market-house to about one hundred people, and afterwards talked with effect to some scoffers at the inn. After this, I set out for, and reached Gloucester about noon, where I was refreshed by a great packet of letters, giving me an account of the success of the Gospel in different parts. God grant I may see it come as powerfully amongst my own countrymen.

GLOUCESTER: Tuesday, April 10. Visited the Religious Society last night, preached at four in the afternoon to a great congregation at St. Michael's Church, visited a Society near the West Gate Street at seven, and another at eight; the last of which was very much crowded. Oh, what unspeakable pleasure does it give me, to see my own townsmen receive the Word with joy!

Wednesday, April 11. Was treated this day as I expected, and as I told my friends I should be used, when I first entered the city. The minister of St. Michael's was pleased to lend me his church yesterday and today; but some wealthy Demetriuses being offended at the greatness of the congregations, and alleging that it kept people from their business, he was influenced by some of them to deny the use of his pulpit any more on a week day. Alas! what an enmity there is in the natural man against the success of the Gospel! How fond are they of Pharaoh's objection, "Ye are idle, ye are idle; therefore ye say, Let us go worship the Lord."

About four I set out for Painswick, a town four miles distant from Gloucester, where the pulpit being denied, I preached to a very large congregation from the stairs belonging to the schoolhouse, in one of the streets. Many were solicitous for me to come and preach at other neighboring places also. At my return to Gloucester, my heart was much refreshed by the reception of near thirty letters from Bristol; all, I hope, from persons whose hearts God hath been pleased to touch, and powerfully convince of self-righteousness.

Thursday, April 12. Spent the morning in answering some of my dear correspondents, and preached in the evening to near three thousand hearers in a field belonging to my brother. Cry out who will against this my frowardness, I cannot see my dear countrymen and fellow Christians everywhere ready to perish through ignorance and unbelief, and not endeavor to convince them of both.

Those who forbid me to speak to these poor baptized heathens that they may be saved, upon them I call to give a reason for their so doing, a reason which may satisfy not man only, but God; I here cite them to answer it to our common Master. What their real reason is, whether envy, or "Master, in so doing Thou reproachest us," or aught else, shall one day be manifested to men and angels.

I am, and profess myself a member of the Church of England. I have received no prohibition from any of the Bishops; and having had no fault found by them with my life or doctrine, have the same general license to preach which the rectors are willing to think sufficient for their curates; nor can any of them produce one instance of their having refused the assistance of a stranger clergyman, because he had not a written license. And have their lordships, the Bishops, insisted that no person shall ever preach occasionally without such special license? Is not our producing our letters or Orders *always judged sufficient?* Have not some of us been *allowed* to preach in Georgia, and other places, by no other than our general commission? Take thou authority to, etc., nay, and therefore ordained that we might preach in Georgia? His lordship of London allowed of my preaching there, even when I had only received Deacon's Orders; and I have never been charged by his lordship with teaching or living otherwise than as a true minister of the Church of England. I keep close to her Articles and Homilies, which, if my opposers did, we should not have so many dissenters from her. But it is most notorious, that for the iniquity of the priests the land mourns. We have preached and lived many sincere persons out of our communion. I have now conversed with several of the best of all denominations; many of them solemnly protest that they went from the Church, because they could not find food for their souls. They stayed among us till they were starved out.

I know this declaration will expose me to the ill-will, not of all my brethren, but of all my idolent, earthly-minded, pleasure-taking brethren. But were I not to speak, the very stones would cry out against them. Speak, therefore, I must, and will, and will not spare. God look to the event!

Friday, April 13. Was much delighted with some more letters I received from some young soldiers of Jesus Christ. Redeemed what time I could to answer some of them; preached at noon to a much larger congregation than yesterday in the field; took a little refreshment, and went, upon invitation, to Chalford, eight miles from Gloucester, where I preached to above 3,000, all which behaved with great decency. It rejoices me much to find that my countrymen also receive the Gospel. Oh, that it may take deep root in their hearts!

Saturday, April 14. Lay at Stroud, about three miles from Chalford; preached in the fields belonging to the inn, at nine in the morning, to above 600 people; went to Stonehouse to pay my dear flock a visit there; and being intreated most earnestly, as I passed through the town yesterday, at three I preached again at Painswick, to double the number I preached to before. God was with us of a truth. As soon as I had done, I hastened to Gloucester, and preached in the Booth Hall to, I believe, near 5,000 people. Extraordinary power God was pleased to give me. God will work, and who shall hinder?

After this, I received another packet of letters from Bristol people, and was comforted by the coming of some more friends, with whom I took sweet counsel, and praised God lustily, and with a good courage. How are His mercies showered down upon me! What enlargements of heart have I experienced this night! Oh that I had a thousand tongues wherewith to praise my God! About three days ago I was much humbled, now am I exalted. Yet a little while and I shall be humbled again. Thus God acts according as He seeth best for our souls.

Sunday, April 15. Preached by eight in the morning to a larger congregation than ever in my brother's field; went to the Cathedral service at ten; and after dinner went to Stonehouse, being invited there by the minister, as well as people. It rained all the way going there, but notwithstanding that, I believe 3,000 were ready to hear me, and behaved with great decency and devotion while I was speaking to them. The church not being large enough to contain a third part of the auditory I preached from a very commodious place on the outside, and though it rained the whole time, yet I did not observe one person leave the place before I had done. Afterwards, many of the children of God came to me, rejoicing that free grace in Christ had been preached unto them, telling me, it was food to their souls, and what they had experienced for some years. The other people also behaved most affectionately, and would have constrained me to abide with them all night, but being engaged to return back to Gloucester, I hastened there through the rain, and expounded in the Booth Hall to about 5,000 people. They behaved excellently well, and hung upon me to hear the Word. All was hushed and solemn, and my delivering the Word from a place just before where the Judges sit rendered it yet more awful. Oh that I could plead the cause of my Lord and King, even Jesus Christ, with greater power!

Monday, April 16. Preached with an extraordinary presense of God among us at my brother's field about ten in the morning. Received a most comfortable packet of letters, giving me an account of the success of the Gospel; visited the prison, took a little refreshment, preached to near a thousand at Oxenhall, seven miles from Gloucester, being invited there by the Rev. Mr. Pauncefoot, a worthy minister of Jesus Christ; then returned, and preached my farewell discourse to more people than ever in the Booth Hall, and afterwards found my strength renewed, and my soul filled with Divine love and joy in the Holy Ghost. Oh what a mystery is the hidden life of a Christian!

Had many merciful deliverances in going to, and returning from Newent. Praise the Lord, O my soul, and all that is within me, praise His holy Name.

Received letters from Abergavenny, acquainting me how many had been convinced since I was there. Heard of one who had received the Holy Ghost immediately upon my preaching Christ. Received a letter from one under strong convictions; and, indeed, there is scare a day passes over my head, but God shows me that He works effectually upon the hearts of many by my ministry — a proof this, I am sure, that the Word preached is not my own, but God's. May He always own it in this manner.

Tuesday, April 17. Spent this morning in visiting a private Society, and conversing with many religious friends, who came from far to take their leave. About eleven, by the Bishop's permission, I baptized, at the Church of St. Mary de Crypt, Mr. Thomas W . . . d, a professed Quaker, about sixty years of age, who was convinced of the necessity of being born of water, as well as the Spirit. Many of Christ's faithful servants attended on the prayers around him; and, I believe, the Holy Ghost was with us of a truth. After the solemnity was over, I gave a word of exhortation from the font; and it being the place where I myself not long since had been baptized, it gave me an opportunity of reflecting on my own frequent breaches of my baptismal vow, and proving the necessity of the new birth from the Office of our Church. God, I believe gave it His blessing.

After this, we returned, and gave private thanks; and having dined, prayed with, and taken leave of my weeping friends, and dispersed a great many of my sermons among the poor, I took horse. But, oh what love did the people express for me! How many came to me weeping, and telling me what God had done for their souls by my ministry! Oh how did they pray for my return among them! Lord, I dared not expect such success among my own countrymen. When I came to the city, I found the Devil had painted me in most horrible colors; for it was currently reported — that I was really mad, that I had said I was the Holy Ghost, and that I had walked bareheaded through Bristol streets singing psalms. But God was pleased to show them that the Devil was a liar, and that the words that I had spoken were not those of a madman, but the words of soberness and truth. It often pleases me to think how God makes way for me into the hearts of His people, nay, even of His enemies wherever I go. My first asking leave for the pulpit and preaching in the fields, notwithstanding they are denied, puts me in mind of the children of Israel first intreating leave of Og, Sihon, etc., to go quietly through their land, but fighting their way through when leave was denied.

CHELTENHAM (7 MILES FROM GLOUCESTER): Being earnestly invited by several of the inhabitants, I came here, attended with about a dozen friends, by five o'clock; and the use of the pulpit being refused me, I preached on the Bowling Green belonging to the Plough Inn. When I came in, the town, I perceived, was alarmed, by the people standing at their doors. At the first, I found myself quite shut up — my heart and head were dead as a stone, but when I came to the inn, my soul began to be enlarged. I felt a freedom in my spirit, and was enabled to preach with power to near two thousand people. Many were convicted. One was drowned in tears, because she had said I was crazy; and some were so filled with the Holy Ghost that they were almost unable to support themselves under it. This, I know, is foolishness to the natural and letter-learned men, but I write this for the comfort of God's children. They know what these things mean.

Wednesday, April 18. Preached this morning with power to a much larger congregation than we had last night. Several servants of God said they never saw the like before. We shall see greater things than these; for almost every day persons of all denominations come unto me, telling how they intercede in my behalf. And it shall now be my particular business, wherever I go, to bring all the children of God, notwithstanding their differences, to rejoice together. How dare we not converse with those who have received the Holy Ghost as well as we?

EVESHAM IN WORCESTERSHIRE (TWELVE MILES FROM CHELTENHAM): Continued at Cheltenham, for the sake of a little retirement, and some private business, till after dinner, and got safe to Evesham (where Mr. Seward's relations live) about seven at night. I found there had been much talk about my coming, God wisely ordering it to engage and excite the people's attention. Several persons came to see me, among whom was Mr. Benjamin Seward, whom God has been pleased to call by His free grace very lately. His circumstances both before and in conversion, much resemble those of St. Paul. For he was bred up at the feet of Gamaliel, being at Cambridge for some years. As touching the law, so far as outward morality went, he was blameless; concerning zeal, opposing the Church. My proceedings he could by no means approve, and he had once a mind, he said, to write against Mr. Law's enthusiastic notions in his *Christian Perfection*. But lately, it has pleased God to reveal His dear Son in him, and to cast him down to the earth, as He did Saul, by eight days' sickness, in which time he scarce ever ate, or drank, or slept, and underwent great inward agonies and tortures. After this, the scales fell more and more from the eyes of his mind. God sent a poor traveling woman, that came to sell straw toys, to instruct him in the nature of the second birth, and now he is resolved to prepare for Holy Orders, and to preach Christ and those truths straightway in every synagogue, which once he endeavored to destroy. He is a gentleman of a very large fortune, which he has now devoted to God. I write this to show how far a man may go, and yet know nothing of Jesus Christ. Behold, here was one who constantly attended on the means of grace, was exact in his morals, humane and courteous in his conversation, who gave much in alms, was frequent in private duties; and yet, till about six weeks ago, as destitute of any saving experimental knowledge of Jesus Christ as those on whom His Name was never called, and who still sit in darkness and the shadow of death. Blessed be God, that although not many rich, not many mighty, not many noble are called, yet some are. Who would but be accounted a fool for Christ's sake? How often has my companion and honored friend, Mr. William Seward, been deemed a madman even by this very brother, for going to Georgia; but now God has made him an instrument of converting his brother. This more and more convinces me, that we must be despised, before we can be vessels fit for God's use. As for my own part, I find by happy experience, the more I am contemned, the more God delights to honor me in bringing home souls to Christ. And I write this for the encouragement of my fellow laborers, who have all manner of evil spoken against them falsely for Christ's sake. Let them not be afraid, but rejoice and be exceeding glad, for the Spirit of God and of glory shall rest upon their souls.

Thursday, April 19. Went to Badsey, about two miles from Evesham, where Mr. Seward's eldest brother lives. We were most kindly received, and I hope, a true Christian church will be in their house. About four in the evening, the churches at Evesham, Bengeworth, and Badsey being denied, I preached from the cross, in the middle of Evesham street, to a great congregation; and then went to Badsey, and preached in Mr. Seward's brother's yard to a great number of people, many of which came from Evesham to hear me again. God grant it may strike home to their hearts.

Friday, April 20. Preached about nine in the morning at the cross, went to public worship, and received the Sacrament. Preached at Badsey at five in the evening, and returned and expounded in the Town Hall, which, though very large, was quite thronged. The Recorder himself procured the keys for us, and great numbers of people were truly affected. The standing in the Judge's place, and speaking from there gave me awful thoughts of God, and the consideration that I was speaking in the Name of our great High Priest and Judge animated me very much. Oh, that I had a thousand tongues, they should all be employed in His service!

OXFORD: Saturday, April 24. Preached in the morning at Badsey to a weeping audience, joined in prayer, and set out for Oxford, which I reached about ten at night. I had been much pressed in spirit to hasten here, and now I found the reason for it; for alas! the enemy had got great advantage over three of our Christian brethren, and driven them to deny Christ's visible Church upon earth. They had so far influenced and deluded Mr. Kinchin, a sincere and humble minister of Jesus Christ, that I found through their persuasion he had actually quitted his fellowship, and intended to resign his living. This, I must needs confess, gave me a great shock. For I knew what dreadful consequences would attend a needless separation from the Established Church. For my own part, I can see no reason for my leaving the Church, however I am treated by the corrupt members and ministers of it. I judge of the state of a Church, not from the practice of its members, but its primitive and public constitutions; and so long as I think the Articles of the Church of England are agreeable to Scripture, I am resolved to preach them up without either bigotry or party zeal. For I love all who love the Lord Jesus.

    Sunday, April 22. Being much concerned about Mr. Kinchin's conduct, this morning I wrote him the following letter:

"Oxon, April 22, 1739.

    "Dearest Mr. Kinchin, — Just now have I received the blessed Sacrament, and have been praying for you. Let me exhort you, by the mercies of God in Christ Jesus, not to resign your parsonage till you have consulted your friends at London. It is undoubtedly true that all is not right when we are afraid to be open to our dear brethren.

    "Satan has desired to sift you as wheat. He is dealing with you as he did with me some years ago, when he kept me in my closet near six weeks, because I could not do anything with a single intention. So he would have you not preach till you have received the Holy Ghost in the full assurance of it; and that is the way never to have it at all. God will be found in the use of means; and our Lord sent out His disciples to preach *before* they had received the Holy Ghost in that most plentiful manner at the day of Pentecost.

    "Besides, consider, my dear brother, what confusion your separation from the Church will occasion. The prison doors at Oxford are already shut against us, our Society is stopped; and most are afraid almost to converse with us. I can assure you, that my being a minister of the Church of England, and preaching its Articles, is a means, under God, of drawing so many after me.

    "As for objecting about the habits, robes, etc., good God! I thought we long since knew that the Kingdom of God did not consist in any externals, but in righteousness, and peace, and joy in the Holy Ghost.

    "Oh! my dear brother, I travail in pain for you. Never was I more shocked at anything than at your proceedings. I doubt not that you will pray to God to be kept from delusion at the reading of this. I am not ignorant of Satan's devices, and I know he never more successfully tempts us, than when he turns himself into an angel of light. Oh! my dearest Mr. Kinchin, do nothing rashly. Consult your friends, and do not break the heart of your most affectionate, though unworthy brother in Christ,

"GEORGE WHITEFIELD"

    Visited two Societies, at the first of which many gownsmen did me the honor of coming to hear. Before I began, I desired them to behave like gentlemen and Christians. I also prayed particularly for them, and applied myself in meekness and love to them at the end of my discourse. I bless God, an awe was impressed upon their minds, and they behaved quietly; but afterwards followed me to my inn, and came uninvited up into my room. I took that opportunity of giving them a second exhortation; and though some no doubt mocked, yet I believe some will remember what was said. Oh how is the faithful city become a harlot! Oh that my head was water, and my eyes fountains of tears, that I might weep day and night for the members of this University! Lord, send forth Thy light and Thy truth, and make them scribes ready instructed to Thy heavenly Kingdom!

Blessed be God for sending me here! Our dear brother Kinchin, falling into such an error, has given such a shock, that, unless I had come, in all probability the brethren would have been scattered abroad like sheep having no shepherd.

Tuesday, April 24. Perceived myself much strengthened yesterday and this morning, and told my friends how these words were impressed upon me, *And more than meet the gathering storm.* About nine o'clock, after I had exhorted the brethren, the Vice-Chancellor came in person to the house where we were assembled, having threatened to do so some time ago, if they continued to build up one another in that manner. He sent for me downstairs, being informed that I was in the house. When I first saw him, I perceived he was in a passion, which he soon expressed in such language as this: "Have you, sir, a name in any book here?" "Yes, sir," said I; "but I intend to take it out soon." "Yes, and you had best take yourself out too," replied he, "or otherwise I will lay you by the heels. What do you mean by going about, alienating the people's affections from their proper pastors. Your works are full of vanity and nonsense. You pretend to inspiration. If you ever come again in this manner among these people, I will lay you first by the heels, and these shall follow." Upon this he turned his back, and went away. I desired the brethren to join in prayer for him. Took my leave, being just about to set out as the Vice-Chancellor came in. I soon found by the comforts God gave me, how glorious it was to suffer anything for the sake of Jesus Christ. However, I must not forget mentioning, that I exhorted all the brethren not to forsake the assembling themselves together, though no pastor should be permitted to come among them; for so long as they continued steadfast in the communion of the Established Church, I told them no power on earth could justify hindering them from continuing in fellowship, as the primitive Christians did, in order to build up each other in the knowledge and fear of God. Oh what advantage has Satan gained over us, by our brother Kinchin's putting off his gown! However, though he is permitted to bruise our heel, yet we shall in the end bruise his head. The gates of hell shall never prevail against the Church of Jesus Christ, either visible or invisible.

About eight at night, I and my friends reached Uxbridge, where we were greatly refreshed by the coming of several brethren, and the receipt of some letters from Savannah. Blessed be God! all is well, and I shall now think the time long till I embark for Georgia. Lord, let that people be precious in Thy sight.

LONDON: Wednesday, April 25. Reached London with my dear friends about ten in the morning, and was received most tenderly by my dear brethren. Received a letter from Gibraltar, giving an account of the success of my labors in that garrison. Expounded to a society of holy women, and afterwards spent about two hours in close conference at Fetter Lane Society. We talked with great sweetness and Christian love, and unanimously declared against the principles of our three brethren who lately made such confusion in Oxford. There must be heresies amongst you, that they which are approved may be made manifest.

Thursday, April 26. Assisted in administering the Blessed Sacrament at Islington, where the vicar, in conformity to the rubric, takes care to observe the octaves of Easter. After this, I expounded to a large roomful of people, and with such power and demonstration of the Spirit as I never saw before. Surely the hearers' hearts were quite melted down by the preaching of the free grace of God in Jesus Christ to poor sinners. Floods of loving tears flowed from their eyes. In the evening I expounded to a Society at St. Mary Hill, and then retired to bed, wishing that all felt the comforts God was then pleased to communicate to my soul. Indeed I can say, that the Lord is gracious.

Friday, April 27. Went this morning to Islington to preach, according to the appointment of my dear brother in Christ, the Rev. Mr. Stonehouse; but in the midst of the prayers, the church-warden came, demanding me to produce my license, or otherwise he forbad my preaching in that pulpit. I believe I might have insisted upon my right to preach, being in priest's orders, and having the presentation of the living at Savannah, which is in the Bishop of London's diocese, — a stronger license than that implicit one by which hundreds of the inferior clergy are by his lordship permitted to preach. However, for the sake of peace, I declined preaching in the church; but after the communion service was over, I preached in the churchyard, being assured my Master now called me out here, as well as in Bristol. The Second Lesson was Acts 24, which contained the plausible speech Tertullus made against Paul, a ringleader of the sect of the Nazarenes, which God applied closely to my heart. He was pleased so to assist me in preaching, and so wonderfully to affect the hearers, that I believe we could have gone singing of hymns to prison. Let not the adversaries say, I have thrust myself out of their synagogues. No; they have thrust me out. And since the self-righteous men of this generation count themselves unworthy, I go out into the highways and hedges, and compel harlots, publicans, and sinners to come in, that my Master's house may be filled. They who are sincere will follow after me to hear the Word of God.

Expounded at night to a very large Society in Wapping, and perceived that the London people were much improved since I left them; indeed, their hearts seem to be quite broken, and I believe they would pluck out their eyes if it were possible to serve me. Lord, sanctify my coming to them, and grant that they may receive a second benefit.

Saturday, April 28. Preached this morning again in Islington churchyard; and blessed be God, the congregation was near as large again as yesterday, and the Word was attended with extraordinary power. The Second Lesson was very applicable, being Acts 25. I can say with St. Paul, that neither against the temple, nor against Caesar have I done anything, and yet I am put out of their synagogues, and reviled as an evildoer; but the Scriptures must be fulfilled, "If they have persecuted Me, they will also persecute you."

About six I expounded to a thronged society of women at Fetter Lane, and at eight on St. Mary Hill. The portion of Scripture that

Providence directed me to, was the nineteenth of Genesis, which was very applicable to what happened, for some wicked men came, and pressed, and broke down the door; but God was pleased to give me such power at the last, that they were forced into an awful silence, and, I believe, they really felt the weight of God's Word. The fierceness of men shall turn to Thy praise, and the remainder of it shalt Thou restrain.

Sunday, April 29. Preached in the morning at Moorfields, to an exceeding great multitude. At ten, went to Christ Church, and heard Dr. Trapp preach most virulently against me and my friends, upon these words, "Be not righteous overmuch: why shouldest thou destroy thyself?" God gave me great serenity of mind; but alas! the preacher was not so calm as I wished him. His sermon was founded upon wrong suppositions (the necessary consequence of his hearing with other men's ears), not to say that there were many direct untruths in it. And he argued so strenuously against all *inward feelings*, that he plainly proved that, with all his learning, he knew nothing yet as he ought to know. I pray God rebuke his spirit, and grant that that sermon may never rise up in judgment against him.

Being weakened by my morning's preaching, in the afternoon I refreshed myself with a little sleep, and at five went and preached at Kennington Common, about two miles from London, where no less than thirty thousand people were supposed to be present. The wind being for me, carried the voice to the extremest part of the audience. All stood attentive, and joined in the Psalm and Lord's Prayer most regularly. I scarce ever preached more quietly in any church. The Word came with power. The people were much affected, and expressed their love to me many ways. All agreed it was never seen on this wise before. Oh what need have all God's people to rejoice and give thanks! I hope a good inroad has been made into the Devil's kingdom this day.

Monday, April 30. Declined preaching today, that I might have leisure to write to some of my correspondents, and make preparations for my poor orphans in Georgia. Received letters this evening from thence, telling me of the affairs of that colony. At present they have but a melancholy aspect; but our extremity is God's opportunity. Lord, Thou calledst me; lo! I come to do Thy will. Heard also that Mr. Kinchin had got over his scruples, and of the wonderful success of my honored friend Mr. John Wesley's ministry in Bristol, and of much opposition at Oxon. Certainly God is about to bring mighty things to pass.

Tuesday, May 1. Preached after public service in Islington churchyard to a greater congregation than ever. In the evening went to expound on Dowgate Hill, at the house of Mr. C . . . h; but when I came to the door, no less than two or three thousand people were gathered round it, so that to avoid a noise, I was obliged to stand up in the Fore Street window, and preach to them in the street. I think they behaved well; and they would have behaved much better, had they not been disturbed. Now know I more and more that the Lord calls me into the fields, for no house or street is able to contain half the people who come to hear the Word. This is a time for doing; yet a little while, and a suffering time will come. I cannot follow Him now, but I shall follow Him afterwards.

Wednesday, May 2. Preached this evening again to above ten thousand, at Kennington Common, and spent the remainder of the evening in conference with our brethren in Fetter Lane Society. I hope we build up one another in our most holy faith. Our brethren who have fallen into errors have left us voluntarily. Now the old leaven is purged out we walk in the comforts of the Holy Ghost, and are edified.

Thursday, May 3. Was fully employed all day in making preparations for my voyage, and preached at six in the evening (a time I choose that people may not be drawn away from their business) at Kennington, and great power was among us. The audience was more numerous and silent than yesterday, the evening calm, and many went affected away. Glory be to God, I begin to find an alteration in the people's behavior already. God grant it may increase more and more.

Saturday, May 5. Preached yesterday and today as usual at Kennington Common, to about twenty thousand hearers, who were very much affected. The remainder of my time I spent in preparing things for Georgia. I am not usually so much engaged in secular work; but I as readily do this as preach, when it is the will of God. It is a great mistake that some run into, to suppose religion consists only in saying our prayers. I think a man is no further holy, than he is relatively holy, and he only will adorn the Gospel of our Lord Jesus Christ in all things, who is careful to perform all the civil offices of life, whether servant, master, or mistress, with a single eye to God's glory, and from a principle of a lively faith in Jesus Christ our Savior. This is the morality which I preach, and which shall stand as long as the Rock on which it is founded, even forever and ever.

Sunday, May 6. Preached this morning in Moorfields to about twenty thousand people, who were very quiet and attentive, and much affected. Went to public worship morning and evening; and, at six, preached at Kennington. Such a sight I never saw before. I believe there were no less than fifty thousand people, and near fourscore coaches, besides great numbers of horses. There was an awful silence among them. God gave me great enlargement of heart. I continued my discourse for an hour and a half, and when I returned home, I was filled with such love, peace, and joy, that I cannot express it. I believe this was partly owing to some opposition I met with yesterday. It is hard for men to kick against the pricks. The more they oppose, the more shall Jesus Christ be exalted. Our adversaries seem to have come to an extremity, while for want of arguments to convince, they are obliged to call out to the civil magistrate to compel me to be silent; but I believe it will be difficult to prove our assemblies in the fields either disorderly or illegal.

Monday, May 7. Had full employment again today in preparing for my voyage. Did not preach, only expounded in a private house, where 10 pounds was collected for the orphans. Though I kept it as secret as possible, numbers of people crowded round the door, so that I find myself more and more under a necessity of going out into the fields. Received several letters of the fruits of my ministry in several places, and had divers come to me, awakened, under God, by my preaching in the fields.

Tuesday, May 8. Preached in the evening, as usual, on Kennington Common. Some considerable time before I set out from town, it rained very hard, so that once I thought of not going; but several pious friends joined in hearty prayer that God would be pleased to withhold the rain, which was done immediately. To my great surprise, when I came to the Common, I saw above twenty thousand people. All the while, except for a few moments, the sun shone out upon us; and I trust, the Sun of Righteousness arose on some with healing in His wings. The people were melted down very much at the preaching of the Word, and put up hearty prayers for my temporal and eternal welfare.

Wednesday, May 9. Waited at noon upon the Honorable Trustees for Georgia. They received me with the utmost civility, agreed to everything I asked, and gave a grant of five hundred acres of land, to me and my successors forever, for the use of the Orphan House. My friend Habersham also writes me word today from Georgia, that the General and officers are very kind to him upon my account, so that there is a comfortable prospect of all things going on as I could wish.

After God had enabled me to preach to about twenty thousand for above an hour at Kennington, He inclined the hearers' hearts to contribute most cheerfully and liberally towards the Orphan House. I was one of the collectors, and it would have delighted anyone to have seen with what eagerness and cheerfulness the people came up both sides of the eminence on which I stood, and afterwards to the coach doors, to throw in their mites. Surely God must have touched their hearts. When we came home, we found we had collected above 46 pounds, among which were 16 pounds in halfpence; for which we endeavored to give thanks. God was pleased to pour into my soul a great spirit of supplication, and a sense of His free distinguishing mercies so filled me with love, humility, and joy, and holy confusion, That I could at last only pour out my heart before Him in an awful silence. It was so full, that I could not well speak. Oh the happiness of communion with God!

Thursday, May 10. Preached at Kennington, but it rained most part of the day. There were not above ten thousand people, and thirty coaches. However, God was pleased so visibly to interpose in causing the weather to clear up, and the sun to shine out just as I began, that I could not avoid taking notice of it to the people in my discourse. Our minute philosophers, nay, and our Christians, falsely so called, laugh at the notion of a particular Providence. But to suppose a general, without holding a particular Providence, is as absurd as to imagine there can be a chain without being composed of links. Search the Scriptures, and we shall find, that not a sparrow can fall to the ground without our heavenly Father; and that even the very hairs of our head are all numbered.

Friday, May 11. Preached at Kennington to a larger audience than last night, and collected 26 pounds 15s. 6d. for the Orphan House. The people offered willingly. They could not have taken more pains, or expressed more earnestness, had they all come to receive an alms from me. Being upon the Publican and Pharisee, I was very earnest in endeavoring to convince the self-righteous Pharisees of this generation, and offering Jesus Christ freely to all, who, with the humble publican feelingly and experimentally could cry out, "God be merciful to me a sinner."

Saturday, May 12. Agreed today, for myself, and eleven more, to go on board the *Elizabeth*, Captain Allen, to Pennsylvania, where I design, God willing, to preach the Gospel in my way to Georgia, and buy provisions for the Orphan House. Many came to me this morning, acquainting me what God had done for their souls by my preaching in the fields. In the evening, I preached to about twenty thousand people at Kennington as usual, the weather continuing remarkably fair while I was delivering my Master's message. I offered Jesus Christ to all who could apply Him to their hearts by faith. Oh that all would embrace Him! The Lord make them willing in the day of His power.

Sunday, May 13. Preached this morning to a prodigious number of people in Moorfields, and collected for the orphans 52 pounds 19s. 6d. above 20 pounds of which was in halfpence. Indeed, they almost wearied me in receiving their mites, and they were more than one man could carry home. Went to public worship twice and preached in the evening to near sixty thousand people. Many went away because they could not hear; but God enabled me to speak so that the best part of them could understand me well, and it is very remarkable what a deep silence is preserved while I am speaking. After sermon, I made another collection of 29 pounds 17s. 8d., and came home deeply humbled with a sense of what God has done for my soul. I doubt not but that many self-righteous bigots, when they see me spreading out my hands to offer Jesus Christ freely to all, are ready to cry out, "How glorious did the Rev. Mr. Whitefield look today, when, neglecting the dignity of a clergyman, he stood venting his enthusiastic ravings in a gown and cassock upon a common, and collecting mites from the poor people." But if this is to be vile, Lord grant that I may be more vile. I know this foolishness of preaching is made instrumental to the conversion and edification of numbers. Ye Pharisees mock on, I rejoice, yea, and will rejoice.

Monday, May 14. Spent most of this day in visiting some friends, and settling my Georgia affairs. Spent the evening very agreeably with several Quakers at the house of Mr. Hy . . .m. How much comfort do those lose who converse with none but such as are of their own communion!

Tuesday, May 15. Preached this evening at Kennington, and God was pleased to send us a little rain. Notwithstanding, the people stood very attentive. The good Lord water us all with the dew of His heavenly blessing.

Wednesday, May 16. Sent a Quaker whom God was pleased to convince, to be baptized by my dear brother, Mr. Stonehouse. Waited upon the Honorable Trustees, who still treated me with the utmost civility. Dined with some serious Quakers, and preached at Kennington, and have reason to bless God, more and more, for the order and devotion of those that come to hear the Word. Indeed, they behave as though they believed God was standing at their right hand.

Thursday, May 17. Preached, after several invitations there, at Hampstead Heath, about five miles from London. The audience was of the politer sort, and I preached very near the horse course, which gave me occasion to speak home to their souls concerning our spiritual race. Most were attentive, but some mocked. Thus the Word of God is either a savor of life unto life, or of death unto death. God's Spirit bloweth when and where it listeth.

Friday, May 18. Dined with several of the Moravian Church, and could not avoid admiring their great simplicity, and deep experience in the inward life. At six, I preached in a very large open place in Shadwell, being much pressed by many to go there. I believe there were upwards of twenty thousand people. At first, through the greatness of the throng, there was a little hurry; but afterwards, all was hushed and silent. Very near 20 pounds was collected for the Orphan House. Blessed be God! we now begin to surround this great city. As the walls of Jericho once fell down at the sound of a few rams' horns; so I hope even this foolishness of preaching, under God, will be a means of pulling down the Devil's strongholds, which are in and about the City of London.

Received several excellent letters, among which was one from Mr. Ralph Erskine, a field-preacher of the Scots Church, a noble soldier of the Lord Jesus Christ. Oh, that all who were truly zealous knew one another! It must greatly strengthen each other's hands.

Saturday, May 19. Had the pleasure of being an instrument, under God, with Mr. Seward, of bringing a young man out of Bethlehem, [Bedlam] who was lately put into that place for being, as they term it, *Methodically mad*. The way I came to be acquainted with him, was by his sending me the following letter: —

"To the Rev. Mr. Whitefield.

"Bethlehem Hospital," No. 50.

"Dear Sir, — I have read your sermon upon the new birth, and hope I shall always have a due sense of my dear Redeemer's goodness to me, Who has so infinitely extended His mercy to me, which sense be pleased to confirm in me by your prayers, and may Almighty God bless and preserve you, and prosper your ministerial function. I wish, Sir, I could have some explanatory notes upon the New Testament, to enlighten the darkness of my understanding, to make me capable of becoming a good soldier of Jesus Christ; but above all, should be glad to see you.

"I am, dear Sir, yours affectionately with my whole heart,

"JOSEPH PERIAM."

According to his request I paid him a visit, and found him in perfect health both in body and mind. A day or two after, I and Mr. Seward went and talked with his sister, who gave me the three following symptoms of his being mad. 1. That he fasted for near a fortnight. 2. That he prayed so as to be heard four stories high. 3. That he had sold his clothes, and given them to the poor. This the young man himself explained to me before, and ingenuously confessed, that under his first awakenings, he was one day reading the story of the young man whom our Lord commanded to sell all, and to give to the poor; and thinking it must be taken in the literal sense, out of love to Jesus Christ he sold his clothes, and gave the money to the poor. This is nothing but what is common to persons at their first setting out in the spiritual life. Satan will, if possible, drive them to extremes. If such converts were left to God, or had some experienced person to consult with, they would soon come into the liberties of the Gospel. But how should those who have not been tempted like unto their brethren, be able to succour those that are tempted?

May the 5th I received a second letter from him.

"Bethlehem, No. 50. May 5, 1739.
"Worthy Sir,

"*Query* 1. If repentance does not include a cessation from sin and turning to virtue; and though notwithstanding I want that deep contrition mentioned by some divines, yet as I live not wilfully in any known sin, and firmly believe the Gospel of our Lord Jesus Christ, may I not thereby be entitled to the benefits of Christ's death and resurrection, in the perseverance of knowledge, and practice of my duty?

"*Query* 2. If I am in prison, whether I may not, without offense to God, make use of endeavors to be discharged, by which I may be enabled to get into a pious family, and consequently be grounded and firmly settled in the love of God, which is my desire; for I am surrounded with nothing but profaneness and wickedness?

"*Query* 3. If my objections to being imprisoned are inconsistent or wicked, which are, that I am obliged to submit to the rules of the house, in going to my cell at seven or eight o'clock at night, and not let out till six or seven in the morning, by which I am debarred the use of candle, and consequently books, so that all the time, except what is spent in prayer and meditation, is lost: which exercises, though good, are by so constant repetition, and for want of change, deadened.

"*Query* 4. If I should, by the goodness of God, be discharged, whether I may, without offense to the Gospel of Jesus Christ, follow the business of an attorney-at-law, to which I was put as a clerk, and by a conscientious discharge of that duty, be thereby entitled to a heavenly inheritance? My fear is this point arises from our Lord's advice about going to law. Matthew 5:40.

"*Query* 5. If I cannot be discharged by proper application (which application pray be pleased to let me have), how can I best spend my time to the glory of God, myself and brethren's welfare? And please to give me rules for the same.

"These questions, whether momentary or not, I leave to your judgment. If you think they deserve an answer, should be glad to have them solved, for as I am sensible of the power of my adversary the Devil, surely I cannot but act with the utmost circumspection, which gives me occasion to trouble you herewith. I hope, Sir, the circumstance of the place I am in may excuse the manner in which I have written to you, and count it not an affront, for God is witness how I love and esteem the ministers of Jesus Christ, for Whose dear sake may the God of infinite love and goodness stablish and confirm you in the daily success of your ministerial labors, which are the daily prayers of your most unworthy but faithful humble servant.

"JOSEPH PERIAM.

"P.S. I am afraid, Sir, I misbehaved myself when you so kindly came to see me; but if I did in any measure, your Christian love and charity will excuse it, for not being warned of your coming, the surprise, though pleasant, so fluttered my spirits, that I was overburdened with joy.

"O how pleased should I be to see you!"

To this I sent the following answer: —

"May 7, 1739.

"Dear Sir, — The way to salvation is by Jesus Christ, Who is the Way, the Truth, and the Life. The way to Christ is by faith. 'Whosoever liveth and believeth in Me,' says our Lord, 'though he were dead, yet shall he live.' This faith, if it is a saving faith, will *work* by love. Come, then, to Jesus Christ as a poor sinner, and He will make you a rich saint. This, I think, serves as an answer to your first query.

"It is, no doubt, your duty, while you are in house, to submit to the rules of it; but then you may use all lawful means to get yourself out. I have just now been with your sister, and will see what can be done further. *Watch and pray.*

"As for the business of an attorney, I think it unlawful for a Christian — at least exceedingly dangerous. Avoid it, therefore, and glorify God in some other station.

"I am, dear Sir, Your affectionate friend and servant,

"GEORGE WHITEFIELD."

A day or two after I received a third letter, which is as follows:

"Wednesday, May 9, 1739.

"Worthy Sir, — I received your letter, which was a full answer to my queries, and give you my hearty thanks for the trouble you have taken upon you (the only gratitude I can at present repay); but He, Whom I have perfectly at heart, will supply the deficiency to you, and will not suffer a meritorious act to go unrewarded. O how do I daily experience the love of Christ towards me, who am so vile, base, and unworthy! I pray God I may always be thankful, and both ready to do and suffer His most gracious will, which I trust through your prayers and God's grace, I shall at all times submit to.

"My father was with me last night, when I showed him your letter. I told him I utterly renounced the business of an attorney. He then asked what profession I chose; which I submitted to him, on condition it might prove agreeable to the will of God. He was pleased to say, he thought me not mad, but very well in my senses, and would take me out, on condition Dr. Monro and the committee were of his opinion. Then he varied again, and thought it convenient for me to stay the summer, and to take physic twice a week, fearing a relapse. I told him, as a father, he should be wholly obeyed; but when, at parting, he mentioned my leaving religion, I was somewhat stirred in my spirit, and told him, nothing should prevail upon me to leave Jesus Christ. This is the substance of what passed between us.

"Upon the whole of the matter, Sir, God gives me perfect resignation, and, I trust, when He shall see fit, will discharge me: I find His love daily more and more shed abroad in my heart. All things will work together for my good. If opportunity will let you, I should be sincerely glad to see you before you set out for America. May Almighty God, in His infinite goodness, prosper, guide, and protect you through this transitory life and hereafter receive you triumphantly into the heavenly Jerusalem, there to converse with, and see the ever-blessed Jesus!

"Your loving and sincere friend,

"JOSEPH PERIAM."

Upon reading this, I was sensibly touched with a fellow-feeling of his misery, and, at my request, Mr. Seward, and two more friends, waited upon the committee. But alas! they esteemed my friends as much mad as the young man, and frankly told them, that both I and my followers, in their opinion, were really beside ourselves. My friend Seward urged the example of the young persons who called the prophet that was sent to anoint Jehu king, a mad fellow; of our Lord, Whom His own relations and the scribes and Pharisees took to be mad, and beside Himself; and Festus's opinion of St. Paul. He further urged, that when young people were under their first awakenings, they were usually tempted by the Devil to run into some extremes; but all such language confirmed the gentlemen more and more that Mr. Seward was mad also. To prove that the young man was certainly mad, they called one of the attendants, who said, when Mr. Periam first came into the place, he stripped himself to his shirt and prayed. The reason of this, as Mr. Periam said afterwards, was that he might inure himself to hardship at once; for being brought from Bethnal Green, where he was taken great care of, into a cold place, without windows, and a damp cellar under him, he thought it best to season himself at first, that he might learn to endure hardness as a good soldier of Jesus Christ. In the midst of the conference, some way or other, they mentioned his going to Georgia, and said, if I would take him with me, they would engage that his father should give leave to have him released. A day or two after, Mr. Seward waited upon his father, who gave his son an excellent character, and consented to his going abroad. After this, he waited upon the Doctor, who pronounced him well. Today he waited again upon the committee, who behaved very civilly, and gave the young man a discharge.

He is now with me, and I hope will be an instrument of doing good. The hardships he has endured at Bethlehem, will, I hope, prepare him for what he must undergo abroad. Being now not ignorant of Satan's devices, he will be better qualified to prevent his getting an advantage over others. Before I leave my account of him, I cannot help telling what usage he met with at first coming into Bethlehem. Being sensible within himself that he wanted no bodily physic, he was unwilling at first to take it; upon which, four or five took hold of him, cursed him most heartily, put a key into his mouth, threw him upon the bed, and said (though I had then never seen or heard of him) "You are one of Whitefield's gang," and so drenched him. I hear also, that there was an order given, that neither I, nor any of my friends, should be permitted to come unto him. Good God! how shortly will that day come when these unhappy men shall be heard to cry out, "We fools counted their lives madness, and their ends to be without honor! Now are they numbered among the children of God! Now is their lot among the saints!"

Dined at Clapham with Mr. B . . .n, a Quaker. Preached in the evening at Kennington Common to about 15,000 people, who were very attentive and affected. Afterwards, I spent two hours at Fetter Lane Society, where we had a most useful conference concerning the necessity of every Christian to have some particular calling, whereby he may be a useful member of the society to which he belongs. We all agreed to this unanimously. For my own part, I think if a man will not labor, neither ought he to eat. To be so intent on pursuing the one thing needful, as to neglect providing for those of our own households, in my opinion, is to be righteous over-much.

Sunday, May 20. Went with our brethren of Fetter Lane Society to St. Paul's, and received the Holy Sacrament, as a testimony that we adhered to the Church of England. Preached at Moorfields and Kennington Common, and, at both places collected very near 50 pounds for the Orphan House. A visible alteration is made in the behavior of the people, for, though there were near fifteen thousand in the morning, and double the number in the afternoon, yet they were as quiet during my sermon, as though there had not been above fifty persons present. I did not meet with a moment's interruption. I could say of the assembly, as Jacob did on another occasion, "Surely God is in this place."

HERTFORD: Monday, May 21. Was fully engaged all the morning in settling my Georgia affairs. Left London about three, called and prayed at a house or two in the way, and reached Hertford between eight and nine at night. I never saw a town so much alarmed. The streets were every way crowded; and, by the behavior of some, I thought we should have had many scoffers, but, blessed be God, I never preached to a quieter congregation. The hearers numbered about four or five thousand, and the place I preached in was a common near the town. Afterwards, a certain gentlewoman, Lydia-like, constrained both me and my friends, if we judged her worthy, to come and abide in her house that night, which we did to our great comfort. The Lord reward her a thousand-fold.

HERTFORD, AND OLNEY IN BUCKINGHAMSHIRE: Tuesday, May 22. Preached about seven in the morning from the same place, and to nearly as large a congregation as I did last night. Breakfasted with Mr. S . . .d's, a Dissenting minister, who kindly invited and received me and my friends. Dined at Hitchin. Promised at the request of many, to preach to them, God willing, on Friday morning, and reached Olney about ten at night, where I had long since promised to come. Here, also, God had prepared a table for us; and here I was not a little comforted in meeting with the Rev. Mr. Rogers of Bedford, who, like me, has lately been thrust out of the synagogues for speaking of justification by faith, and the new birth, and has commenced a field-preacher. Once he was shut in prison for a short time, but thousands flock to hear him, and God blesses him more and more. I believe we are the first professed ministers of the Church of England that were so soon, and without cause, excluded every pulpit. Whether our reverend brethren can justify such conduct, the last day will determine.

Wednesday, May 23. Being denied the pulpit, I preached this morning in a field near the town, to about two thousand people, with much freedom and power. They were very attentive, and I could have continued my discourse much longer, but the bells ringing for prayers, I adjourned my hearers to public worship, where many of them went, and God was pleased to speak to us much in the Second Lesson. How powerfully does the Word of God come to our hearts, when we experience it; otherwise, it is a dead letter.

NORTHAMPTON: Reached Northampton about five in the evening, and was most courteously received by Dr. Doddridge, Master of the Acadamy there.

At seven, according to appointment, I preached to about three thousand hearers on a common near the town, from the starting-post. I preached with wonderful pleasure, because I thought I had then actual possession of one of the Devil's strongholds. Oh, that we may all run so as to obtain the Crown of Life, which God, the righteous Judge will give, at the last day, to all who love our Lord Jesus in sincerity.

Thursday, May 24. Preached again in the same place, at about eight in the morning, but to a much larger audience. Breakfasted with some pious friends. Was greatly comforted by several choice children of God, who came to me from different parts, and left Northampton about eleven, rejoicing with my friends at the mighty things God had already done, and was yet about to do for us. Many rightous souls live in and about Northampton, and nothing confirms me more than God intends to work a great work upon the earth, than to find how His children of all denominations everywhere wrestle in prayer for me.

OLNEY: Being much solicited thereto, after sermon yesterday, I hastened, in company with near a dozen friends, to Olney, eight long miles from Northampton, and got there about ten o'clock. Great numbers were assembled together; but on account of it being a rainy day, it was judged inconvenient to preach in the fields. I therefore stood upon an eminence in the street, and preached from there with such power as I have not for some time experienced. Though it rained all the time, yet the people stood very attentive and patient. All, I really believe, felt, as well as heard the Word, and one was so pricked to the heart, and convinced of sin, that I scarce ever saw the like instance. The Word of God is quick and powerful, and sharper than a two-edged sword.

BEDFORD: Hasted away as fast as possible from Olney to Bedford, where I had promised, God willing, to preach tonight. About eight, I preached from the stairs of a windmill (the pulpit of my dear brother and fellow-laborer, Mr. Rogers) to about three thousand people; and God was pleased to give me such extraordinary assistance, that I believe few, if any, were able to resist the power wherewith God enabled me to speak. My heart was full of God. God caused me to renew my strength, and gave me such inward support, that my journey did not affect me. As my day is, so shall my strength be.

Friday, May 25. Preached at seven in the morning, and had rather a larger congregation than before. Took an affectionate leave of many gracious souls, and reached Hitchin, ten miles from Bedford, about one o'clock noon. The town, I perceived, was much alarmed, and many devout souls came from far to hear me. About two, I got upon a table in the market-place, near the church; but some were pleased to ring the bells in order to disturb us. Upon this, not having begun, we removed into a most commodious place in the fields; but being a little fatigued with my ride, and the sun beating most intensely upon my head, I was obliged, in a short time, to break off, being exceedingly sick and weak. A kind gentlewoman offered me her house, where I went, and lay down for about two hours, and then came and preached near the same place, and God was with us. It was surprising to see how the hearts of the people were knit to me. I could have continued longer with them; but being under an engagement to go to St. Albans, I hastened there, but could not preach on account of my coming in so late. Great numbers had been expecting me; and it grieved me to think how little I could do for Christ, for He is a gracious Master, and had I a thousand lives, they should be spent in His service.

ST. ALBANS AND LONDON: Saturday, May 26. Had a comfortable night's rest, which much refreshed me. Preached at seven in the morning to about fifteen hundred people in a field near the town, and got safe to London by two in the afternoon. Blessed be God this had been a week of fat things. Many further inroads have been made into Satan's kingdom. Many sinners convicted, and many saints much comforted and established in their most holy faith. I find there are some thousands of secret ones yet living among us, who have not bowed the knee to Baal; and this public way of acting brings them out. It much comforts me, wherever I go, to see so many of God's children, of all communions, come and wish me good luck in the Name of the Lord. I perceive the people would be everywhere willing to hear, if the ministers were ready to teach the truth as it is in Jesus. Lord, do Thou stir up more of my dear friends and fellow-laborers to go out into the highways and hedges, to compel poor sinners to come in! Amen!

Received an excellent letter from the Rev. Mr. Ebenezer Erskine of Scotland, brother to Mr. Ralph Erskine, acquainting me of his preaching last week to fourteen thousand people. Blessed be God! there are other field-preachers in the world besides myself. The Lord furnish us all with spiritual food wherewith to feed so great multitudes.

Preached in the evening at Kennington Common to about fifteen thousand people, and we had an extraordinary presence of God among us. Oh! that all who object to this way of preaching would come and see; all sincere persons must go convicted away.

Sunday, May 27. Preached this morning at Moorfields to about twenty thousand, and God manifested Himself still more and more. My discourse was near two hours long. My heart was full of love; and people were so melted down on every side, that the greatest scoffer must have owned that this was the finger of God. Went twice to public worship, received the blessed Sacrament, and preached, as usual, in the evening at Kennington Common, to about the same number of people as I did last Lord's Day. I was a little hoarse; but God strengthened me to speak so as not only to be heard, but felt by most that stood near me. Glory be to God on high!

Monday, May 28. Preached, after earnest and frequent invitation, at Hackney, in a field belonging to one Mr. Rudge, to about ten thousand people. I insisted much upon the reasonableness of the doctrine of the new birth, and the necessity of our receiving the Holy Ghost in His sanctifying gifts and graces, as well now as formerly. God was pleased to impress it most deeply upon the hearers. Great numbers were in tears; and I could not help exposing the impiety of those letter-learned teachers, who say, we are not now to receive the Holy Ghost, and who count the doctrine of the new birth, enthusiasm. Out of your own mouths will I condemn you. Did you not, at the time of ordination, tell the bishop, that you were inwardly moved by the Holy Ghost to take upon you the administration of the Church? Surely, at that time, you acted the crime of Ananias and Sapphira over again. You lied, not unto man, but unto God.

Tuesday, May 29. Went to public service at Westminster Abbey. Afterwards dispatched business for my orphans, and preached at Kennington to a most devout auditory with much sweetness and power. The subject I treated of, was our Lord's miracle of the loaves and fishes; and I hope He Who fed so many thousands with bodily bread, fed my hearers' souls with the Bread of Life which cometh down from heaven.

Wednesday, May 30. Waited upon the Bishop of Bristol (who treated me with the utmost civility), and received his lordship's benefaction for Georgia. At the request of many, I preached in the evening at Newington Common, to about fifteen thousand people. A most commodious place was erected for me to preach from. The Word came with power; and seeing a great multitude, I thought proper to collect for the Orphan House; and 16 pounds 9s. 4d. was gathered on that occasion.

Thursday, May 31. Was taken very ill this afternoon; but God was pleased to strengthen me to go to Kennington, where I preached to my usual congregation; and three of my brethren in the ministry were pleased to accompany me, which filled the people with exceeding great joy. Thou

Lord of the harvest, send forth, we beseech Thee, more laborers into Thy harvest.

Friday, June 1. Dined at Old Ford, and gave a short exhortation to a few people in a field, and preached, in the evening, at a place called Mayfair, near Hyde Park Corner. The congregation, I believe, consisted of near eighty thousand people. It was, by far, the largest I ever preached to yet. In the time of my prayer, there was a little noise; but they kept a deep silence during my whole discourse. A high and very commodious scaffold was erected for me to stand upon; and though I was weak in myself, yet God strengthened me to speak so loud, that most could hear, and so powerfully, that most, I believe, could feel. All love, all glory be to God through Christ!

> So weak, so frail an instrument,
>> If Thou, my God, vouchsafe to use;
> 'Tis praise enough to be employed,
>> Reward enough, if Thou excuse.
>
> If Thou excuse, then work Thy will
>> By so unfit an instrument;
> It will at once Thy goodness show,
>> And prove Thy power Omnipotent.

Saturday, June 2. Sent another Quaker to be baptized by Mr. Stonehouse. Collected by private contributions, nearly 50 pounds for the orphans, and preached in the evening to about ten thousand at Hackney, where 20 pounds 12s. 4d. was gathered on the same occasion. Before I went out to preach, I was very sick and weak; but power was given me from above, so that I continued preaching for an hour and a half. It rained some considerable time, but almost all were unmoved; and I was so enlarged by talking of the love and free grace of Jesus Christ, that I could have continued my discourse till midnight. This promise, "They that wait on the Lord shall renew their strength," is fulfilled in me daily. Oh free grace in Christ Jesus our Lord!

Sunday, June 3. Preached at Moorfields to a larger congregation than ever, and collected 29 pounds 17s. 9d. for the Orphan House. Went twice to public worship, and received the Sacrament. Preached in the evening at Kennington Common, to the most numerous audience I ever yet saw in that place, and collected 34 pounds 5s. When I mentioned my departure from them, they were melted into tears. Thousands of ejaculations and fervent prayers were poured out to God on my behalf, which gave me abundant reason to be thankful to my dear Master. Oh what marvelous great kindness has God shown me in this great city! Indeed, I have seen the Kingdom of God come with power, and cannot but say, "Blessed are the eyes which see the things that we see, and hear the things which we hear; for many righteous souls have desired to see the things which we see, ... and to hear the things which we hear, and have not heard them."

I now go, I trust, under the conduct of God's Holy Spirit, to

Pennsylvania and Virginia, and from thence to Georgia, knowing not what will befall me, save that the Holy Ghost witnesseth in every place, that labors, afflictions, and trials of all kinds abide me. O my dear friends, pray that none of these things may move me, and that I may not count even my life dear unto myself, so that I may finish my course with joy, and the ministry which I have received of the Lord Jesus. Into His hands I commend my whole spirit, soul and body; His will be done in me, by me, and upon me, for time, and for eternity. Let me do or suffer just as seemeth good in His sight. Only do Thou, O Lord, give me that wisdom which dwelleth with prudence, that I may never suffer for my own misconduct, but only for righteousness' sake. Reward, O Lord, my dear friends for all their works of faith, and labors of love. Forgive my enemies; and grant we may all effectually be called by Thy free grace, and after death be translated to sit on Thy right hand.

Prepare me for the fiery trial wherewith I must be tried, and make me faithful to the trust committed to my charge. May I carefully watch the flock over which the Holy Ghost hath made me overseer, and may I, in all things, behave as a good steward of the manifold gifts of God. May the past mercies make me humble and truly thankful, and may I be prepared for these greater things which I am yet to see. May the souls of all to whom I have preached be precious in Thy sight, and may we all meet to be one another's joy and crown of rejoicing in the Day of the Lord Jesus. Though absent in body, may we be present in spirit, and always have reason to triumph because of the truth. May we go from conquering to conquer, and see Satan, like lightning, fall from heaven. May God pour into our hearts a spirit of prayer and supplication, and may our prayers ascend up as an acceptable sacrifice through Jesus Christ, to Whom, with Thee, O Father, and Thee, O Holy Ghost, Three Persons, and One God, be all glory, might, majesty, and dominion, now and forevermore. Amen.

> Captain of my salvation, hear!
> Stir up Thy strength, and bow the skies;
> Be Thou the God of battles near;
> In all Thy majesty arise!
>
> The day, the dreadful day's at hand!
> In battle cover Thou my head:
> Pass'd is Thy word: I here demand:
> And confident expect Thine aid.
>
> Now arm me for the threatening fight,
> Now let Thy power descent from high,
> Triumphant in Thy Spirit's might,
> So shall I every foe defy.
>
> I ask Thy help; by Thee sent forth
> Thy glorious Gospel to proclaim,
> Be Thou my mouth, and shake the earth,
> And spread by me Thy awful Name.

Steel me to shame, reproach, disgrace,
    Arm me with all Thy armour now,
Set like a flint my steady face,
    Harden to adamant my brow.

Bold may I wax, exceeding bold
    My high commission to perform,
Nor shrink Thy harshest truth t'unfold,
    But more than meet the gathering storm.

Adverse to earth's rebellious throng,
    Still may I turn my fearless face,
Stand as an iron pillar strong,
    And steadfast as a wall of brass.

Give me Thy might, Thou God of power,
    Then let or men or fiends assail!
Strong in Thy strength, I'll stand a tower,
    Impregnable to earth or hell.

THE FOURTH JOURNAL

DURING THE TIME WHITEFIELD WAS DETAINED IN ENGLAND BY THE EMBARGO

(June, 1739 — August, 1739)

BLACKHEATH, IN KENT: Monday, June 4, 1739. Went a second time to pay my respects to the Archbishop of Canterbury, but his Grace was gone out, as before. Waited upon the Bishop of London, who used me very civilly. Finished all my affairs according to my mind. Took leave of my weeping friends, and went in company with many of them to Blackheath, where there was nearly as large a congregation as at Kennington the last Lord's Day. I think I never was so much enlarged since I have preached in the fields. My discourse lasted nearly two hours, and the people were so melted down, and wept so loud, that they almost drowned my voice. I could not but cry out, "Come, ye Pharisees, come and see the Lord Jesus getting Himself the victory." Afterwards went to an inn upon the Heath, where many came drowned in tears to take a last farewell. The remainder of the evening I spent with several of my brethren, and went to bed about 12 o'clock — I hope, in some measure, thankful for the great things we had seen and heard.

BLENDON: Tuesday, June 5. Went in the morning to Blendon, five miles from Blackheath, and enjoyed a sweet retreat at the house of Mr. Delamotte. Preached with unusual power at Bexley Common, at 11 in the morning, to about three hundred people, and in the evening, near Woolwich, to several thousands. I returned to Blendon rejoicing, and spent the evening most delightfully with many dear Christian friends, who came from London to see me. Oh, how does their sweet company cause me to long for communion among the spirits of just men made perfect! Accomplish, O Lord, the number of Thine elect, and hasten Thy Kingdom.

BEXLEY AND GRAVESEND: Wednesday, June 6. Breakfasted with many friends, and gave a word of exhortation to many more who came from London to bid me adieu. Their hearts were ready to break with sorrow. But God, I hope, will supply in my absence, by raising up more ministers to go in and out before them. About 10 o'clock in the morning, read prayers, and preached at Bexley church, Mr. Piers, the vicar, my brother and fellow-laborers in Christ, having given me a pressing invitation. The congregation was large, and my soul was so filled with God, that the Word came with very great power to all who heard me. After sermon we dined with Mr. Piers, and having taken a farewell, we left our friends in tears, and hasted to Gravesend, where I read prayers, and preached in a church near the town to about six hundred people. I have no objection against, but highly approve of the excellent Liturgy of our Church, would ministers lend me their churches to use it in. If not, let them blame themselves, that I pray and preach in the fields.

GRAVESEND, BEXLEY AND BLENDON: Thursday, June 7. Received two letters from persons, confessing, that they came to hear me out of a bad motive, but were apprehended by the free grace of Jesus Christ. Answered them, and some others. Read prayers, and preached in the same church as I did last night. Took some refreshment, and returned in the evening, and preached in Bexley church, being much excited to do so by the kind solicitations of Mr. Piers. The congregation was much larger than we could expect, and most, I believe, were much affected. Here some of Mr. Delamotte's family gave us the meeting. After sermon I returned to their house at Blendon, praising and blessing God, that we had once more an opportunity of building up each other in our most holy faith. Oh, how sweet is this retirement to my soul! God is pleased to meet me in it, and vouchsafe me great measures of His Divine Presence. I must expect some fresh trials. Dearest Lord, sweeten all Thy dispensations with a sense of Thy love, and then deal with me as it seemeth good in Thy sight!

Friday, June 8. Preached at Bexley in the morning, and at Charlton in the afternoon, where I was invited by the Earl and Countess of Egmont. Both before and after sermon they entertained me with the utmost civility. My heart was much comforted by God, and at night I returned with my friends to my sweet retreat at Blendon. Oh, the comforts of being all of one mind in a house! It begins our heaven upon earth. Were I left to my own choice, here would be my rest. But a necessity is laid upon me, and woe unto me if I preach not the Gospel!

Saturday, June 9. Was much pleased and edified in reading Bishop Hall's *Christ Mystical*, and Erskine's *Sermons*, both whose works, with Boehme's *Sermons*, I would earnestly recommend to every one. Preached in the evening at Dulwich, to not a very large congregation, and went afterwards to Blackheath, and spent a most agreeable evening with many Christian friends, who came here on purpose to give me the meeting.

BLENDON, BEXLEY AND BLACKHEATH: Sunday, June 10. Hastened back to Blendon, where more of our brethren came last night to see me. Preached with more power than ever, and assisted in administering the Sacrament to about two hundred communicants in Bexley Church. Dined, gave thanks, and sang hymns at Mr. Delamotte's. Preached with great power, in the evening, on Blackheath, to above twenty thousand people, and collected 16 pounds 7s. for the orphans. After sermon I went to the *Green Man*, near the place where I preached, and continued till midnight instant in prayer, praise, and thanksgiving, and Christian conversation. I believe there were nearly fifty or sixty of us in all. Numbers stood by as spectators. God enlarged my heart much in prayer and exhortation.

Many of them watched unto prayer and praise all night. I think it every Christian's duty to be particularly careful to honor and glorify God where He is most dishonored. Some can sing the songs of the drunkards in public houses; others can spend whole nights in chambering and wantonness; why should Christians be ashamed to sing the songs of the Lamb, and spend nights, as their Lord did before them, in exercises of devotion?

> Silent have we been too long,
> Awed by earth's rebellious throng,
> Thee if we should still deny
> Lord, the very stones would cry.
>   Hallelujah.

BLACKHEATH, BEXLEY, DULWICH AND BLENDON: Monday, June 11. Prayed, sang with and gave a warm exhortation to those that continued at Blackheath all night. Read prayers at Bexley Church; dined with Mrs. S . . . at Lewisham, a gentlewoman who gladly received both me and my friends into her house. Preached in the evening to a much larger audience than before at Dulwich, and then hastened back to Blendon, in company with some who love our Lord Jesus in sincerity. Oh how swiftly and delightfully do those hours pass away which are spent in Christian conversation!

BLENDON, BEXLEY AND BLACKHEATH: Tuesday, June 12. Read prayers at Bexley Church. Began (being pressed thereto both in spirit and by my friends) to put some of my extempore discourses into writing. Preached at Blackheath in the evening to about twenty thousand people, and spent the remaining part of the night with more friends. Several people of different ranks stood by as before. Some, I hope, went away edified, for God gave me great enlargement of soul, and the exhortation, I believe, reached their hearts. God grant we may thus always continue to let our light shine before men: it cannot but bring glory to our Father Who is in Heaven.

Wednesday, June 13. Retired in the morning to Blendon; preached as usual, at Blackheath, and went with my fellow-travelers to Lewisham, about a mile off, to the house of Mrs. S . . ., who has frequently pressed me to abide there. How does God raise me up friends unsought for in every place! After supper I expounded to, and prayed with, several gentlemen and ladies whom Mrs. S . . . had invited to hear the Word. Oh that it may take deep root in their hearts!

Thursday, June 14. Spent the whole day in my pleasant and profitable retreat at Blendon; and, in the evening had the pleasure of introducing my honored and reverend friend, Mr. John Wesley to preach at Blackheath. The Lord give him ten thousand times more success than He has given me! After sermon, we spent the evening most agreeably together with many Christian friends at the *Green Man*. About ten we admitted all to come in who would; the room was soon filled — God gave me utterance. I exhorted and prayed for nearly an hour, and then went to bed, rejoicing that another fresh inroad had been made into Satan's territories, by Mr. Wesley's following me in field-preaching in London as well as in Bristol. Lord, give the word, and great shall be the company of such preachers. Amen, Amen.

Friday, June 15. Continued at Blendon all day. Preached with great power in the evening at Blackheath to about as many as usual, and afterwards retired to Lewisham, where I and my friends were again most kindly received by Mrs. S .... May the Lord bless her house as He did the house of Obed-edom, and make each of our souls an ark of the Holy Spirit.

Saturday, June 16. Returned in the morning to Blendon; finished some writings I had in hand, and preached in the evening at Blackheath, on Abraham's offering up his son Isaac. God make us partakers of such a working obedient faith!

Sunday, June 17. Preached in Bexley Church, and helped to administer the Sacrament to nearly three hundred communicants, most of whom came from London. Baptized a person, twenty-eight years of age, whom God had worked upon by my ministry. Dined at Blendon, and took sweet counsel with many Christian friends. Preached to above twenty thousand people at Blackheath; and afterwards supped again at the *Green Man*. There were nearly three hundred in the room. I continued in exhortation and prayer till eleven o'clock, and then retired to bed, much pleased to think that religion, which had long been skulking in corners, and was almost laughed out of the world, should now begin to appear abroad, and openly show herself at noonday. Let them count us vainglorious for thus confessing Christ before men. It is a small thing with us to be judged with the judgment of men — to our own Master we stand or fall.

HERTFORD: Monday, June 18. An embargo being laid upon the shipping for some weeks, I had time to go to Hertford, where I was invited by several pressing letters, declaring how God had worked by my ministry, when I was there last. We dined and prayed with Madame Cook, of Newington, and her family, and reached the place intended by seven at night. A most kind reception I met with from many Christians. At eight, I preached, according to appointment, to about four thousand people, who were quite silent and attentive. I found myself much stronger that when I was here last.

Tuesday, June 19. Preached this morning about 7 o'clock, to nearly three thousand people. Many came to me under strong convictions of their fallen estate, and their want of a God-Man to be their Mediator. Many, I heard of besides, who had been much worked upon by my preaching; several Christian families, I find, had been comforted, and such immediate effects produced, that I could not help rejoicing exceedingly. Breakfasted, dined, prayed, and sang hymns with Mr. S ..., a dissenting minister; was visited by some Quakers, and, in the afternoon waited upon Mr. T ..., a Baptist teacher, who, unknown to me, had sent a horse to fetch me from London. Preached at 7 o'clock in the evening to about five thousand souls, upon the faith of Abraham, in which God was pleased to give me great freedom, and the people great attention. I believe God has much people in and near Hertford.

BROAD-OAKS, IN ESSEX: Wednesday, June 20. Set out about 5 o'clock in the morning, and hasted to Broad-Oaks, about twenty miles from

Hertford. About midway, at Bishop-Stortford, as we were passing through, a person unknown to us constrained both me and my friends to come and refresh ourselves a little at his house. We accepted his offer, and found he was the son of a gentleman, who had sent to engage me to preach at this place on Friday night next. Having spent an hour very agreeably with some Christian friends, he went with us, to Broad-Oaks, the way being intricate. About 12 o'clock we got there, and perceived that Providence had sent us most opportunely to a family, some of whom being born after the Spirit, are, for that reason, most violently opposed and persecuted by those foes of their own household who are only born after the flesh. A clergyman has been employed to divert them from their present madness, as they call it; and has done them the honor of preaching against them. For this week past, they have been continually beset with numbers of such, who are lovers of pleasure more than lovers of God, and who would tell them that a decent, genteel and fashionable religion is sufficient to carry them to Heaven. They knew nothing of me paying them this visit, which made them more thankful. No one can tell what a comfortable meeting God gave us. Surely it was Heaven begun upon earth. We found the sweets of opposition, and rejoiced greatly in the prospect of suffering for Christ's sake. To increase our satisfaction, Mr. Delamotte, a convert of Mr. Ingham's, came from Cambridge to meet us. He is scandalously opposed at that University. The students make him a proverb of reproach, and abuse him in the rudest manner. He has been forbidden coming into one college; and two or three who associate with him have been threatened much by their tutors for keeping him company. And here I cannot but remark what wonderful mercies God has shown this Mr. Delamotte's family. About three or four years ago, God was pleased to touch the heart of his brother Charles, who hearing that Mr. Wesley was going to Georgia (though his father would have settled him in a very handsome way), offered to go abroad with him as a servant. His parents' consent was asked, but they, and almost all their relations, opposed it strenuously. However, the young man being resolute, and convinced that God called him, they at length somewhat consented. He went abroad, lived with Mr. Wesley, served under him as a son in the Gospel, did much good, and endured great hardships for the sake of Jesus Christ. Behold, how God rewarded him for leaving all. While he was absent, God was pleased to make use of the ministry of Mr. Ingham and Mr. Charles Wesley in converting his mother, two sisters, and this young gentleman at Cambridge; who, I pray God, may stand as a barrier against the profaneness, debauchery, lukewarmness, and deism of that seat of learning, and prove both a Barnabas and Boanerges in the Church of England.

But to return: after having spent some comfortable hours together, we went to Wimbish Green, where Mr. Charles Wesley had preached some time ago. I rode there in a chaise, and preached from it to about four hundred people, with great freedom and power. About 9 o'clock we returned to Broad-Oaks, and spent the most heavenly night I have known for a long while. Oh, how doubly sweet are opportunities when we have been debarred of them for some time. I believe the saints of old never had so much comfort, as when they were obliged to shut the doors for fear of the Jews, and to hide themselves in dens and caves of the earth. The Lord prepare us all for such an hour.

SAFFRON WALDEN: Thursday, June 21. Preached at Saffron Walden, eight miles from Broad-Oaks, to about two thousand people; dined with my friends at Mr. F's; preached at 5 o'clock in the evening to a congregation as before, and returned to Broad-Oaks singing and praising God. Wherever I go, people fly to the doctrine of Jesus Christ. "My sheep," says our Lord, "hear My voice. A stranger will they not follow."

THAXTED AND BISHOP STORTFORD: Friday, June 22. Read part of Jenks' *Submission to the Righteousness of Christ*, a most excellent book. Preached at 9 o'clock in the morning at Thaxted, about two miles from Broad-Oaks, to upwards of a thousand people, and with such sweetness and power, as I have not felt since I came into Essex. All around me were melted into tears. After sermon, Mr. S. kindly entertained me, and my fellow-travelers, and many others who came to hear me. We spent our time most Christianly together, and afterwards went to Bishop Stortford, about twelve miles from Thaxted, where I promised, God willing, to preach at night. About 5 o'clock we got there, and at six, God enabled me to preach with power to nearly four thousand people. Many devout souls were present, and several invitations were given me in the Name of Christ to other parts of Essex, which I promised to accept, supposing the embargo on the shipping continued. Blessed be God, this itinerant preaching brings me acquainted with numbers of His children, which otherwise I might never have seen or heard of in this life. The united fervent prayers of so many righteous souls undoubtedly will avail much.

BLACKHEATH: Saturday, June 23. Set out betimes from Bishop Stortford, and reached Blackheath about 3 o'clock in the afternoon. Preached at 7 o'clock in the evening to about a thousand people. The smallness of the congregation was occasioned by a report that I was dead, Wherever I went I found the people much surprised and rejoiced to see me alive. God knows I long to be dissolved and to be with Christ, but as I have scarcely begun my testimony, I believe I shall not yet die, but live, and declare the works of the Lord. Hereafter I hope He will enable me to say, "I have fought a good fight, I have finished my course, I have kept the faith. Henceforth there is laid up for me a crown of righteousness, which the Lord, the Righteous Judge, shall give me at that day: and not to me only, but unto all them also that love His appearing."

BEXLEY: Sunday, June 24. Read prayers and assisted in administering the Sacrament at Bexley Church. Many came from afar, and expected to hear me, but the Diocesan had been pleased to insist on the Vicar's denying me the pulpit. Whether for just cause God shall judge at the last day. If we have done anything worthy the censures of the Church, why do not the Right Reverend the Bishops call us to a public account? If not, why do not they confess and own us? It is well we can appeal to the great Bishop of souls. They say it is not regular, our going out into the highways and hedges, and compelling poor sinners to come in. We ought not so to beseech them to be reconciled to God. They desire to know by what authority we preach, and ask, "What sign showest thou that thou dost these things?" But, alas! what further sign would they require? We went not into the fields till we were excluded from the churches; and has not God set His seal to our ministry in an extraordinary manner? Have not many that were spiritually blind received their sight? Many that have been lame strengthened to run the way of God's commandments? Have not the deaf heard? The lepers been cleansed? The dead raised? And the poor had the Gospel preached unto them? That these notable miracles have been wrought, not in our own names, or by our own power, but in the Name and by the power of Jesus of Nazareth cannot be denied. And yet they require a sign.

Preached in the afternoon to about three hundred people in Justice Delamotte's yard; and in the evening on Blackheath to upwards of twenty thousand, on these words, "And they cast him out." I recommended to the people the example of the blind beggar; reminded them of preparing for the gathering storm, and exhorted them in the Name of Christ Jesus to follow the example of the Lamb of God, supposing my enemies should think that they did God good service by killing me. I dread nothing more than the false zeal of my friends in a suffering hour. God grant that we may learn when we are reviled, not to revile again; when we suffer, may we threaten not, but commit our souls into the hands of Him Who judgeth righteously. Lord, endue us with the spirit of Thy first martyr, St. Stephen, that we may pray most earnestly even for our very murderers.

LONDON: Monday and Tuesday, June 25 and 26. Came here privately last night. Went to a love-feast in Fetter Lane, and intended setting out the next morning (being greatly importuned thereto) for Gloucester in the stage coach; but there were no vacant places. Spent the day in writing letters and settling some affairs. Preached in the evening to about as many as usual on Kennington Common, with great and visible success. Spent a delightful hour with many Christian friends. Took coach about 11 o'clock at night, and reached Cirencester by 10 the next evening. Justly may I say, I am a stranger and pilgrim upon earth; for I have here no continuing city. May I always be preparing myself for that which is to come, a city not made with hands, eternal in the Heavens, whose Builder and Maker is God.

CIRENCESTER AND GLOUCESTER: Wednesday, June 27. Waited on the minister of the parish, and asked him for the use of his pulpit; but he refused it, because I had not my letters of orders. Went to public worship at eleven; and preached to about three thousand people, in a field near the town, about twelve. Was afterwards visited by several of the Baptist congregation, who brought me five guineas for the Orphan House. Set out about four in the afternoon, and reached Gloucester about seven in the evening, to the inexpressible joy of many. The late report of my being dead has only served to make my present visits more welcome. Thus all things work together for good to those that love God. Soon after I came into the town, I visited the Society, and expounded for the space of an hour to more p eople than the room (though it was large) would contain. Blessed be God all heard the Word most gladly. I now see the seed sown when I was here last, was not all sown on stony, thorny ground; no, some has been received into honest and good hearts. This is the Lord's doing; to Him be all the glory through Jesus Christ.

GLOUCESTER: Thursday, June 28. Preached in the morning to about a thousand people in my brother's field. Went to public prayers at the Cathedral. Waited upon the Bishop, who received me very civilly. Visited some sick persons in the afternoon who sent for me. Preached at night to upwards of three thousand. Great numbers were melted into tears; and most, I believe, went convicted away. Thanks be to God Who thus giveth us the victory through our Lord Jesus Christ.

GLOUCESTER AND PAINSWICK: Friday, June 29. Preached in my brother's field in the morning to a large and very affected congregation. Went to the Cathedral service. Visited some religious friends; and preached to above three thousand souls in the street at Painswick. All was hushed and silent. The Divine Presence was amongst us. All rejoiced to see me alive again, and thanked God abundantly on my behalf.

STROUD AND GLOUCESTER: Saturday, June 30. Spent the evening with some Christian friends. Slept at Painswick; and preached about ten in the morning to nearly two thousand people, in the bowling-green belonging to the George Inn at Stroud, three miles from thence. God was with us. After sermon, I went in company with many friends to Gloucester, where I preached at seven o'clock in the evening, to a larger and more affected congregation than ever. Blessed be God, the Word has free course. Oh, that it may run and be glorified through all the earth.

GLOUCESTER, RANDWICK AND HAMPTON COMMON: Sunday, July 1. Preached at seven o'clock in the morning to a much increased audience in my brother's field. Breakfasted at Gloucester; preached at eleven in the morning, read prayers in the afternoon, and preached again in the afternoon at Randwick Church, about seven miles from Gloucester. The church was quite full, and about two thousand were in the churchyard, who, by taking down the window that lay behind the pulpit, had the convenience of hearing. Many wept sorely.

After this service I hastened to Hampton Common, and to my great surprise, found no less than twenty thousand, on horseback and foot, ready to receive me. I spoke with greater freedom than I had done all the day before. About twelve at night, I reached Gloucester much fresher than when I left it in the morning. Surely Jesus Christ is a gracious Master. They that wait upon Him shall renew their strength.

Monday, July 2. Preached this morning in my brother's field to a larger audience than ever. Found my spirits much exhausted by yesterday's labors, but notwithstanding, a sweet power was among us. After dinner I went to Tewkesbury, where I found much opposition had been made by the bailiff against my coming. Upon my entrance into the town, I found the people alarmed; and as soon as I was got into the inn, four constables came to attend me. But a lawyer being there who was my friend, demanded the constables' warrant, who not being able to produce one, he sent them about their business. At eight o'clock I went into a field loaned me by one Mr. H . . .s, which lay without the liberties of the town. My audience consisted of two or three thousand people. I spoke with freedom, and most went affected away. The remainder of the evening I spent most agreeably with many Christian friends, who accompanied me on my journey. I rejoiced that God led me on from conquering to conquer.

TEWKESBURY AND EVESHAM: Tuesday, July 3. Waited this morning upon Mr. J . . .s, one of the town bailiffs, and asked him in meekness, "for what reason he had sent the constables after me?" He said, "It was the determination, not of himself, but of all the council." He then said, "the people were noisy, and it reflected upon the bailiffs." I answered, "that was owing to their sending the constables with their staves to apprehend me, when I should come into the town." Upon this he began to be a little angry, and told me, "a certain judge said, he would take me up as a vagrant, were I to preach near him." I answered, "he was very welcome to do as he pleased; but I apprehended no magistrate had power to stop my preaching, even in the streets, if I thought proper." "No, sir," said he, "and if you preach here tomorrow, you shall have the constables to attend you." After this, I took my leave, telling him, "I thought it my duty as a minister to inform him, that magistrates were intended to be a terror to evildoers, and not to those who do well." And I desired he would be as careful to appoint constables to attend at the next horse races, balls, and assemblies.

About nine in the morning we left Tewkesbury, and reached Evesham about noon. The poor people were much alarmed, hearing that I had been abused at Tewkesbury, and that the magistrates of Evesham had threatened to apprehend me if I preached within their liberties. Upon this, Mr. Benjamin Seward thought it advisable to preach near his house, which I did from a wall to nearly a thousand hearers; and, I believe, to good effect. On my return to the inn, I could not but observe to my friends how gradually the opposition increased. At present, it seems to be like the cloud which Elijah's servant saw no bigger than a man's hand; but, by and by; it will gather apace, and break upon the Church of God. But the God whom we serve is able to deliver us.

About eight o'clock at night I preached again from the same place, and had the satisfaction of seeing my morning congregation trebly increased. After this I went to a friend's house to eat bread, and came to my inn, wishing that all felt the love of God shed abroad in their hearts, as I did.

EVESHAM, PERSHORE, TEWKESBURY AND GLOUCESTER: Wednesday, July 4. Preached by seven in the morning at Evesham. Breakfasted at a hospitable Quaker's house; and went in company of about thirty to Pershore, where I was kindly invited by Mr. Parks, the present incumbent. He gave me the meeting as I was going to the church; I read prayers, and preached. Several clergymen were present, and after sermon Mr. Parks sent me his thanks, and gave me another invitation to Pershore. The inhabitants were much affected, and I was received gladly into some of their houses, and requested to come to others. About five in the evening I took an affectionate leave of Evesham friends, and in company with about one hundred and twenty on horseback, went to Tewkesbury, and never saw a town so much alarmed. The streets were crowded with people from all parts. I rode immediately through the town, and preached to about six thousand hearers in a field loaned us by Mr. P., but saw no constables either to molest or attend on me.

Immediately after sermon, I took horse, and reached Gloucester near midnight. We went on our way rejoicing in the Lord, Who still causes us to triumph in every place. Oh, forever be adored His free grace in Christ!

GLOUCESTER AND CHAFFORD: Thursday, July 5. Preached about ten in the morning, as usual, to a numerous and exceedingly affected audience. My own heart was full of love to my dear countrymen, and they sincerely sympathized with me. Many friends after this came to take leave of me, and told me what God had done for their souls. Having written my journal, and dispatched my private business, after joining in prayer and singing with many, I left Gloucester. About five in the evening I reached Chafford Common; at seven preached till it was nearly dark to upwards of ten thousand people — a glorious increase since I was there last.

BRISTOL: Friday, July 6. Slept at the house of Mr. W . . .n, a clothier, two miles from Chafford. Rose at six, and after family duty and taking a little breakfast, we set out towards Bristol. At Petty France some friends met us; and before we came within two miles of Bristol, our company increased very considerably. The people were much rejoiced at the news of my coming: their hearts seemed to leap for joy, and many thanksgivings were rendered to God on my behalf. The bells were rung unknown to me. I was received as an angel of God. At seven o'clock in the evening, I preached at Baptist Mills, to about six or seven thousand people, who were much melted by the power of God's Word. I hope they will receive a second benefit.

Saturday, July 7. Breakfasted with Mr. L . . .y. Settled some affairs concerning our brethren, and had a useful conference about many things with my honored friend, Mr. John Wesley. Dined at my sister's; gave the Sacrament to a sick sister, and paid another visit upon a matter of importance. Preached at Baptist Mills to near the same number of people as last night, and found that Bristol had great reason to bless God for the ministry of Mr. John Wesley. The congregations I observed to be much more serious and affected than when I left them; and their loud and repeated Amens, which they put up to every petition, as well as the exemplariness of their conversation in common life, plainly show that they have not received the grace of God in vain. That good, great good, is done is evident. Either this is done by an evil or good spirit. If you say by an evil spirit, I answer in our Lord's own words, "If Satan be divided against Satan, how can his kingdom stand?" If by a good spirit, why do not the clergy and the rest of the Pharisees believe our report? It is little less than blasphemy against the Holy Ghost to impute the great work, that has been wrought in so short a time in this kingdom, to delusion and the power of the devil.

Sunday, July 8. Preached at the bowling-green to about ten thousand people, greatly affected indeed. About eleven, I preached again at Hannam Mount, to nearly as many hearers; and at seven in the evening to about twenty thousand at Rose Green. I find such a visible alteration in the congregation for the better, since I was here last, that convinces me more and more that God is with us of a truth. As our opposition increases, I doubt not but the manifestations of God's Presence amongst us will increase also.

Monday, July 9. On Thursday I received a letter from the Bishop of Gloucester, in which his lordship affectionately admonished me to exercise my authority I received in the manner it was given me; his lordship being of opinion that I ought to preach the Gospel only in the congregation wherein I was lawfully appointed thereunto.

Today I sent his lordship the following answer: —

"Bristol, July 9, 1739.

"My Lord, — I thank your lordship for your lordship's kind letter. My frequent removes from place to place prevented my answering it sooner.

"I am greatly obliged to your lordship, in that you are pleased to watch over my soul, and to caution me against acting contrary to the commission given me at ordination. But, if the commission we then receive, obliges us to preach nowhere but in that parish which is committed to our care, then all persons act contrary to their commission when they preach occasionally in any strange place; and consequently, your lordship equally offends when you preach out of your own diocese.

"As for inveighing against the clergy, without a cause, I deny the charge. What I say, I am ready to make good whenever your lordship pleases. Let those, who bring reports to your lordship about my preaching, be brought face to face, and I am ready to give them an answer. St. Paul exhorts Timothy not to receive an accusation against an elder under two or three witnesses. And even Nicodemus could say, the law suffered no man to be condemned unheard. I shall only add, that I hope your lordship will inspect the lives of your other clergy, and censure them for being over-remiss, as much as you censure me for being over-righteous. It is their falling from their Articles, and not preaching the truth as it is in Jesus, that has excited the present zeal of those, whom they, in derision, call the Methodist preachers.

"Dr. Stebbing's sermon (for which I thank your lordship) confirms me more and more in my opinion, that I ought to be instant in season and out of season; for, to me, he seems to know no more of the true nature of regeneration than Nicodemus did when he came to Jesus by night. Your lordship may observe that he does not speak a word of original sin, or the dreadful consequences of our fall in Adam, upon which the doctrine of the new birth is entirely founded. No; like other polite preachers, he seems to think that St. Paul's description of the wickedness of the heathen is only to be referred to them of past ages; whereas I affirm, we are all included as much under the guilt and consequences of sin as they were.

"Again, my lord, the doctor entirely mistakes us when we talk of the *sensible* operations of the Holy Ghost. He understands us just as those Jews understood Jesus Christ, who, when our Lord talked of giving them that Bread which came down from Heaven, said, 'How can this man give us his flesh to eat?' I know not that we use the word *sensible* when we talk of the operations of the Spirit of God; but if we do, we do not mean that God's Spirit manifests itself to our *senses*, but that it may be perceived by the soul, as really as any sensible impression made upon the body. But to disprove this the doctor quotes our Lord's allusion to the wind in the third chapter of St. John, which is one of the best texts he could urge to prove it. For if the analogy of our Lord's discourse be carried on, we shall find it amounts to this much: that although the operations of the Spirit of God can no more be accounted for than how the wind cometh and where it goeth; yet they may be as easily felt by the soul as the wind may be felt by the body.

"But, says the doctor, 'These men have no proof to offer for their *inward* manifestations.' What proof, my lord, does the doctor require? Would he have us raise dead bodies? Have we not done greater things than these? I speak with all humility. Has not God, by our ministry, raised many dead souls to a spiritual life? Verily, if men will not believe the evidence God has given that He sent us, neither would they believe though one rose from the dead.

"Besides, my lord, the doctor charges us with things we are entire strangers to, — such as denying men the use of God's creatures; and encouraging abstinence, prayer, etc., to the neglect of the duties of our station. Lord, lay not this sin to his charge!

"Again, my lord, the doctor represents as my opinion concerning Quakers in general, that which I only meant of those I conversed with in particular. But the doctor, and the rest of my reverend brethren, are welcome to judge me as they please. Yet a little while, and we shall all appear before the great Shepherd of our souls. There, there, my lord, shall it be determined who are His true ministers, and who are only wolves in sheep's clothing. Our Lord, I believe, will not be ashamed to *confess us publicly in that day*. I pray God, we may all approve ourselves such faithful ministers of the New Testament, that we may be able to lift up our heads with boldness!

"As for declining the work in which I am engaged, my blood runs chill at the very thoughts of it. I am as much convinced it is my duty to act as I do, as I am that the sun shines at noonday. I can foresee the consequences very well. They have already, in one sense, thrust us out of the synagogues. By-and-by they will think it is doing God service to kill us. But, my lord, if you and the rest of the Bishops cast us out, our great and common Master will take us up. Though all men should deny us, yet will not He. However you may censure us as evil-doers and disturbers of the peace, yet, if we suffer for our present way of acting, your lordship, at the great day, will find that we suffer only for *righteousness' sake*. In patience, therefore, do I possess my soul. I will willingly tarry the Lord's leisure. In the meanwhile, I shall continually bear your lordship's favors upon my heart, and endeavor to behave, so as to subscribe myself,

"My Lord, your lordship's obedient son and obliged servant,

"GEORGE WHITEFIELD."

Tuesday, July 10. Preached yesterday evening, at the brickyard to about eight thousand people. Dined today with my honored fellow-laborer, Mr. Wesley, and many other friends at Two Mile Hill, in Kingswood; and preached afterwards to several thousand people and colliers in the schoolhouse, which has been carried on so successfully, that the roof is ready to be put up. The design, I think, is good. Old as well as young are to be instructed. A great and visible alteration is seen in the behavior of the colliers. Instead of cursing and swearing, they are heard to sing hymns about the woods; and the rising generation, I hope, will be a generation of Christians. They seem much affected by the Word, and attend the churches and societies when Mr. Wesley is absent from them. The prospect of their future welfare filled me with joy. They took a most affectionate leave of me.

Went immediately after sermon was ended, with Mr. Wesley and several other friends, to Bath, and preached there to about three thousand people at seven o'clock in the evening. It rained a little all the while, but the people were patient and attentive, and I never had such power given me to speak to the polite scoffers before. Oh, that the scales were removed from the eyes of their minds!

Heard today that the town clerk of Bristol did my brother Wesley and me the honor, to desire the grand jury, at their quarter sessions, to prevent our meetings, and to have the riot act read; but they did not regard him — nay one, who was called to serve on the petty jury offered to subscribe to any fine, rather than do anything against us, who, he said, were true servants of Jesus Christ.

BATH AND BRISTOL: Wednesday, July 11. Preached at eleven in the morning, to a larger audience than last night. Hastened to Bristol, and preached in the evening at Baptist Mills to a large congregation. It rained much, but, blessed be God, the people's hearts are so far influenced by the Gospel of Christ, that they care but little whether it rains or shines.

After this, my brother Wesley and I went to the women's and men's Societies, settled some affairs, and united the two leading Societies together. How can I be thankful enough to God, for sending me here to see that the seed has been sown in good ground, and that by the ministry of Mr.

Wesley it has received great increase. May it still increase with all the increase of God.

Thursday, July 12. Was busied most of the day in preparing a sermon for the press *On the Indwelling of the Spirit*, which I would recommend to all. Preached, in the evening, to eight or nine thousand people in the bowling-green; and afterwards spent an hour most delightfully with some Christian friends. Blessed be God for the communion of saints. Oh, when shall I be translated to the communion of the spirits of just men made perfect! As the hart panteth after the water brooks, so doth my soul long after that perfect fellowship with the sons of God.

Friday, July 13. Preached my farewell sermon, at seven in the morning, to a weeping and deeply affected audience. My heart was full, and I continued nearly two hours in prayer and preaching. The poor people shed many tears, and sent up thousands of prayers on my behalf, and would scarce let me go away. Their mites they most cheerfully contributed for the schoolhouse at Kingswood. Blessed be God for allowing me to see this increase of His mercy. Blessed be God for my coming here to behold some fruits of my labors. Many souls have been strengthened and comforted, many convinced of sin, and myself also, more established and strong in the Lord. As oppositions abound, so do my consolations much more abound. Who is so good a master as Jesus Christ?

Dined with and took a most affectionate leave of a whole roomful of weeping friends. Set out at four o'clock, and reached Thornbury about eight in the evening. It raining exceedingly hard most part of the day, there were but few country people; however, I preached to about six hundred from a table in the street. I hope God gave His blessing.

THORNBURY AND GLOUCESTER: Saturday, July 14. Preached at eight this morning to an attentive congregation. Breakfasted at a Quaker's, and reached Gloucester, with my honored friend, Mr. John Wesley, and some others, in the afternoon. Went to the Cathedral prayers, and afterwards preached to a congregation a third part larger than I have had in this place before. Blessed be God, wherever I go, I find my audiences are always more numerous by far at the last than at the first. Lord, make me truly humble and thankful.

Sunday, July 15. Left my honored friend, Mr. Wesley, to preach to about seven thousand souls in Gloucester. Preached twice in Randwick Church, and assisted in administering the Sacrament to two hundred and seventy communicants. My body being weak, I spoke with very little power in the morning; but in the afternoon, God caused my strength to return, and I preached with much freedom in the evening at Hampton Common, where I was enabled to lift up my voice like a trumpet, and preach to about twenty thousand, all of whom behaved with great reverence and devotion. After I had done, I received fresh invitations to different places, which I proposed to comply with, if the Lord should permit. Never did I see people more eager after the milk of the Word. Their souls were much rejoiced when I told them Mr. John Wesley intended to come after to feed them. Lord, grant he may be preferred before me wherever he goes.

Monday, July 16. Slept last night at the house of Mr. E . . . s, of Ebly. Went to Tedbury, about six miles from thence, having been earnestly invited several times, and preached at noon to about four thousand people. Many, of divers denominations, came to meet me, with whom I took sweet counsel. The scoffers, before I came, had threatened to do something, but the power of God's Word overcame them. Visited, in the afternoon, Mr. O . . ., a Baptist teacher, and went afterwards, in company with several friends, to Malmesbury in Wiltshire, about three miles from Tedbury, where I had been invited by a letter, signed by fifty-two persons. At seven, I preached to about three thousand people. Much opposition had been made by the Pharisees, against my coming; and the minister, in particular, had written to the churchwarden to stop me. But he was more noble. Numbers, as I heard afterwards, who were greatly prejudiced against me by lying reports, went away convinced that I spoke the words of truth and soberness.

Tuesday, July 17. Stopped with my fellow-travelers at the house of Mr. Line, who gladly received us for our Master's sake. I had a thorn in the flesh sent to buffet me, being weak in body and deserted in mind. With great reluctance I rose and preached to about two thousand, at eight o'clock in the morning; then I retired to my bed again, with an unspeakable pressure upon my heart till noon. I was somewhat better after dinner, and much revived to see what an effectual door was likely to be opened in Wiltshire for preaching the Gospel. Went to pay my respects to the chief magistrate, who was my friend, and reached Cirencester about six in the evening.

Here also men breathed out threatenings against me, but were not empowered to put them in execution. Numbers came from neighboring towns. My congregation was as large again as when I preached here last. God enabled me, weak as I was, to speak boldly. How heavily do I drive when God takes off my chariot wheels, that I may learn to be meek and lowly in my own eyes. Lord, give me humility, or I perish.

CIRENCESTER AND ABINGDON: Wednesday, July 18. Found more than ever the truth of the wise man's saying, "Woe be to him that is alone, for when he falleth he hath not another to lift him up." Breakfasted with one Mr. H . . .; and preached at seven in the morning to about as numerous a congregation as last night. The place where I preached was exceedingly convenient. I stood in the valley, and the people on an ascent, that formed a most beautiful amphitheater. After I had done, God gave me some most extraordinary instances of the power of His Word.

Left Cirencester about eleven; dined at Letchlade, where the inhabitants were very importunate to hear me, would time have permitted. I reached Abingdon, twenty-two miles from Cirencester, about seven, and preached to several thousands soon after I came in. Much opposition had been made against my coming. The landlord, whose house we offered to put up at, genteelly told us he had not room for us; and numberless prejudices had been industriously spread to prevent my success. But God strengthened me after my journey, and enabled me to speak, I trust, to the hearts of many. God's Word will make its own way, let men say what they please. Our weapons are not carnal, but mighty through the Divine Power, to the pulling down of Satan's strongholds.

ABINGDON AND BASINGSTOKE: Thursday, July 19. At the request of several well-disposed people, preached again this morning, though not to so great a number as before. A sweet power was felt among us. The hearers melted into tears under the Word. Oh, what a sudden alteration doth this foolishness of preaching make in the most obstinate hearts. 'Tis but for God to speak the word, and the lion is turned into a lamb. Oh, that we were like that dear Lamb of God, Who died to take away the sins of the world.

Breakfasted with Mr. F . . . Set out at eleven, dined at Ilsly, and reached Basingstoke about seven at night. Being languid and wearied, I lay down upon the bed soon after our coming to the inn; but soon received the news, that the landlord, one of whose children was wrought upon when I was there last, would not let us stay under his roof; upon which I immediately rose and went to another inn. The people made a mock of both me and my friends as we passed along, and shot out their arrows, even bitter words against us, and fire-rockets were thrown around the door. It was now nearly eight o'clock and too late to preach; I therefore retired from my friend, gave God thanks for accounting me worthy to suffer reproach for His Name's sake, and about an hour after, received the following letter by the hands of the constable from the mayor: —

"Basingstoke, July 19, 1739.

"Sir, — Being a civil magistrate in this town, I thought it my duty, for the preservation of the peace, to forbid you, or, at least dissuade you, from preaching here. If you persist in it, in all probability, it may occasion a disturbance, which I think it is your duty, as a clergyman, as well as mine, to prevent. If any mischief should ensue (whatever pretense you may afterwards make in your own behalf), I am satisfied it will fall on your own head, being timely cautioned by me, who am, sir, your most humble servant,

"JOHN ABBOT.

"P.S. The Legislature has wisely made laws for the preservation of the peace; therefore, I hope, no clergyman lives in defiance of them."

To this I immediately sent the following answer: —

"Honored Sir, — I thank you for your kind letter, and I humbly hope a sense of your duty, and not a fear of man, caused you to write it.

"If so, give me leave to remind you, honored sir, as a clergyman, that you ought to be not only a terror to evil-doers, but a praise to them that do well. I know of no law against such meetings as mine. If any such law exists, I believe you will think it your duty, honored sir, to apprise me of it, that I may not offend against it. If no law can be produced, as a clergyman, I think it my duty to inform you that you ought to protect, and not in any way to discourage, or permit others to disturb an assembly of people meeting together purely to worship God.

"Tomorrow, honored sir, I hear there is to be an assembly of another nature. Be pleased to be as careful to have the public peace preserved at that; and to prevent profane cursing and swearing, and persons breaking the sixth commandment, by bruising each other's bodies by cudgelling and wrestling. If you do not this, I shall rise up against you at the great day, and be a swift witness against your partiality.

"I am, honored sir, your very humble servant,

"GEORGE WHITEFIELD."

Friday, July 20. After breakfast I waited in person on the mayor, to see what law could be produced against my meetings. As soon as I began to talk with him, I perceived he was a little angry. He said, "Sir, you sneered at me in the letter you sent last night. Though I am a butcher, yet sir," said he, "I — " I replied, I honored him as a magistrate, and only desired to know what law could be produced against my preaching; in my opinion there could be none, because there was never any such thing as field-preaching before. I then instanced the trial of P . . . , the Quaker, where the jury, notwithstanding they were so hardly used, gave a verdict in favor of him. "Sir," said he, "you ought to preach in a church." "And so I would," I replied, "if your minister would give me leave." "Sir," said he, "I believe you have some sinister ends in view; why do you go about making a disturbance?" I answered, "I make no disturbance. It was hard I could not come into your town without being insulted. It was your business, sir, to wait, and if there was any riot in my meetings, then, and not till then, to interpose." He then said, "Sir, you wrote to me about the revel today — I have declared against it." "But," said I, "you ought, sir, to go and read the riot act, and put an entire stop to it." I then pressed him to show me a law against meetings, urging, that if there had been any law, they would have been stopped long since. He answered, "It was an odd way of preaching. But sir, I must go away to a fair; before you came I had written you another letter, which I will send you yet, if you please." Upon this, I thanked him, paid him the respect due to a magistrate, and took my leave. Soon after I had returned to my company, he sent me the following letter:

"Basingstoke, July 20, 1739.

"Rev. Sir, — I received your extraordinary letter, and could expect no other from so uncommon a genius.

"I apprehend your meetings to be unlawful, having no toleration to protect you in it. My apprehension of religion always was, and I hope always will be, that God is to be worshiped in places consecrated and set apart for His service; and not in brothels, and places where all manner of debauchery may have been committed; but how far this is consistent with your actions, I leave you to judge.

"As for the other assembly you were pleased to mention, 'tis contrary to my will, having never given my consent to it, nor approved of it, but discouraged it before your reverendship came to this town; and if these cudgellers persist in it, I shall set them upon the same level with you, and think you all breakers of the public peace. You very well know there are penal laws against cursing and swearing, and I could wish there were the same against deceit and hypocrisy.

"Your appearing against me as a swift witness, at the day of judgment, I must own, is a most terrible thing, and may serve as a bugbear for children, or people of weak minds; but, believe me, reverend sir, those disguises will have but little weight among men of common understanding.

"Yours,
"JOHN ABBOT.

"P.S. I told you I had a letter written. I make bold to send it."

To this I sent the following answer: —

"Basingstoke, July 20, 1739.

"Honored Sir, — Does Mr. Mayor do well to be angry? Alas! what evil have I done? I honor you as a magistrate; but, as a minister, I am obliged to have no respect of persons. Your *apprehending* my meetings to be unlawful, does not make them so. There is no need of a toleration to protect me, when I do not act unconformable to any law, civil or ecclesiastical. Be pleased to prove that my meetings are schismatical, seditious, or riotous, and then I will submit.

"But you say they are upon unconsecrated ground. Honored sir, give me leave to inform you, that God is not now confined to places, but seeketh such to worship Him, who worship in spirit and in truth. Where two or three are gathered together in Christ's Name, there will Christ be in the midst of them. The Church, by our ministers in their prayer before their sermons, is defined to be, not the church walls, but a congregation of Christian people. Such is mine.

"As for judging me, to my own Master I stand or fall. At His dreadful tribunal I will meet you; and then you shall see what is in the heart of, honored sir, your very humble servant,

"GEORGE WHITEFIELD."

About eight o'clock I went into a field, loaned me by Mr. H . . . ; and though one said, I should not go out of Basingstoke alive if I preached there, and another said, the drum should beat just by me, yet I had little or no interruption, and God gave me power to speak against reveling; and those few scoffers that were there, were not able to gainsay or resist it. As I came from the field, passing through the churchyard, the boys, headed by some of the baser sort, saluted me as before, calling me strange names, which, I trust, was received in the spirit of our dear Master.

After this, I prayed and sang psalms, at the inn, with some few disciples, and then took my leave. As I passed by on horseback, I saw a stage built for the cudgellers and wrestlers; and as I rode further, I met divers coming to the revel, which affected me so much, that I had no rest in my spirit. And therefore, having asked counsel of God, though I had gone above a mile from the town, I could not bear to see so many dear souls for whom Christ died, ready to perish, and no minister or magistrate interpose, so I told my dear fellow-travelers that I was resolved to follow the example of Howell Harris in Wales, and to bear my testimony against such lying vanities, let the consequences, as to my own person, be what they would. They immediately consenting, I rode back to the town, got upon the stage erected for the wrestlers, and began to show them the error of their ways. Many seemed ready to hear what I had to say; but one, more zealous for his master than the rest, and fearing conviction every time I so much as attempted to speak, set the boys upon repeating their huzzas. I felt willing to be offered up, if I might save some of those to whom I was about to speak. While I was on the stage, one struck me with his cudgel.

At last, finding the devil would not permit them to give me audience, I got off, and after much thronging and pushing me, I mounted my horse, with the inward satisfaction, that I had now begun to attack the devil in his strongest holds, and had borne my testimony against the detestable diversions of this generation. Ye magistrates, who are called gods in scripture, why sleep you? Why do you bear the sword in vain? Why count me a troubler of Israel, and why say I teach people to be idle, when you connive at, if not subscribe to, such meeting as these, which not only draw people from their bodily work, but directly tend to destroy their precious and immortal souls. Surely I shall appear against you at the judgment seat of Christ; for these diversions keep people from true Christianity as much as paganism itself. I doubt not, it will require as much courage and power to divert people from these things, as the Apostles exerted in converting the heathen from their dumb idols. However, in the strength of my Master, I will now enter the lists, and begin an offensive war with Satan, and all his host. If I perish, I perish; but I shall have the testimony of a good conscience, and be free from the blood of all men.

From Basingstoke I intended to go to Windsor, but not having sent to any in that place, and longing for a little retirement, I went to Staines, and spent some hours in sweet fellowship with my dear fellow-travelers. O what a blessed thing it is for brethren to dwell together in unity!

LONDON: Saturday, July 21. Set out a little after four in the morning, and reached London by breakfast time. Settled my affairs, and preached in the evening to upwards of ten thousand at Kennington Common. The Word sank deep into their hearts; great numbers melted into tears, and my own heart overflowed with love to them. Blessed be God for what has been done here since I left London, by my honored friend and fellow-laborer, Mr. Charles Wesley. Surely, we can see the fruits of our labors. All love, all glory be to God, for giving so great an increase!

Sunday, July 22. Ever since I was abused at Basingstoke, I have had sweet communion with God. When men cast us out, then does Jesus Christ chiefly take us up. Who would not be a Christian? There is nothing I desire on earth in comparison with that. Received a letter from Mr. Ralph Erskine, of Scotland. Some may be offended at my corresponding with him, but I dare not but confess my Lord's disciples. Had a pressing invitation to come into Lincolnshire. Preached, at seven in the morning, to about twenty thousand at Moorfields. A greater power than ever was among us. Scoffers and curious persons daily drop off; most who come now, I hope, do not attend out of curiosity. Never were souls more melted down by the power of God's words; never did people offer their mites more willingly. I collected 24 pounds, 17s. for the school-house being erected at Kingswood, and all seemed solicitous to express their affection. Ye scoffers, ye blind Pharisees, come and see, and then call these tumultuous, seditious assemblies, if you can. Would to God, they behaved so decently in any church in London!

Went to St. Paul's, and received the Blessed Sacrament; preached in the evening, at Kennington Common, to about thirty thousand hearers, and collected 15 pounds 15s. 6d. for the colliers. God gave me great power, and I never opened my mouth so freely against the letter-learned clergymen of the Church of England. Every day do I see the necessity of speaking out more and more. God knows my heart, I do not speak out of resentment. I heartily wish all the Lord's servants were prophets; I wish the Church of England was the joy of the whole earth; but I cannot see her sinking into papistical ignorance, and refined Deism, and not open my mouth against those who, by their sensual, lukewarm lives, and unscriptural superficial doctrines, thus cause her to err. O Lord, send out, we beseech Thee, send out Thy light and Thy truth.

Monday, July 23. This day I received the following letter from the Quaker at Basingstoke, at whose house I lodged: —

Basingstoke, July 21, 1739.

"My Dear Friend, — When I yesterday went up to thy inn, and found thee just gone, I was sorry that I missed an opportunity, both of taking my leave of thee, and expressing the sense I had of the power and presence of God with thee, especially in the latter part of thy sermon, and in thy prayer after it. However, I am truly glad that thou wert preserved out of the hands of cruel and unreasonable men. Thou heardest of the threatenings of many; but the malice of some went further. For hadst thou gone to my friend H . . . to bed, or elsewhere towards that part of the town, which I believe was expected, there were ten or twelve men lying in wait to do thee a private mischief. I know this, by the testimony of one of those very men, who boasted to me, 'We would have given him a secret blow, and prevented his making disturbances.' This confession he made to me in the warmth of his zeal, thinking, perhaps, that I could hate at least, if not destroy (like him) all that were not of my own party.

"O thy noble testimony against the profaneness and vanity of the age! It rejoiced me not a little. But when thou camest to the necessity, the nature, and the rewards of the new birth, thou were carried beyond thyself. I, for one, am a monument of free grace and mercy. O God, how boundless is Thy love! I have often drunk of the spiritual Rock, and been a witness of the joys of God's salvation; of that sweet presence of Christ, which carries men above the fear of the world, and enables them to overcome the world; that baptizeth into the spirit and nature of the Son of God, and maketh disciples indeed. It is a sense of God ever near, the influences of His quickening Spirit, that is only able to deter from evil, crucify the old nature, create again to God, and perform His good and acceptable will. This will make a thorough reformation, beginning at the heart, sanctifying it, guarding it, and making it a holy temple for the Holy Spirit to dwell in; then producing holy thoughts, longings after Divine enjoyments, love, joy, solidity, watchfulness, etc.

"But, why this to thee? Thou hast drunk deep of Divine love; but I know that the good experiences of God's children are often causes of mutual comfort. I have often been sensible of it myself, and therefore, not only thus privately, but publicly I have been strengthened by telling to others, that God is good, and that He has done great things for my soul. Ministers not thus qualified, and thus sent, may indeed be ministers of those who sent them, but ministers of Christ they cannot be.

"May we, my dear friend, though absent in body, be present in spirit in Him Who is Omnipresent. May we unitedly go on in the cause of our common Lord and Master, to promote His honor in winning souls to Him! May we bear a faithful and undaunted testimony to Him before all men in the midst of a perverse generation. May we not flinch, but declare the truth as it is in Jesus, not daubing nor daring to make the way to the Kingdom of God wider than it is. And may we finally be received up into the mansions of glory, there to live with all the righteous generations; with those who have washed their garments white in the blood of the Lamb, and with those who have laid down their lives for the testimony of Jesus, and to sing with them hallelujahs, glory and praise, forever and ever. May the Ancient of Days, the Alpha and Omega, keep thee in His arms, direct thee by His Spirit, support, comfort, and watch over thee, is the fervent prayer of thine in great sincerity,

"J. PORTSMOUTH."

My friend, Mr. William Seward, received also a letter from his brother, in which were the following paragraphs: —

"I had a letter per last post from Mr. . . , wherein he speaks of one Mr. . . , of Corpus Christi College, whom his uncle, a clergyman, had entirely discarded, and concerning whom he had written to the College to expel for his methodistical notions.

"The old clerk at Bretforton, whom I before spoke of, having heard Mr. Whitefield at Badsey, was so affected, that he told me, he had no rest in his spirit; but after searching the Church Homilies, Articles, etc., and finding the doctrine every way agreeable to them, he met with the landlord of Contercup, who discoursing about Mr. Whitefield, told him, he had some old books that set forth the very same doctrine. Soon after this he went to work, being a tailor by trade, and asking for one of these books, (the others being loaned out), he said he had not read above a page or two, before the truth broke in upon his soul like lightning. He said he could not go on with his work with any satisfaction, but his fingers itched to be at the book again, which the man loaned him to take home. A few days after, he got the other, which strengthened and confirmed him. He says, the Gospel appears to him as though he had never read a line in it before; and it is a greater miracle to him, that he, an old sinner, with one foot in the grave, should be called at these years, than if he had seen the dead raised.

"By what I can learn, he always bore a fair character, and was esteemed by his neighbors; but is now threatened with the loss of his bread, for coming to Badsey Society, and declaring his testimony to the truth of Mr. Whitefield's doctrine, or rather, I should say, the doctrine of the Gospel. The books he met with are very old, and were thrown by as waste paper from a clergyman's library, that was sold after his death, whereby the Contercup man met with them, and they seemed providentially reserved for his use."

Persons wonder at me, because I talk of persecution, now that the world has become Christian; but alas! were Jesus Christ to come down from Heaven at this time, He would be treated as formerly. And whoever goes forth to preach the Gospel in His spirit, must expect the same treatment as His first Apostles met with. Lord, prepare us for all events.

Preached this evening at Hackney Marsh, to about two thousand people. I prayed and discoursed for above two hours, and with greater demonstration of the Spirit than ever. Every day have I more and more reason to rejoice in what God has done for my own and others' souls. Thousands at the great day will have reason to bless God for field-preaching. Then our Pharisees will believe; but Lord, grant the veil may be taken from their hearts, and the scales from their eyes, before that dreadful day! For then convictions will come too late.

Tuesday, July 24. Dispatched my private affairs, and preached in the evening at Kennington Common, to about fifteen thousand.

Wednesday, July 25. Preached this evening at Edmonton. The congregation was large and attentive, and I rejoiced in having an opportunity of offering salvation freely to the rich. Oh, that all in high stations were rich towards God!

Thursday, July 26. Preached to upwards of ten thousand at Hackney Marsh, where I had appointed purposely to discourse because there was to be a horse-race in the same field. I had the pleasure of bearing my testimony against such unchristian entertainments. Very few left the sermon to see the race, and some of those soon returned, to whom I took the occasion of speaking to. By the help of God, I will still go on to attack the devil in his strongest holds. The common people go to these diversions for want of knowing better. If we can once draw them from these, their minds will be better prepared to receive the Gospel. Prosper, O Lord, this work.

Friday, July 27. Preached at Kennington Common, to my usual number of hearers. Went to Lewisham.

Saturday, July 28. Visited the family of Justice Delamotte at Blendon, where we exhorted and built up each other in the knowledge and fear of God. Preached at Blackheath in the evening, and came home rejoicing. The bills which are sent to me, plainly prove that God has worked on numbers of souls. At the judgment day, we shall see what good has been done by this foolishness of preaching. Many, I believe, come to the fields to worship the Father in spirit and in truth. God seeketh such to worship Him.

Sunday, July 29. Preached this morning in Moorfields, to a much larger congregation than we had last Sunday, and collected 24 pounds, 9s. for the school at Kingswood. Received the Sacrament at St. Paul's, and preached at Kennington Common in the evening, where 20 pounds was collected. God sent us a little rain, but that only washed away the curious hearers. Nearly thirty thousand stood their ground, and God, I believe, watered them with the dew of His heavenly blessing. A visible alteration for the better is made in the people daily, and it would be endless to recount how many come after preaching under strong convictions of their lost estate. God has begun, God will carry on the good work in their souls.

Monday, July 30. Was busied all the morning in directing those to believe in Jesus Christ, who came asking me what they should do to be saved? Preached at Plaistow, about six miles from London. An uncommon power was in the congregation. My heart was much enlarged, and I returned home rejoiced that the Lord Jesus was pleased still to manifest Himself more and more among us.

Tuesday, July 31. Preached at Newington, near Hackney, to about twenty thousand people, from Genesis 3:15. I hope the Seed of the woman is now bruising the serpent's head. Amen, Lord Jesus, Amen.

Wednesday, August 1. Preached this evening at Marylebone Fields, to near thirty thousand, and went afterwards to take my leave of Fetter Lane Society. We parted in love, and I hope the next time we meet, we shall be in, or, at least, nearer Heaven.

Thursday, August 2. Preached at Newington, to upwards of twenty thousand people, and came home rejoicing to see what a great work God has done in this city. Scoffers seem afraid to show their heads, being frequently overpowered by God's Word. I hope the time is coming which the prophet speaks of: "Behold ye despisers, and wonder, and perish; for I will work a work in your days, which you shall in no wise believe, though a man declare it unto you."

Friday, August 3. Spent the day in completing my affairs and taking leave of my dear friends. Preached in the evening, to nearly twenty thousand, at Kennington Common. I chose to discourse on St. Paul's parting speech to the elders at Ephesus, Acts 20, at which the people were much affected, and almost prevented my making any application. Many tears were shed when I talked of leaving them. I concluded with a suitable hymn, but could scarcely get to the coach for the people thronging me, to take me by the hand, and give me a parting blessing.

And here I cannot but finish this part of my Journal with a word or two of exhortation to my dear brethren, whoever they are, whom God shall stir up to go forth into the highways and hedges, into the lanes and streets, to compel poor sinners to come in. You see, my dear brethren, what great things God has already done. I do not know how many have come to me under strong convictions of their fallen estate, and what numbers of bills I have received from persons seeking Christ, desiring to be wakened to a sense of sin, and giving thanks for the benefits God has imparted to them by my ministry. Letters of invitation have been sent me from different parts of the kingdom. O my brethren have compassion on our dear Lord's Church, which He has purchased with His own blood. Suffer none of them to be as sheep having no shepherd, or with worse than none, those blind leaders of the blind, who let them perish for lack of knowledge, and are no better than wolves in sheeps' clothing. If you are found faithful, you must undergo strong persecution. A person told me, nothing but the fear of strengthening my interest, kept off the storm. The enmity of the natural man is so great against God, that if the good work, which is begun is carried on, it will soon break through all restraints, though thereby our enemies will confound themselves.

Oh, arm people against a suffering time: exhort them always to be obedient to the higher powers; remind them again and again, that our Lord's Kingdom is not of this world, and that it does not become Christians to resist the powers that are ordained of God, but patiently to suffer for the truth's sake. At present God calls me to trials of a different nature; but I am persuaded, ere long, it will be given me not only to believe, but also to suffer for our Lord's sake. Oh let us strive together in our prayers, that we may fight the good fight of faith, that we may have that wisdom which cometh from above, that we never suffer for our own faults, but only for righteousness' sake. Then will the spirit of Christ and of glory rest upon our souls, and being made perfect by suffering here, we shall be qualified to reign eternally with Jesus Christ hereafter. Amen. Amen.

Eternal, Universal Lord,
    Maker of Heaven and earth art Thou,
All things sprang forth t'obey Thy word,
    Thy powerful word upholds them now.

Why then with unavailing rage,
    Did heathen with Thy people join,
And impotently fierce engage,
    To execute their vain design?

Indignant kings stood up t'oppose
    The Lord, and His Messiah's reign,
And earth's confederate rulers rose,
    Against their God in counsel vain.

Surely against Thy Holy Son,
    (Son of Thy love and sent by Thee,
One with th'anointing Spirit, One,
    With Thy co-equal Majesty).

Herod and Pilate both combin'd,
    Thy sov'reign purpose to fulfil,
Gentiles and Jews unconscious join'd,
    T'accomplish Thy eternal will.

And now their idle fury view,
    And now behold their threatenings, Lord,
Behold Thy faithful servants too,
    And strengthen us to speak Thy word.

Embolden'd by Thy outstretch'd Arm,
    Fill us with confidence Divine,
With heavenly zeal our bosom warm.
    That all may own the work is Thine;

May see the tokens of Thy hand,
    Its sovereign grace, its healing pow'r,
Nor more their happiness withstand,
    And fight against their God no more.

Now let their opposition cease,
    Now let them catch the quick'ning flame,
And forc'd to yield, the signs increase,
    The wonders wrought, by Jesus' Name.

THE FIFTH JOURNAL

FROM WHITEFIELD'S DEPARTURE AFTER THE EMBARGO TO HIS ARRIVAL IN SAVANNAH, GEORGIA

(AUGUST 1739 – JANUARY 1740)

LEWISHAM, DEPTFORD AND BLENDON: Saturday, August 4. Stayed last night at the house of Mrs. S .... Went in the morning to Deptford; prayed, sang psalms, and gave a word of exhortation at two or three houses. Returned to dine with Mrs. S ... Expounded to a room full of people. Preached at Blackheath to about ten thousand; and returned to Blendon. Oh, that my mouth was ever filled with the Divine praise!

BLENDON, BEXLEY AND BLACKHEATH: Sunday, August 5. Expounded, prayed, and sang psalms at Mr. Delamotte's door, with many who came last night from London. Read prayers and assisted in administering the Sacrament to several hundred communicants at Bexley Church. Preached in the afternoon, to about fifteen hundred, in Justice Delamotte's yard; and again in the evening, to about twenty thousand, at Blackheath. It rained, but few were driven away by it. God watered us with the dew of His heavenly blessing. Oh that we may all grow in grace, and in the knowledge of our Lord and Savior Jesus Christ.

BLENDON AND CHATHAM: Monday, August 6. Spent the former part of the day at Blendon, and preached in the evening at Chatham, about eighteen miles from thence, to nearly twelve thousand people. I never observed more decency and order in any place at my first preaching, than at that. Had a conference after sermon with one, who I fear with some others, maintained antinomian principles. From such, may all that know them turn away; for though, (to use the words of our Church Article) good works, which are the fruits of faith, cannot put away our sins, or endure the severity of God's judgment (that is, cannot justify us), yet they follow after justification, and do spring out necessarily of a true and lively faith, insomuch that by them a lively faith may be as evidently known as a tree discerned by the fruit.

CHATHAM, BLENDON, BLACKHEATH AND LEWISHAM: Tuesday, August 7. Left Chatham early this morning. Dined at Blendon, and preached in the evening at Blackheath. It rained very much the whole day; but there were about two thousand present. I discoursed on the conversion of Zacchaeus the publican. I hope there was joy in Heaven over some of my hearers repenting. Lord, in doing Thy commandments there is great reward.

LEWISHAM, DEPTFORD AND BLACKHEATH: Wednesday, August 8.

Slept at Lewisham. At Deptford, went on board the ship; which we now hallowed by the Word of God, and prayer. Preached at Blackheath to nearly twenty thousand people, on the Pharisee and the Publican. I felt I could not but take notice of a fundamental mistake his lordship of London was guilty of, in a Pastoral Letter published this day; for in it he exhorts his clergy, so to explain the doctrine of justification by faith *alone*, as to make our good works a *necessary condition* of it. St. Paul, in his Epistle to the Galatians, pronounces a dreadful anathema against the maintainers of such doctrines.

ON BOARD SHIP, LEWISHAM AND BLACKHEATH: Thursday, August 9. Preached at Blackheath to a very large congregation, and went and lay on board the ship, in order to be ready to finish my affairs in the morning. Several companies of friends came to see me, and some continued with me all night. In answer to their prayers, I doubt not but we shall be as safe as Noah in the ark. Every place is alike to those who have the presence of God with them.

> Heaven is, dear Lord, where'er Thou art,
> O never then from me depart;
> For to my soul 'tis hell to be,
> But for one moment void of Thee.

LEWISHAM, BLACKHEATH AND BLENDON: Friday, August 10. Finished my ship business, and preached in the evening at Blackheath, to a greater congregation than ever. The people expecting it would be the last time, were much affected; but great rejoicing was heard among them, when I told them I should continue to preach till Monday. God has made Himself a willing people in the day of His power. O all ye servants of the Lord, bless ye the Lord, praise Him and magnify Him forever.

BLENDON AND BLACKHEATH: Saturday, August 11. Began in the spirit of meekness to answer the Bishop of London's Pastoral Letter. Continued all day at Blendon. Preached in the evening at Blackheath, and returned to Blendon with an earnest longing for the approaching sabbath. O how I long for that rest which awaits the children of God.

BLENDON, BEXLEY, BLACKHEATH AND LEWISHAM: Sunday, August 12. Preached early in the morning to some hundreds, in Justice Delamotte's yard, most of whom came there last night, singing and praising God. Read prayers, heard a truly Christian sermon from Mr. Piers, and assisted him in administering the blessed Sacrament, in his own church, to nearly six hundred communicants. Preached at three in the afternoon, to nearly three thousand, in Mr. Delamotte's yard, and to about thirty thousand at Blackheath. At each place, the people were exceedingly affected. Much devotion and reverence was to be seen during the time of the administration of the Holy Eucharist. In the afternoon at Blackheath, when I said, "Finally, brethren, farewell!" thousands immediately burst out into

206

strong crying and tears. I continued my discourse till it was nearly dark, and collected nearly 15 pounds for Kingswood School. With great difficulty I got away in a coach to Lewisham, where a hospitable entertainment had been prepared for me and my friends. Their company was sweet to my soul; but my body being weak, and God being pleased to visit me with some inward trials, I retired to rest with a deeper sense of my own vileness, than I have felt for some time.

Monday, August 13. Rose early, and hastened to Blendon. Finished, and sent to the press, my answer to his lordship's Pastoral Letter. Dined, and took leave of my dear weeping friends. Rode with many of them to Erith; took my final and sorrowful farewell, and went from there in a boat with my dear fellow travelers to Gravesend, where our ship was fallen down. In the way I was much edified by reading an extract from Bishop Hopkins' and Dr. Hammond's sermons on the doctrine of the new birth, and thought it my duty to recommend them publicly to all my friends. Blessed be God for detaining me in England by the embargo. Many others, as well as myself, I hope, have reason to rejoice thereat. Lord, teach me in all things simply to comply with Thy will, without presuming to say, even in my heart, "What doest Thou?"

> My bondage of corruption break,
> For this my spirit groans;
> Thy only will I fain would seek,
> O save me from my own!

ON BOARD THE ELIZABETH, CAPT. STEVENSON, COMMANDER, BOUND FROM ENGLAND TO PHILADELPHIA: Tuesday, August 14. Went on board about eight last night, and received the following letter from Thomas Webb, Clerk of the parish of Bretforton, Worcestershire, whom Mr. Benjamen Seward mentioned in a letter published in my last Journal.

"August 11, 1739.

"Reverend and Worthy Sir, — Although I am unknown to you in person, yet as I trust I am, by the grace of God, awakened to a new and spiritual life through the powerful influence of your ministry, I think myself under an obligation to give my testimony to the truth as it is in Jesus; and to pay my grateful acknowledgments to the freedom of that Divine Grace, which has made you so wonderfully instrumental in calling me, a most unworthy sinner, at this last hour of the day, from a state of darkness and insensibility, to the marvelous light of His glorious Gospel. The circumstances of my conversion were as follows: I heard you were to preach on Thursday, the 19th of April last, at Mr. Seward's of Badsey; and living at Bretforton, a village about a mile from there (where I have been Clerk of the Parish for about thirty years, being now in the sixty-third year of my age), my curiosity, as I then should have termed it, but as it is since evident by the consequence, *the wonderful goodness and providence of Almighty God*, let me to hear you, which I did with great attention, and was much affected.

"The next day, being Good Friday, I attended your ministry again, when you spoke with such demonstration of the Spirit and power, from these words, 'What I say unto you, I say unto all, Watch,' that I was soon convinced I was in the state of the foolish virgins, who were unprepared to meet the bridegroom, having all my life long taken up a lamp of an outward profession, thinking it sufficient that I duly and constantly attended public worship, sacraments, and the like; but I soon found, to my great confusion, that I had all my life long been offering to God the sacrifice of fools, being destitute of the pure oil of grace in the heart, which alone could make me meet to attend the marriage supper of the Lamb. The new birth, justification by faith only, the want of free will in man to do good works without the special grace of God, and the like, was as it were, a new language to me; for though I remembered the letter of these doctrines, yet the spiritual sense thereof I was an utter stranger to.

"But being very much oppressed in thought concerning those important truths which you delivered, as soon as I returned home, I searched an old Exposition of the Catechism, the Church Articles, and Book of Homilies, which I found exactly to correspond with what I had heard you deliver. Some days after this, being a tailor by trade, I was sent for to work at a little alehouse called Contercup, where (though one of the last places in which I should have expected food for the soul) the man of the house told me he had some books, which he had of one Mr. F . . ., a glazier and plumber, in Tewkesbury, who had thrown them by, in order to send them to the paper mills, as fit for no other purpose, but that he begged they might be given to him; that he had heard Mr. Whitefield, got his sermon on the new birth, and that these old books spoke to the very same purpose as Mr. Whitefield did. I desired to see one of them (the other then being lent out) the title whereof was, 'General Directions for a comfortable Walking With God,' by Robert Boulton, an old divine of our Church. I had not read long, before the light broke in upon my soul with such powerful evidence, that I was from that instant clearly convinced, and I hope, by the grace of God, determined not to know anything, save Jesus Christ, and Him crucified.

"Upon this, I avoided all carnal acquaintance and reasoning as much as possible, and constantly attended the Religious Society at Badsey, where, by hearing your sermons, and other religious exercises, I was daily strengthened and comforted. Soon after this, I got the other old book, which was so providentially preserved from the paper mill, the title whereof is as follows: 'Six Evangelical Histories. — Water turned into Wine — The Temple's Purgation — Christ and Nicodemus — John's last Testimony — Christ and the Woman of Samaria — The Ruler's Son Healed: Contained in the Second, Third, and Fourth Chapters of St. John's Gospel, opened and handled by the late faithful servant of God, Daniel Dykes, Bachelor in Divinity. Printed Anno Dom., 1617.' The old book has been a very grateful cordial to my soul; and though I have lived under the sound of the Gospel for so many years, and thought I did not want to be taught the first principles of Christianity at this age, (being, as I apprehended, well thought of, and esteemed by all my neighbors), yet I am fully convinced, that I knew nothing as I ought to know, the Gospel being to me a sealed book; but by the wonderful free grace of God, though I before had eyes and saw not, ears and heard not, I now read it as the savor of life unto life, and can say *experimentally* that the Word of God is 'a light to my feet, and a lamp to my path.'

"For this declaration of the truth, I have suffered the reproach and derision of them that were round about me; but I trust that the grace of God, which hath called me, when so old and dead in trespasses and sins, will also touch the hearts of my opposers, and work in them both to will and to do of His good pleasure. I have been even threatened with the loss of my bread for the profession of the truth, but hope God will turn the hearts of my enemies. If not, and it were His blessed will, I hope I should be enabled to lay down my life in defense of that Gospel, which I can truly say is glad tidings of great salvation to my soul; and could, I think, be content with old Simeon to cry out in transport, 'Lord, now lettest Thou Thy servant depart.' The inward light and comfort I have felt is to me more miraculous than if I had seen one risen from the dead. May the Lord prosper your labors, and make them successful to the turning of many souls to righteousness; and as you know in Whom you have believed, so I am confident you will join with me in giving all glory to that God, Who I trust hath created us anew in Christ Jesus; in Whom I most humbly and thankfully beg leave to subscribe myself, your most unworthy servant,

"THOMAS WEBB."

Rose early, and settled my family affairs. Wrote some letters. After much entreaty, went to Gravesend, and read prayers, and preached at Mitton Church, near the town. The congregation was large, I spoke with freedom, and returned to the ship by eight in the evening. I was much rejoiced at retiring from the world. Oh, that God may now fully show me myself.

> Search, try, O Lord, my reins and heart,
> If evil lurks in any part;
> Correct me where I go astray,
> And guide me in Thy perfect way.

Wednesday, August 15. Began to put those of my family, who, I thought, were prepared for it, into bands. In all, we are eight men, four women, one boy, and two children, besides Mr. Seward and myself. The conversion of one of the men was particularly remarkable. Not long since he was master of a ship, which was lost near the Gulf of Florida. Providence was pleased to throw him and his crew upon a sand-bank, where they continually expected the waters to overwhelm them. At the end of ten days they saw a ship, and made a signal of distress. The ship made towards them; the captain (now with me) went out with his boat, and begged for a passage for himself and men. It was granted him, on condition he would leave some of his crew behind upon the sand-bank; but he would not consent. At length, the other commander agreed to take all; but as soon as my friend put off his boat to fetch them, the commander of the ship made sail and left them.

All this seemed quite against, but in the end God showed it was intended for the good of my friend. After thirty days' continuance upon the sand-bank, having fitted up the boat with some planks they had taken out of a ship, which had been lost five months before, nine of them committed themselves to the Providence of God, (the others not caring to venture in so small a boat). They sailed about one hundred-and-forty leagues, and at length came to Tyby Island, ten miles off Savannah. An inhabitant being near that place, saw them, and brought them home with him. Being then in Georgia, and informed of what had happened, I invited the captain to breakfast with me, and reminded him of the goodness of God. He then seemed serious, and coming very providentially in the same ship with me, when I returned to England, God was pleased to work more effectually in his soul, and he is now returning with me to Georgia again. Many offers have been made him to go back into the world, but he chooses rather to suffer affliction with the people of God. Most of my other assistants have left good places, and are willing freely to spend and be spent for the good of the Orphan House. Several of them have already found, all I hope are seeking Christ. We seem perfectly settled already, and whatever storms God may permit to attack us without, I hope we shall have a constant calm within and among ourselves. Blessed be God, I find myself composed, and perfectly resigned, nay, much rejoiced at my present situation. Oh that I could always have no other will but God's.

Thursday, August 16. Had still greater reason to rejoice at the regulation of my family. Wrote several letters, and began to have public prayers morning and evening, and spent above an hour in examining and exhorting my fellow travelers. Went to bed almost forgetful that I had ever been out in the world. Forever blessed be God's Holy Name through Christ.

Friday, August 17. Had a brisk gale, which carried us directly through the Downs. Sent some farewell letters on shore, and rejoiced much in my happy settlement on shipboard. In the morning, most of my family were sick, and I did not entirely escape. God enabled us to give thanks, and as we came to sail more directly before the wind, our disorder gradually went off. I bless God we are in good order, and if the voyage ends as happily as it begins, we shall have abundant reason to thank God for it. Grant this, O Lord, for Thy dear Son's sake.

Saturday, August 18. Made but small advance on our way, there being but little wind, and that not very fair, till about six this evening, at which time it favored us very much. Was enlightened in reading God's Word. Had my heart warmed with a sense of His love and distinguishing mercies. I prayed several times with and for my friends, and was very earnest with God to give me grace to improve my present retirement to His glory, the good of His Church, and the edification of my own soul. My bodily strength increased, and I enjoyed such unspeakable peace and tranquility within, that I was often filled with a holy confusion, and obliged to retire.

Our Lord, I am sure, is with us in the ship. O Thou infinitely condescending God!

Sunday, August 19. Administered the Holy Sacrament early in the morning, sang a hymn, and continued in prayer for nearly an hour afterwards, on behalf of ourselves and absent friends. A spirit of love was among us. May it increase evermore and more.

Both at morning and evening prayers, the captain and ship's company attended. The remainder of the day was spent in reading, prayer, singing, and praising God. The ship continued to sail directly before the wind, at the rate of about five or six miles an hour. Most seemed sensible of, and thankful for the Divine mercies.

Monday, August 20. Fair wind all night, by which our ship was carried to the Bay of Biscay, and went before the wind at the rate of six miles an hour, almost the whole day. The wind being brisk, and a great swell coming from the Bay, most of us grew sick, and could do little else but lie down. This rejoiced me much, for I had a glorious opportunity of spending many hours in close communion with God, to ask pardon for the defects of my public ministry, and to pray for strength to prepare me for future work and trials. A sense of my actual sins and natural deformity humbled me exceedingly; and then the freeness and riches of God's everlasting love broke in with such light and power upon my soul, that I was often awed into silence, and could not speak. A dear companion was with me, and helped me to lament, pray, and give praise. Oh the comforts of religious friendship. Sanctify it, O Lord, to me, for Thy dear Son's sake.

Tuesday, August 21. Contrary winds all day, and the swell continuing, kept all my family, as well as myself, a little sickish. I conversed with God by prayer, and His Word, most of the time. Oh that by conversing with God I may be changed from glory to glory, and fitted for whatever He has appointed for me to do or suffer, during my pilgrimage here on earth.

Saturday, August 25. Had but little regular sleep since Tuesday, the wind continuing contrary. Last night it blew a gale. Most of my family still continued sick. I waited on them as well as I could, and prayed to God to make me willing to become the servant of all. Had two or three conferences with the captain of the ship, and some of his men. Read Dr. Guise's Paraphrase on the Evangelist St. Matthew, and think it the best I ever met with. Endeavored to keep close to God by watching unto prayer, for direction and help in time of need. I was frequently enlightened to see the pride and selfishness of my heart, and as frequently longed for that perfect liberty wherewith Jesus Christ sets His servants free. The sea was calmer today than before. My family grew better, and we spent nearly two hours this evening in talking of the inward state of our souls, and preparing for the reception of the Blessed Sacrament. Lord, grant that we all may have on the wedding garment.

Sunday, August 26. Administered the Holy Sacrament early in the morning. Spent the remainder of the day in reading, intercession, etc. The wind was still contrary, and the sea rough; but I had a great calm and joy in my own soul. How can I be thankful enough for the opportunities I now enjoy for improvement. Let all that is within me praise God's Holy

Name.

Monday, August 27. Had the pleasure of seeing three Jamaica ships all together, two of which spoke to us, and by them we sent news of our situation to England. Commenced writing an account of God's dealings with me from my infant days, which I have wanted to do these three years. The weather was more calm, the wind more fair, and my family better; so that I trust we shall receive strength to bear future crosses. As yet this is the most comfortable voyage I have made. Oh, that I may grow in grace and then my happiness will increase daily.

Tuesday, August 28. Calm weather and smooth sea. Rejoiced much in the good behavior of those about me. One part of the day felt some irregular passion arise in my heart, but in the evening was so visited from above, that my soul was quite confounded in the sense of the Divine goodness. This day twelvemonth I left Savannah. Lord, how hast Thou multiplied Thy mercies upon me since that time; and Thou dost still delight to honor me, and makest this retirement so sweet and profitable to my soul. My time is in Thy hands. Lord, let me have no will of my own for Thy dear Son's sake.

Friday, August 31. Very light winds for last two days, and an entire calm today. I had many inward strugglings, and could do nothing but lay down and offer my soul to God. At night, I prayed before all my family, for them and all those dear people who have recommended themselves to my prayers. Afterwards I received comfort. Oh that these inward conflicts may purge, humble, and purify my polluted, proud, and treacherous heart.

I observe these inward trials always follow inward communications. For these two days past I have been much assisted. Lest I should be puffed up, and that my mind may be prepared to receive greater degrees of light, God out of love, has sent me a thorn in the flesh. Lord, grant this loving correction of Thine may make me truly great. Amen.

Sunday, September 2. Still very light winds and fair weather. Weak and sick in body these two days. Administered the Holy Sacrament in the morning. Had public prayers as usual. All attended very orderly. Examined in the evening particularly into the inward state of my companions. I hope we grow in grace, and learn more and more to bear one another's burdens. Grant we may forever thus fulfill Thy law, O Christ.

Saturday, September 8. Advanced about a hundred leagues this week on our way to Philadelphia. Boisterous weather most part of the time, which caused many of us to be ill again. Finished the Account of my Life before mentioned. Father, bless it for Thy dear Son's sake. I groan daily to be set at liberty. Dearest Redeemer, I come unto Thee weary and heavy laden. O do Thou bring me into the full freedom of the sons of God.

Sunday, September 9. Had a comfortable Sacrament, and a love feast afterwards, at which we were not unmindful to pray for our dear friends on shore. Read public prayers, and expounded, as usual, to the ship's company in the morning; but gave a Quaker preacher (at his desire) the use of my cabin in the afternoon. He spoke chiefly concerning the false pretenses and education of those who run before they are called of God into the ministry of the Church of England. Woe be unto those who give the adversaries cause thus to speak reproachfully of us.

Saturday, September 15. Had a pleasant prospect today of some of the western islands. Gave myself to reading the Word of God, and to prayer, the greatest part of this week. Was exceedingly strengthened in reading Professor Francke's account of the Orphan House at Halle, near Glauchau. It seems, in many circumstances, to be so exactly parallel to my present undertaking for the poor of Georgia, that I trust the Orphan House about to be erected there, will be carried on and ended with the like faith and success. Amen. Amen.

Sunday, September 16. Administered the Sacrament, and had a love feast afterwards. Expounded, as usual, at Morning and Evening Prayer, and the power of God was among us. The day was calm and clear. We do not go forward much in our course.

Saturday, September 22. Underwent inexpressible agonies of soul for two or three days, at the remembrance of my sins, and the bitter consequences of them. All the while I was assured God had forgiven me; but I could not forgive myself for sinning against so much light and love. I felt something of that which Adam felt when turned out of Paradise; David, when he was convicted of adultery; and Peter, when with oaths and curses he had thrice denied his Master. At length, my Lord looked upon me, and with that look broke my rocky heart, and I wept most bitterly. When in this condition, I wondered not at Peter's running so slowly to the sepulchre, when loaded with the sense of his sin. Were I always to see myself such a sinner as I am, and as I did then, without seeing the Savior of sinners, I should not be able to look up.

This latter part of the week, blessed be the Lord, He has restored me to the light of His countenance, and enabled me to praise Him with joyful lips. Our ship having got southwardly into the trade winds, and the weather being warm, I and some of my companions, lay upon deck. We had the Holy Sacrament on the Festival of St. Matthew. We are likely to have a long voyage, yet I trust a profitable one to our souls.

Sunday, September 23. Had a sweet Sacrament, and love feast afterwards. Was much strengthened, both in my morning and evening exercises; but at night, a sense of my sins weighed me down again. Alas! how mistaken are they, who go out of the world to avoid temptations. I never am so much tempted, as when confined on shipboard: a mercy this from God to keep me in action. Luther says, he never undertook fresh work, but that he was either visited with a fit of sickness, or some strong temptation. Prayer, meditation, and temptation are necessary accomplishments, in his account, for every minister. May I follow Him, as he did Christ.

Saturday, September 29. Administered the Holy Sacrament this morning. Had fair winds, and lay upon deck with my companions the greatest part of the week. This afternoon, I was greatly strengthened by perusing some paragraphs out of a book called The Preacher, written by Dr. Edwards, of Cambridge, and extracted by Mr. Jonathan Warn, in his books entitled, The Church of England-Man turned Dissenter, and Arminianism the Backdoor to Popery. There are such noble testimonies given before that

University, of justification by faith only, the imputed righteousness of Christ, our having no free-will, etc., that they deserve to be written in letters of gold. I see more and more the benefit of leaving written testimonies behind us, concerning these important points. They not only profit the present, but will also edify the future age.

Sunday, September 30. Administered the Holy Sacrament, and had a love feast. Expounded with power in the morning to the sailors, and lent my cabin to the Quaker preacher in the afternoon. He spoke with much earnestness, but in my opinion his foundation was wrong. He seemed to make the light of conscience, and the Holy Spirit, one and the same thing, and represented Christ within, and not Christ without, as the foundation of our faith; whereas, the outward righteousness of Jesus Christ imputed to us, I believe, is the sole fountain and cause of all the inward communications which we receive from the Spirit of God. Oh, that all of that persuasion were convinced of this; till they are, they cannot preach the truth as it is in Jesus.

Saturday, October 6. Contrary winds most part of this week. Made very slow progress towards Philadelphia. Held a close band for some hours this evening with my whole family, wherein we opened our hearts, confessed our faults to, and prayed for one another. Do Thou, O great and mighty Physician of souls, hear and heal us! Amen.

Sunday, October 7. Administered the Holy Sacrament. Had a love feast, and expounded as usual. The wind blowing very fresh, the shipmen were obliged to attend to the sails, and so could not come to public worship. Sailed sometimes nearly nine miles an hour, for which we endeavored to praise the Lord. Every day more and more convinces me that the Lord will fulfill the desires of them that fear Him. He is the Father of mercies; He is the God of all consolations; He can create comfort out of nothing, and bring light and order out of the greatest confusion. This my soul knoweth right well. O my soul, be not slack to praise Him and love Him forever and ever!

Tuesday, October 9. This morning, our whole ship's company was brought to an allowance of bread, two biscuits a day for each person; but, blessed be God, through the bounty of friends in England, as yet my family have enough provisions. The Lord, in return, feed our benefactors with that Bread which cometh down from Heaven.

Friday, October 12. Kept a family fast this day, that we might afflict ourselves before our God, to seek a right way for us and our little ones, and for all our substance. His Divine Presence was among us, and we had good reason to hope and believe that the Lord was entreated for us. Oh, that we may find more and more reason to say so when we come on shore. I dread going into the world; but wherefore do I fear? Lord, I believe (Oh help my unbelief) that Thou wilt keep me unspotted from it.

Saturday, October 13. Still God is pleased to send us contrary winds, but very warm and pleasant weather. The power of writing has been in a great measure, taken from me, but God has been with me in reading, expounding, and other exercises of devotion. I have experienced some blessed teachings of His Holy Spirit, in convicting me of the pride, sensuality, and blindness of my own heart, and of the advantages Satan has gained over me by working on them. I have also been more enlightened to see into the mystery of godliness, God manifest in the flesh, and behold more and more of God's goodness, in letting me have this time of retirement to search my spirit. I would not have lost this voyage for a thousand worlds; it has been sweet and profitable to my soul. Lord I want to know myself and Thee. Oh let not the hurry of business, which awaits me on shore, prevent my hearing the still small voice of Thy Holy Spirit. Enable me, as Thou didst Thy servant Enoch, whether in public or private life, to walk with Thee, my God.

Sunday, October 14. Felt God's power with us, both at Sacrament and public worship, morning and evening. Was enlarged in intercession, and had reason to believe there was sweet communion kept up between us and our friends on shore. The assurance of their prayers often lifts up my hands when they hang down, and strengthens my feeble knees. The prospect of the many changes and trials, which I must necessarily be exposed to and undergo, sometimes fills me with fear and trembling; but when I reflect that God has stirred up the hearts of His servants to pray for me, my fears vanish. Methinks, I could then leap into a burning, fiery furnace, or bear to be thrown into a den of devouring lions. Lord, make me thus minded in the hour of trial. My dear friends, continue to pray for me, that my faith fail not.

Saturday, October 20. On Tuesday and Wednesday had the roughest weather we have yet met with; but the latter part of the week has been warm and calm. All our fresh livestock of every kind is now gone, but through the Divine bounty in raising us friends, we have not only food enough for ourselves, but some to spare for the ship's company. I experience fresh teachings from God's Holy Spirit, and have received some remarkable answers to prayer, both in respect to myself and family. The Lord is pleased to fill me out of His Divine fulness, and to show me more of the glories of the upper world. I can never be thankful enough for this sweet retreat. How wonderfully does the great and infinitely wise God cause everything to work together for our good. I want a thousand tongues to praise Him. Let every thing that hath breath praise the Lord.

Saturday, October 27. Came into soundings on Sunday last; saw land on Monday, and were within a few leagues of Cape-Lopen, which opens into the Bay where we are bound; but Providence was pleased to keep us back by contrary winds. Met with a Jamaica brig on Thursday, and had an opportunity of sending a packet by her to my dear friend Mr. Noble, of New York. Came within sight of the land again today, but still are kept back. Our provisions grow scanty, the people are put to an allowance of about half-a-pound of beef for each in a day, and we have diminished our family stock in helping them. However, we have got plenty of water, and very fair weather. The Lord has been especially gracious unto me, as He always is in the time of any necessity. I have abundant reason to cry out, "Surely the Lord is in this place."

   Lo! God is here! My soul adore
    And own how dreadful is this place;
   Let all within thee feel His power,
    In silence bow before His face;
   To Him let all thy thoughts arise,
   Ceaseless accepted Sacrifice.

   Sunday, October 28. I have been engaged in writing my extempore sermon on the marriage at Cana. Though I have well drunk of Divine comforts since my retirement already, yet I may say with the governor of the feast, "Lord, Thou has kept the good wine until now." Hasten that time, O Lord, when I shall drink it new in Thy heavenly Kingdom.

   Monday, October 29. Had an opportunity offered me today of giving a few sermons, and something out of my little stock of provisions to a captain of a sloop and his company, who had been driven to great extremity. Oh how gently does God deal with me and mine. How has He considered our weakness, and not permitted us to fall into great dangers or wants. Blessed be His Name forevermore. Amen.

PENNSYLVANIA – LEWIS TOWN: Tuesday, October 30. Had sweet communion with God last night. Prayed with, exhorted, and solemnly recommended my family to the grace of our Lord Jesus, expecting to go on shore this morning. Being near Cape-Lopen, a pilot came on board, in whose boat, brother Seward, myself, and another dear friend, went to Lewis Town, in order that we might go to Philadelphia by land, and get a house in readiness before the ship arrived at the place. When we reached Lewis Town about evening, I took the first opportunity of retiring, to vent my heart in praises and thanksgiving for His abundant mercies conferred on me and mine. Oh, how can I be thankful enough for this blessed voyage! I have been on board just eleven weeks, but they have seemed to me only as so many days. My knowledge, I trust, in spiritual things has been increased, my understanding enlightened, and my heart much enlarged. The remembrance of my humiliations is sweet unto my soul, and the freedom which God has given me over some darling failings, fills me with joy unspeakable and full of glory.

   I cannot say any remarkable conversions have been wrought on board; but many have had strong convictions. Lord, cause them to end in sound conversions. Amen. But to return. About five in the evening, we landed at Lewis Town, situated in the southern part of the Province of Pennsylvania, and about one hundred-and-fifty measured English miles from Philadelphia. Most of the houses are built of wood; it is not above half as big, but more plentiful, in respect of provision, than Savannah in Georgia. We had not been long in the inn, before God showed us He had prepared our way; for news had been brought a fortnight ago of my coming here, and two or three of the chief inhabitants being apprized of my arrival, came and spent the evening with us, and desired me to give them a sermon on the morrow, which I promised to do. We supped together, and after prayers, and singing with the family, I and my dear companions went to rest, admiring more and more the goodness and Providence of the All-wise God. He is the Great Householder of the whole world, and I look upon all places and persons as so many little parts of His great family. I pray to Him before I go, and I find in answer to my prayer He always commands some or other of His household to take care of, and provide for me. As there is here the same sun, so there is here the same God — in America as in England. I bless God all places are equal to me, so that I am where God would have me to be. I hope I shall never account myself at home till I arrive at my Heavenly Father's house above. My heart is there already. I long to shake off this earthly tabernacle! It sadly confines my soul. However, I desire patiently to tarry till my blessed change comes! I would not desire to reign till I have suffered with my Master. Heaven will be doubly sweet when I am worn out with distresses and persecutions for the sake of Jesus Christ. Lord, grant that I may be continually looking up to the glory which is to be revealed hereafter, and then deal with me as it seemeth good in Thy sight, during my pilgrimage here.

> If rough and thorny be my way,
>   My strength proportion to my day;
> 'Till toil and grief, and pain shall cease,
>   Where all is calm, and joy, and peace.

Wednesday, October 31. Spent the morning in writing, and sent some provisions on board for my fellow travelers. Wrote some letters, and preached at two in the afternoon, to a serious and attentive congregation. Persons of different denominations were present; and the congregation was larger than might be expected in so small a place, and at so short notice. After sermon, the High Sheriff, Collector, and chief men of the place, came and took leave of me; and by their means we were provided with horses and a guide for our journey at a reasonable expense. About five in the evening we left Lewis Town, and rode very pleasantly near twenty-seven miles through the woods. At ten, we called at what they call a tavern, which was not very commodious; but the host and hostess were plain, well-meaning people. They made us a cake of unleavened bread, let us have a little cider, and a few eggs, and we went to bed rejoicing in all the mercies of God. I know not when I have felt more intenseness of love, peace, and joy in my soul since I left England. How does God delight to visit us when we are out of the world. Oh that my heart may be made meet for such a Divine Guest to reside in! Amazing condescension that the High and Lofty One that inhabiteth eternity should condescend to dwell in earthly tabernacles! What shall I say unto Thee, O Thou preserver of men. I am lost in wonder. A sense of Thy mercies strikes me dumb.

> A guilty, weak and helpless worm,
>   Into Thy arms I fall;
> Be Thou my Strength and Righteousness,
>   My Jesus and my All.

Thursday, November 1. Set out from our little inn about eight; dined at Dover, a small town (nineteen miles distant from our lodging), from where (having left a few books), we rode as pleasantly and with as much ease as though we were riding through Hyde Park. About eight in the evening, we came to a more convenient inn, nearly fifty miles distant from the place where we stopped last night. Our Lord was with us as we came on our way. Our hearts burned within us while we talked to one another in psalms and hymns and spiritual songs. Oh how gloriously must the children of Israel have passed through the wilderness, when they saw God's Presence go along with them. Lord, let it always accompany us, Thy unworthy servants, in as sure though not in the same visible manner; for without it we can do nothing.

Friday, November 2. Rode nearly sixty miles without fatigue, and reached Philadelphia before eleven at night. As I traveled, I observed the country was more and more open, and many fruitful plantations lay on each side of the road; so that I frequently thought I was, as it were, in England. Going abroad, if duly improved, cannot but help to enlarge our ideas, and give us exalted thoughts of the greatness and goodness of God. Lord, enable me to learn this, and every other good lesson for Thy dear Son's sake.

PHILADELPHIA: Saturday, November 3. Delivered the letters committed to my charge. Went on board the *Elizabeth* to see my family, who arrived last night. Visited the Proprietor, Commissary, and some others, who received me very civilly. Met with some gracious souls, who discoursed with me concerning the things which belong to the Kingdom of God. Hired a house at a very cheap rate, and was entirely settled in it before night. Methinks going thus from place to place with my friends, somewhat resembles the patriarch Abraham's frequent removes, when called to leave his kindred and his native country. Oh that, like him, we may erect an altar for God wherever we go! Blessed be His Holy Name! He hath sent His angel before us to prepare our way. All things have been ordered for us far above our expectation, and everything is so convenient, that I fear we shall be tempted to say, "It is good for us to be here": but we must move soon, and learn hardness like good soldiers of Jesus Christ. Lord, for Thy infinite mercies' sake keep us striving till we die.

Saturday, November 4. Read prayers and assisted at the Communion in the morning. Dined with one of the churchwardens, and preached in the afternoon to a large congregation. Went in the evening to the Quakers' meeting, and felt somewhat in sympathy with the man that spoke. But I heartily wish that they would talk of an outward as well as an inward Christ; for otherwise, we make our own holiness, and not the righteousness of Jesus Christ the cause of our being accepted by God. From such doctrine may I always turn away.

Monday, November 5. Read prayers and preached to a large auditory. Dined with the other churchwarden, and had some close and edifying conversation about our justification by faith in Christ. I was visited in the afternoon by the Presbyterian minister, and went afterwards to see the

Baptist teacher, who seems to be a spiritual man; and spent part of the evening most agreeably with two Quakers. Had remarkable instances of God's answering our prayers which we put up on board ship; and that in the minutest particulars. Oh that I may watch God's particular Providence more and more! It comforts and builds up my soul. How unhappy must they be who would exclude it from the world; surely such must wander about in worse than Egyptian darkness. To live without a sense of God's particular Providence, is in effect, to live without God in the world. From such a state, good Lord deliver me.

Tuesday, November 6. Read prayers and preached in the morning, having had the use of the pulpit granted me for the whole week. Went at the invitation of its father, to the funeral of a Quaker's child; and thought it my duty, as there was a great concourse of people at the burying place, and none of the Quakers spoke, to give a word of exhortation. I hope this will be a means of making them more free in coming to hear the Word, though preached within church walls. Oh that bigotry and prejudice were banished from the Christian world: Lord, let it not be once named among us, as becometh saints. Amen.

Was visited again in the evening by the Presbyterian and Baptist preachers, who were much rejoiced to hear Jesus Christ preached in the Church. While I was conversing with them, some women came desiring to be admitted to prayers with my family. Looking on this as from Providence, I called them up, and felt much enlargement of heart in exhorting them, and pouring out my heart before God in their behalf. Many came up afterwards, whom I desired, if they thought proper, to come again every night. Who knows but the Lord may be about to open a yet more effectual door? O prepare me to do Thy will, O God.

Wednesday, November 7. Read prayers and preached in the church. Dined with Mr. Penn, the proprietor, and prayed with and gave a word of exhortation to more than a roomful of people, who came, as last night, to hear the Gospel of Christ. I found much liberty of spirit; but having taken cold, was obliged to leave off sooner than otherwise I should have done. However, in the midst of the weakness and disorder of my body, seeing people come so gladly to hear the Word, refreshed and comforted my soul. Lord, make it my only joy to see Thy Kingdom advanced and carried on. Amen and Amen.

Thursday, November 8. Read prayers and preached to a more numerous congregation than I have yet seen here. Dined with an honest, open-hearted, true Israelitish Quaker; and had a sweet opportunity with him and his family, of talking about Jesus Christ and Him crucified. Preached at six in the evening, from the Court House stairs to about six thousand people. I find the number that came on Tuesday to my house greatly increased and multiplied. The inhabitants were very solicitous for me to preach in another place besides the church; for it is quite different here from what it is in England. There, the generality of people think a sermon cannot be preached well without; here, they do not like it so well if delivered within the church walls. Lord, grant that I may become all things to all men, that I may gain some; and preach the Gospel in every place and in every manner, as well as to every creature.

Friday, November 9. Read prayers and preached as usual in the morning; and perceived the congregation still increased. Visited a sick person, for whom I was sent for, and felt the power of the Lord was present, both with him and those who attended him. Most wept at the preaching of faith. I was visited in a kind manner by the minister of the parish; and preached again at six in the evening, from the Court House steps. I believe there were nearly two thousand more present tonight than last night. Even in London, I never observed so profound a silence. Before I came, all was hushed exceedingly quiet. The night was clear, but not cold. Lights were in most of the windows all around us for a considerable distance. The people did not seem weary of standing, nor was I weary of speaking. The Lord endured me with power from on high. My heart was enlarged and warmed with Divine love. My soul was so carried out in prayer, that I thought I could have continued my discourse all night. After I came home, some desired to join me in family prayer; and in that exercise the Divine Presence was manifest among us. Surely God is favorable unto this people. At present they seem most gladly to receive the Word. Lord, I beseech Thee, show forth Thy glory more and more; and grant that much people in this place may be enabled to believe on Thee.

Saturday, November 10. Before it was light, there came a young person whom I had observed much affected last night, desiring to join in prayer; and after our devotions were ended, she put into my hands the following letter: —

"Oh what shall I say to express my thanks I owe to my good God, in and from you through Jesus Christ, which you have been the happy instrument of beginning in my soul; and if you have any regard for a poor, miserable, blind and naked wretch, that is not only dust, but sin, as I am confident you have, you will in nowise reject my humble request, which is that I, even I, may lay hold of this blessed opportunity of forsaking all, in order to persevere in a virtuous course of life.

"Despite not thou thine handmaiden; but, oh let me say, as Ruth the Moabitess said to her mother-in-law, 'Intreat me not to leave thee, or to return from following after thee, for where thou goest I will go, and where thou art, there will I be also, thy people shall be my people, and thy God my God.' Thus am I fully determined. I pray and beg that you will not despise thy poor forlorn and destitute fellow creature; and the Lord recompense thy work, and a full reward be given unto thee of the Lord Jesus Christ, under Whose wings I am come to trust."

Soon after came a little maid about seven years of age, telling me she had heard I took little children to Georgia, and desired me to take her. In the remaining part of the morning, several gracious souls of different communions paid me a visit, and my heart was much refreshed with their conversation. About eleven, I read prayers and preached in the church to a larger audience than before. Dined with the minister of the parish; and at my return home, was much comforted by the coming of Mr. Tennent, an old grey-headed disciple and soldier of Jesus Christ. He keeps an academy twenty miles from Philadelphia. He is a great friend of Mr. Erskine, of

Scotland, and, as far as I can find, both he and his sons are secretly despised by the generality of the Synod, as Mr. Erskine and his brethren are hated by the judicatories of Edinburgh, and, as the Methodists preachers are by their brethren in England. Though we are but few, and stand alone, as it were like Elijah, yet I doubt not, but the Lord will appear for us, as He did for that prophet, and make us more than conquerors.

About three I went to the prison, and preached on the trembling jailer. The place was crowded, and many wept. Returned home with the Swedish minister and old Mr. Tennent. Conversed with them of the things of God; and, in the evening, preached to as large a congregation as there was the night before, from the Court House stairs. Satan endeavored to interrupt us about the middle of the discourse; for the people were frightened with they knew not what, but they were soon at peace again. I preached above an hour, and, when I had finished, the people seemed unwilling to go away, so I began to pray afresh, and I hope the Lord sent them home with His blessing. Many, to my knowledge, have been quickened and awakened to see that religion does not consist in outward things, but in righteousness, peace, and joy in the Holy Ghost. Oh that they may not only receive the Word with joy for a season, but bring forth fruit unto perfection.

After preaching, my house was filled with people who came in to join in psalms and family prayer. My body was weak, but the Lord strengthened me. Many wept most bitterly while I was praying. Their heart seemed to be loaded with a sense of sin, the only preparative for the visitation of Jesus Christ. Blessed be the Lord for sending me here! This has been a day of fat things. Lord, give me humility, and make me truly thankful. Amen, Lord Jesus.

Sunday, November 11. Read prayers in the morning, and preached in the afternoon to a very thronged congregation. Visited one sick person, and administered the Holy Sacrament to another. For ever adored be the Divine goodness, the Gospel has taken root in many hearts. As soon as I come home, my house is generally filled with people desirous to join in psalms and prayers. They are so eager for the Bread of Life, that they scarcely give me time to take bodily refreshment and proper retirement in my closet. This afternoon I was carried out much in bearing my testimony against the unchristian principles and practices of our clergy. Three of my reverend brethren were present; I know not whether they were offended. I endeavored to speak with meekness as well as zeal. Were I to convert Papists, my business would be to show that they were misguided by their priests; and if I want to convince Church of England Protestants, I must prove that the generality of their teachers do not preach or live up to the truth as it is in Jesus. In vain do we hope to set people right till we demonstrate that the way which they have been taught is wrong.

My life, my blood, I here present,
If for Thy cause they may be spent,
Fulfill Thy sovereign counsel, Lord,
Thy will be done, Thy name adored.
Give me Thy strength, O God of power;
Then let winds blow, or thunders roar,
Thy faithful witness will I be;
'Tis fixed: I can do all for Thee!

PHILADELPHIA, BURLINGTON, AND TRENT TOWN IN THE JERSEYS:

Monday, November 12. Left a large packet of letters, and some things for the press, to be sent by the *Constantine*, Captain Wright, to London. A man came to me this morning, telling me what God had done for his soul, by my preaching of faith. He seemed deeply convinced of sin, and said he was drawn by God's Spirit to pray last night, for which he was immediately looked upon by his master and the family as a madman. I never yet knew one truly awakened, who did not commence a fool for Christ's sake. I have great reason to believe a good work is begun in many hearts. Lord, carry it on for Thy dear Son's sake. At my first arrival at Philadelphia, I received a letter, which had been left for me three months, and in which was a pressing invitation, sent me by Mr. Noble, (a spiritual man), on behalf of many others, to come to New York. On Friday, I received another from the same person; which, looking like the call given St. Paul, when the man appeared to him, saying, "Come over to Macedonia, and help us," I, this morning, set out for that place. Four horses were lent to me and my friends; and more we might have had, had there been occasion. About one, we got safe to Burlington, in the Jerseys, (twenty miles from Philadelphia), where I was importuned to preach as I went along. Immediately after dinner, I read prayers and preached in the church, to a mixed but thronged and attentive congregation. The poor people were very importunate for my staying with them all night, and giving them another discourse; but it being inconvenient with my business, with great regret, about five in the evening, we took our leave, and by eight o'clock reached Trent, another town in the Jerseys. It being dark, we went out of our way a little, in the woods; but God sent a guide to direct us aright.

Tuesday, November 13. Left Trent at six in the morning, and reached Brunswick, thirty miles distant, at one. Here we were much refreshed with the company of Mr. Gilbert Tennent, an eminent Dissenting minister, about forty years of age, son of that good old man who came to see me on Saturday at Philadelphia. God, I find, has been pleased greatly to own his labors. He and his associates are now the burning and shining lights of this part of America. Several pious souls came to see me at his house, with whom I took sweet counsel. At their request, and finding there was a general expectation of hearing me, I read the Church Liturgy, and preached in the evening at Mr. Tennent's meeting house; for there is no place set apart for the worship of the Church of England, and it is common, I was told, in America, for the Dissenters and Conformists to worship at different times, in the same place. Oh, that the partition wall were broken down, and we all with one heart and one mind could glorify our common Lord and Savior Jesus Christ!

At my first getting up, I was somewhat weak, but God renewed my strength, and enabled me to speak with freedom and power. I was above an hour in my sermon, and I trust I shall hear it was not preached in vain. Paul may plant, Apollos water; Thou, Lord, only canst give the increase.

Wednesday, November 14. Set out from Brunswick, in company with my dear fellow travelers, and my worthy brother and fellow laborer, Mr. Tennent. As we passed along, we spent our time most agreeably in telling one another what God had done for our souls. He recounted to me many instances of God's striving with his heart, and how grace, at last, overcame all his fightings against God. About noon, we got to Elizabeth Town, twenty-two miles from Brunswick. Here we took boat, and at four reached New York, where we were most affectionately received by the family of Mr. Noble. I waited upon Mr. Vessey, the Commissary, but he was not at home. Then I went to the meeting house to hear Mr. Gilbert Tennent preach, and never before heard such a searching sermon. He convinced me more and more that we can preach the Gospel of Christ no further than we have experienced the power of it in our own hearts. Being deeply convicted of sin, by God's Holy Spirit, at his first conversion, he has learned experimentally to dissect the heart of a natural man. Hypocrites must either soon be converted or enraged at his preaching. He is a son of thunder, and does not fear the faces of men. After sermon, we spent the evening together at Mr. Noble's house. My soul was humbled and melted down with a sense of God's mercies, and I found more and more what a babe and novice I was in the things of God. Blessed Jesus, grant I may make continual advances, until I come to a perfect man in Thee.

Thursday, November 15. Several came to see me at my lodgings, who also gave me kind invitations to their houses. Waited upon Mr. Vessey; but wished, for his own sake, he had behaved in a more Christian manner. He seemed to be full of anger and resentment, and before I asked him for the use of his pulpit, denied it. He desired to see my Letters of Orders, and, when I told him they were left at Philadelphia, he asked me for a license. I answered, I never heard that the Bishop of London gave any license to any one who went to preach the Gospel in Georgia; but that I was presented to the living of Savannah by the trustees, and upon that presentation had letters Dismissory from my lord of London, which I thought was sufficient authority. But this was by no means satisfactory to him; he charged me with breaking my oath, with breaking the Canon, which enjoins ministers and churchwardens not to admit persons into their pulpit without a license. How can I break that, when I am neither a churchwarden, nor have any church hereabouts to admit any one into? Upon this, knowing that he was a frequenter of public houses, I reminded him of that Canon which forbids the clergy to go to any such places. This, though spoken in the spirit of meekness, stirred him up more. He charged me with making a disturbance in Philadelphia, and sowing and causing divisions in other places. "But you," he said, "have a necessity laid upon you to preach." I told him I had, for the clergy and laity of our Church seemed to be settled on their lees; but that my end in preaching was not to sow divisions, but to propagate the pure Gospel of Jesus Christ. He said, "they did not want my assistance." I replied, if they preached the Gospel, I wished them good luck in the Name of the Lord; but as he had denied me the church without my asking to use of it, I would preach in the fields, for all places were alike to me. "Yes," he said, "I find you have been used to that." After this, he taxed me with censuring my superiors. I told him I was no respecter of persons; if a bishop committed a fault, I would tell him of it; if a common clergyman did not act aright, I would be free with him also, as well as with a layman. While we were talking, he called for some wine, and I drank his health. Soon after, he rose up, saying he had business to do, and, as we were going out, full of resentment, he said to Mr. Noble, who accompanied me and brother Seward, "Mr. Noble, as you sent for this gentleman, so I desire you will find him a pulpit." Alas! alas! what manner of spirit are the generality of the clergy possessed with? Is this the spirit of the meek Lamb of God? Are these the fruits of the Holy Ghost? It cannot be. Their bigotry, if it was nothing else, in time would destroy them. Lord, for Thy mercy's sake, lighten their darkness, and grant that many of the priests also may be obedient to the faith.

Dined with Mr. Pemberton, the Presbyterian minister. Preached in the fields, to upwards of two thousand, at three in the afternoon; and expounded, at six in the evening, to a very thronged and attentive audience in Mr. Pemberton's meeting house. At first, for the sake of my weak brethren, I was unwilling to preach there; but hearing that Mr. Vessey, the commissary, himself had preached in the Dutch Calvinistic Meeting house, when there was no place of worship for the people of our own communion, and the Dutch Meeting house being denied me, as well as the church, I thought it my duty to accept the kind offer made me by Mr. Pemberton and his friends. In the field, a few mocked, but, after speaking to them, they grew more serious. At night, the people seemed exceedingly attentive, and I have not felt greater freedom in preaching, and more power in prayer, since I came to America, than I have had here in New York. I find that little of the work of God has been seen in it for many years. Oh that this may be the accepted time! Oh that this may be the day of salvation!

Friday, November 16. Preached at three in the afternoon, to a congregation in the meeting house; it being too cold to go into the fields. Expounded in the evening, at the same place, to a far greater congregation than I have seen here yet. Great multitudes returned home for want of room. God enabled me to preach with power, and I hope some good will be done, because Satan is disturbed. After evening service, I was told by several persons, that the constables of the town had been placed at the door of the English Church, lest my adherents, encouraged by me, should break it open and take it by force.

Saturday, November 17. Preached as usual, in the afternoon, at the meeting house, to a full congregation; and again at night, to a great multitude standing round the doors, besides those that were within. Woe be unto those, who by their bigotry, prejudice, and party zeal, oblige us to preach the Gospel in so confined a place. But no matter, this, as well as everything else, shall be overruled for the good of Christ's Church. Had the pleasure of hearing that some blessed effects had been produced by the preaching of the Word, and several expressed a strong inclination to go with me. When God will work, who can hinder? Praised be the Lord, Who daily shows me this is the way wherein I should go. Lord, make me ever humble and thankful.

Sunday, November 18. Preached, this morning at eight o'clock to a very attentive auditory. Went to the English Church, both morning and evening, and felt my heart almost bled within me, to consider what blind guides were sent forth into her. If I have any regard for the honor of Christ, and good of souls, I must lift up my voice like a trumpet, and show how sadly our Church ministers are fallen from the doctrines of the Reformation. Her prophets prophesy lies, and I fear many of the people love to have it so.

In the Second Lesson this morning were these verses, and some, I found, made an immediate application of them, by looking on me: "There was a division therefore again among the Jews for these sayings. And many of them said, he hath a devil, and is mad; why hear ye him; Others said, these are not the words of him that hath a devil." In the evening, a vast multitude flocked to hear the Word. Some petitioned the mayor to allow the use of the Town Hall, but it was denied; then we thought of expounding from a window, and let the people stand in the street; but at last, with much difficulty, I got into the meeting house, and the windows being open, numbers could hear that stood outside. I was pressed in spirit to bear my testimony against the doctrine delivered in the English Church, both morning and evening. Though it may seem a hard saying to many, yet our people need to be cautioned against the scribes and Pharisees of our communion, as much as the Jews were cautioned to beware of the scribes and Pharisees by our Lord Jesus. After sermon, many persons came to pray with me, and take their farewell. They also gave me tokens of their love, and I had great reason to believe God has begun a good work in New York. I saw my sermon on regeneration advertised in the New England paper, and gave leave for my Answer to the Bishop of London to be printed at New York.

About ten at night, I took boat with my friends, and had a pleasant passage to a place about half-way to Elizabeth Town, where we lay down with joy and thankfulness for the great things the Lord had shown us. Oh, that I was duly sensible of His distinguishing mercies!

Monday, November 19. Took boat about five in the morning, and reached Elizabeth Town at seven. Paid a visit to Mr. Vaughan, the minister of the Church of England in Elizabeth Town, who, I heard afterwards, had preached against me, and said I should not have the use of his pulpit. Dined with Mr. Dickinson, the Dissenting minister, who had sent a letter of invitation to New York, offering me the use of his meeting house. About twelve, I preached in it, according to appointment, to upwards of seven hundred people. God was pleased to open my mouth against both ministers and people among the Dissenters, who hold the truth in unrighteousness, contenting themselves with a bare, speculative knowledge of the doctrines of grace, but never experiencing the power of them in their hearts.

NEW BRUNSWICK: Tuesday, November 20. Reached here about six last night; and preached today, at noon, for near two hours, in worthy Mr. Tennent's meeting house, to a large assembly gathered together from all parts; and among them, Mr. Tennent told me, was a great number of solid Christians. About three in the afternoon, I preached again; and, at seven, I baptized two children, and preached a third time. Among others who came to hear the Word, were several ministers, whom the Lord has been pleased to honor, in making them instruments of bringing many sons to glory. One was a Dutch Calvinistic minister, named Freeling Housen, a pastor of a congregation about four miles from New Brunswick. He is a worthy old soldier of Jesus Christ, and was the beginner of the great work which I trust the Lord is carrying on in these parts. He has been strongly opposed by his carnal brethren, but God has appeared for him, in a surprising manner, and made him more than conqueror, through His love. He has long since learned to fear him only, who can destroy both body and soul in hell.

Another was Mr. Cross, minister of a congregation of Barking Bridge, about twenty miles from Brunswick. He himself told me of many wonderful and sudden conversions that had been wrought by the Lord under his ministry. For some time, eight or nine used to come to him together, in deep distress of soul; and, I think, he said, three hundred of his congregation, which is not a very large one, were brought home to Christ. They are now looked upon as enthusiasts and madmen, and treated as such by those who know not God, and are ignorant of the hidden life of Jesus Christ in their hearts. He is one, who, I believe, would rejoice to suffer for the Lord Jesus. Oh that I may be likeminded! A third minister was a Mr. Camel, who has been a preacher of the doctrines of grace for these four years; was a regular and moral liver, and accounted a very good man; but within these last few years, being convinced of sin, and that he knew nothing experimentally of Jesus Christ, (though he had pretended to preach Him so long), after many struggles with himself, told the Synod he was unconverted, and therefore dare not preach until he was; accordingly, he has left off preaching these two months, and has labored under unspeakable anguish and distress of soul. By some he is looked upon as melancholy, and beside himself; but I have had much discourse with him, and really believe these humiliations will prepare him for great and eminent services in the Church of God.

His case reminds me of Professor Francke, who having agreed on Easter Day to preach on the nature of Divine faith, and finding he had not that faith himself, was convicted by God of his unregenerate state; upon which he ran into the woods, was there deeply humbled, and at last became a most exalted instance of faith. At our persuasion, Mr. Camel promised to preach next Sunday, and, I believe, will be instrumental in convicting many heart hypocrites among the Dissenting ministers. For that there are many such, is evident from this: though they hold, have been bred up in, and preach the doctrines of grace, yet whenever the power of

God appears in any congregation, they cry it down as much as our ministers of the Church of England. Oh, that the Lord may comfort poor Mr. Camel, and cause him to detect these wolves in sheep's clothing. With these ministers, and many other disciples of our Lord Jesus, I took sweet counsel, and comforted ourselves with this consideration, that though we must be separated from each other on earth, yet we should sit down to eat bread with Abraham, Isaac, and Jacob, in the Kingdom of Heaven. Hasten, O Lord, this blessed time! O when will Thy Kingdom come!

MAIDENHEAD AND TRENT TOWN: Wednesday, November 21. Set out early, with about a score in company, for Maidenhead, a little more than twenty miles from Brunswick, where, at Mr. Tennent's request, I had appointed to preach today. At noon we got there, and I preached from a wagon to about fifteen hundred persons, on the conversion of Saul. Here one Mr. Rowland, another faithful minister of Jesus Christ, gave us the meeting. He has been a preacher about two years, has gone about doing good, and has had many seals to his ministry. Much of the simplicity of Christ was discernible in his behavior. Blessed be God for sending forth such burning and shining lights in the midst of the thick darkness that is upon the face of this generation. Thou Lord of the harvest, send forth more such laborers into Thy harvest.

After sermon, we were kindly entertained at a house, near the place where I preached, and being strongly desired by many, and hearing that a condemned malefactor was to suffer there that week, I went to Trent Town, in company with above thirty horse. It is ten miles from Maidenhead, and we reached there by five in the evening. Knowing that God called, I went out trusting in His Divine strength, and preached in the Court House. The unhappy criminal seemed hardened, but I had great reason to believe some good was done in the place. Lord, send forth others to carry it on, for Thy dear Son's sake.

TRENT TOWN AND NESHAMINY: Thursday, November 22. Set out for Neshaminy (twenty miles distant from Trent Town), where old Mr. Tennent lives, and keeps an academy, and where I was to preach today, according to appointment. We came here about twelve, and found above three thousand people gathered together in the meeting house yard, and Mr. William Tennent preaching to them, because we were beyond the appointed time. When I came up, he soon stopped, and sang a psalm, and then I began to speak. At first the people seemed unaffected, but, in the midst of my discourse, the hearers began to be melted down, and cried much. After I had finished, Mr. Gilbert Tennent gave a word of exhortation. At the end of his discourse, we sang a psalm, and then dismissed the people with a blessing. Oh, that the Lord may say Amen to it!

After our exercises were over, we went to old Mr. Tennent, who entertained us like one of the ancient patriarchs. His wife seemed to me like Elizabeth, and he like Zacharias; both, as far as I can find, walk in all the ordinances and commandments of the Lord blameless. We had sweet communion with each other, and spent the evening in concerting measures for promoting our Lord's Kingdom. It happens very providentially, that Mr. Tennent and his brethren are appointed to be a Presbytery by the Synod, so that they intend breeding up gracious youths, and sending them out into our Lord's vineyard. The place wherein the young men study now is, in contempt, called *the College*. It is a log house, about twenty feet long, and nearly as many broad; and, to me, it seemed to resemble the school of the old prophets. That their habitations were mean, and that they sought not great things for themselves, is plain from that passage of Scripture, wherein we are told, that at the feast of the sons of the prophets, one of them put on the pot, while the others went to fetch some herbs out of the field. From this despised place, seven or eight worthy ministers of Jesus have lately been sent forth; more are almost ready to be sent; and a foundation is now being laid for the instruction of many others. [It was to develop into Princeton University and Theological Seminary. Cf. *The Log College*, by Archibald Alexander.] The devil will certainly rage against them; but the work, I am persuaded, is of God, and will not come to nought. Carnal ministers oppose them strongly; and, because people, when awakened by Mr. Tennent, or his brethren, see through them, and therefore leave their ministry, the poor gentlemen are loaded with contempt, and looked upon as persons who turn the world upside down.

NESHAMINY, ABINGDON AND PHILADELPHIA: Friday, November 23. Parted with dear Mr. Tennent and his worthy fellow laborers; but promised to remember each other publicly in our prayers. Rode to Abingdon, about ten miles from Neshaminy, and preached to above two thousand people from a porch window belonging to the meeting house. It is surprising how such bodies of people, so scattered abroad, can be gathered at so short a warning. At Neshaminy, I believe there were nearly a thousand horses. The people, however, did not sit upon them to hear the sermon, as in England, but tied them to the hedges; and thereby much disorder was prevented. As soon as I had done, I had fresh invitations to go to several places, should time and business permit. Though it was cold, the people stood very patiently in the open air, and seemed in no hurry to return home after the discourses were ended.

When I had finished at Abingdon, I hastened to Philadelphia, where I found my family in good order, and all things carried on according to my desire. Oh, how can I express my thankfulness for this little excursion! The Lord has done great things for us in it, whereat the people of God are much rejoiced. Oh that I may now begin to do something for Christ, not to justify my person, but my faith, and to show my love and gratitude for what God has done for my soul.

Saturday, November 24. Preached this morning in the church. Afterwards, several came to me, inquiring about inward feelings and receiving the Holy Ghost; and I found many began to be awakened out of their carnal security by the Word preached. Received an excellent letter from one grievously vexed with temptations, to whom God has been pleased to make me an instrument of comforting. Preached again, at four in the afternoon, in the church, that building being judged more convenient than the market place, as the weather was so cold. A vast concourse of all denominations were present. After sermon, I visited two sick persons, supped with my family, and laid me down with a strong desire to see my own unworthiness, and the freeness and riches of that grace, which alone has made me to differ from the most abandoned of men. Therefore, whenever I glory, I desire only to glory in Thee, O Lord.

Sunday, November 25. Had great travail of soul, and struggling within myself, about a text to preach on. At last, I fixed on one for the morning, and trusted to God to direct me to one for the evening; but before I came from church God showed me what I should do, for after I had done preaching, a young gentleman, once a minister of the Church of England, but now secretary to Mr. Penn, stood up with a loud voice, and warned the people against the doctrine I had been delivering, urging, "That there was no such term as *imputed righteousness* in Holy Scripture; that such a doctrine put a stop to all goodness; that we were to be judged for our good works and obedience, and were commanded *to do and live.*" When he had ended, I denied his first proposition, and brought a text to prove that "imputed righteousness" was a scriptural expression; but, thinking the church an improper place for disputation, I said no more at that time. The portion of Scripture appointed for the Epistle, was Jeremiah 23, wherein are these words, "The Lord our Righteousness." Upon these, I discoursed in the afternoon, and showed how the Lord Jesus was to be *our whole righteousness.* I proved how the contrary doctrine overthrew all Divine revelation, and answered all the objections. I produced the Articles of our Church to illustrate it, and concluded with an exhortation to all to lay aside reasoning infidelity, and to submit to Jesus Christ, Who is the end of the law for *righteousness*, to every one that believeth. The verses at the beginning of the chapter, from which the text was taken, are very remarkable (Jeremiah 23:1,2,3,4). God was pleased to fulfill that promise in me; for, blessed be His Name, I was not dismayed. The church was thronged within and without; all were wonderfully attentive; and many, as I was informed, were convinced that the Lord Christ was *our Righteousness.* In the evening, the gentleman came to me; but alas! was so very dark in all the fundamentals of Christianity, and such an entire stranger to inward feelings, that I was obliged to say to him, "Art thou a master of Israel, and knowest not these things?" Lord, convict and convert him for Thy infinite mercy's sake.

Went to the Quakers' meeting for a short time. Gave the Sacrament at a private house, and came home and exhorted, prayed and sang psalms with a room full of people. They follow me wherever I go, as they used to do in London, and, I believe, a noble gathering of souls might be in this place. Here, as elsewhere, they only want somebody to preach the truth as it is in Jesus. Lord, remember Thy Church, and revive Thy work among us in the midst of the days.

Monday, November 26. Read prayers and preached twice in the church, to very large and attentive congregations. The Word came with great power, and people now apply to me so fast for advice under convictions, and so continually crowd in upon me, that I have not enough time to write to my English friends. Some little presents have been sent for the Orphan House, and a large collection, I believe, might be made for it; but I choose to defer that till my return here again. As yet, it seems necessary for the good of the Church in general, and my orphans in particular, that I should visit every place in America where I have been before. Good Lord, direct my goings in Thy way.

PHILADELPHIA AND GERMAN TOWN: Tuesday, November 27. According to appointment, I preached at German Town, seven miles from Philadelphia, from a balcony, to above six thousand people. God strengthened me to speak nearly two hours, with such demonstration of the Spirit, that great numbers continued weeping for a considerable time. I have not seen a more gracious melting for a considearble time. After I had done, people came to shake me by the hand, and invited me to their houses, and fresh places. A German most kindly entertained me. I had sweet converse, and felt a blessed union and communion with many souls, though of different nations and professions. I think there are no less than fifteen denominations of Christians in German Town, and yet all agree in one thing, that is, to hold Jesus Christ as their Head, and to worship Him in spirit and in truth. I talked with one who had been banished from Switzerland for preaching Christ. Numbers are scattered round about the town, who were driven out of their native countries for the sake of their holy religion. About four in the afternoon, we went with many dear disciples of the Lord, to see one Conrad Mattheus, an aged hermit, who has lived a solitary life nearly forty years. He was heir to a great estate, but chose voluntary poverty. He has worked hard, but always without wages. He is now unable to do much, but God sends somebody or other to feed him. A friend built him the little house wherein he lives; and Jesus, I am persuaded, dwells with him. He talked most feelingly of inward trials; and when I asked him whether he had not many such in so close a retirement, he answered, "No wonder that a single tree that stands alone is more exposed to storms, than one that grows among others." After half-an-hour's conversation, we took our leave. He kissed me and my friends, and was rejoiced to hear what was being done in England. Our hearts were knit together, and the God of love was with us of a truth. The Germans, I find, are about to translate my *Journals* into High Dutch.

About eight in the evening we reached Philadelphia, and found great numbers waiting round my door to hear the Word of life. After I had paid a visit, and talked closely to two persons, who were doubtful of the principles of the Quakers, I returned home, and though I was weak, I could not bear to let so many go away without a spiritual morsel; I therefore gave them a word of exhortation, sang a hymn, and prayed and dismissed them with a blessing. Many wept bitterly, and the people's behavior more and more convinces me that God has begun a good work in many souls. Were proper encouragement given, I am persuaded Georgia might soon be peopled. Many would gladly go with me there. I cannot but hope that it will be in time a fruitful soil for Christians. One great reason, I believe, why Pennsylvania flourishes above other provinces, is the liberty of conscience which is given all to worship God in their own way; by this means, it has become, as it were, an asylum or place of refuge for all persecuted Christians. I want to go up in the woods, but time will not permit. O when shall the children of God sit down together in the Kingdom of their Father? There we shall all speak *one language*, and join in singing the Song of the Lamb forever!

PHILADELPHIA: Wednesday, November 28. Wrote a letter or two to my dear friends in England. I have not had time before, since my return from New York. People are continually coming in, and inquiring with many tears how they must come to Christ. It grieves me to send them away with such short answers; but necessity compels me. Oh, that the Lord may send forth more laborers into His harvest! Read prayers and preached, as usual, in the morning, to a thronged congregation. Heard of more who were under convictions, and as I was walking out to dinner, a German came to me saying, "Thou didst sow some good seed yesterday in German Town, and a grain of it fell into my daughter's heart. She wants to speak with thee, that she may know what she must do to keep and increase it." The young woman being near at hand, came at her father's call. Both melted into tears immediately, and after I had exhorted her to watch and pray, and keep close to Christ by faith, I took my leave, beseeching God to water the good seed His own right hand had planted in her heart.

In the morning, notice had been given that I should preach my farewell sermon in the afternoon. But the church, (though as large as most of our London churches), being not large enough to contain a fourth part of the people, we adjourned to the fields, and I preached for an hour-and-a-half from a balcony, to upwards of ten thousand hearers, who were very attentive and much affected. The mention of my departure was a grief to many, and it almost melted me down, to see with what eagerness and earnest affection they follow after the preaching of the Word. If I could preach, they would attend all the day long. Blessed be God for this effectual door. I wonder we have no more adversaries. By and by, I expect Satan and his emissaries will rage horribly. I endeavored to forewarn my hearers of it. Lord, prepare us against a day of spiritual battle! Took my leave of the Governor and Proprietor. Supped with one of the churchwardens and his friends; and when I came home, exhorted and sang psalms, and prayed with a great company of people who were waiting at my door. After I was in bed, I received the following letter from New York: —

"Reverend and Dear Sir, — I was heartily sorry that the disorder of a cold should hinder me from waiting upon you in the Jerseys. I found the next day that you had left the town under a deep and universal concern. Many were greatly affected, and I hope, abiding impressions are left upon some. Some who were before very loose and profligate, now look back with shame upon their past lives and conversations, and seem resolved upon a thorough reformation. I mention these things to strengthen you in the blessed cause you are engaged in, and support you under your abundant labors. When I heard so many were concerned about their eternal welfare, I arranged a lecture for Wednesday evening, though it was not in the usual season. And though the warning was short, we had a numerous and attentive audience. In short I cannot but hope that your coming among us has been the means of awakening some among us to a serious sense of practical religion, and may be the beginning of a good work in this secure and sinful place. Dear Sir, let your prayers be joined with mine for this desirable blessing.

"I desire your prayers for me in particular, that I may be faithful in my Master's work; that I may be an instrument in the hands of Christ for pulling down the strongholds of sin and Satan, and building the Redeemer's Kingdom in this place. Pray for us, that the good impressions any have received may not wear off and prove as the morning cloud, and as the early dew; but that He would grant a resurrection of religion in the midst of us that many may flock to Christ. I pray God to take you under His gracious protection, sustain you under your many trials, and make you gloriously successful in converting sinners from the error of their ways, and turning them to the wisdom of the just. My wife joins with me in affectionate regard to you, Mr. Seward, and your other friends, whom we love in sincerity. I am, your affectionate brother, and very humble servant,

"E. PEMBERTON."

Blessed be God for such success at New York! Nor is He working less here. One of the printers [No doubt this was Benjamin Franklin, at that time publisher of the *Pennsylvania Gazette*.] has told me he has taken above two hundred subscriptions for printing my *Sermons* and *Journals*. Another printer told me he might have sold a thousand *Sermons*, if he had them; I therefore gave two extempore discourses to be published. Lord, give them Thy blessing. Numbers of letters have been sent me from persons under convictions, and it is unknown what deep impressions have been wrought in the hearts of hundreds. An opposer told me I had unhinged many *good sort* of people. I believe many that contented themselves with good desires, are now convinced they must have good habits also, and be thoroughly born again ere they can see the Kingdom of God. As I have sown spiritual things, the people were willing I should reap carnal things. They have, therefore, sent me butter, sugar, chocolate, pickles, cheese, and flour, for my poor orphans; and indeed, I could almost say they would pluck out their own eyes and give them me. Blessed be God, for the great work begun in these parts. Oh, that what God says of the Church of Philadelphia in the Revelation, may be now fulfilled in the city called after her name! "I know thy works. Behold I have set before thee an open door, and no man can shut it. Behold I will make them of the synagogue of Satan to come and worship before thy feet, and to know that I have loved thee."

PHILADELPHIA, CHESTER AND WILMINGTON: Thursday, November 29. Had the satisfaction of settling all my family affairs: gained considerably by the goods that were sold for the poor, and had a sloop loaned me, which Mr. Seward bought and named *Savannah*, in which I left orders for my family to set sail, immediately after my leaving Philadelphia. My friend Gladman (the Captain mentioned before at the beginning) has been a helpmeet to me, and done everything without giving me any (or but little) trouble. About eleven in the morning, having corrected two sermons for the press, I took an affectionate leave of my family and Philadelphia people. From seven in the morning they thronged round the door, and when we parted, oh, how bitterly did the poor souls weep! As I passed along the street, they came running out to the doors, and I discovered the concern that was in their hearts by the sorrow of their countenances. Nearly twenty gentlemen accompanied me on horseback out of town. About seven miles off, another company was waiting to meet us, so that at last we were nearly two hundred horse. By three we reached Chester, a town fifteen miles distant from Philadelphia; and after we had taken a little food, I preached to about five thousand people from a balcony. It being courtday, the Justices sent word they would defer their meeting till mine was over; and the minister of the parish, because the church could not contain the people, provided the place from which I spoke. The people were very quiet and attentive; I was told that near a thousand of the congregation came from Philadelphia. After sermon, many of them took their last farewell of me, and wished me good luck in the Name of the Lord.

About six in the evening, we left Chester, and came to Wilmington (thirteen miles) before nine. The evening was warm, the moon shone bright, and the discourse we had on the way, made the time imperceptibly glide away. Two loving Quakers received us into their house. God was pleased to refresh my heart with a sense of His love, and after I had given a word of exhortation, and prayed with my own friends and some others who came in, I went to bed, admiring the great work that God had begun in these parts. I have not seen greater things, considering the places, even in England. Oh, that the Lord, in answer to the people's prayers, and in His own due time, may bring me back hither again. I hope to see there some substantial fruits of my present weak endeavors. Dearest Redeemer, make me humble, prepare me for Thy future mercies; and whenever Thou seest me in danger of being exalted above measure, graciously send me a thorn in the flesh, so that Thy blessings may not prove my ruin.

WILMINGTON: Friday, November 30. Preached at noon, and again at three in the afternoon. Received several fresh and pressing invitations to preach at various different places, but was obliged to refuse them all. Oh, that I had a hundred tongues and lives, they should be all employed for my dear Lord Jesus! Spent the evening in sweet conversation with Mr. William Tennent, brother to Mr. Gilbert Tennent, a faithful minister of Jesus Christ, and with several Germans, whose hearts God has been pleased to knit to me in a close and intimate union. Blessed be God for the communion of saints! Lord, why am I thus highly favored? Who dares despair, when such mercies are daily poured on such a wretch as I am?

NEWCASTLE AND CHRISTIAN BRIDGE: Saturday, December 1. Reached Newcastle, seven miles from Wilmington, by ten in the morning. Was met on the way by Mr. Ross, the minister of the place, and kindly entertained by Mr. G..., who sent to invite me and my friends yesterday. On my arrival, I preached to about two thousand people from a balcony, but did not speak with so much freedom and power as usual, God being pleased to humble my soul by inward visitations, and a bodily indisposition. Lay on the bed after sermon, which much refreshed me; and at four o'clock rode and preached at Christian Bridge, to about the same number as at Newcastle. Near two hundred came on the road with us. I had some edifying conversation with some children of God, as we went on the way, and great power from God descended on me and the congregation, in the latter part of my sermon. I always observe inward trials prepare me for, and are the certain forerunners of *fresh mercies*. Oh what a gracious melting of hearts was there; enough to convince (one would imagine) the greatest of infidels. With what earnestness did people beseech me to visit other places. Surely the divine Herbert's prophecy is now being fulfilled.

> Religion stands a tiptoe in our land,
> Ready to pass to the American strand, etc.
> (See his Church Militant.)

Sunday, December 2. Returned last night to Newcastle, that I might see my dear family, who came there in the sloop just after I had left. Lay at the house of Mr. Gladman, and this morning went on board, prayed, sang psalms, gave a word of exhortation, and rejoiced much to see all things in such excellent order. My dear friend the Captain, told me how kind the people of Philadelphia had been to my family after my departure. One brought them butter, another beer, etc., and the collector would not take his perquisite for clearing the sloop. The two children, the people were particularly fond of, and gave them so many things that I was obliged to desire them to desist. About ten, we came to Christian Bridge again, where we had left some of our friends last night. Here we took a little refreshment, and by twelve reached Whiteclay Creek, the place appointed for my preaching. The weather was rainy, but upwards of ten thousand people were assembled to hear the Word. It surprised me to see such a number of horses: there were several hundreds of them. I preached from a tent, erected for me by order of Mr. William Tennent, whose meeting-house lay near the place. I continued in my first discourse an hour and a half, after which we went into a log-house near by, took a morsel of bread, and warmed ourselves. I preached a second time from the same place. My body was weak, but God magnified His strength, and caused His power to be known in the congregation. Many souls were melted down. Here I had the pleasure of meeting with one Mr. Gillespie, another faithful minister of Jesus Christ. He, as well as Mr. Tennent, was very solicitous for my going to his house; but being previously engaged, I rode three miles, and was kindly and hospitably entertained by Mr. Howell, who came with his family, some years ago, from Cardiff in Wales. One in the house had heard me preach in Kingswood, and everything was carried on with so much freedom and love, that I rejoiced much that God had sent me there. I stayed up as long as I could; but finding my body weakened by the posture in which I stood to preach, about ten o'clock, after family prayer, I went to bed thoroughly weary, but full of that peace which the world cannot give, but which I wish the whole world were partakers of.

MARYLAND: NORTH EAST: Monday, December 3. Came to North East in Maryland, where I had appointed to preach today. Little notice having been given, there were not above fifteen hundred people; but God was with us, and many were deeply affected. Several repeated invitations were sent me to preach at other places. Immediately after sermon, we passed over Susquehannah Ferry, about a mile broad, and were received at a gentleman's house that lay on our way. Though we were eight in company, all things were carried on with great freedom and generosity; and I hope God sent us providentially there, for the gentleman told us he had been a little melancholy, and had therefore sent for some friends to help him to drive it away. The bottle and the bowl, I found, were the means to be employed; but, blessed be God, the design was, in a good measure, prevented by our coming; another turn was soon given to the conversation, while I endeavored to talk of God as much as I could. All joined in family prayer; and I went to bed pitying the miserable condition of those who live a life of luxury and self-indulgence. They are afraid to look into themselves; and, if their consciences are at any time awakened, they must be lulled to sleep again by drinking and evil company. None but a sincere Christian can with pleasure practice the duty of self-examination. Lord, grant I may always so live that I may keep a conscience void of offense, both towards Thee and towards man. Then I shall never be less alone than when alone; for Thou, Father of mercies, and God of all consolations, will everywhere be with me.

JOPPA: Tuesday, December 4. Set out about eight in the morning, and took leave of two dear friends, who parted from us with weeping eyes. Partook of refreshments at Joppa, a little town about fifteen miles from the place where we lay. I gave a word of exhortation to about forty people in the church. Oh, that the Holy Ghost may fall on all them who heard the Word, in as real though not in so visibly miraculous a manner as it did once on Cornelius and his household! Maryland, as far as I can hear, seems to be a place as yet unwatered with the true Gospel of Christ, and with no likelihood of much good being done in it, unless one could abide there for some time. There is scarcely any town worth mentioning, because almost every planter has a landing-place, from which he exports his tobacco at his own house, which generally lies very near the river. By this means the people are much dispersed, and consequently cannot be gathered together without much previous notice, which, notwithstanding, is difficult to be given, because there are many large ferries between place and place. I trust the time will come when God will visit these dark corners of the earth.

NEWTOWN AND ANNAPOLIS: Wednesday, December 5. Lay last night at Newtown, fifteen miles from Joppa; ate what was set before us; joined in family prayer; and, as opportunity offered, put in a word for God. In the morning we sang and prayed; at noon we partook of refreshments at a house lying about fifteen miles off, and by four in the afternoon, we reached Annapolis, a little town, by the metropolis of Maryland. The house where we lodged was very commodious, considering it was in Maryland, but the people of it seemed to be surprised when they heard us talk of God and Christ. Notwithstanding, both they and the other strangers attended very orderly at family prayer, and I endeavored to recommend them, as I was enabled, to the mercy of our gracious and good God. Oh that I may prevail in their behalf! It grieves me in my soul to see poor sinners hanging as it were by a single hair, and dancing (insensible of their danger) over the flames of hell. Oh, that God may make me instrumental in plucking them as firebrands out of the fire! For here is the misery of man; he is miserable, poor, and blind, and naked, and yet *knows it not*. Lord Jesus, send forth, we beseech Thee, Thy light, and lighten our darkness, for Thy mercies' sake!

ANNAPOLIS: Thursday, December 6. Had an opportunity of writing some letters last night and this morning to England. Waited on Governor Ogle, and was received with much civility. Went to pay my respects to Mr. Stirling, the minister of the parish, who happened not to be within; but while we were at dinner, he came and offered me his pulpit, his house, or anything he could supply me with. About four, he came and introduced me and my friends to a gentleman's house, where we had some useful conversation. Our conversation ran chiefly on the new birth, and the folly and sinfulness of those amusements, whereby the polite part of the world are so fatally diverted from the pursuit of the one thing needful. Some of the company, I believe, thought I was too strict, and were very strenuous in defense of what they called *innocent* diversions; but when I told them everything was sinful which was not done with a single eye to God's glory, and that such entertainments not only discovered a levity of mind, but were contrary to the whole tenor of the Gospel of Christ, they seemed somewhat convinced; at least, I trust it set them *doubting*, and I pray God they may *doubt* more and more, for cards, dancing, and such like, draw the soul from God, and lull it asleep as much as drunkenness and debauchery. Every minister of Christ ought, with the authority of an apostle, to declare and testify the dreadful snare of the devil, whereby he leads many captive at his will, by the falsely called *innocent* entertainments of the polite part of the world; for women are as much enslaved to their fashionable diversions, as men are to their bottle and their houds. Self-pleasing, self-seeking is the *ruling principle* in both; and therefore, such things are to be spoken against, not only as so many trifling amusements, but as things which show that the heart is wholly alienated from the life of God. If I may speak from my own, as well as others' experience, as soon as ever the soul is stirred up to seek after God, it cannot away with any such thing, and nothing but what leads towards God can delight it; and therefore, when in company, I love to lay the axe to the root of the tree, show the necessity of a thorough change of heart, and then all things fall to the ground at once. My friend, C Wesley, well describes the misery of a modern fine lady in the following verses.

I TIMOTHY 5:6

She that liveth in pleasure is dead while she lives.

How hapless is th'applauded virgin's lot,
Her God forgetting, by her God forgot!
Stranger to truth, unknowing to obey,
In error nurs'd and disciplin'd to stray;
Swoln with self-will, and principled with pride,
Sense all her good, and passion all her guide:
Pleasure its tide, and flatt'ry lends it breath,
And smoothly waft her to eternal death!

A goddess here she sees her vot'ries meet,
Crowd to her shrine, and tremble at her feet;
She hears their vows, believes their life and death
Hangs on the wrath and mercy of her breath;
Supreme in fancied state she reigns her hour,
And glories in her plenitude of power.
Herself the only object worth her care,
Since all the kneeling world was made for her.
For her creation all its stores displays;
The silkworm's labour, and the diamond's blaze;
Air, earth, and sea conspire to tempt her taste,
And ransack'd Nature furnishes the feast.
Life's gaudiest pride attracts her willing eyes,
And balls, and theatres, and courts arise:
Italian songsters pant her ear to please,
Bid the first cries of infant reason cease,
Save her from thought, and lull her soul to peace.

Deep sunk in sense th'imprison'd soul remains,
Nor knows its fall from God, nor feels its chains:
Unconscious still, sleeps on in error's night,
Nor strives to rise, nor struggles into light:
Heaven-born in vain, degen'rate cleaves to earth,
(No pangs experienc'd of the second birth)
She only fallen, yet unwaken'd found,
While all th'enthrall'd creation groans around!

Friday, December 7. A visible alteration has taken place in the behavior of the people of the house. Preached in the morning and evening to small polite auditories. The Governor put aside his court to come to morning service, and at noon, upon an invitation sent last night, I and my friends dined with him. In the evening, two of the chief inhabitants favored me with a visit. The minister seemed somewhat affected, and under convictions; but I fear a false politeness, and the pomps and vanities of the world, eat out the vitals of religion in this place. I bless God I did not spare to tell my hearers of it in my discourses, and the minister told me they took it kindly. At night, four persons came to join in family prayer, to whom I gave a warm exhortation. Here are but few inhabitants, but God, I hope, will show that He hath some chosen ones in this place.

UPPER MARLBOROUGH: Saturday, December 8. Had more last night come to family prayer. Left Annapolis this morning. Partook of refreshments at Upper Marlborough, about fifteen miles distant, intending to go further; but being desired by some gentlemen to stay and preach on the morrow, I was prevailed upon, and spent the remainder of the day in sweet conversation with my friends, and in writing letters to some under convictions at Philadelphia. I supped with a gentleman who kindly entertained both me and my fellow-travelers. Our talk ran upon the fall of man. I fear Deism has spread much in these parts. I cannot say I have yet met with *many* here who seem truly to have the fear of God before their eyes.

UPPER MARLBOROUGH, PORT TOBACCO: Sunday, December 9. Preached at Upper Marlborough, to a small, polite, and seemingly very curious audience. Dined with the gentleman with whom we supped last night. There being no sermon in the afternoon, we took horse, and went a Sabbath-day's journey as far as Piscataway, where we were kindly entertained. Wrote some letters to our English friends. Conversed to the use of edifying, and felt an uncommon freedom and sweetness in each other's spirits. Well might our Lord say, "The kingdom of God is within you"; for they who are truly born of God, carry Heaven in their hearts.

POSCATAWAY, PORT TOBACCO, AND POTOMAC: Monday, December 10. Partook of refreshments at Port Tobacco and reached Potomac by three in the afternoon. Potomac is a river which parts the two provinces of Maryland and Virginia. It is six miles broad. We attempted to go over it; but after we had rowed about a mile, the wind blew so violently, and night was coming on so fast, that we were obliged to go back and lie in the person's house who kept the ferry, where they brought out such things as they had. God showed us the benefit of returning, for the wind was very boisterous, and the night snowy; so that without a miracle, (which in such a case we had no right to expect), both we and our horses must have been lost. Lord, grant we may always keep between the two extremes of distrusting or tempting Thee.

VIRGINIA: SEALS CHURCH: Tuesday, December 11. Had a short and delightful passage over the river this morning, which we could not pass last night. Observed the country to be much more open, and the roads better than in Maryland. Passed over two more ferries in the day's journey, and were put to some little inconvenience for want of finding a public-house in the way. However, at last, we met a poor woman, who was going to sell cakes to the trained bands, of which we bought some; and, a few miles further, a planter let us have some provender for our beasts, and a little milk and small beer for ourselves. By six at night, we got to a place called Seals Church, twenty-nine miles from Potomac. Here we called at a person's house to whom we were recommended; but the mistress of it was not at home, and the overseer of the slaves, at first, was unwilling to receive us. However, finding we were wet and strangers, he was at last prevailed upon to let us abide there all night; and in a little time furnished us with a good fire, with some meat, milk, and a cake baked on the hearth, which was exceedingly refreshing, and afforded us no small matter for praise and thanksgiving. Oh, that we may abound in that duty more and more.

Wednesday, December 12. Went on, having pleasant roads and a warm day, till we came to Piscataway ferry, eighteen miles from Seals Church, where the man of the house spared us some corn and sheaves for our horses, but had neither milk nor bread in the house for ourselves. However, I endeavored to feed him with spiritual bread; but he seriously asked one of us if I was not a Quaker, because (as I supposed) he heard me talk of the necessity of being born again of the Spirit. If I talk of the Spirit, I am a Quaker! if I say grace at breakfast, and behave seriously, I am a Presbyterian! Alas! what must I do to be accounted a member of the Church of England? About one we set out, and before four in the afternoon reached an ordinary. Here we were most opportunely refreshed with what meat they had in the house. There being no other public-house for some miles, and being wearied more than common for want of usual sustenance, we tarried all night. In the evening, some gentlemen came disordered in liquor; but the woman of the house kept them from us, so we slept very comfortably on the bed that she made us in the kitchen. I talked to her of religion, and told her that we must be born again. She said that was true, but it was to be done *after* death; also she thought God was very merciful, and that it would be no harm to swear by her faith. I could not help remarking how the devil loves to represent God as *all mercy* or *all justice*. When persons are awakened, he would, if possible, tempt them *to despair*; when dead in trespasses and sins he tempts them *to presume*. Lord, preserve us from making shipwreck against either of these rocks. Give us such a sense of Thy justice as to convince us that we cannot be saved if we continue in sin, and such a sense of Thy mercy as may keep us from despair, through a living faith in Thy dear Son Who is the Savior of sinners!

Thursday, December 13. Set out just as the sun rose; got to an ordinary by noon; ate what was set before us with some degree of thankfulness; and reached the house of Colonel Whiting, father of my dear friend Captain Whiting, long before night. Here God spread a plentiful table for us, and, what was more desirable, sent to us a well-inclined person, to whom, I trust, my conversation was blessed. That passage in St. John, wherein it is said that our Lord must needs go through Samaria (when the poor woman was to be converted) has often been affecting to my mind. The same good Providence, I trust, led me through these parts, for the sake of the person before mentioned. Oh that, like the woman at the well, he may have Christ revealed in his heart, and be filled with a holy zeal to go and invite his neighbors to Him. Amen.

GLOUCESTER, YORK AND WILLIAMSBURGH: Friday, December 14. Left Colonel Whiting's about seven in the morning, and passed through Gloucester Town, a very small place. Crossed a ferry a mile wide. Dined at York and reached Williamsburgh, the metropolis of Virginia, by the evening. The gentleman before mentioned kindly accompanied us; with him I discoursed much on the things pertaining to the Kingdom of God. He seemed to be one to whom God had given a hearing ear and an obedient heart. I have not met with a temper more resembling that of Nathaniel for a great while. Oh that the Lord may make him an Israelite indeed!

Saturday, December 15. Waited on, and afterwards (at his invitation) dined with the Governor, who received me most courteously. Paid my respects to the Rev. Mr. Blair, the Commissary of Virginia, and by far the most worthy clergyman I have yet conversed with in all America. He received me with joy, asked me to preach, and wished my stay was to be longer. He has been chiefly instrumental in raising a beautiful college at Williamsburgh, in which is a foundation for about eight scholars, a president, two masters, and professors in the several sciences. Here the gentlemen of Virginia send their children, and as far as I could learn by inquiry, they are under about the same regulation and discipline as in our Universities at home. The present masters came from Oxford. Two of them, I find, were my contemporaries there. I rejoiced in seeing such a place in America. It may be of excellent use, if learning Christ be made one end of their studies, and arts and sciences only introduced and pursued as subservient to that. For want of this, most of our English schools and Universities have sunk into mere seminaries of paganism. Young men's heads are stuffed with heathen mythology, and Christ or Christianity is scarcely so much as named among them; so that when they come to be converted, they are obliged to undo what they have been doing for many years. Revive, O Lord, a primitive spirit, and then we may hope for some primitive schools to be erected and encouraged among us.

Sunday, December 16. Preached in the morning. Several gentlemen came from York, fourteen miles off, to hear me, and were desirous of my going back to preach at their town, on the morrow. A large audience, I found might have been expected, could timely notice have been given; but being in great haste, and there being no sermon customarily in the afternoon, I dined with the Commissary, and left Williamsburgh in the afternoon, promising, if possible, to visit these parts again some time in the summer. About three miles from the town we took leave of our friend from Gloucester, whose heart God has much melted by the foolishness of preaching. Here also, as well as at Williamsburgh, we left some letters to be sent to England. I could not but think, that God intended, in His own time, to work a good work in these southern parts of America. At present they seem more dead to God, but far less prejudiced than in the northern parts. At his request, I gave the printer leave to print my *Journals and Sermons* and I trust that God Who loves to work by the meanest instruments, will be pleased to bless them to the conviction and edification of these His people. Visit them, O Lord, with Thy salvation.

> Stretch out Thine Arm, victorious King,
>   Their raging sins subdue,
> Drive the old dragon from his seat,
>   With his infernal crew.

Monday, December 17. Got over a ferry three miles broad last night, and met with a young man who showed us the way to Captain R....n's, who entertained us with much generosity, and was so kind as to go with us this morning fourteen miles on our way. On first getting up, I perceived myself much indisposed, but God was pleased to strengthen me, and I held out my journey till we came to an ordinary about thirty miles from the place where we lay last night. Here we met with what some would account very indifferent entertainment; but God enabled us to be resigned and thankful. Bashfulness, and a fear of being troublesome, have kept us from embracing offers of gentlemen's houses; but we have heard a good report of the generosity of the Virginia gentlemen. I find they are so willing, and accustomed to entertain strangers, that few think it worth their while to keep public ordinaries. It is good to find people given to hospitality.

Tuesday, December 18. Was very restless and indisposed with a fever all night, which continuing upon me, and one of our horses being foundered, it was thought advisable to stay at the ordinary the whole day. Being very weak I could scarce lift up my head, or eat any food; but God caused me to rejoice in it, so that my greatest concern was about the trouble I gave my dear friends. I never feel the power of religion more than when under outward or inward trials. It is that alone which can enable any man to sustain with patience and thankfulness his bodily infirmities. Lord, let me feel the power of it more and more, and then, though Thou slay me, yet will I put my trust in Thee.

NORTH CAROLINA: Wednesday, December 19. Finding myself somewhat stronger, and the horse also being in better order, we took a short day's journey of about twenty-six miles, and were most affectionately received by Colonel O...n, in North Carolina. A little while after our coming in, I begged leave to lie down to rest my weary limbs. In some way or other, in my absence, my friends acquainted our host who I was; upon which he was so rejoiced that he could not tell how to express his satisfaction. His wife also seemed most anxious to oblige, and they were only concerned that they could do no more for us. The honest old man told us, that his son-in-law, who lived about three miles off, ever since he heard of me in the *News*, wished that I would come there. This is not the first time, by many, that I have found the advantage of the things my adversaries have inserted in the public papers: they do but excite people's curiosity, and serve to raise their attention, while men of seriousness and candor naturally infer that some good must be doing where such stories and falsities are invented. It often gives me unspeakable comfort, to see how wisely God overrules everything for the good of His Church.

> The world, sin, death, oppose in vain,
> Christ by His dying, death hath slain!
> My great Deliverer, and my God.
> In vain does the old dragon rage,
> In vain all hell its pow'rs engage;
> Nought can withstand Thy conquering Blood!

EDEN TOWN: Thursday, December 20. Found myself better in the morning than I have been for some days past. Took leave of our kind host, and traveled cheerfully onwards. About noon, we alighted in the woods, to give our horses provender, and to take a little refreshment ourselves, which we have done every day this week, because there are no ordinaries in the way. We praised God for spreading us a table in the wilderness. By four in the afternoon, we reached Eden Town, a little place, beautifully situated by the waterside. Here we were well entertained at a publichouse; and though God was pleased to humble my body by weakness, and my soul by conviction of past sin, yet before we went to rest, He was pleased to refresh me with exceeding peace, and in the midst of my humiliations exalted me, by giving me a more lively sense of His favor and lovingkindness, which is better than life itself. I think I often feel what our Lord meant, when He said the Publican went down to his house justified rather than the Pharisee. I doubt not, but that while he was pouring out his soul and smiting upon his breast, the Holy Spirit overshadowed him, and sealed to him his pardon. It is a dreadful mistake to deny the doctrine of assurances, or to think it is confined to a time of persecution, or to the primitive ages of the Church. Not only righteousness and peace, but joy in the Holy Ghost, which is the consequence of assurance, is a necessary part of the Kingdom of God within us; and though all are not to be condemned who have not an immediate assurance, yet all ought to labor after it. I really believe one great reason why so many go mourning all their life long, is owing to ignorance of their Christian privileges. They have not assurance, because they ask it not; they ask it not, because they are taught that it does not belong to Christians of these last days; whereas I know numbers whose salvation is written upon their hearts as it were with a sunbeam. They can rejoice in God their Savior, and give men and devils the challenge to separate them, if they can, from the love of God in Christ Jesus their Lord. Dear Redeemer, enlighten all Thy followers to see their privileges, and never let them cease wrestling with Thee till Thou dost bless them, by assuring them of their eternal salvation.

Why should the children of a King,
   Go mourning all their days?
Great Comforter, descend, and bring
   The tokens of Thy grace!
Assure each conscience of its part
   In the Redeemer's blood;
And bear Thy witness with each heart,
   That it is born of God!

BELL'S FERRY: Friday, December 21. Was much refreshed both in body and spirit: and the weather being too hazy to pass over the Sound, I had an opportunity of writing. I intended, had I stayed, to preach to those few people who were in the town; but, about noon, the sun shining bright and dispelling the mist, at three o'clock we went in a pettiagua over the sound, and were nearly seven hours in our passage. It was about twelve miles across. God favored us with a calm and pleasant night, and we praised Him as we went over by singing hymns, and met with a convenient ordinary when we got on the other side. How short a way can a boat go in a long time, when there is no wind or tide to carry it forward. Thus it is with the soul. When God withholds the gentle gales and breathings of His Spirit from us, we sail but slowly towards the haven of eternal rest. Happy the man who gets out of himself, and lives upon the promises of the Gospel; he is sure whether he is becalmed, or in a storm, that all will work together for his good.

BATH-TOWN: Saturday, December 22. Set out at break of day, and arrived by eight at night at Bath-Town, which is nearly fifty miles from Bell's Ferry. It is by far the longest stage, and the roads are the worst we have had since we began our journey. The ground, most part of the way, was wet and swampy, the country uninhabited, and a very great alteration was discernible in the climate. It was as hot as it is generally at Midsummer in England; but we had a sweet breeze, which made our riding through the woods in the daytime exceedingly pleasant. About midway, we met with an ordinary, where we refreshed ourselves and beasts. We observed a variety of birds; and, in the evening, heard the wolves howling like a kennel of hounds, which made me reflect on what the Psalmist says, "The lions roaring after their prey do seek their meat from God."

They range all night on slaughter bent,
   Till summoned by the rising morn,
To skulk in dens, with one consent,
   The conscious ravagers return.

God's Providence sent us a guide, and we had better entertainment at our inn than we have had for some time. As we rode along, one of my friends said, "How dreadful must it be for a natural man to be placed in such a howling wilderness, surrounded with those many wolves, bears, and tigers, which come forth at night roaring upon him?" And then he added, "But how infinitely more dreadful must it be to be cast into hell, and surrounded continually with the howlings of damned spirits!" When we came to the inn, we were told of a man and woman, who one night were surrounded with a company of these wolves, and pursued by them a long way.

> Though in a bare and rugged way,
> Through desert lonely wilds I stray,
> Thy bounty shall my pains beguile;
> The barren wilderness shall smile
> With sudden greens and herbage crown'd,
> And streams shall murmur all around.

Sunday, December 23. Sent to the minister of the place, and had some conversation with him last night. Preached about noon to nearly a hundred people, which, I found, was an extraordinary congregation, there being seldom more than twenty at church. I felt the Divine Presence, and did not spare to tell my hearers that I thought God was angry with them, because He had sent a famine of the Word among them for a long while, and not given them a teaching priest. All seemed attentive to what was spoken. After sermon, one poor woman came with a full heart, desiring my prayers. I asked her whether she had been convicted by the sermon, or whether she knew Christ; she answered, she had been seeking Him for some time, but wanted to find a minister who had understanding in Divine things. This case is not uncommon. Most that handle the law know not what they say, nor whereof they affirm. Lord Jesus, in Thy mercy purify the sons of Levi; accomplish the number of Thine elect, and hasten Thy Kingdom! O make no long tarrying, our Lord and our God!

NEWBORN TOWN: Monday, December 24. Crossed Pamplico River, about five miles wide yesterday evening. Lay at an ordinary at the waterside. Set out by break of day, crossed New River about four in the afternoon, and reached Newborn Town, thirty-two miles from Bath Town, by six at night. Had sweet communion in spirit, after I came to the inn, with my dear friends in England, who, I supposed were joining with one accord in fervent prayer, and ushering in the festival of our dear Lord's nativity, by the singing of hymns and spiritual songs. This time, twelve months ago, I was with them, and even now I am not absent from them; my soul is closely united with them, and all God's children, by the Spirit of His dear Son, and however separated here, this is my comfort, that neither men nor devils can keep us from meeting and dwelling together eternally hereafter. Oh, that the cry was made, "Behold the Bridegroom cometh!" As the hart panteth after the water brooks, so doth my soul long for that time when I shall be summoned to go forth to meet Him.

Tuesday, December 25. Endeavored still to keep my mind as much as possible in union with all those who I knew were rejoicing in the glad tidings of salvation by Jesus Christ. Went to public worship, and received the Holy Sacrament, which was celebrated in the Court House; but mourned much in spirit, to see in what an indifferent manner everything was carried on. I cried mightily to the Lord in my secret devotions, and in the afternoon when I read prayers and preached, He was pleased to show that He had heard me, for I scarcely know when we have had a more visible manifestation of the Divine Presence since our coming into America. The people were uncommonly attentive, and most were melted into tears. After sermon, a poor woman, with a heart full of concern, ran to me, desiring that I would come and preach where she lived, and another told me I had given him a home stroke. The woman where we lodged would take nothing for our Christmas dinner, and wished we could stay with them longer. This unexpected success rejoiced me the more, because I looked upon it as an earnest of future and more plentiful effusions of God's Spirit in these parts. I believe, whenever the Gospel is preached in these parts with power, it will be remarkably blessed. I have scarcely heard of one faithful minister sent over among them; and how shall they believe on Him of Whom they have not heard? And how shall they hear without a preacher? And how shall they preach, unless they are sent by and taught of God? Oh, how it will rejoice me to hear that some poor soul this day was born again. Then it would be a Christmas Day indeed! And why should I doubt? I have great reason to think

> In many a soul the Saviour stirred;
> I trust some yielded, and believed.

Soon after evening service, I and my friends took horse, rode about eight miles, and were entertained by a German, who kept an ordinary, and who had been one of my hearers. The people of that nation, (as far as I can find), are the most industrious as well as serious people that ever came into America. Wrote this morning to the minister of Newborn, who I heard countenanced a dancing-master, by suffering his own son to be one of his learners. Several of the inhabitants, I was informed, had subscribed to his assemblies, and they were generally attended with ill consequences, which made me the more desirous to leave my testimony against them. It grieves me to find that in every little town there is a settled dancing-master, but scarcely anywhere a settled minister to be met with; such a proceeding must be of dreadful consequence to any, especially a new settled province. All Governors, if it were only from a policy of human policy, ought to put a stop to it; for such entertainments altogether enervate the minds of people, insensibly leading them into effeminacy, and unfitting them to endure those hardships, and fatigues, which must necessarily be undergone, to bring any province to perfection. True religion alone exalts a nation; such sinful entertainments are a reproach, and will, in time, be the ruin of any people.

Wednesday, December 26. Set out early, and rode very pleasantly till dinner time. Had some refreshment at an ordinary on the road, and lodged at a little house in the woods, about thirty-five miles from where we lay last night. I had a good deal of discourse with the people of the house, and after much previous and suitable conversation, I baptized two children of strangers, who lay at the same house that night. I believe there may be hundreds of children in this province unbaptized, for want of a minister.

Oh, that the Lord would send forth some who, like John the Baptist, might preach and baptize in the wilderness! I believe they would flock to him from all the country round about.

Thursday, December 27. Set out about eight in the morning; crossed Trent River, a ferry about half a mile wide, and got to an ordinary a little way out of the road, and about thirty-three miles distant, before six at night. As soon as I came in, a young man welcomed me to America, who, upon enquiry, I found had been one of my parishioners at Savannah; this gave me an immediate opportunity of falling into religious conversation, and afterwards I went, as my usual custom is, among the Negroes belong to the house. One man was sick in bed, and two of his children said their prayers after me very well. This more and more convinces me that Negro children, if early brought up in the nurture and admonition of the Lord, would make as great proficiency as any white people's children. I do not despair, if God spares my life, of seeing a school of young Negroes singing the praises of Him Who made them, in a psalm of thanksgiving. Lord, Thou hast put into my heart a good design to educate them; I doubt not but Thou will enable me to bring it to good effect.

NEW TOWN ON CAPE FEAR RIVER: Friday, December 28. Had a very boisterous night, and the weather continued rainy most part of the day. After about fifteen miles' ride, we refreshed both ourselves and beasts at a poor widow's ordinary, who, a few days ago, had buried her husband, which made her better prepared for religious discourse. After dinner, we had a pleasant ride to New Town on Cape Fear River, nearly eighteen miles from the place where we partook of refreshments. It is a little but thriving place for trade. We rejoiced greatly that the Lord had brought us so far on our journey, and had not suffered us to go out of our way through so many almost uninhabited woods, nor so much as to hurt our feet against a stone. The little wet weather today made our inns more acceptable, and we could not help reflecting that it is in our spiritual as in our temporal journeys; sometimes the Sun of Righteousness arises with great luster upon our hearts, sometimes a cloud overshadows us, and storms surround us. Lord enable us through all, continually to press forward, and suffer us not to grow weary and faint in our minds; for we know that one moment of the Beatific Vision will make amends for all.

Saturday, December 29. Thought proper to rest today for the ease of our beasts. Had another opportunity of writing some letters to England. Dined with Mr. Murray, the naval officer, who gave us an invitation last night to his house, and spent the remainder of the day in writing down some things that lay upon my heart. Sanctify them, O Lord, to the promoting Thy glory, and the good of mankind.

Sunday, December 30. Wrote more letters to my friends in England. Read prayers, and preached, both morning and evening, in the Court House, to as many as could be expected at so short a warning. There being many of the Scotch among the congregation, who lately came over to settle in North Carolina, I was led in the afternoon to make a particular application to them, and to remind them of the necessity of living holy lives, that so they might prove a blessing to the province, and giving proof of their zeal for those truths which they had heard preached to them, with great purity and clearness, in their native country. After service, two gentlemen came and pressed me to stay longer; but being intent on my journey, about five in the evening I and my friends passed the ferry, about three miles distant, and lay at the house of the High Sheriff of the county. Here we met with some other persons, whom I prayed with, and instructed to the best of my power, for which they seemed thankful. Much good may be done by an earnest and circumspect endeavoring always to introduce proper religious conversation. Our Lord did so wherever He was; and every true minister of Jesus Christ ought to live so exemplarily, that wheresoever he comes people should expect some edifying discourse immediately from him. Every Christian ought to bring light and heat with him, like the sun, wheresoever he comes. Wicked men will show us an example of boldness.

> They can brave th'eternal laws,
> Zealous in their master's cause;
> Jesus, shall Thy servants be
> Less resolv'd or bold for Thee?

Monday, December 31. Set out early and met with more perils by land than we have been exposed to yet. It had rained almost the whole night, the swamps and creeks which lay in the way were filled with water; and the bridges, being out of repair, rendered traveling very dangerous. In one place, we were obliged to swim our horses; in many, the waters were very high, and were not to be passed without much difficulty. But the Lord sent us two good guides, by whose assistance we were carried through all, and brought at night, to a little house, where with pleasure we reflected on the dangers and deliverances of the day, and reminded one another of the unspeakable satisfaction we might expect hereafter on reviewing those many crosses, difficulties, and temptations, which we must necessarily endure while in our pilgrimage here. Oh that we may learn to endure any pain, despise any shame, submit to any difficulties, from a believing prospect of what we shall hereafter enjoy, when raised to glory at the right hand of God our Savior!

SOUTH CAROLINA: Tuesday, January 1, 1740. Rode about ten miles, and where we partook of refreshments, met with one who I had great reason to believe, was a child of God. It grieved me that I could stay no longer, but being in haste, we passed over a half-mile ferry. About sunset, we came to a tavern, five miles within the province of South Carolina. Here I immediately perceived the people were more polite than those we generally met with; but I believe the people of the house wished I had not come to be their guest that night; for, it being New Year's Day, several of the neighbors were met together to divert themselves by dancing country dances. By the advice of my companions, I went in among them while a woman was dancing a jig. At my first entrance I endeavored to show the folly of such entertainments, and to convince her how well pleased the devil was at every step she took. For some time she endeavored to outbrave me; neither the fiddler nor she desisted; but at last she gave over, and the musician laid aside his instrument. It would have made any one smile to see how the rest of the company, one by one attacked me, and brought, as they thought, arguments to support their wantonness; but Christ triumphed over Satan. All were soon put to silence, and were, for some time, so overawed, that after I had discoursed with them on the nature of baptism, and the necessity of being born again, in order to enjoy the Kingdom of Heaven, I baptized, at their entreaty, one of their children, and prayed afterwards as I was enabled, and as the circumstances of the company required. I and my companions then took a little refreshment; but the people were so bent on their pleasure, that notwithstanding all that had been said, after I had gone to bed, I heard their music and dancing, which made me look back upon my own past follies with shame and confusion of face; for such an one, not long since, was I myself. Lord, for Thy mercies' sake, show all unhappy formalists the same favor, and suffer them not to go in such a carnal security till they lift up their eyes in torment! Draw them, O draw them from feeding upon such husks. Let them know what it is to feast upon the fatted calf, even the comforts of the Blessed Spirit. Amen.

Wednesday, January 2. Rose very early, prayed, sang a hymn, and gave a sharp reproof to the dancers, who were very attentive, and took it in good part. At break of day, we mounted our horses, and, I think, never had a more pleasant journey. For nearly twenty miles we rode over a beautiful bay as plain as a terrace walk, and as we passed along were wonderfully delighted to see the porpoises taking their pastime, and hear, as it were, shore resounding to shore the praises of Him Who hath set bounds to the sea that it cannot pass, and hath said, "Here shall your proud waves be stayed." At night we intended to call at a gentleman's house, where we had been recommended, about forty miles distant from our last night's lodging; but the moon being totally eclipsed, we missed the path that turned out of the road, and then thought it most advisable, as we were in the main road, to go on our way, trusting to the Almighty to strengthen both our beasts and us. We had not gone far when we saw a light. Two of my friends went up to it, and found a hut full of Negroes; they inquired after the gentleman's house where we had been directed, but the Negroes seemed surprised, and said they knew no such man, and that they were newcomers. From these circumstances, one of my friends inferred that these Negroes might be some of those who lately had made an insurrection in the province, and had run away from their masters. When he returned, we were all of his mind, and, therefore, thought it best to mend our pace. Soon after, we saw another great fire near the roadside, and imagining there was another nest of such Negroes, we made a circuit into the woods, and one of my friends at a distance observed them dancing round the fire. The moon shining brightly, we soon found our way into the great road again; and after we had gone about a dozen miles, (expecting to find Negroes in every place), we came to a great plantation, the master of which gave us lodging, and our beasts provender. Upon our relating the circumstances of our travels, he satisfied us concerning the Negroes, informed us whose they were, and upon what occasion they were in those places in which we found them. This afforded us much comfort, after we had ridden nearly threescore miles, and, as we thought, in great peril of our lives. Blessed be Thy Name, O Lord, for this, and all other Thy mercies, through Jesus Christ!

Thursday, January 3. Had a hospitable breakfast; set out late in the morning, passed over a three mile ferry near George Town; and for the ease of our beasts, rode not above nineteen miles the whole day. "A good man," says Solomon, "is merciful to his beast."

Friday, January 4. Lay at a little house on Santa River, where I met a soldier, formerly one of my catechumens, who had been discharged, but retained a grateful sense of the instructions which had been given him. Passed over two ferries in the morning, partook of refreshments at dinner time, after we had ridden about eighteen miles and were then obliged to ride twenty-five miles farther, there being no proper place to stay at by the way. About eight in the evening, we came to a tavern, five miles from Charleston, where we were refreshed with food. We then had family prayer, and endeavored to express our thankfulness to God for thus causing us to renew our strength, and bring us so near the place where we would be. Oh, that our hearts may be excited more and more to praise the Lord for these and all other mercies which He daily pours down on us, the unworthiest of the sons of men!

CHARLESTON: Saturday, January 5. Left our lodging before daylight, and reached Charleston, after we had passed over a three mile ferry, about ten in the morning. Went to the house of one Mr. L . . . re, where we dined, and were entertained with great civility. In the afternoon, several gentlemen of the town were so kind as to come and see me, and expressed great willingness to hear me preach. Letters and papers were also brought me from New York, informing me how mightily the Word of God grew and prevailed there. The accounts in the English papers of the war being daily carried on there between Christ and Belial, afforded us fresh matter for praising that God, Who we hoped would, in His Kingdom of grace, bring mighty things to pass, while the world was busied in wars and rumors of wars.

Sunday, January 6. Went to public service in the morning, but did not preach, because the curate had not a commission to lend the pulpit, unless the Commissary (then out of town) were present. Most of the town, however, being eager to hear me, I preached, in the afternoon, in one of the Dissenting meeting-houses, but was grieved to find so little concern in the congregation. The auditory was large, but very polite. I question whether the court-end of London could exceed them in affected finery, gaiety of dress, and a deportment ill-becoming persons who have had such Divine judgments lately sent among them. I reminded them of this in my sermon; but I seemed to them as one that mocked. This made me more importunate in secret prayer, and I hoped God would let me see that He intended to visit the inhabitants with mercy as well as with judgments; for nothing is a greater sign of a people's being hardened, than their continuing unreformed under Divine visitations. Thus it was with Pharaoh and the Egyptians. Lord, for Thy mercy's sake, let it not be the case of this people! Amen, Lord Jesus, Amen.

Monday, January 7. Finding the inhabitants desirous to hear me a second time, I preached at the French church, at eleven in the morning, and blessed be God, I saw a glorious alteration in the audience, which was so great that many stood without the door. I felt much more freedom than I did yesterday. Many were melted into tears. One of the town, most remarkably gay, was observed to weep. Instead of the people going out (as they did yesterday) in a light, unthinking manner, a visible concern was in most of their faces. After sermon, I and my friends dined at a merchant's; and, as I was passing along, a letter was put into my hands, wherein were these words: "Remember me in your prayers, for Christ's sake, Who died for me a sinner. I appeal to you for help in the way to salvation. Pray fail me not; I beseech you to pray for my soul; and the Lord bless you, and grant you may win many souls to God by your preaching." Many of the inhabitants, with full hearts, entreated me to give them one more sermon, and, though I was just about to take the boat, I thought it my duty to comply with their request, and put off my journey till the morrow. Notice was immediately given, and, in about half an hour, a large congregation was assembled in the meeting-house, where I preached yesterday, because it was the largest place. God strengthened me to speak, I trust, as I ought to speak. In the evening, I supped at another merchant's house, and had an opportunity, for nearly two hours, to converse of the things of God with a large company, and retired to my lodgings, full of joy at the prospect of a good work having begun in that place. It grieves me to see people humane, hospitable, willing to oblige, and in every way accomplished, excepting that they are yet ignorant of *the one thing needful*. Lord, send forth Thy servants, and let there be now a great cry made, "Behold the Bridgroom cometh," and incline all formal professors, all polite and foolish virgins, to trim their lamps, that they may be ready to go forth to meet Thee.

BEAUFORT IN PORT ROYAL: Tuesday, January 8. Rose a good while before day, left our horses in Charleston, and set out for Georgia in an open canoe (having five Negroes to row and steer us), God being pleased to give us, for the most part, fair weather. The poor slaves were very civil, diligent, and laborious. We lay one night on the water; and, about five on Wednesday evening, arrived at Beaufort in Port Royal (one hundred miles from Charleston), within the province of South Carolina. We drank a little tea at our inn, and then waited upon the Rev. Mr. Jones, the minister of the place, who received us with great civility, and was very desirous that I should take a bed at his house, as I did when I passed through the place after I left Georgia last. But intending to set out by two in the morning, we thought it best to lie at our inn; and, therefore, after supper, and a little friendly conversation, we took our leave.

Wednesday, January 9. The wind being very high, and sailing impracticable, we stayed at Beaufort all the morning, and dined with kind Mr. Jones. Afterwards, the weather being fair, and the tide serving, we took boat, and refreshed ourselves at a plantation on the way. In the night, we made a fire on the shore, and slept round it for about four hours. A little after midnight, we prayed with the Negroes; took boat again; and reached Savannah before noon the next day, where I had a joyful meeting with my dear friends, who I found, had arrived three weeks ago. Blessed be God, the work of our dear Emmanuel is everywhere being carried on. I expect, ere long, that mighty things will be brought to pass. Oh, that the Lord may strengthen me to make full proof of my ministry in this place, to the glory of His great Name, and the good of His dear Church!

Here I would stop, but I think it may not be amiss to put down some remarks which I have made on the state of religion in those provinces, which I have lately passed through. And here I cannot but give Pennsylvania the preference. To me it seems to be the garden of America. Their oxen are strong to labor, and there seems to be no complaining in their streets. What is best of all, I believe they have the Lord for their God. This, I infer, from their having so many faithful ministers sent forth among them; and, except Northampton in New England, the work of conversion has not been carried on with so much power in any part of America, that I can hear of, as under the ministry of Messrs. Tennents, Cross, and the other laborers before mentioned. The Constitution is far from being arbitrary; the soil is good, the land exceedingly fruitful, and there is a greater equality between the poor and rich than perhaps can be found in any other place of the known world. For my part, I like it so well, that, God willing, I purpose taking up some land to erect a school for Negroes, and settle some of my English friends, whose hearts God shall stir up, or whom the fury of their enemies shall oblige to depart from their native land.

Philadelphia is one of the most regular planned towns I ever saw. Above seventy new houses were built in it last year, and it is likely to increase in inhabitants every day. It is rightly called Philadelphia, i.e., brotherly love; for by the charter all are permitted to worship God their own way, without being branded as schismatics, dissenters, or disturbers of the established constitution. The Quakers have the pre-eminence in the government. The Assembly is made up of them, with the exception of about four, which prevents all preparations for martial defense, it being one of their principles not to fight at all. Much of the simplicity of dress and manners, which may be observed among the inhabitants, I think is, in a great measure, owing to them. I saw less of the pride of life in Pennsylvania than elsewhere. But it has happened to them, as it will to all other religious societies, when they flourish and have the upper hand. I mean that many, for profit's sake, have been known to dissemble with them. I fear numbers among them, as among us, can give no other reason why they are Quakers, than that their fathers were so before them. I say this, because I find little of Divine Power stirring among them; and most of them are too stiff and rigid about external things, I was credibly informed. One of their own preachers warned them lately of their backsliding, and told them, that without a reformation, God would remove the candlestick from them, and work no more by their hands. In the city of Philadelphia they have two large meeting-houses, where they assemble frequently together; and, all things considered, are the most regular society of men I have seen or heard of. Besides this, there are Baptist and Presbyterian meetings. I had the pleasure of conversing with the ministers of both; and found there were some in their congregations, particularly in the Baptist, who loved the Lord Jesus in sincerity. The Church of England is at a low ebb in the province in general, and in Philadelphia in particular. In all the places that I passed through, the Presbyterians and Quakers had larger congregations than any of our missionaries; and we may guess that the love of many of the Church of England in Philadelphia must have waxed cold, for the church, which was begun, if I mistake not, some years ago, is now far from being finished within. Many of late, however, have been convinced what true Christianity is; and I hope a church of Jesus Christ will, ere long, be selected out of the members of our own communion.

The little time I was in New York would not permit me to make as many observations of the situation of affairs of religion in the province, as otherwise I might have done. A great complaint was made to me by some of the most serious inhabitants of it, that it was a very secure place, and that a work of God had never been carried on in it, since its first settlement. The heads of the Church of England seemed resolved to shut out the Kingdom of God from among them; but our Lord Jesus has been pleased to get Himself the victory; for though I was mostly opposed in New York, yet, if I may judge of what I saw myself, and have heard since my departure, as much, if not more good has been done there, than in any other place, in so short a time. In Maryland religion seems to be at a very low ebb. There are Roman Catholics in some parts, four congregations of Presbyterians, and a few Quakers; but by far the greatest part call themselves of the Church of England, which might, no doubt, greatly flourish were her ministers found faithful. But the Government, I fear, spoils them by giving them too much tobacco; for some, I hear, have thirty thousand, others fifty thousand, and others sixty thousand pounds of tobacco per annum. It is gathered by the High Sheriff of the County, and every person taxable is obliged to pay forty pounds of tobacco yearly to the ministers, though great numbers never hear or see them. In Virginia matters are not so bad. The ministers' stipends are not so large; the Commissary seems to have more power, and to exercise more discipline; but almost all are quite settled upon their lees. In Virginia, there are no Dissenters from the Established Church, except one or two meetings of Quakers. The importation of so many Negroes and convicts is one great reason why there is so little religion to be seen; but the main cause of irreligion, both in Virginia and Maryland, I take to be their not incorporating into towns: for hereby people living at a distance from the church, are apt to make every little thing serve as an excuse to keep them from public worship. While in this condition, religious societies cannot well be settled, and without control, wicked men may more easily revel and get drunk. Ministers, had they a will, cannot visit from house to house; and, what is as bad as anything, schools for the education of children cannot be so conveniently erected when the houses are so far apart. The greatest probability of doing good in Virginia is among the Scots-Irish, who have lately settled in the mountainous parts of that province. They raise little or no tobacco, but things that are useful for common life. I hear the Governor has given leave for a minister of their own religious persuasion, to come whenever he can be procured.

In North Carolina there is scarcely so much as the form of religion. Two churches were begun, some time since, but neither is finished. There are several dancing-masters, but scarcely one regular settled minister; so that in most places they have readers, who read a sermon every Sunday to the people, for which they pay five shillings a quarter of their currency, which is ten shillings sterling for one. However, the Governor, I hear, has made proposals to the Society for Propagating the Gospel in Foreign Parts, to send missionaries. But I should rather that people had no minister than such as are generally sent over; and I cannot see the charity of contributing towards sending out missionaries, unless greater care be taken in the choice of those who are sent. All the accounts most of them have given for some time is, that they have baptized so many, and that so many have received the Sacrament; and, upon the whole, if it be asked why there is so little religion in the Church of England, it may be answered, the missionaries, who, for the most part, lead very bad examples. In South Carolina they have many ministers, both of our own and other persuasions; but I hear of no stirring among the dry bones. Mr. Garden, the present Commissary, is strict in the outward discipline of the Church. And now I am come to Georgia, what shall I say? Many of the inhabitants have left it since we were here last; but I hope blessings are in reserve. Oh, that all who remain would acquaint themselves with God, and be at peace with Him; then would they be more than conquerors over all their enemies.

Thus have I put down a few thoughts that have occurred to my mind. May God enlighten me where I am in the dark, correct me wherever I am wrong, and bless this further account of His dealings with me to all who shall read it. Amen.

I cannot express my desire for the advancing of our dear Lord's Kingdom, both in the hearts of my friends and all mankind, better than in the hymn altered from Dr. More, by one of the Reverend Mr. Wesleys.

I   When Christ had left His flock below,
        The loss His faithful flock deplored:
    Him in the flesh no more they know,
        And languish for their absent Lord.

II   Not long — for He gone up on high,
        Gifts to receive, and claim His crown,
    Beheld them sorrowing, from His sky,
        And poured the mighty blessing down.

III   He, for the presence of His flesh,
        The Spirit's seven-fold gifts imparts,
    And living streams their souls refresh,
        And joy Divine o'erflows their hearts.

IV   While all in sweet devotion joined,
        Humbly to wait for God, retire,
    The promised grace in rushing wind
        Descends, and cloven tongues of fire.

V   God's mighty Spirit fills the dome,
        The feeble dome beneath Him shook,
    Trembled the crowd to feel Him come,
        Soon as the Sons of Thunder spoke.

VI   Father, if justly still we claim
        To us, and ours, the promise made,
    To us be graciously the same,
        And crown with living fire our head.

VII   Our claim admit, and from above,
        Of holiness the Spirit shower,
    Of wise discernment, humble love,
        And zeal, and unity, and power.

VIII   The Spirit of convincing speech,
        Of power demonstrative impart,
    Such as may every conscience reach,
        And sound the unbelieving heart.

IX   The Spirit of refining fire,
        Searching the inmost of the mind,
    To purge all fierce and foul desire,
        And kindle life more pure and kind.

X   The Sp'rit of faith, in this Thy day,
        To break the power of cancelled sin,
    Tread down its strength, o'erturn its sway,
        And still the conquest more than win.

XI   The Spirit breathe of inward life,
        Which in our hearts Thy laws may write;
    Then grief expires, and pain, and strife:
        'Tis nature all, and all delight.

XII   On all the earth Thy Spirit shower,
        The earth in righteousness renew;
    Thy kingdom come, and hell's o'erpower,
        And to Thy sceptre all subdue.

XIII   Like mighty wind, or torrent fierce,
        Let it opposers all o'er-run,
    And every law of sin reverse,
        That faith and love may make all one.

XIV   Yea, let Thy Sp'rit in ev'ry place
        Its richer energy declare,
    While lovely tempers, fruits of grace,
        The Kingdom of Thy Christ prepare.

XV   Grant this, O holy God, and true!
        The ancient seers Thou didst inspire:
    To us perform the promise due,
        Descend and crown us now with fire.

THE SIXTH JOURNAL

FROM WHITEFIELD'S ARRIVAL AT GEORGIA TO A FEW DAYS AFTER HIS SECOND RETURN THERE FROM PHILADELPHIA

(JANUARY 1740 – JUNE 1740)

SAVANNAH: Friday, January 11, 1740. Went this morning, with some friends, to view a tract of land, consisting of five hundred acres, which Mr. Habersham, whom I left schoolmaster of Savannah, was directed, I hope by Providence, to make choice of for the Orphan House. It is situated on the northern part of the colony, about ten miles from Savannah, and has various kinds of soil in it; a part of it very good. Some acres, through the diligence of my friend, are cleared. He has also stocked it with cattle and poultry. He has begun the fence, and built a hut, which will greatly forward the work. I choose to have it so far off the town, because the children will be more free from bad examples, and can more conveniently go up on the land to work. For it is my design to have each of the children taught to labor, so as to be qualified to get their own living. Lord, do Thou teach and excite them to labor also for that meat which endureth to everlasting life!

Thursday, January 24. Went this morning and took possession of my lot. I called it Bethesda, that is, the House of Mercy; for I hope many acts of mercy will be shown there, and that many will thereby be stirred up to praise the Lord, as a God Whose mercy endureth forever.

Tuesday, January 29. Took in three German orphans, the most pitiful objects, I think, I ever saw. No new Negroes could look more despicable, or require more pains to instruct them. They have been used to exceedingly hard labor, and though supplied with provisions from the trustees, were treated in a manner unbecoming even heathens. Were all the money I have collected, to be spent in freeing these three children from slavery, it would be well laid out. I have also in my house near twenty more, who, in all probability, if not taken in, would be as ignorant of God and Christ as the Indians. Blessed be God, they begin to live in order. Continue this and all other blessings to them, for Thy mercies' sake, O Lord.

This day I began the cotton manufacture, and agreed with a woman to teach the little ones to spin and card. I find annual cotton grows fairly well in Georgia; and to encourage the people, I bought today, three hundred pounds weight, and have agreed to take all the cotton, hemp, and flax that shall be produced the following year through the whole province. Though there are fewer inhabitants in Savannah, yet I think they are in a better situation than when I was here last. They now live independent on a public store. Provisions, (flour especially) are much cheaper, cattle more plentiful; and if any manufacturer can be raised among themselves, to prevent them exporting so much money, thay may yet do well. My congregations are as large as usual. The Court House is generally full; and I keep as near as possible to my old way of proceeding. We have the Sacrament every Sunday, and public prayer and exposition twice every day in the week.

Wednesday, January 30. Went with the carpenter and surveyor, and laid out the ground whereon the Orphan House is to be built. It is to be sixty feet long and forty wide. The foundation is to be brick, and is to be sunk four feet within, and raised three feet above the ground. The house is to be two stories high, with a hip roof: the first ten, the second nine feet high. In all, there will be nearly twenty commodious rooms. Behind are to be two small houses, the one for an infirmary, the other for a workhouse. There is also to be a still-house for the apothecary; and, I trust, before my return to England, I shall see the children and family quite settled. I find it will be an expensive work; but it is for the Lord Christ. He will take care to defray all charges. The money that will be spent, on this occasion, will keep many families from leaving the colony, and in all probability, bring many others over. There are nearly thirty working at the plantation already, and I would employ as many more, if they were to be had. Whatsoever is done for God, ought to be done speedily, as well as with all our might.

Monday, February 4. Met, according to appointment, all the magistrates, who heard the Recorder read the grant given me by the Trustees, and took a minute of their approbation of the same. Lord, grant I may carefully watch over every soul that is or shall be committed to my charge.

Monday, February 11. Took in four fresh orphans, and set out with two friends, to Frederica, in order to pay my respects to General Oglethorpe, and to fetch the orphans in the southern parts of the colony.

PROVIDENCE (Fourteen miles from FREDERICA): Tuesday, February 12. Lay here last night, at a planter's house, expecting to meet the scout boat this morning; but finding it did not come at the time appointed, I and my friends went to Bethesda. At night, we returned to Providence. About eight o'clock the scout boat came; but it being late, we deferred going till next morning. In the meanwhile, God was pleased to give us refreshing sleep, and to fill my soul, after it had been much cast down, with unspeakable peace and joy in the Holy Ghost. Oh, that I was careful always to behave, so as to provoke not that Blessed Guest to depart from me. But I find that I have yet a body of sin and death.

DARIEN NEAR FREDERICA: Friday, February 15. On the water two nights, and reached the Scots' settlement today, at noon. Was kindly received by Mr. MacLeod, the minister, and those of his house. Engaged to take four orphans of his flock; and, about seven in the evening, after some conversation and friendly offices of love, I took boat for Frederica, where we arrived about two in the morning. Having warmed and refreshed ourselves, we retired to bed, blessing God for the bodily and spiritual comforts which He from time to time imparted to us. Oh, that my eyes were open to see the length, and breadth, and depth, and height of the loving kindnesses of the Lord! I can only adore — comprehend it, I cannot;

it is past my finding out.

FREDERICA: Saturday, February 16. Waited upon, and was courteously received by General Oglethorpe with whom I and my friends breakfasted and dined, and spent most part of the day. At night I had a fever, which obliged me to go to bed sooner than usual. My mind was also exercised with inward trials; but, in a few hours, my pain both of body and mind, was somewhat abated, and the remainder of the night I was blessed with sweet repose. Forever adored be the Keeper of Israel, Who neither slumbereth nor sleepeth!

> 'Tis He sustains my feeble powers
> With His Almighty arms:
> He watches my unguarded hours,
> Against invading harms.
>
> No scorching sun, nor sickly moon,
> Have leave from Him to smite:
> He shields my head from burning noon,
> From blasting damps at night.
>
> He guards my soul, He keeps my breath,
> When thickest dangers come:
> Still I'll go on, secure from death,
> Till He commands me home.

Sunday, February 17. Found myself better in body, though somewhat weak. Preached in the morning in a room belonging to the storehouse. God was pleased to give me much freedom. The General, soldiers, and people attended very orderly. After sermon I married a couple baptized a child, and spent the remainder of the evening with my two friends. Oh, what a happy thing it is for brethren to dwell together in unity!

Monday, February 18. Rose this morning by one o'clock. Took boat in order to go to St. Andrews; but the rudder breaking, we were obliged to return back and desist from our intended voyage. Went to bed and slept for a few hours. Spent a good part of the day with the General. Received from him a bill of exchange for 150 pounds, which he advanced me in order to begin a church at Savannah. About 7 o'clock set off for Darien, where I had promised to return, to take Mr. McLeod and the orphans with me to Savannah. The passage to that place takes generally about four hours; but the wind being contrary, we were obliged to come to a grappling, near an open reach, and did not get to Darien till the next day at noon. Mr. MacLeod and his friends received us with joy, and finding me ill, advised me to lie down; by which I was much refreshed. Oh, who can express the loving kindness of the Lord, or show forth all His praise!

DARIEN: Wednesday, February 20. Preached at ten in the morning to Mr. MacLeod's congregation. About two o'clock, took boat for Savannah. After we had rowed about twelve miles, the wind grew rough, and the water beat so fast into our boat, which was but small, and very heavily laden, that we were obliged to put in at a place called Doboy Island; where we sat round a large fire, and praised the Lord with joyful lips, for providing such a place for our safety. Oh God, Thou and Thou only art our Refuge against every storm. Be Thou my Guide even unto death.

DOBOY AND DARIEN: Friday, February 22. Continued all day yesterday on Doboy Island, and finding the wind still continued high and contrary, we thought it best to return to Darien, where we arrived about noon. The people were much pleased at our return.

Sunday, February 24. Preached once yesterday, and twice today. Prayed with a sick person. Spent some hours in discoursing with a well-disposed family. Upon many accounts, both bodily and spiritual, had reason to bless God for bringing me to, and detaining me at Darien. I have reason to say, "It is good for me that I have been here." Retirement is a sweet means to keep up and quicken the Divine life. Lord, grant I may never be afraid to converse with Thee and myself.

SAVANNAH: Thursday, February 28. Preached on Monday, and on Tuesday settled a school both for grown persons and children at Darien, to the great satisfaction of the inhabitants. Set out with my friends and four orphans on Tuesday evening. Had pleasant weather. Lay two nights in the woods. Reached Bethesda about noon; and was pleased with the improvements that had been made there in my absence. Took horse and came home to my family at Savannah, who received me with love and joy. The people of the parish also rejoiced at my coming. They flocked to and seemed very attentive at public worship.

Tuesday, March 11. Buried this evening one of the women who came over with me, who I trust, died in the Lord. The orphans sang before the corpse, from our house to the Court House, where I preached; and I afterwards gave another word of exhortation at the grave. My soul was much affected with the awfulness of the solemnity. The Word came with power. I pray God it may make such a deep impression upon all our hearts, that we may be wise and practically consider our latter end!

CHARLESTON: Friday, March 14. Arrived last night at Charleston, being called there to see my brother, who lately came from England, and had brought me a packet of letters from my dear friends. Blessed be God, His work goes on among them! Waited on the Commissary, with my brother and other companions; but met with a cool reception. After I had been there a little while, I told him I was informed he had some questions to propose to me, and that I had now come to give him all the satisfaction I could in answering them. Upon this, I immediately perceived passion to arise in his heart. "Yes, Sir," he said, "I have several questions to put to you. But," he added, "you have got above us," or something to that effect. Then he charged me with enthusiasm and pride, for speaking against the generality of the clergy, and desired I would make my charge good. I told him, I thought I had already; though as yet I had scarce begun with them.

He then asked me wherein the clergy were so much to blame? I answered, they did not preach justification by faith alone; and upon talking with the Commissary, I found he was as ignorant as the rest. He then sneered me with telling me of my modesty, expressed in my letter to the Bishop of Gloucester; charged me with breaking the Canons and Ordination vow; and, notwithstanding I informed him I was ordained by Letters Dismissory from the Bishop of London, in a great rage, he told me, if I preached in any public church in that province, he would suspend me. I replied, I should regard that as much as I would a Pope's bull. "But, Sir," I said, "why should you be offended at my speaking against the generality of the clergy; for I always spoke well of you?" "I might as well be offended," added my brother, "at you saying, 'the generality of people were notorious sinners,' and come and accuse you of speaking evil of me, because I was one of the people." I further added, "You did not behave thus, when I was with you last." "No," he said, "but you did not speak against the clergy then." I then said to him, "If you will make an application to yourself, be pleased to let me ask you one question, 'Have you delivered your soul by exclaiming against the assemblies and balls here?'" "What," said he, "must you come to catechize me? No, I have not exclaimed against them; I think there is no harm in them." "Then," I replied, "I shall think it my duty to exclaim against you." "Then, Sir," he said in a very great rage, "Get you out of my house." I and my friends then took our leave, pitying the Commissary, who I really thought was more noble than to give such treatment. After this, we went to public prayers, dined at a friend's house, drank tea with the Independent minister, and preached at four in the afternoon, to a large auditory in his meeting-house.

Saturday, March 15. Breakfasted, sang a hymn, and had some religious conversation on board my brother's ship. Preached in the Baptist meeting-house; and was much pleased, when I heard afterwards, that from the same pulpit, a person not long ago had preached, who denied the doctrine of original sin, the Divinity and Righteousness of our Lord, and the operation of God's Blessed Spirit upon the soul. I was led to show the utter inability of man to save himself, and absolute necessity of his dependence on the rich mercies and free grace of God in Christ Jesus for his restoration. Some, I observed, were put under concern; and most seemed willing to know whether those things were so. In the evening, I preached again in the Independent meeting house to a more attentive auditory than ever; and had the pleasure, afterwards, of finding that a gentlewoman, whose whole family had been carried away for some time with Deistical principles, began now to be unhinged, and to see that there was no rest in such a scheme for a fallen creature to rely on. Lord Jesus, for Thy mercies' sake, reveal Thyself in her heart, and make her willing to know the faith as it is in Thee. Amen.

Sunday, March 16. Preached at eight in the morning, in the Scots' meeting house, to a large congregation. Visited a sick person. Went to church and heard the Commissary represent me under the character of the Pharisee, who came to the Temple, saying, "God, I thank Thee that I am not as other men are"; but whether I do what I do, out of a principle of pride, or duty, the Searchers of hearts shall discover ere long, before men and angels. I was very sick and weak at dinner. Went to church again in the afternoon; and, about five, preached in the Independent meeting house yard, the house not being capacious enough to hold the auditory.

> With restless and ungoverned rage,
>> Why do the clergy storm?
> Why in such rash attempts engage,
>> As they can ne'er perform?

> The great in counsel and in might,
>> Their various forces bring;
> Against the Lord they all unite,
>> And His anointed King.

> Must we submit to their commands,
>> Presumptuously they say?
> No, let us break their slavish bands,
>> And cast their chains away.

> But God, Who sits enthroned on high,
>> And sees how they combine,
> Does their conspiring strength defy,
>> And mocks their vain design.

Felt much freedom after sermon, in talking to a large company at a merchant's house. Supped with another friend, expounded part of a chapter, prayed, and went to our lodgings with my dear companions, praising and blessing God. Hasten that time, O Lord, when we shall join the Heavenly Choir that is now about Thy throne.

Monday, March 17. Preached, in the morning, in the Independent meeting house, and was more explicit than ever in exclaiming against balls and assemblies. Preached again in the evening, and, being excited thereto by some of the inhabitants, I spoke on behalf of my poor orphans, and collected upwards of 70 pounds sterling, the largest collection I ever yet made on that occasion: a further earnest to me, that we shall yet see greater things in America, and that God will carry on and finish the work, begun in His Name at Georgia.

Tuesday, March 18. Preached twice again this day, and took an affectionate leave of my hearers, thanking them for their great liberality. Many wept, and my own heart yearned much towards them; for I believe a good work is begun in many. Generally, every day several came to me, telling me how God had been pleased to convince them by the Word preached, and how desirous they were of laying hold on and having an interest in the complete and everlasting righteousness of the Lord Jesus Christ. Numbers desired privately to converse with me. Many sent me little presents, as tokens of their love, and earnestly entreated that I would come among them again. Invitations were given me from some of the adjacent villages; and people daily came to town more and more from their plantations to hear the Word. The congregations grew larger on week days, and many things concurred to induce us to think that God intended to visit some in Charleston with His salvation.

SAVANNAH: Friday, March 21. On Wednesday morning, went on board the sloop, prayed, sang a hymn, and took an affectionate leave of my dear brother and other friends. Got over the bar, and reached Savannah about noon this day, to the great joy of my friends and family, who immediately joined with me, in giving thanks to God for the signal mercies vouchsafed unto us since our last parting. O how plentiful is Thy goodness, O Lord, which Thou hast laid up for them that fear Thee, even before the sons of men!

Tuesday, March 25. Went to Bethesda, and, with full assurance of faith, laid the first brick of the great house. The workmen attended, and with me kneeled down and prayed. After we had sung a hymn suitable to the occasion, I gave a word of exhortation to the laborers, and bid them remember to work heartily, knowing that they worked for God. Much satisfaction seemed to be among them, and blessed be God's Holy Name, His work prospers much in our hands. Nearly twenty acres of land are cleared, and almost ready for planting. Two houses are already raised, and one nearly finished. All the timber of the great house is sawn, and most of it brought to the place where it is to be built. A good part of the foundation is dug, and many thousands of bricks ready for use. Nearly forty children are now under my care, and nearly a hundred mouths are daily supplied with food from our store. The expense is great, but our great and good God, I am persuaded, will enable me to defray it. As yet, I am kept from the least doubting. The more my family increases, the more enlargement and comfort I feel. And though what has been done hitherto, comparatively speaking, may be only like a grain of mustard seed, yet I believe it will, in God's good time, take root and fill the land, and many poor distressed souls will come and lodge under the branches of it.

Sunday, March 30. Found myself very sick and weak in body, but was strengthened to go through most of the duties of the day, and to take an affectionate leave of my parishioners, because it appeared that Providence called me towards the northward. An unspeakable trouble and agony of soul did I feel most part of the day, and was enabled to wrestle with my Lord in behalf of the people in general, and those belonging to the Orphan House in particular. Blessed be God, He has already, and I trust in a great measure, heard my prayer. All things belonging to the Orphan House succeed beyond expectation, and some of my little flock have lately (as far as I can judge) been effectually called of God. One woman, who had been a constant attender on the means of grace, and thought herself a Christian for many years, came to me acknowledging that she had been a self-deceiver, and knew nothing of the righteousness of or true living faith in Jesus Christ. A tradesman, of the same stamp, having felt the power of the doctrines of grace, sent me seventeen volumes of Archbishop Tillotson's *Sermons*, of which he had been a great admirer, to do what I would with them. A captain of a ship, who had been a strong opposer of the truth, wrote and came to me under great convictions, confessing his sin, and desirous of being a Christian indeed. Some others, also, there are who have received the love of God in the truth of it; so that I hope, if ten saints could preserve Sodom, the few righteous souls left behind will prevent the utter desolation of declining Savannah. Blessed Jesus, let our extremity be Thy opportunity, and for Thy mercies' sake, take the colony into Thine own hands; so shall we sing and praise Thy power!

Wednesday, April 2. Read prayers, as usual, as soon as it was light; expounded the Lesson, and then went on board with several of my family and my parishioners, whose hearts God had touched by His grace. The weather was very pleasant, and we spent the day to our mutual edification and comfort. In the evening, we took leave of each other; and the Searcher of Hearts only knows what yearnings I felt in my own soul. I have always observed, that I am under a greater concern, when leaving Savannah, than any other place in the world; for it has proved a blessed place for my soul; and leaving my companions, and more particularly familiar friends, gives nature a deeper wound than any other outward trial. Dearest Redeemer, guide and preserve them in my absence, for Thy infinite mercy's sake! Amen.

PENNSYLVANIA — NEWCASTLE: Sunday, April 13. After a short passage of ten days, (in which God was pleased to exercise my body with sickness, and my soul with spiritual conflicts), we cast anchor about eight this morning at Newcastle, in the province of Pennsylvania. Mr. Grafton, at whose house I lodged when last here, very courteously received both me and my friends. The minister of the parish, who has been an advocate for me, but was now sick, readily accepted my offer to officiate for him. I read prayers and preached twice in his church. People were surprised, but much rejoiced at the news of my arrival, which they expressed by flocking, as soon as they were apprised of my coming, to hear the afternoon sermon. Mr. Charles Tennent, mentioned in my last, came with great part of his congregation. People began to invite me several ways to come and preach to them; but being in haste to go to Philadelphia, I appointed to preach on the morrow at Wilmington, which lay in the way. There I went, with Mr. Tennent and other friends, after evening service; and my soul was much rejoiced, in hearing how mightily the Word of God had prevailed since I was at Pennsylvania last. The Lord was also pleased to give new strength to my body, and I wanted words to express my gratitude for this and all His other innumerable mercies from time to time showered down upon me.

> My soul, inspired with sacred love,
>   God's Holy Name for ever bless:
> Of all His favours mindful prove,
>   And still thy humble thanks express.
>
> 'Tis He Who all thy sins forgives,
>   And after sickness makes thee sound:
> From danger He thy life retrieves,
>   By Him with grace and mercy crowned.

The Lord abounds with tender love,
    And unexampled acts of grace;
His weakened wrath doth slowly move,
    His willing mercy flies apace.

Let every creature jointly bless,
    The mighty Lord; and thou, my heart,
With grateful joy thy thanks express,
    And in this concert bear thy part.

WILMINGTON AND PHILADELPHIA: Monday, April 14. Preached to near three thousand people, at eleven in the morning; and God was pleased to be among us, as in the holy place of Sinai. Many went away refreshed and comforted, and several importunate invitations were given me to preach in several country places round about. After sermon, I and my friends dined at a Quaker's, who seemed to have a right spirit within him, and could speak as one experienced in the things of God. As soon as dinner was over, we took horse, partook of refreshments at Chester, (where the landlord of the house would take nothing either for the entertainment of ourselves or horses), and reached Philadelphia about eight in the evening. It is impossible to express the joy many felt when they saw my face again. O how did they comfort my heart with the account of what God had done for their own and many other people's souls. The Baptist minister in particular, who has been instrumental in watering what God had planted, recounted to me many noble instances of God's power of free grace, shown in the conviction and conversion of some ministers, as well as common people. Oh that the Lord may revive His work in the midst of the years. The world is now up in arms. Blessed Jesus, while the kings of the earth are striving to extend their dominions, do Thou secretly carry on Thy Kingdom in believers' hearts, till the earth be filled with the knowledge of Thee, our Lord, as the waters cover the sea!

PHILADELPHIA: Tuesday, April 15. Paid my respects to the Governor and Proprietor. Went to the Commissary's house, who was not at home; but, afterwards, speaking to him in the street, he told me that he could lend me his church no more, because I had not treated the Bishop of London well, in my Answer to his late Pastoral Letter; and also, because I had misquoted and misrepresented Archbishop Tillotson, in a letter published in the last week's *Gazette*. I told him he had best show that in public. He replied, the printers would not publish anything for them, and that the press was shut against them. I answered, it was without my knowledge. Upon this we parted. In the afternoon, I was much pressed in spirit to preach upon the blind beggar, to whom the scribes and Pharisees said, "Dost thou teach us?" I stood upon a balcony, on Society Hill, from whence I preached my farewell sermon last fall. Towards the conclusion of my discourse, I read to the people some extracts I had taken from Dr. Edwards against Archbishop Tillotson's writings; and then appealed to them, where was the presumption in pretending to teach even him.

Wednesday, April 16. Talked in the morning with three or four who were convicted, and I believe I can say, converted by my ministry last fall. In the afternoon, two men came to me; one of which, with a full heart, cried out, "Blessed be God, for you, under Him, have begotten me again to a lively hope." Preached upon Society Hill twice; in the morning to about six thousand, and in the evening to near eight thousand people. God was with me in both exercises. In the afternoon, I was particularly assisted in speaking from these words, "Yea, and all that will live godly in Christ Jesus must suffer persecution." The storm is gathering apace. As the Word of God increases, so will the rage and opposition of the devil. Lord, support us in a suffering hour, and overshadow us with Thy wings. Amen.

ABINGDON AND PHILADELPHIA: Thursday, April 17. Rode last night after sermon about eight miles. Lay at a friend's house, and preached this morning to near three or four thousand people at Abingdon, a district under the care of Mr. Treat, a Presbyterian minister, to whom God has been pleased lately to show mercy. He has been a preacher of the doctrines of grace for some years; but was deeply convinced, when I was here last, that he had not experienced them in his heart. Soon after I went away, he attempted to preach, but could not; he therefore told his congregation how miserably he had deceived both himself and them, and desired those who were gifted, to pray for him. Ever since, he has continued to seek Jesus Christ sorrowing, and is now under deep convictions, and a very humbling sense of sin. He preaches as usual, though he has not a full assurance of faith; because he said it was best to be found in the way of duty. I believe God is preparing him for great services, and I hope he will also be a means of awakening some dead, false-hearted preachers among the Dissenters, who hold the form of sound words, but have never felt the power of them in their own souls. When I had done, I took a little refreshment, baptized a child, and hastened to Philadelphia, where I preached to upwards of ten thousand people, upon the woman who was cured of her bloody issue. Hundreds were graciously melted; and, many, I hope, not only thronged round, but also touched the Lord Jesus Christ by faith. About ten came to me after sermon, under deep convictions, and told me the time when, and manner how, the Lord Jesus made Himself manifest to their souls. What gives me greater hope that this work is of God, is, because these convictions have remained on many since I was here last. Blessed be God, there is a most glorious work begun in this province. The Word of God every day mightily prevails, and Satan loses ground apace. Lord Jesus, stretch out Thy arm, and let not this work be stopped till we see that new Heaven and new Earth wherein dwelleth righteousness.

GERMAN TOWN AND WHITEMARSH: Friday, April 18. Was employed for two hours this morning, in giving answers to several who came to me under strong convictions; among whom was a Negro or two, and a young girl of about fourteen years of age, who was turned out of the house where she boarded, because she would hear me, and would not learn to dance. Set out about nine o'clock for Whitemarsh, about twelve miles from

Philadelphia. Had near forty people on horse in our company, before we reached the place. Preached to upwards of two thousand people, and great numbers were melted down, and brought under convictions, when I made free offers to them of Jesus and His benefits, if they would believe on Him. Took a little refreshment at a Quaker's, and baptized two children, belonging to the Church of England, at his house. Returned back to, and preached at German Town to near four thousand hearers; and came to Philadelphia, about seven in the evening, refreshed both in body and soul.

PHILADELPHIA: Saturday, April 19. Was still much engaged in giving answers, and praying with divers persons who applied to me under deep convictions. Preached morning and evening to seven or eight thousand people each time; and I was much rejoiced to see with what order and devotion they constantly attend. Scoffers seem to be at a stand what to say. They mutter in coffee houses, give a curse, drink a bowl of punch, and then cry out against me for not preaching up more morality. Poor men! where is the morality they so much boast of? If God judges them, as He certainly will do, by their morality, on which they so much rely, out of their own mouths will He condemn them. They say, but do not. And how can they, since they are ignorant of a living faith in Jesus Christ, which alone can enable us to do anything acceptable in the sight of God.

Sunday, April 20. Preached at seven o'clock, with much freedom, to about ten thousand people, and collected 110 pounds sterling for my poor orphans. The people threw in their mites willingly, and thereby reminded me much of what God had done for me at Moorfields and Kennington Common, when I was last in England. Went to church morning and evening, and heard the Commissary preach a sermon upon Justification by Works, from James 2:18. Many people seeing me go in, followed; and numbers of them told me afterwards, the Commissary (though undesignedly) had confirmed them in the truths which I had delivered. In the evening, I preached from the same words, to about fifteen thousand people, and confuted the false doctrines and many fundamental errors contained in the Commissary's discourse; for he all along took faith to be only an assent to the truths of the Gospel. He said, St. Paul and St. James spoke of the same kind of justification; that works mentioned by St. Paul were only the works of the ceremonial law; that the doctrine of an imputed righteousness had done much harm, and hindered the conversion of the heathen; and that we were to be justified by our works at the last day, and consequently were to be justified in the same manner now. To all these things I endeavored to answer distinctly. After sermon, we collected 80 pounds currency, for my children in Georgia. Little do my enemies think what service they do me. If they did, one would think, out of spite they would even desist from opposing me. Oh what a good Master is Jesus Christ!

GREENWICH AND GLOUCESTER IN THE WEST JERSEYS: Monday, April 21. Had fresh application made to me by persons under convictions. Went by water about four miles, and then rode, in company with many others, who came to meet me, to Greenwich in the West Jerseys, and about twelve miles from Philadelphia. There being a mistake made in the *News*, about the place where I was to preach, I had not above fifteen hundred hearers. At first I thought I was speaking to stocks and stones; but before I had done, a gracious melting was visible in most that heard. Sermon being ended, I dined with my friends; and being taken very ill in the way, lay down for an hour. Rode back to Gloucester; where I took horse in the morning, and preached to about fifteen hundred people. It being but four miles distant from Philadelphia, many came in boats from there. The moon shining very bright, we went back to town very pleasantly. We sang hymns good part of the way. About eight at night we reached Philadelphia, with satisfaction in my own soul that I had this day been plowing up some fallow ground, and opening a way into a place where I find there has been a great famine of the Word of God. I am, in that respect, like-minded with St. Paul, and desire to go chiefly where Christ has not been named.

PHILADELPHIA: Tuesday, April 22. Hearing a sloop was going to Georgia, I shut up myself for some time, in the morning, in order to write some letters to my friends at Savannah. Preached both morning and evening to rather larger congregations than I have yet seen on a weekday. There were not less than ten thousand people. When I came to take my farewell, being about to depart for New York on the morrow, a great number wept sorely. Many of the Negroes were also much affected. This day I bought five thousand acres of land on the forks of the Delaware, and ordered a large house to be built thereon, for the instruction of these poor creatures. The land, I hear, is exceedingly rich. It is a manor, and pays only a white rose yearly for chief rent. I took up so much, because I intend settling some English friends there, when I come next from England. I have called it Nazareth; and, I trust, in a few years, the Lord will let us see much good come out of it. Amen, Lord Jesus, Amen.

Went in the evening to visit a young woman under deep convictions. She was struck down by the power of God's Word on Sunday, and has continued, as Paul did, ever since sick in body, and under great agony of soul. I talked and prayed with her, and with near twenty more that came into the room. I also gave them a strong exhortation. They wept sorely and prayed earnestly; and I have not seen circumstances more like those of the Apostles, when the Holy Ghost shook the room, wherein they were lifting up their voice with one accord to the Most High God.

NESHAMINY: Wednesday, April 23. Was more than ordinarily employed the first part of the morning, in writing letters, answering people, and preparing for my journey. Set out about eight with many friends, and partook of refreshments at a friend's house about midway. Reached Neshaminy near three in the afternoon, and preached to upwards of five thousand people, in old Mr. Tennent's meeting-house yard. When I got there, my body, through heat and labor, was so weak and faint, that my knees smote one against another, my visage changed, and I was ready to drop down as soon as I had finished my prayer. But God was pleased to revive me. Great numbers were melted; and one in particular, who after sermon came to me with tears, saying, "You have brought me under deep convictions; what shall I do to be saved?" I gave him the Apostle's answer, "Believe on the Lord Jesus Christ, and thou shalt be saved." Upwards of fifty, I hear, have been lately convicted about this place. The Lord grant his arrows may stick fast in them, till they have got a closing interest with Jesus Christ; for many, I find, receive the Word with joy for a season, but having no root in themselves, soon fall away. Lord, if it be Thy will, have mercy on these and such-like unhappy apostates, and let them be renewed again unto repentance. Amen and Amen.

MONTGOMERY AND SHIPPACK: Thursday, April 24. Was hospitably entertained with my friends last night at Montgomery, about eight miles from Neshaminy, where I came to make this day's journey the easier. Preached at Shippack, sixteen miles from Montgomery, where the Dutch people live. It was seemingly, a very wilderness part of the country but there were not less, I believe, than two thousand hearers. When I had done, Peter Bohler, a deacon of the Moravian Church, a dear lover of our Lord Jesus Christ, preached to his countrymen in Dutch. Traveling and preaching in the sun again, weakened me much and made me very sick; but by the Divine assistance, I took horse, rode twelve miles, and preached in the evening to about three thousand people at a Dutchman's plantation, who seemed to have drunk deeply of God's Holy Spirit. The German Brethren were exceeding loving to me, and I spent the evening with many of them in a most agreeable manner. The order, seriousness, and devotion of these people in common life, is most worthy of imitation. They prayed and sang in *their* language, and then God enlarged my heart to pray in *ours*.

AMWELL IN THE EAST JERSEYS: Friday, April 25. Rose before day. Sang and prayed with my own friends and the German Brethren. Set out before sunrising, and reached Amwell, thirty-five miles from Shippack, where I had appointed to preach by six at night. Some thousands of people were gathered together, expecting I would have been there by noon; but Mr. Gilbert Tennent, and Mr. Rowland, mentioned in my last *Journal*, coming there to meet me, had given the people three sermons. In my way there, I was brought low by inward trials, and very great weakness of body, occasioned by the heat of the sun, want of sleep, and the length of the journey; but before I had preached six minutes, bodily and spiritual strength was given me, and the Lord set His seal to what He enabled me to deliver. After sermon, a friend took me in his chaise to an old Christian's, who invited me and my company to his house, five miles distant from the place where I preached.

NEW BRUNSWICK: Saturday, April 26. Was much conforted and refreshed both in body and soul last night, after I went to rest. Sang psalms, prayed, and set out for New Brunswick about eight. Reached there by four in the afternoon, and preached to about two thousand hearers in the evening. Many were affected. Here, also, my true Christian friend and host, Mr. Noble, from New York, gave me the meeting, and brought me a packet of letters from Savannah. I trust, many of my friends in the Orphan House will be friends of God. Grant this, O Lord, for Thy mercies' sake!

Sunday, April 27. Was told last night by Mr. Gilbert Tennent, of two that were savingly brought home by my ministry, when here last. Got a little time to write a letter to my English friends, giving them a short account of what God was doing here. Preached morning and evening to near seven or eight thousand people. In the afternoon sermon, had I proceeded, I believe the cries and groans of the congregation would have drowned my voice. One woman was struck down, and a general cry went through the assembly. We collected both times upwards of 20 pounds sterling for my orphans. At night a woman came to me under strong convictions. She told me she had often been somewhat moved; but now, she hoped God had struck her home. She cried out, "I can see nothing but hell!" Oh that all were in as good a way to Heaven.

BRUNSWICK, WOODBRIDGE, ELIZABETH TOWN AND NEW YORK: Monday, April 28. Underwent great conflicts in my soul last night and this morning. Wrote some letters to my dear English friends, who are continually upon my heart. Took a sorrowful leave of Captain Gladman, and my dear brother and fellow-traveler, Mr. Seward, whom I have dispatched to England to bring me over a fellow laborer, and to transact several affairs of importance. Captain Gladman is the person mentioned in my last *Journal*, who was cast away in the Gulf of Florida, and whom God made me the instrument of converting in my passage to England. Hitherto he has had the command of our sloop; but being obliged to dispatch him on business to England, I have now committed the care of it to his mate, whom God was pleased to bring home to Himself when I was last at Philadelphia. Not long since he was an abandoned prodigal, and ringleader in vice; but God struck him to the heart. Captain Gladman had prayed that God would send him a mate. This young man was strongly drawn to come and offer himself; the Captain hired him; and now, I believe, he is a child of God.

Set out about eight in the morning, and reached Woodbridge by ten, where I preached to about two thousand people. Here, again, my bodily strength was small; but God enabled me to speak home to many hearts; for many were affected. After sermon, I and my friends dined at the Dissenting minister's house, who invited me to preach; and then we hastened to Elizabeth Town, where the people had been waiting for some hours. I preached in the meeting house, as when I was there last. It was full, and was supposed to contain two thousand people. Ten Dissenting ministers were present, and two Church ministers; but they did not tarry very long. God gave me much freedom of speech. I dealt very plainly with the Presbyterian clergy, many of whom, I am persuaded, preach the doctrines of grace to others, without being converted themselves. No doubt, some were offended: but I care not for any sect or party of men. As I love all who love the Lord Jesus, of what communion soever; so I reprove all, whether Dissenters, or not Dissenters, who take His Word into their mouths, but never felt Him dwelling in their hearts.

After sermon, I took leave of Mr. Gilbert Tennent and Mr. Cross, who accompanied me thus far and told me their souls were much refreshed by this day's work.

After I parted from them, I intended to ride six miles; but being overruled by the advice of friends, I stopped, and lay at an inn all night, near the waterside, where people take boat to go to New York. Here I had an appetite for my food, which I have not had before for some time. Surely this frail body cannot hold me long. When, O Lord, wilt Thou set my imprisoned soul at liberty! When shall I be dissolved and be with Thee, O Christ! Lord, give me patience to wait till that blessed time come.

NEW YORK: Tuesday, April 29. Took boat about nine in the morning, and was blessed with a fair gale of wind, which brought us to New York before noon. Here my dear friends kindly received me, and here also, I met with Mr. William Tennent, who refreshed my heart by telling me what the Lord was doing for numbers of souls in the Highlands, where he has lately been. Surely Jesus Christ is getting Himself the victory indeed! About five in the evening, I preached on the common to five or six thousand people, but observed no scoffers, as there were when I was here last. The people were still and quiet after I began; and, though I did not perceive much power in the congregation, yet God enabled me to speak with all boldness. Oh that I may never be ashamed of Christ or of His Gospel; for it has been the Power of God to my salvation. O grace! grace!

Wednesday, April 30. Preached this morning from a scaffold, erected for that purpose, to a somewhat less congregation than last night, but with much greater power; for towards the conclusion of my discourse, God's Spirit came upon the preacher and the people, so that they were melted down exceedingly. Afterwards, I began to collect money from private hands for my orphans, and met with success. Blessed be God, Who has the hearts of all men in His hands. Dined at Mr. P . . . 's, but was obliged to retire as soon as dinner was over; for my body was weak, and my soul was in an unspeakable agony for near an hour. At length I dropped asleep, but rose about five in the evening, and preached to upwards of seven thousand people on our Lord's temptations. Oh that I may follow the Captain of my salvation, and be willing to be tempted in all things like unto my brethren, that I may be experimentally able to succor such as apply to me when tempted! Amen, Lord Jesus, Amen.

FLAT BUSH ON LONG ISLAND: Thursday, May 1. Went in a ferry this morning, over to Flat Bush on Long Island, on the east part of which God has lately begun a most glorious work, by the ministry of two young Presbyterian ministers, who have walked in the light of God's countenance for a long while together. Prosper Thou, O Lord, more and more the work of their hands upon them. Oh prosper Thou their handiwork!

At our coming to Flat Bush, the Dutch ministers received me with all civility, and gave me the use of their church. There were also seven or eight Dissenting ministers present. I continued discoursing on the knowledge of Jesus Christ, near an hour and a half. Many people, and some of the ministers wept. My own soul was wonderfully carried out; and, at last I applied myself to the ministers themselves. Oh that we all were a flame of fire!

About two in the afternoon, having a fair wind, we returned to New York; where I received another packet of letters from Charleston and Savannah, among which were two or three from my little orphans. I preached in the evening at New York to as large a congregation as ever; but my spirits being exhausted, I preached, as I thought, but heavily. But I have been too apt to build on my frames, and think I do no good, or do not please God, only because I do not please myself; for I have often found, that my seemingly less powerful discourses have been much owned by God. I find it absolutely necessary, that Gospel ministers should meet with such thorns in the flesh, that both ministers and hearers may know themselves to be but men. Lord, show that Thou dost love me, by humbling and keeping me humble as long as I live! The means I leave to Thee. I am Thy clay, Thou art the Potter; mould me as it seemeth good to Thy sovereign goodwill and pleasure! Amen and Amen.

NEW YORK: Friday, May 2. Preached twice in the field, and once in the meeting house; and was agreeably refreshed in the evening with one, Mr. Davenport, whom God has lately highly honored, by making use of his ministry for the conversion of many at the east end of Long Island. He is looked upon as an enthusiast and a madman by many of his reverend pharisaical brethren; and, as far as I can find, there is as great an enmity against the work of God in the hearts of most even of the Dissenters, (though they preach the doctrines of grace), as there is in our clergy, who, for the generality, entirely disown them. As Jannes and Jambres withstood Moses, so do these also resist the truth. But I trust they will not proceed much further; for their folly shall be manifest unto all men, as theirs also was.

Sunday, May 4. Preached at seven in the morning, in the meeting house. Went to the English church twice, and heard two legal sermons, though not quite so bad as those I heard when here last. Preached in the evening to about eight thousand in the field, and had evidence that the Lord was among us.

> Give me Thy strength, O God of power,
> Then let or men or friends assail:
> Strong in Thy strength, I'll stand a tower
> Impregnable to earth or hell.

After evening sermon, numbers came to me, giving God thanks for what they had heard. They were desirous of my return among them again, and brought several large contributions for my poor orphans. By public collections and private donations, I have received upwards of 300 pounds since I came here; and I doubt not but my dear Lord will always provide for my little ones. Oh what a blessed thing it is to live upon God! I believe Elijah never lived more comfortably than when fed by the ravens. Lord, increase my faith, and accept my poor thanks for what Thou has done for me and Thy people during my short stay here.

STRATTON ISLAND, FREEHOLD, AND AMBOY: Monday, May 5. Prayed with, and parted from my dear New York friends last night. About ten o'clock, took boat with my worthy host, Mr. Noble, and some others, and came by midnight to Stratton Island, where we were kindly received by one of our Lord's true disciples. Not long after our coming ashore, the wind blew, and the weather grew very tempestous, and so continued all the morning; but God strengthened my weak body. About eleven I set out; preached at a place appointed on the island, about seven miles distant, and afterwards hastened to Amboy, about twelve miles further, where I preached again a little after six in the evening. I sent to the minister of the place for the use of his pulpit; but he was very angry, and said he wondered at my assurance in asking such a thing. It being such rainy weather, only a few people came. After sermon, my friends advised me to stay at Amboy all night; but my dear brother and fellow laborer, Mr. William Tennent, coming to fetch me, I passed over a ferry with him and his brother Gilbert, who also came to Amboy to meet me. With them I set out for Freehold, twenty miles from Amboy, the place where God has more immediately called Mr. William Tennent. Oh how sweetly did the time glide on, and our hearts burn within us, when we opened the Scriptures, and communicated our experiences to each other! Our Lord was with us, as with the two disciples going to Emmaus. About midnight, we reached Freehold, and about two in the morning, retired to rest. My body was weak, but my soul much comforted; and I think I sleep with double satisfaction when lying in a good man's house. For the angels of the Lord encamp about the dwellings of the righteous. Oh that we may be like them, and be unwearied in administering to, and watching over, those who are heirs of everlasting salvation!

FREEHOLD, AMBOY AND BURLINGTON: Tuesday, May 6. Preached at Freehold in the morning to about three thousand, and the power of God was much manifested, and many, I believe, brought under convictions. Took a little refreshment, and went in company with many of God's children to Allen's Town, about sixteen miles from Freehold. Preached to about three thousand more, and afterwards reached Burlington, about twenty miles further, by midnight. As I came along, a man who had been dissuaded from coming to hear me, came to me under strong convictions, and desirous of following me wheresoever I went. I scarce know a day wherein I have not had several apply to me for the same purpose, and under the same circumstances. It is natural for persons to be desirous of being with those, who have, under God, brought them from darkness to light. Thus the man out of whom the devil had been cast, desired to go with Jesus. But our Lord's answer I find best to be given; "Go home to thy house, and tell what great things the Lord hath done for thee." Dear Redeemer, teach me in this, and all other respects, to follow Thy perfect, unerring example. Amen and Amen.

BRISTOL IN PENNSYLVANIA, AND PHILADELPHIA: Wednesday, May 7. After a little refreshing sleep, crossed the ferry into Pennsylvania province. Preached to about four thousand at Bristol, and made all possible haste to Philadelphia, twenty miles off, where I was received with great joy by my kind host, Mr. Benezet, and many other friends. After dispatching some private affairs, I went and heard Mr. Jones, the Baptist minister, who preached the truth as it is in Jesus. He is the only preacher that I know of in Philadelphia, who speaks feelingly and with authority. The poor people are much refreshed by him, and I trust the Lord will bless him more and more.

PHILADELPHIA: Thursday, May 8. Had what my body much wanted, a thorough night's repose. Was called up early in the morning, as I always am, to speak to poor souls under convictions. The first who came was an Indian trader, whom God was pleased to bring home by my preaching when here last. He is just come from the Indian nation, where he has been praying with and exhorting all he met who were willing to hear. He has hopes of some of the Indians; but his fellow traders endeavored to prejudice them against him. However, he proposes to visit them again in the autumn, and I humbly hope the Lord will open a door among the poor heathen. The conversion of one of their traders, I take to be one great step towards it. Lord, carry on the work begun. Fulfill Thy ancient promises, and let Thy Son have the heathen for His inheritance, and the utmost parts of the earth for His possession.

I conversed also with a poor Negro woman, who has been visited in a very remarkable manner. God was pleased to convert her by my preaching last autumn; but being under dejections on Sunday morning, she prayed that salvation might come to her heart, and that the Lord would be pleased to manifest Himself to her soul that day. While she was at meeting, hearing Mr. M . . . n, a Baptist preacher, the Word came with such power to her heart, that at last she was obliged to cry out; and a great concern fell upon many in the congregation. The minister stopped, and several persuaded her to hold her peace; but she could not help praising and blessing God. Many since this have called her mad, and said she was full of new wine; but the account she gave me was rational and solid, and, I believe in that hour the Lord Jesus took a great possession of her soul. Such cases, indeed, have not been very common; but when an extraordinary work is being carried on, God generally manifests Himself to some souls in this extraordinary manner. I doubt not, when the poor Negroes are to be called, God will highly favor them, to wipe off their reproach, and show that He is no respecter of persons, but that whosoever believeth in Him shall be saved.

Preached, at eleven, to six or seven thousand people, and cleared myself from some aspersions that had been cast upon my doctrine, as though it tended to Antinomianism. I believe God has much people in the city of Philadelphia. The congregations are very large and serious, and I have scarce preached this time among them without seeing a stirring among the dry bones. At five in the evening I preached again, but to a rather larger audience; and, after sermon, rode ten miles to a morning, according to appointment. How differently am I treated from my Master! He taught the people by day, and abode all night upon the Mount of Olives. He had not where to lay His head; but go where I will, I find people receiving me into their houses with great gladness.

PENNYPACK AND PHILADELPHIA: Friday, May 9. Preached at Pennypack, about three miles' distance from the house where I lay, to about two thousand people, and came back to Philadelphia, about two in the afternoon. Agreed to build my Negro schools on the land which I have lately purchased. Preached in the evening, and afterwards began a Society of young men, many of whom I trust, will prove good soldiers of Jesus Christ. Amen.

Saturday, May 10. Though God has shown me great things already in this place, yet today I have seen greater. I preached twice, and to larger congregations than ever. In the evening, I went to settle a Society of young women, who, I hope, will prove wise virgins. As soon as I entered the room, and heard them singing, my soul was delighted. When the hymn was over, I desired to pray before I began to converse; but, my soul was so carried out, that I had not time to talk at all. A wonderful power was in the room, and with one accord, they began to cry out and weep most bitterly for the space of half an hour. They seemed to be under the strongest convictions, and did indeed seek Jesus sorrowing. Their cries might be heard a great way off. When I had done, I thought proper to leave them at their devotions. They continued in prayer for above an hour, confessing their most secret faults; and, at length, the agonies of some were so strong, that five of them seemed affected as those who are in fits. The present Captain of our sloop going near the waterside, was called in to a company, almost in the same circumstances; and, at midnight, I was desired to come to one who was in strong agonies of body and mind, but felt somewhat of joy and peace, after I had prayed with her several times. Her case put me in mind of the young man whom the devil tore, when he was coming to Jesus. Such-like bodily agonies, I believe, are from the devil; and, now the work of God is going on, he will, no doubt, endeavor by these to bring an evil report upon it. O Lord, for Thy mercy's sake, rebuke him; and, though he may be permitted to bite Thy people's heel, fulfill Thy promise, and let the Seed of the Woman bruise his head! Amen, Amen!

Sunday, May 11. Preached to about fifteen thousand people in the morning. Went twice to church, and heard myself taken to task by the Commissary, who preached from these words: "I bear them record, they have a zeal for God, but not according to knowledge." I could have wished he had considered the next words: "For they being ignorant of God's righteousness, have not submitted themselves to the righteousness of God." Had he considered these words, I might justly have said, "Speaketh Mr. Commissary of this false zeal in reference to himself, or of some other man?" He exclaimed loudly against me in the pulpit, and, I soon found, obliged many of his hearers to do what they were before inclined to do, viz., resolve to leave me entirely. I bear him record, that experience will soon convince him, that whatever mine may be, his own zeal is by no means according to knowledge. After he had done, I preached my farewell sermon to very near twenty thousand hearers. Though the Commissary's sermon was chiefly of personal reflections, I thought it not proper to render railing for railing. However, I considered it my duty, in an especial manner to recommend the Messrs. Tennents and their associates, being most worthy preachers of our Lord Jesus. One passage out of the Second Lesson for the morning, much affected me: "And the Lord had compassion on the multitude, because they were scattered, as sheep having no shepherd." I then reminded them of our Lord's command, "Pray ye therefore the Lord of the harvest that He may send out labourers into His harvest." For though "the harvest is plenteous, the labourers are few."

The poor people were much concerned at my bidding them farewell; and, after I had taken my leave, many came to my lodgings, sorrowing that they were to see my face no more for a long season. Near fifty Negroes came to give me thanks for what God had done to their souls. How heartily did those poor creatures throw in their mites for my poor orphans. Some of them have been effectually wrought upon, and in an uncommon manner. Many of them have begun to learn to read. One, who was free, said she would give me her two children, whenever I settle my school. I believe masters and mistresses will shortly see that Christianity will not make their Negroes worse slaves. I intended, had time permitted, to have settled a Society for Negro men and Negro women; but that must be deferred till it shall please God to bring me to Philadelphia again. I have been much drawn out in prayer for them, and have seen them exceedingly wrought upon under the Word preached. I cannot well express how many others, of all sorts, came to give me a last farewell. I never saw a more general awakening in any place. Religion is all the talk; and, I think I can say, the Lord Jesus has gotten Himself the victory in many hearts. I have scarce had time to eat bread from morning to evening; some one or other was generally applying to me under deep soul-concern, and others continually pressing upon me to baptize their infants. I did comply with as many as I could; but I was obliged sometimes to say, "The Lord sent me not to baptize, but to preach the Gospel."

Many of the Quakers have been convinced of the righteousness of Jesus Christ, and openly confess the truth as it is in Jesus; for which, I believe, they will shortly be put out of their synagogues. Some of their head men are zealous against me, and are much afraid their foundation will be sadly shaken. Great numbers of the inhabitants would have built me immediately a very large church, if I would have consented; but the Lord, I am persuaded, would have His Gospel preached in the fields; and building a church would, I fear, insensibly lead the people into bigotry, and make them place the Church again, as they have done for a long time, in the church walls. For these reasons I declined it; though notwithstanding, I believe they will build some place. What I mostly fear is, now there is such a general awakening, the people will not know where to go for proper food, and thereby fall into different sects and parties. Lord Jesus, look upon them, and let not Satan divide them again; but raise them up pastors after Thy own heart. Amen and Amen.

With preaching, and praying, and conversing, I was truly weary by eight at night; but I went and baptized two children; took my leave of both the Societies; and I had not prayed long in the women's Society, before two of them fell down in violent fits, so that I was obliged to leave them. At my return home, I supped with some Christian friends, and went to bed, astonished at, and desirous to be humbly thankful for the great things the Lord had done at Philadelphia. Blessed be the Lord God of Israel, for He hath wonderfully visited this people, and raised up for them a means of salvation, from where it was least expected. Oh grace, grace!

DERBY, CHESTER, AND WILMINGTON: Monday, May 12. Rose early to answer those who came for private advice. Visited three persons, one of whom was under such deep convictions, that she had taken scarce anything to eat for a fortnight. Another had a prospect of hell set before her last night in the most terrifying colors; but, before morning, received comfort. When I came to my lodgings, my friends were waiting to accompany me on horseback, and great numbers of the common people were crowding about the door. About nine, I left Philadelphia, and when I came to the ferry, was told that people had been crossing over, as fast as two boats could carry them, ever since three in the morning. After we had waited some time, I and my friends got over, and I preached at Derby, seven miles from Philadelphia, to about four thousand; and collected there and at Derby upwards of 40 pounds for my orphans. Here I parted with more friends; but several went with me to Wilmington, fifteen miles from Chester. We got in about eleven at night. My body was weak; but God strengthened me to pray, to sing psalms, and to exhort a roomful of people for about an hour. At this place I lay at a Quaker's house for the night.

WILMINGTON AND WHITECLAY CREEK: Tuesday, May 13. In the morning, preached at Wilmington to five thousand; and, at Whiteclay Creek, about ten miles distant, in the evening, to three thousand. The Word, I believe, was both like a fire and a hammer; for many were melted, and one cried out most bitterly, as in great agonies of soul. At both places, we collected about 24 pounds for the Orphan House, and the people were very solicitous for me to bring our sloop up their Creek, the next time I came, that they might put in provisions. Never did I see a more plentiful country than Pennsylvania. I have seen but very few poor objects since my arrival. Almost every one enjoys peace and plenty. The rich do not swallow up the poor, as in other provinces; but there seems to be a proper balance. After sermon at Whiteclay Creek, I rode towards Nottingham with Mr. Craghead, and Mr. Blair, all worthy ministers of the Lord Jesus. Many others belonging to Philadelphia accompanied us, and we rode through the woods, singing and praising God. We were all rejoiced to see our Lord's Kingdom come with such visible power, and endeavored to strengthen one another against a suffering time, should it come. May the Great Shepherd make us willing, if called to it, to lay down our lives for His sheep. Amen.

NOTTINGHAM: Wednesday, May 14. Got to a Quaker's house, which lay in our way to Nottingham, about midnight (May 13), and met with a hospitable reception. Preached at Nottingham both morning and evening, with such demonstration of the Spirit, and such a wonderful movement among the hearers, as few ever saw before. I was invited there, by some of the inhabitants, who had a good work begun among them, some time ago, by the ministry of Mr. Blair, the Messrs. Tennents, and Mr. Cross, the last of which had been denied the use of the pulpit by one of his own brethren, and was obliged to preach in the woods, where the Lord manifested forth His glory, and caused many to cry out, "What shall we do to be saved?" It surprised me to see such a multitude gathered together, at so short a warning, and in such a desert place. I believe there were near twelve thousand. I had not spoken long before I perceived numbers melting. As I proceeded, the influence increased, till, at last, (both in the morning and the afternoon), thousands cried out, so that they almost drowned my voice. Never did I see a more glorious sight. Oh what tears were shed and poured forth after the Lord Jesus. Some fainted; and when they had got a little strength, they would hear and faint again. Others cried out in a manner as if they were in the sharpest agonies of death. Oh what thoughts and words did God put into my heart! After I had finished my last discourse, I was so pierced, as it were, and overpowered with a sense of God's love, that some thought, I believe, I was about to give up the ghost. How sweetly did I lie at the feet of Jesus! With what power did a sense of His all-constraining, free, and everlasting love flow in upon my soul! It almost took away my life. At length, I revived, and was strengthened to go with Messrs. Blair, Tennent, and some other friends to Mr. Blair's house, twenty miles from Nottingham. In the way, we refreshed our souls by singing psalms and hymns. We got to our journey's end at midnight. Oh Lord, was ever love like Thine!

FAGG'S MANOR: Thursday, May 15. Preached at Fagg's Manor, three miles from Mr. Blair's house, where he had earnestly invited me to come. The congregation was about as large as that at Nottingham. As great, if not a greater commotion was in the hearts of the people. Most were drowned in tears. The Word was sharper than a two-edged sword. The bitter cries and groans were enough to pierce the hardest heart. Some of the people were as pale as death; others were wringing their hands; others lying on the ground; others sinking into the arms of friends; and most lifting up their eyes to Heaven and crying to God for mercy. I could think of nothing, when I looked upon them, so much as the Great Day. They seemed like persons awakened by the last trump, and coming out of their graves to judgment. One would imagine, none could have withstood the power, or avoided crying out, "Surely God is in this place"; yet Mr. El . . . son, a Dissenting minister, a virulent opposer of Mr. Tennent and his brethren, after sermon was over, while thousands were under the deepest distress of soul, came desiring to have a public disputation. I told him I was going to Newcastle, and that the place we were now in was not proper to dispute in. But he thinking that was only to evade the trial, I desired him to begin, and I would answer such questions as he should propose. He then charged me with saying, "That such as had only a faith of adherence, were in a damnable condition." I answered, such a thing never entered my thoughts. I only said, a faith of adherence was not to be rested in, but that all should ask for, and labor after a full assurance of faith. He then quoted a passage from Isaiah, Chapter 1 verse 10, to prove that a person might be in Christ, and yet not know it. I told him, if he were a spiritual person, he would have known, there was a time when God withdraws His sensible presence from a believer's soul, and yet that soul may even then be kept from doubting of his interest in Christ. He was about to quote some other passage of Scripture, but, by this time, the people were exasperated, and one cried out in haste, that he would take Mr. El . . . son, out of the place. For this I rebuked him, telling him that was not the Spirit of Christ, and, at the same time blamed Mr. El . . . son, for coming at such an improper time to dispute, when he saw the power of God so obviously among us. I also told him, that if he had any objections to make, I would answer them, as I rode to Newcastle, or in a letter, if he would send them on to me. Upon this, he seemed somewhat sensible of his fault, and said he thought it was best to withdraw. The people hung so close upon me, that with difficulty I got upon a horse; and after I had given them a word of exhortation, to answer those who opposed themselves, I rode to a friend's house, who had invited me to dinner. After dinner, I rode (at the rate of eight miles an hour) to Newcastle, twenty-four miles from Fagg's Manor, preached to about four thousand, prayed with several who came many miles under violent convictions, and then went on board our sloop, the *Savannah*.

After supper, and singing a hymn and prayer, many who have accompanied me ever since I left Philadelphia, as well as Messrs. Tennent, Blair, and Craghead, took their final leave. Their hearts were melted with love towards me; but being much fatigued, I could only sigh out my heart's desire for them, and commend them to God. Then, as soon as possible, I betook myself to rest.

ON BOARD THE *Savannah*: Friday, May 16. Rose by break of day, parted with two more friends, and put my things and little family in order as soon as I could. Was pleasingly surprised to see the variety and quantity of provisions and sea-stores which had been sent on board by Philadelphia people. I found that in goods and money I had received near 500 pounds sterling. Blessed be the Lord God of Israel, Who alone bringeth mighty things to pass. I am now going to make an addition to my family, of half a dozen persons, a bricklayer, a tailor, two maidservants, and two little girls, whose father kept a dancing-school, assembly and concert room in Philadelphia. Their mother, I believe, had a work of grace in her heart, was well-bred, and much concerned, for some time, at the business in which her husband was engaged. When last at Philadelphia, I did what I could, but now God opened Mr. Seward's heart to relieve the parents. I took these two children, and an end will entirely be put to the assembly, etc., at least in that house. It is a shame they should be permitted in any Christian country. They enervate people's minds, unfit them for business, as well as religion, and grieve the Holy Spirit exceedingly.

Saturday, May 17. Felt much of the presence of God in my heart, and had several captains and ship-carpenters (the wind being contrary) come to hear me pray and exhort. I observed the tears trickling down their stern faces plentifully. Three seemed to be under strong convictions; and, one especially, not long since remarkably wicked, I have great hopes will be effectually brought home. Grant it, O Lord, for Thy dear Son's sake! Amen and Amen.

ON BOARD SHIP, AND REEDY ISLAND: Sunday, May 18. The weather not permitting us to sail, at the people's and sailors' desire, I went on shore and preached twice on Reedy Island, near which our sloop, and several other ships came to an anchor. Having but a few hours' notice, not above two hundred came together. It pleased me to see the ships' companies haste in their boats to hear the sermon. Many people wept bitterly. In the evening I returned to the sloop, and was enabled to finish my *Journal* to this day, not having had time to write a word of it before I came on board, for a fortnight.

Monday, May 19. Was much refreshed today, by reading the *Journal* of an Indian trader, mentioned a little before, and could not help thinking that God would open a door for preaching the Gospel among the Alleghanian Indians. Being much pressed thereto in spirit, I wrote them a letter, wherein I laid down the principles of our Holy Religion, told them the promises of the Gospel, that had especial reference to them, and cautioned them against such things as I thought might be a hindrance to their embracing Christianity. The Head or Chief of them is well inclined, and the white people thereabouts have heard of me, and have got my sermons. Who knows but God may now begin to give His Son the heathen for His inheritance, and the uttermost parts of the earth for His possession. This trader, I really believe is called of God, and God never sends any of His servants on a needless errand. I long to see that time when the earth shall be filled with the knowledge of the Lord, as the waters cover the sea. Even so, come Lord Jesus, come quickly!

Wednesday, May 21. Preached for these three days past, once every day on shore at Reedy Island, and the congregations increased much every time. Felt much of the Divine assistance, both on shore and on board, and was enabled to exhort and pray with the captains and sailors that came to our sloop. I found they had all made an agreement to come constantly, so long as the wind continued against us; but after evening sermon, the weather clearing up, and the wind being somewhat fair, we weighed anchor, and went a few miles towards the bay. Blessed be God for retarding us at Reedy Island. Though I long to see my flock and family at Georgia, yet I rejoice in this delay, because I hope some servants of God have been refreshed, and others brought into a fair way of coming to Jesus Christ. Draw them, O Lord, with the cords of Thy love, and then they cannot fail to follow after Thee! The love of Christ is a constraining love, oh, shed it abroad in the hearts of all poor unbelieving sinners! Amen and amen.

LEWIS TOWN: Friday, May 23. Came this morning to Old Kilroad, and dropped anchor, the wind being contrary. Went ashore at Lewis Town, read prayers, and preached in the church to a small and unaffected congregation. The minister hearing our sloop was coming, stayed to give me the meeting. I quickly found he was one of those who subscribed to the Articles of the Church of England in his own sense. He inveighed bitterly against the doctrines of grace in private; but seemed struck dumb after he heard me in public, for he did not open his lips about the doctrines afterwards. Oh how Divine truths make their own way, when attended by Divine power! They either convict or confound gainsayers. I think the Church of England is by no means beholden to Bishop Burnet for his Exposition on her Articles. He has opened a door for the most detestable equivocation; and, were it possible for the compilers of our Articles to rise again from the dead, I am persuaded they would insist on their being taken in the grammatical sense. They cannot, in my opinion, admit of a two-fold interpretation.

Saturday, May 24. Wrote some letters to England to go by way of Lisbon. Read prayers, and preached twice in the church, to a much larger and more affected auditory than yesterday. Many people stood without the church door. In the evening, I retired and looked towards Georgia; but this text was much upon my mind, "They assayed to go into Bithynia, but the Spirit suffered them not." Lord, I submit. Thy will be done! Oh when shall I learn to have no other will but Thine!

Sunday, May 25. Preached twice from a balcony, to about two thousand, the church not being capable of holding them. In the evening, discoursing on Abraham's faith, a great many, and some even of the most polite, wept much; but, alas! when I came to turn from the creature to the Creator, and to talk of God's love, in sacrificing His only begotten Son, Jesus Christ, their tears, I observed, dried up. I told them of it. We can weep at the sufferings of a martyr, a man like ourselves; but when are we affected at the relation of the sufferings of the Son of God? Pascal, I have been informed, always wept when he read of our dear Lord's passion. Though weeping be not always a sign of grace, yet, I think it is an evidence of the hardness of our hearts, and a want of a due sense of sin, when we can remain unmoved at the account of the sufferings of a dying Savior. The divine Herbert, modernized by my dear brother, Mr. Charles Wesley, furnishes me with a sweet prayer on this occasion.

> Sin is still spreading o'er my heart,
>   A hardness void of love:
> Let suppling grace, to cross her art,
>   Drop gently from above!

After evening service, thinking it time to visit my little family, (in all seventeen souls) I went on board, and prayed with and exhorted them. I was much carried out for them and my Savannah friends, and had some thoughts that the Lord would now send me to them. Whether that be His good pleasure or not, I desired to be resigned and thankful for this delay. It has been made very beneficial to many souls, especially to some of our own sloop, and particularly to one most profligate sinner, who, I trust, will make an eminently courageous saint. I think I have now preached sixty-eight times since my arrival at Newcastle, and have been near forty days on shore.

> While in these regions here below,
>   No other good will I pursue,
> I'll bid this world of noise and show,
>   With all its flatt'ring snares, Adieu!
>
> That path with humble speed I'd seek,
>   Wherein, O Lord, Thy footsteps shine:
> Nor will I hear, nor will I speak,
>   Of any other love than Thine.

TYBEE ISLAND: Wednesday, June 4. Cast anchor at midnight, off Tybee Island fifteen miles from Savannah, after a short passage of nine days, a very extraordinary thing at this time of the year.

SAVANNAH: Thursday, June 5. Took boat at Tybee, about one in the morning, and arrived at Savannah about eight. What a sweet meeting had I with my dear friends! When I parted, my heart was ready to break with sorrow, but now it almost burst with joy. All things concurred to render our meeting exceedingly happy. None of my letters had come to hand, so that my family did not expect me for a long season. They had also been informed, that I was cast away; so that they received me as one risen from the dead. All that Joseph felt, when he wept over his brother Benjamin, or David, when making a covenant with Jonathan, did I feel. In short, my soul was quite filled with peace, and love, and joy; and, I took the first opportunity of kneeling down with my family, and venting my heart before them. My soul felt so full of a sense of the Divine love, that I wanted words to express myself. O dearest Jesus, why am I thus highly favored? Oh unspeakable, free, almighty, and everlasting love! And yet these are only earnests and foretastes of future bliss! Hasten, Lord, hasten that happy hour, when I shall be received into Abraham's bosom, and praise Thee to all eternity for what Thou has done for our souls! Even so, come, Lord Jesus!

Friday, June 6. Blessed be the God of all grace, Who continues to do for me marvelous things. This day, I hope salvation is come to many in my house. Long have I interceded for poor Savannah. Strong wrestlings have I had with God, time after time, both in public and private, on behalf of the inhabitants; and this night God has most remarkably answered my requests. About four, I prayed earnestly, and particularly for my friends, who were in the room with me. Many came into the passage near us, and wept much before the Lord, deeply laboring in their souls. After this, I went up and prayed for half an hour with some of the women of the house, and three girls, who seemed to be weary with the weight of their sins. But when we came to public prayer, the Holy Ghost seemed to come into the congregation like a mighty rushing wind, carrying all before it. I had not long begun, before several fell a-weeping sorely; and the number still increased, till young men and maidens, old men and children, were all dissolved in tears, and mourning after Jesus. I believe there were scarcely half a dozen in the whole congregation, but what were deeply affected. I never saw the like before. Being come home, I laid myself upon the bed, weak in body, and astonished at the power of God; but finding so many came up in such a condition, I rose from bed, and betook myself to prayer again. This continued for nearly an hour, till at last, finding their concern rather increase than abate, I desired all to retire. I was delighted afterwards, to hear some praying most earnestly to God in every corner of the house and it surprised me to hear what a spirit of supplication was put into the hearts of some of the boys and girls. It happened to thunder and lighten, which added much to the solemnity of the night, and reminded us of the coming of the Son of Man. Exerting myself so much, threw my body into a fever, and I slept but little the whole night. The next day, the concern continued, especially among the girls, four of whom I have great reason to believe are coming home truly to Jesus Christ, with as many boys. One has been so filled with love, peace, and joy, that she has continued almost all nights in prayer. Her heart burns with longing desire for the salvation of her dear relations and fellow creatures.

Our affairs are now carried on with decency and order, and I believe, Savannah will yet become the joy of the earth. Before long, I trust, the Lord will take it into His own hands, and then the curse, which has hereto been lying on it, will be taken off. I am beginning to build a church, and when matters are brought to a sufficient extremity, then, I believe, will be the Lord's opportunity to save and deliver us. He seems to be purging the province apace. The children are industrious. We have now in the house near one hundred yards of cloth spun and woven. We have several tradesmen belonging to the House, much cattle on our plantation, and, I hope, before long we shall live among ourselves. There are several masters set over the children, who watch over them, both in and after school hours. Generally once a day, if I do not, they walk with their respective charges, tell them of the glory of God in creation, and praise Him by singing a hymn. But I shall give a more particular account when I send my next *Journal*. As it is uncertain when I shall return to my native country, I thought it my duty to send this in the meanwhile, that my dear friends may give thanks, and by their prayers strengthen my hands: for an effectual door is opening in America, and I trust the time is coming when the earth shall be filled with the knowledge of the Lord, as the waters cover the sea. We hear of wars and rumors of wars; but let not the servants of Jesus Christ be troubled. May the Lord be glorified in all His dispensations, and may that happy time now hasten on, wherein the leopard shall lie down with the kid, and the lion eat straw like the ox, and the people learn war no more! The concern I have for the Church in general, and Savannah and the Orphan House in particular, lies much upon my heart; but I commit myself to God in a hymn composed by Gerhardt, and translated by my friend, Mr. Wesley.

I   Commit thou all thy griefs,
        And ways into His hands;
    To His sure truth and tender care,
        Who earth and heaven commands.

II   Who points the clouds their course,
        Whom winds and seas obey;
    He shall direct thy wandering feet,
        He shall prepare thy way.

III   Thou on the Lord rely,
        So safe shalt thou go on;
    Fix on His work thy steadfast eye,
        So shall thy work be done.

IV   No profit canst thou gain
        By self-consuming care;
    To Him commend thy cause; His ear
        Attends the softest prayer.

V   Thy everlasting truth,
        Father, Thy ceaseless love,
    Sees all Thy children's wants, and knows
        What best for each will prove.

VI   And whatso'er Thou will'st
        Thou dost, O King of Kings;
    What Thy unerring wisdom choose,
        Thy power to being brings.

VII   Thou everywhere hast sway,
        And all things serve Thy might;
    Thy every act pure blessing is,
        Thy path unsullied light.

VIII   When Thou arisest, Lord,
        What shall Thy work withstand?
    Whate'er Thy children want, Thou giv'st,
        Who, who shall stay Thy hand?

IX   Give to the winds thy fears;
        Hope, and be undismayed;
    God hears thy sighs, and counts thy tears,
        God shall lift up thy head.

X   Through waves, and clouds, and storms,
        He gently clears thy way;
    Wait thou His time, so shall this night
        Soon end in joyous day.

XI   Still heavy is thy heart?
        Still sink thy spirits down?
    Cast off the weight, let fear depart,
        Bid every care be gone.

XII   What though thou rulest not?
            Yet heaven, and earth, and hell
       Proclaim, God sitteth on the throne,
            And ruleth all things well.

XIII   Leave to His sovereign sway
            To choose and to command;
       So shalt thou wondering own His way,
            How wise, how strong His hand.

XIV   Far, far above thy thought,
            His counsel shall appear,
       When fully He the work hath wrought
            That caused thy needless fear.

XV   Thou seest our weakness, Lord;
            Out hearts are known to Thee;
       O lift Thou up the sinking hand,
            Confirm the feeble knee.

XVI   Let us in life, in death,
            Thy steadfast truth declare,
       And publish with our latest breath,
            Thy love and guardian care.

                                     Amen and Amen.

THE SEVENTH JOURNAL

FROM A FEW DAYS AFTER WHITEFIELD'S RETURN TO GEORGIA TO HIS ARRIVAL AT FALMOUTH MARCH 11, 1741

EBENEZER: Wednesday, June 25, 1740. Went on Monday to, and returned this evening from Ebenezer, which I have seen with no small satisfaction. Surely there is a difference, even in this life, between those that serve the Lord, and those that serve Him not. All other places of the colony seem to be like Egypt, where was darkness, but Ebenezer, like the land of Goshen, wherein was great light. For near four miles did I walk in almost one continued field, with a most plentiful crop of corn, peas, potatoes, etc., growing upon it, — all the product of a few months' labor. But God blesses the laborers; they are unanimous; the strong help the weak, and all seem hearty for the common good. In a few years, the Saltzburghers, I believe, will be a flourishing people. Their land is good, and lies very near the river. They already provide food, and before long, will be capable of providing raiment for themselves. I shall send them up cotton, spinning wheels, and a loom to begin a manufactory for themselves; and next year they hope their own land will produce enough flax, cotton, etc., to carry it on. I had communications with their ministers. Our sister Orphan House there, is blessed by their means. Yesterday was set apart as a day of thanksgiving for assistance sent the orphans from Germany and Savannah. The people seemed very grateful. They willingly received me into their clean, but little huts, and seemed proud when I accepted anything from their hands. As I said formerly, so I say again, they who help the Saltzburghers will do a good work. They want assistance. Lord, raise them up benefactors.

SAVANNAH: Friday, June 27. Received Captain Grant, who has been to Cape Fear, to fetch a load of boards, and returned with his sloop, in fourteen days. He was welcomed very courteously by the chief inhabitants; and, many, he tells me, were in expectation of seeing me at North Carolina. Lord, send me wheresoever and whensoever it shall seem good to Thy Divine Majesty. Amen.

Monday, June 30. God has often been pleased, since my return, to make Himself known in our sanctuary and has caused a mighty power to attend the Word preached, both in public and private. Providence seems to smile upon the Orphan House, and to prosper everything I take in hand. A wealthy, moral, civilized planter, of South Carolina, came lately to see us, and God, I believe, has been pleased to give him a true knowledge of Himself, and a true faith in His dear Son, Jesus Christ. His wife, also, was quickened, having been wrought upon by God, sometime last winter. She was a great admirer of Archbishop Tillotson; but, having her eyes now opened, to discern spiritual things, can no longer take up with such husks. With this happy pair, (hearing that Charleston people were in expectations of seeing me, before I went to the North, and that God had been pleased to work by my ministry among them), I and a friend left Savannah this morning, in a large boat, and arrived at Beaufort, in Port Royal, about midnight. Our friend and his wife went to a relation's house, but my companion and I chose to continue in the boat, where our Lord caused us to lie down, and sleep in peace and safety. Blessed, forever blessed, be the Keeper of Israel, Who neither slumbereth nor sleepeth.

BEAUFORT IN PORT ROYAL: Tuesday, July 1. Went, as soon as it was light, to a relation of our fellow travelers', and, afterwards had some conversation with Mr. Jones, the minister of the parish, about the great doctrines of the Gospel. He received us with much tenderness and respect, but thought I went too far in condemning Archbishop Tillotson. I think the arguments I brought, were conclusive, and the account my new convert (one of his parishioners) gave of God's dealing with his soul, rational, and, as he confessed, satisfactory; but, he could not see clearly into the doctrine of *free justification*, without regard to anything foreseen in the creature. However, being more noble than most of his brethren, he was candid, courteous, and, notwithstanding he was in danger of incurring the Commissary's displeasure thereby, he read prayers, and requested me to preach in the evening, at his church. I preached, but to a small auditory, there being but little notice given of it. After sermon, Mr. J . . . . thanked me, and, having promised to preach again, God willing, in my return to Savannah, I took my leave, and spent the evening with my fellow travelers, at their relations' houses. May God convert every one related to them, and make them all members of the household of faith. Amen.

CHARLESTON: Thursday, July 3. Set out yesterday, at one in the morning, and reached Mr. Bryan's plantation about ten. Stayed, and dined together. Rode through extreme heat. Put in, and lay at a planter's house, by reason of the thunder, lightning, and rain. Breakfasted this morning, at Mr. B . . .'s, of Ponpon. Prayed, talked of the things of God; and was enabled to hold out, notwithstanding the weather was exceeding hot, till I came to Charleston, about eighty miles from Beaufort. Here, again, my spirits were much raised, and my heart comforted by a packet of letters from the North, giving me an account how the Word of God runs and is glorified in Philadelphia, and other adjacent places. The Lord's Name be praised, from the rising of the sun to the going down of the same.

Friday, July 4. Lay at a gentlewoman's house, who came last night to give me an invitation. Was visited by many friends, who were rejoiced to see me. Received a letter from the Commissary, which I immediately answered. Wrote some letters to Savannah; dispatched some affairs for the Orphan House; and, preached in the evening in the Independent meeting house, to as large and attentive congregations as usual. Blessed be God for giving the people a hearing ear. Lord give them also an obedient heart for Thy dear Son's sake. Amen.

Sunday, July 6. Preached twice yesterday, and twice today, and had great reason to believe our Lord got Himself the victory in some hearts.

Went to church in the morning and afternoon, and heard the Commissary preach as virulent, unorthodox, and inconsistent a discourse as ever I heard in my life. His heart seemed full of choler and resentment; and, out of the abundance thereof, he poured forth so many bitter words against the Methodists (as he called them) in general, and me in particular, that several, who intended to receive the Sacrament at his hands, withdrew. Never, I believe, was such a preparation sermon preached before. I could not help thinking the preacher was of the same spirit as Bishop Gardiner in Queen Mary's days. After the sermon, he sent his clerk to desire me not to come to the Sacrament, till he had spoken with me. I immediately retired to my lodgings, rejoicing that I was accounted worthy to suffer this further degree of contempt for my dear Lord's sake. Blessed Jesus, lay it not to the Commissary's charge! Amen and Amen!

ASHLEY FERRY: Monday, July 7. Set out early this morning, in company with several, whose hearts the Lord had lately opened, and went to the house of Mr. Chandler, a gracious Baptist minister, who lives about fourteen miles from Charleston. After dinner, according to appointment, I preached at his meeting house, to the conviction of some, and comfort of others, who came to me rejoicing that the exploded doctrines of the Gospel were so publicly and successfully preached. Sermon being ended, and much importunity used, I went with some Charleston friends to the house of Mrs. P . . . rs, about five miles from the meeting house; but was obliged to lie down (as I now am generally every day) by reason of the violent heat of the weather, and great expense of sweat. God strengthened me much, and so assisted me in giving an exhortation to the company who came with me, that all seemed to be put under great concern. Three or four in particular, came out telling me how powerfully God was working in their souls. Father, show that it is Thy especial work, by carrying it on and perfecting it till the Day of our Lord Jesus. Amen.

DORCHESTER AND ASHLEY FERRY: Tuesday, July 8. Left my lodgings at eight in the morning, and hastened to Dorchester, where I preached twice to a large audience in Mr. Osgood's meeting house, a young Independent minister. At four in the afternoon, we set out again; took a little refreshment at a gentleman's house in the way, and lay at Mr. C's at night. Here my bodily strength failed me again; and, therefore, being very weak, I retired to bed as soon as possible, but slept very little. Lord, hasten that blessed time when I shall sleep no more.

> Oh when shall I, in endless day,
> For ever chase dark sleep away,
> And hymns, with the supernal choir,
> Incessant sing, and never tire.

ASHLEY FERRY AND CHARLESTON: Wednesday, July 9. Found myself still weaker; but was strengthened to preach under a tree near Mr. C's meeting house, at ten in the morning, it being now too small to contain

the congregation. People seemed to come from all parts, and the Word
came with convincing power. Having changed my linen (which I am obliged
to do after every sermon, by reason of my prodigious sweating), I hastened
to Charleston; but my body was so exceeding weak, and the sun shone so
intensely hot, that five miles before I reached town, I called in at a public
house, and lay for a considerable time, almost breathless and dead. But God
comforted me; and, being thereby strengthened in the inner man, I once
more set forward with my fellow travelers, reached town about four, and
preached at six in the usual place, with more freedom and power than
could have been expected, considering the great weakness of my body. But
I can do all things through Christ strengthening me. I thank Thee, Holy
Father, that I have so often the sentence of death within myself. Oh, let
me be daily taught thereby, not to trust to myself in the least, but in
Thee, the Everliving God.

CHRIST'S CHURCH, CHARLESTON, AND JOHN'S ISLAND: Saturday,
July 12. Went over the water on Thursday, and read prayers and preached
at the request of the churchwardens and vestry, at Christ's Church.
Returned in the evening to Charleston; preached twice there yesterday, and
went this morning to John's Island, about twenty miles up the river, where
I was invited by Colonel G . . . s. He received me and my friends most
hospitably, and provided several horses, chairs, etc., for us and his family.
We rode to the church, where there was a great congregation. God
strengthened me to read prayers and preach twice with much freedom.
About four we returned to the Colonel's. I was enabled to give a warm and
close exhortation to the rich that sat about me, and returned to town in
the evening, praising and blessing God. Glory be to His Most Holy Name,
Dagon seems daily to fall before the ark. A lasting impression, I am
persuaded, is made on many hearts; and, God, I believe, will yet show that
He hath much people in Charleston, and the countries round about. Lord,
Thou hast visited them with Thy judgments, melt them down with Thy
mercies. Stretch out the golden sceptre of Thy favor, and bruise them no
more with Thy iron rod. Amen.

Sunday, July 13. Preached this morning, and collected in the evening
for my poor orphans. Great numbers stood without the doors, and, it
raining very hard during the time of Divine service, many of them were
driven away. However, God caused the other people's hearts to devise
liberal things. Upwards of 50 pounds sterling was collected on the occasion,
most showing a readiness to assist me.

In the morning I went to church, and heard the Commissary preach.
Had some infernal spirit been sent to draw my picture, I think it scarcely
possible that he could have painted me in more horrid colors. I think, if
ever, then was the time that all manner of evil was spoken against me
falsely for Christ's sake. The Commissary seemed to ransack church history
for instances of enthusiasm and abused grace. He drew a parallel between
me and all the *Oliverians, Ranters, Quakers, French Prophets*, till he came
down to a family of the *Dutarts*, who lived, not many years ago, in South
Carolina, and were guilty of the most notorious incests and murders. To the

honor of God's free grace be it spoken, while the Commissary was representing me thus, I felt the Blessed Spirit strengthening and refreshing my soul. God, at the same time, gave me to see what I was by nature, and how I had deserved His eternal wrath; and, therefore, I did not feel the least resentment against the preacher. No; I pitied, I prayed for him; and wished, from my soul, that the Lord would convert him, as He once did the persecutor Saul, and let him know that it is Jesus Whom he persecutes. In the evening, many came, I was informed, to hear what I would say; but as the Commissary hinted that his sermons would be printed, and as they were full of invidious falsehood, I held my tongue, and made little or no reply.

Saturday, July 19. Preached twice every day this week at Charleston, except on Wednesday and Thursday evening, the last of which days I was called upon to go to St. James's Island, to preach at the house of Madame W . . . d. This gentlewoman, as she informed me herself, was at one time much prejudiced against me, insomuch that she thought it dangerous to come and hear me; but, having read my sermons, she changed her mind, and coming both to town, and to St. John's Island to hear me preach, was, with her daughter and another gentlewoman, much melted down. Being given to hospitality, she provided food sufficient for a great multitude. People came from town and the neighboring places. Her barn was put into proper order, and I read prayers and preached in it. A lovely melting was visible in several parts of the auditory. After sermon, God enabled me to speak many Gospel truths amidst a polite set of people. At the request of Madame W . . . d, I stayed all night, which gave me an opportunity of teaching her family the way of God more perfectly, and also of resting my weary body, which seems to be declining more every day. Blessed be God, I hope it will not be long before worms destroy it, and my soul carried to see God.

> Jesus, to Thy dear faithful hand,
> My naked soul I trust;
> My flesh awaits Thy blest command,
> To drop into my dust.

Here would follow a particular account of my trial, but it is judged proper not to publish it, while the cause is depending.

Sunday, July 20. Preached in the morning as usual, and went afterwards to church, to hear the Commissary. His text was, "Take heed how ye hear." At first, I thought we should have a peaceable sermon, especially, since we had conversed the night before so amicably; but the gall soon began to flow from his tongue, though not with such bitterness as last Sunday. He endeavored to apologize for his proceedings, condemned all that followed me, and gave all hopes of Heaven who adhered to him and the Church. In the evening (though I went off my bed to do it, and was carried in a chaise) the Lord Jesus strengthened me to take my last farewell of the people of Charleston. Many seemed to sympathize with me.

Blessed be God for sending me once more among them. Though the heat of the weather, and frequency of preaching, have perhaps given an irrecoverable stroke to the health of my body; yet, I rejoice, knowing it has been for the conviction, and I believe conversion of many souls. Glory be to God on high, the fields here, as well as elsewhere, are now white, ready to harvest. Numbers are seeking after Jesus. Two or three Dissenting ministers, by my advice, agreed to set up a weekly lecture. I advised the people, since the Gospel was not preached in the church, to go and hear it in the meeting houses. May the Lord be with both ministers and people, and cause them to preach and hear as becomes the Gospel of Christ. At my first coming, the people of Charleston seemed to be wholly devoted to pleasure. One, well acquainted with their manners and circumstances, told me that they spent more on their polite entertainments than the amount raised by their rates for the poor. But now the jewelers and dancing masters begin to cry out that their craft is in danger. A vast alteration is discernible in ladies' dresses; and some, while I have been speaking, have been so convinced of the sin of wearing jewels, that I have seen them, with blushes, put their hands to their ears, and cover them with their fans. But the reformation has gone further than externals. Many moral, good sort of men, who before were settled on their lees, have been awakened to seek after Jesus Christ; and many a Lydia's heart hath the Lord opened to receive the things that were spoken. Indeed, the Word often came like a hammer and a fire. Several of the Negroes did their work in less time than usual, that they might come to hear me; and many of the owners, who have been awakened, have resolved to teach them Christianity. Had I time and proper schoolmasters, I might immediately erect a Negro school in South Carolina, as well as in Pennsylvania. Many would willingly contribute both money and land. Almost every day something was sent for my orphans at Georgia. The people were very solicitous about my health, when they saw me so weak, and sent me many small presents. I sometimes feared they would be too hot against the Commissary; but I endeavored to stop their resentment, as much as possible, and recommended peace and moderation to them, in most of my discourses. May the Lord Jesus reward them for all their works of faith, and labors which have proceeded of love. May He never leave them without a teaching priest, and grant that the seed sown in their hearts may grow up into an eternal harvest! Amen and Amen!

ASHLEY FERRY AND PONPON: Monday, July 21. Left Charleston very early, accompanied by many of the inhabitants. Read prayers and preached at Ashley Ferry, to a large congregation. The weather continuing extremely hot, sweating and preaching weakened me very much. I went in a carriage to Madam B's, who kindly invited me and my friends to dinner. I ate but little; took leave of my dear fellow travelers, as well as I could; took horse, and put in for shelter from the rain at Major B's, in the evening; and reached Mr. B's, of Ponpon, nearly forty miles from town, about midnight. Here I had the pleasure of meeting Mr. Hugh B . . . n; but nature being quite worn out, I went to rest, as soon as possible, not doubting that the Lord would cause me to renew my strength before the morning. Why should I doubt it, since the Lord hath said, "I will never leave thee nor forsake thee"?

Tuesday July 22. Slept fairly well, but found I was not strong enough to engage in family duty. Met with Mr. S. and Mr. S., two Scots' Presbyterian ministers, and Mr. T., a Church of England missionary, who refused to preach or sit in judgment against me. About noon, God strengthened me to ride a mile, and preach, under a great tree, to an attentive auditory. Some were affected. I would willingly have preached a second time; but my body was so weak, that, by the advice of friends, I resolved to continue where I was all night. Surely it cannot be long before this earthly tabernacle will be dissolved.

HOOSPANAH CHAPEL AND GOOD HOPE: Wednesday, July 23. Rose some time before day, and about noon got to Hoospanah Chapel, near thirty miles from Mr. B's. Here I preached to a very small auditory, few people living thereabouts. Sermon being over, I went on horseback to Good Hope, where Mr. Hugh B . . . n lived, and several followed, hoping I would preach again in the evening. But here my bodily strength so failed me, and I had such longings after God; that I sometimes hoped He was about to set my imprisoned soul at liberty. Surely God then placed me upon Mount Pisgah, and gave me a distant prospect of the Heavenly Canaan. I stretched for immortality, and longed for the blessed angels to come and carry me to Abraham's harbor. These words, "I know that my Redeemer liveth," came with wonderful sweetness and power to my soul; and the thoughts of my Savior's dying love, and of the Lord being my Righteousness, melted me into tears. My dear friend and companion was in tears, and seemed willing to take his flight with me into the arms of our beloved Jesus. The poor Negroes crowded round the windows, and expressed a great concern for me. Their master had acquainted them, I believe, that I was their friend. He himself sat by and wept. But the time of my departure was not yet at hand. In a short time, I felt my body grow stronger, and I was enabled to walk about. I joined in family prayer, as well as I could, and asked God, if I was not to die, but live, that it might be to declare the works and lovingkindness of the Lord. Grant this, O Father, for Thy dear Son's sake. Amen.

GOOD HOPE AND BEAUFORT: Thursday, July 24. Being too weak to ride on horseback I went in Mr. B's boat to Beaufort. We got there about ten in the morning, but the heat of the sun almost struck me down, and took away my senses, as soon as I put my foot on shore. Kind Mr. J . . . s courteously received me. In the cool of the evening, I preached in his church, to a larger auditory than when there last. Mr. J. thanked me for my sermon, disapproved entirely of the Commissary's treatment of me, and kindly entertained me and my friends all night.

BEAUFORT AND SAVANNAH: Friday, July 25. Took boat before day, and having fine weather and a favorable breeze, reached Savannah, and saluted my family about five in the evening. In the evening I expounded, and, thinking it was the Lesson for the night, read the last chapter of St. Paul's Second Epistle to Timothy, in which were these encouraging words: "But watch thou in all things, endure afflictions, do the work of an evangelist, make full proof of thy ministry. Alexander the coppersmith did me much evil: the Lord reward him according to his works. Of whom be thou ware also; for he hath greatly withstood our words. At my first trial, no man stood by me. Notwithstanding, the Lord stood by me, and strengthened me, that by me the preaching might be fully known. And I was delivered out of the mouth of the lion. And the Lord shall deliver me from every evil work, and will preserve me unto His heavenly Kingdom: to Whom be glory forever and ever. Amen."

Thursday, July 31. Continued very weak, ever since my return from Charleston. Was much refreshed this morning with the sight of some friends (among whom was Mr. Tilly, a Baptist minister) who came in our sloop to see the Orphan House.

Sunday, August 3. Last night, through weakness of body, just as I began family prayer, I was struck, as I thought, with death. I put up a few broken accents and breathed out, "Lord Jesus, receive my spirit." This morning, soon after I rose, I found that Mr. J. and his wife, of Port Royal, Mr. Jonathan B., brother of Mr. Hugh B, and Mr. B . . . ll, were all come to pay us a visit. Though exceedingly weak, and I had almost laid aside thoughts of officiating this day, yet, upon Mr. J's intimating that friends came expecting to hear me, I promised, if I could, to preach, and begged him to read prayers. He did, but I found myself so ill, that I would fain have persuaded Mr. T. to preach for me. He refused, urging that God would strengthen me if I began. Before I had prayed long, Br. B dropped down, as though shot with a gun. Afterwards he got up, and sat attentively to hear the sermon. The influence spread. The greatest part of the congregation were under great concern. Tears trickled down apace, and God manifested Himself much among us at the Sacrament.

Monday, August 4. Was sent for at noon to see Mr. Jonathan B. At my coming, I found him under great concern and strong convictions of sin. He reflected much on his misspent life, and blessed God for bringing him now to Savannah, and hoped that he might be found in Christ before he returned home. His wife sat weeping by. Mr. B . . . ll lay on a bed groaning in bitterness of soul, under a sense of guilt, and crying out for an interest in Jesus. I asked, "what caused him to fall down yesterday?" He answered, "The power of God's Word." After half an hour's conversation on the nature of the new birth, and the necessity of closing in with Christ, I kneeled down, prayed with them, and took my leave, hoping the Lord would pluck them as brands from the burning. Amen and Amen.

Sunday, August 10. Went on Tuesday with Mr. B., Mr. J., etc. to Bethesda, and had the pleasure of seeing the work of God going on in most of our visitors' hearts. This morning I expounded early as usual, and read part of the prayers at ten o'clock; but got Mr. T. to preach, who (though a Baptist minister) joined with us in receiving the Sacrament, in the Church of England way. The King was pleased to sit at His Table; He brought us into His Banqueting House, and caused it to be a feast of fat things to our souls. Many, I believe, fed on Jesus in their hearts with thanksgiving. I went home much refreshed in soul, but so weak in body that I declined going to public worship in the afternoon. In the evening, when my friends were sitting together, I began to speak to them of the things of God. Their concern increased, till many burst into tears, and one fell on the ground. Before I had done, some of my parishioners came up, and the rest of my family. When I had done speaking to them from God, I spoke in prayer to God for them. My soul was carried, as it were, out of the body, and I wrestled with our Lord in prayer on their behalf. He did not let us go without a blessing. The room was filled with the cries of those around me, and many at that time sought Jesus sorrowing. The concern continued after the Duty was over a Cherokee Indian trader, who was present, desired to speak with me, saying, "I never saw or felt the like before."

Saturday, August 16. Parted with Mr. B. and Mr. B . . . n, on Tuesday, who, I hope, could say, "Lord now lettest Thou Thy servants depart in peace; for our eyes have seen, our hearts have felt, Thy Salvation." Several times this week I was obliged to come out through weakness of body, in the midst of our public worship. But, as troubles abounded, consolations abounded also. These words, "But David strengthened himself in the Lord his God," and, also, the eleventh chapter of Hebrews were blessed to me. I found the benefit of being afflicted. God enabled me to sanctify Him in my heart. Lord, I adore Thy infinite, condescending goodness. O do not leave me to myself, but purge, O purge me, for Thy mercy's sake, that I may bring forth more fruit!

> Correct me when I go astray,
> And lead me in Thy perfect way.

Monday, August 18. Preached yesterday morning, and took leave of my parishioners. Administered the Blessed Sacrament, and gave an exhortation afterwards. Settled everything to the best of my power, for the Orphan House, which succeeds beyond expectation. In this evening's exposition, and my private farewell discourse, my hearers were vastly affected; and, a strange woman was so touched, that she came to me confessing her sins, and crying out, "What shall I do to be saved?" When I came to converse with her, I found God had struck her the last time I preached at Port Royal, and, I hope, He will now effectually call her by His grace. I am thankful to the Lord of all lords for setting such seals to my ministry at departure. About ten at night I went on board our sloop with my other visitors, in order to go to Charleston; where the Captain is to take in freight for Boston, for the benefit of the Orphan House. The Lord preserve my dear lambs and flock, in my absence; bring them into green pastures, and lead them beside the waters of comfort, for His own Name's sake!

CHARLESTON: Friday, August 22. Had a comfortable passage with my friends. Found the sea air improved my health. Arrived at Charleston about four this afternoon. Many came to the wharf, and welcomed me most kindly. I retired as soon as possible, to my lodgings, and spent the evening at the house of Mr. F., where many were met together. The Lord, Who once came to the eleven by night, and said, "Peace be unto you," I am persuaded, by His Spirit spoke to many of them. The Lord has made a willing people in this day of His power. Praised be His Name, from the rising of the sun unto the going down of the same!

Monday, August 25. Being weak in body, I have preached only once each day (except on Sundays); but, I think, with greater success. I scarce know the time wherein I did not see a considerable melting in some part of the congregation, and often it spreads over the whole of it. Several times I was so weak before I began to preach, that I thought it almost impossible for me to get through half the discourse; but the Lord quickened, enlightened, and supported me above measure. Out of weakness, I became strong. The audiences were more numerous than ever, and it was supposed, not less than four thousand were in and about the meeting house, when I preached my farewell sermon. The Commissary, having run his utmost length, thought it best to say no more. Finding, when I was here last, that Jesus Christ was not preached in the church, my conscience would not suffer me to attend on those that preached there any more. I therefore went to the Baptist and Independent meeting houses, where Jesus Christ was preached. I have administered the Sacrament thrice in a private house. Never did I see anything more solemn. The room was large, and most were in tears, as though they were weeping at their Savior's Cross. Surely Christ Crucified was set forth before them. Many, at their request, stood by that did not receive; but they wept bitterly. I prayed for them all, and I hope the Lord will clothe them with the wedding garment. What was best, Baptists, Church folks, and Presbyterians, all joined together, and received according to the Church of England, except two, who desired to have it sitting: I willingly complied, knowing that it was a thing quite indifferent. Many others, hearing how God was among us yesterday, desired I would administer today. I did, and our Lord was with us again. Having more leisure from my private studies, through my weakness not permitting me to read much, I had better opportunities of conversing with, and confirming those who were under convictions. Most of them, I found grown in grace, and their hearts softened by Redeeming Love. Mr. Jonathan B. came much established. Mr. Hugh B. was left sick at home; but his wife came to Charleston. By my advice, they have resolved to begin a Negro school. A young stage player, who was convinced when I was at New York last, and who providentially came to Georgia, when Mr. Jonathan B. was there, is to be their first master. The time would fail me were I to relate every particular.

Great, a very great alteration is made in the life and manners of several of the polite ladies. The rooms that were usually employed for balls and assemblies are now turned into society rooms. Every night, where I was invited to supper, it became customary to have the house filled with company, with whom the Lord enabled me to pray and exhort. Once I was so sick that I was obliged to be led home. Many came to me in private under the deepest convictions. Several were esteemed mad by their relations.

One young lady was for some time turned out of doors, but afterwards was recalled; and, one, who was looked upon as a very good man, was convinced of self-righteousness in an extraordinary manner, and burnt near forty pounds' worth of books written by such authors as Chubb, Foster, etc. The people here were often sending me something or other, and so loaded our sloop with sea stores, that I was constrained to send much of them to the Orphan House. Being obliged to be absent from them for a long season, I exhorted them with all my power to continue in the grace of God: I forewarned them of their danger, and told them how they must deny themselves, and take up their daily crosses, if they would follow Jesus Christ. Having our sloop freighted, and the wind favoring us, after dinner, I embarked with several Charleston friends for Rhode Island, intending to go from there by land to Boston. In the evening, we got over the bar, and the pilot would take nothing for his trouble. Here I parted with all my friends, except four, two of whom, God willing, intend to accompany me during this excursion. O Lord, Who claspest the winds in Thy fists, and holdest the waters in the hollow of Thy hand, accept our thanks for past mercies, sanctify our voyage, and, if it be best, carry us with speed to the haven where we would be. Amen.

NEWPORT IN RHODE ISLAND: Sunday, September 14. Was sick part of the passage, but, afterwards the sea air, under God, much improved my health. Arrived at Newport just after the beginning of evening service. We came purposely there first with our sloop. Almost all the morning the wind was contrary. With a strong assurance that we should be heard, we prayed that the Lord would turn the wind, that we might give Him thanks in the great congregation; and, also, that He would send such to us, as He would have us to converse with, and who might show us a lodging. Though the wind was rough when we began; yet, when we had done praying, and come up out of the cabin, it was quite fair. With a gentle breeze, we sailed pleasantly into the harbor; got to public worship before they had finished the Psalms, and sat, as I thought, undiscovered. After service was over, a gentleman asked me whether my name was not Whitefield? I told him yes; he then desired me to go to his house, and he would take care to provide lodgings for me and my friends. I went, silently admiring God's goodness in answering my prayer so minutely. Several gentlemen of the town soon came to pay their respects to me, among whom was Mr. Clap, an aged Dissenting minister, and the most venerable man I ever saw in my life. He looked like a good old Puritan, and gave me an idea of what stamp those men were, who first settled in New England. His countenance was very heavenly, and he prayed most affectionately for a blessing on my coming to Rhode Island.

In the evening, with him and some more friends, I waited on Mr. H . . . n, the minister of the Church of England, and desired the use of his pulpit. At first he seemed a little unwilling, and wished to know "what extraordinary call I had to preach on weekdays," which he said, "was disorderly?" I answered, "St. Paul exhorted Timothy to be instant in season and out of season; that, if the Orders of the Church were rightly complied with, our ministers should read public prayers twice every day, and then it would not be disorderly at such times, to give them a sermon." As to an extraordinary call, I claimed none otherwise than the Apostle's injunction, "as we have opportunity let us do good unto all men." He still held out, and did not give any positive answer; but, at last, after he had withdrawn and consulted with the gentlemen, he said, "If my preaching would promote the glory of God, and good of souls, I was welcome to his church, as often as I would, during my stay in town." We then agreed to make use of it at ten in the morning, and three in the afternoon. After this, I waited on the Governor, who seemed to be a very plain man, and had a plain house. By profession, he is a Seventh Day Baptist; and he is a man of good report, as to his conduct and dealing with the world. After a short visit, I returned to take leave of Mr. H., and to fetch my friends, who were at his house, waiting for me. We then went to the house of Mr. B., who first spoke to me when coming out of the church. The house was soon filled with company. I expounded and prayed for about an hour, and then retired to a lodging, which the Lord in His good Providence had provided for me. His distinguishing repeated mercies quite melted me down, and I called upon all that was within me to praise His Holy Name. O Lord, in the night season, let me arise and give thanks unto Thee, and let my talking be of Thy loving kindness and tender mercies all the day long!

Monday, September 15. Breakfasted this morning with old Mr. Clap, and was much edified with his conversation. I could not but think while at his table, that I was sitting with one of the patriarchs. He is full of days; a bachelor, and has been minister of a congregation in Rhode Island upwards of forty years. People of all denominations respect him. He abounds in good works; gives all away, and is wonderfully tender of little children; many of different persuasions come to be instructed by him. Whenever he dies, I am persuaded he will be enabled to say with old Simeon, "Lord, now lettest Thou Thy servant depart in peace." At ten in the morning, and three in the afternoon, according to appointment, I read prayers and preached in the church. It is very commodious, and will contain three thousand people. It was more than filled in the afternoon, persons of all denominations attending. God assisted me much. I observed numbers affected, and had great reason to believe the Word of God had been sharper than a two-edged sword in some of the hearers' souls. After evening service, I received the following letter: —

"Newport in Rhode Island, September 15, 1740.

"Reverend Sir and Beloved Brother, — Although mine eyes never saw your face before this day, yet my heart and soul have been united to you in love, by the bond of the Spirit. I have longed and expected to see you for many months past: blessed be God, mine eyes have seen the joyful days. I trust, through grace, I have some things to communicate to you, that will make your heart glad. I shall omit writing anything; and only hereby present my hearty love, and let you know, that I am waiting now at your door for admission. Though I am unworthy, my Lord is worthy, in

Whose Name, I trust I come.
"I am your unworthy brother,

"JONATHAN B . . . R."

On reading it, I could not but think this was one of those young ministers, whom God had lately made use of, in such a remarkable manner, at the east end of Long Island. I sent for him, and found he was the man. My heart rejoiced. We walked out, and took sweet counsel together; and, among other things, he told me, that he came to Rhode Island, hoping he should see me there, and had been waiting for me about a week. What rendered this meeting more remarkable was, I had not intention of sailing into Rhode Island, till about three days before I left Carolina; and, also, I had a great desire to put in, if I could, at the east end of Long Island, to see this very person, whom the Great God now brought unto me. Lord, accept our thanks, sanctify our meeting, and teach us both what we shall do for Thy own Name's sake! After a long conference, we took leave of each other for the present, but agreed, that we should now be companions in travel, till the Lord should make our way more plain. In the evening, I went to venerable Mr. Clap's, and exhorted and prayed with a great multitude, who, not only crowded into the house, but thronged every way about it. The dear old man rejoiced to see the things which he saw; and after my exhortation was over, dismissed me with his blessing. Lord Jesus, do Thou say Amen to it. Amen and Amen.

Tuesday, September 16. Although a little low in the morning, I was enabled to read prayers and preach to still greater auditories than yesterday. It being assembly time, the gentlemen adjourned in order to attend the service, and several invitations were given me to come to other adjacent places. The people were exceedingly attentive; tears trickled down their cheeks; and they so far prevailed with me by their importunity, that I promised, God willing, to call upon them in my return from Boston. When I came home to my lodgings, the woman of the house saluted me with "Blessed art thou of the Lord." I looked round to see the reason of such a salutation, and found it on the couch, where there lay a young woman under great distress of soul. After a little conversation, I found she had a gracious discovery of the Lord Jesus made to her soul, when I was speaking from these words, "Come, see a man that told me all things that ever I did." She told me, she had often grieved the Spirit of God, but now she believed the Lord was calling her home effectually. "The Word" she added, "came with such power, that I was obliged to go out of the church, otherwise I must have disturbed the congregation. When I came from home, contrary to my parents' inclinations, I insisted, I knew not why, on staying at Newport six weeks. They wanted me to stay only a month, but at last consented that I should stay my own time. Tomorrow is the last day of the six weeks, and, oh the goodness of God in sending you just now, before my time was out," or words to that effect.

Afterwards, one or two more came under similar circumstances, crying out, in the bitterness of their souls, after the Lord Jesus. I prayed with each of them, and exhorted them not to rest till they found rest in Jesus

Christ. In the evening I went, privately as I thought, to a friend's house; but the people were so eager to hear the Word, that in a short time, I believe, more than a thousand were before the door, besides those that were within, and filled every room in the house. I therefore stood upon the threshold, and spake for near an hour on these words, "Blessed are they that hunger and thirst after righteousness, for they shall be filled." It was a very solemn meeting. Glory be to God's great Name! Before I retired to bed, I went to take leave of Mr. H., and had some talk with him about the new birth. He was very civil, and would have liked me to stay with him longer; but, having to go a journey on the morrow, I took my leave, after we had conversed near half an hour. At my return to my lodgings, good old Mr. Clap went with me into a private room, gave me something for my orphans, and spoke many kind things to me. Although very old, yet he followed me from one end of the town to another; so that people said I had made old Mr. Clap young again. Oh what a crown of glory is a hoary head, when found in the way of righteousness! He was exceedingly desirous of my coming to Rhode Island again, which, God willing, I promised to do: for Rhode Island seems to be a place where much good may be done.

They are very plain people in general; though I observed there were some foolish virgins at church, covered all over with the pride of life. I find they are sadly divided among themselves as to outward things. I think there are no less than four different congregations of Baptists, two of the Independents, and one of the Quakers. Dean Berkeley's name is much respected among them. The Established Church is in excellent order as to externals; but many of the chief members were bigots. They seemed very fearful lest I should preach in Mr. Clap's meeting house, and gloried much in my bringing the good old man to church. Nor is there less bigotry among those of other communions. All, I fear, place the Kingdom of God too much in meats and drinks, and have an ill name abroad for running of goods. One day, when I said in my sermon, "What will become of you, who cheat the King of his taxes?" — the whole congregation seemed surprised, and looked at one another, as though they should say, "We are guilty." Lord Jesus, give them to know Thee, and the power of Thy Resurrection, and teach them to live soberly, righteously and godly in this present evil world. Amen and Amen.

NEWPORT AND BRISTOL: Wednesday, September 17. Left Newport in Rhode Island about nine in the morning, and reached Bristol, a town twelve miles distant, about noon. Several friends from Rhode Island accompanied me, and before we came to the town, a Dissenting minister (as I afterwards found) met me, and in the name of the Court, which was then sitting at Bristol, invited me and my friends to dine with them, and also desired me to give them a sermon. I complied. The gentlemen received us with much civility; and, after dinner, I preached in the meeting house to more people than might have been expected on such sudden notice. My heart was much shut up in the exercise. However, the gentlemen seemed very thankful. I took my leave about four in the afternoon, and lay at an inn about ten miles further on the road. Thanks be to God for His unspeakable mercies.

Thursday, September 18. Rose a long while before day, and set out as soon as it was light. Breakfasted at a minister's house on the road. Found the people were apprised of my coming, and solicitous for my preaching; but, being resolved, if possible, to reach Boston, we traveled on for near fifty miles, and came to Boston about eight in the evening. When we were within four miles of the city, the Governor's son, with one or two ministers and several other gentlemen, waited at a gentleman's house to give me the meeting. They received me with great gladness, and told me many more would have come, had there not been a large funeral in the city, or if there had been more certain notice of my arriving. I think I can stand anything better than this: it favors too much of human grandeur; but I must be tried every way. The Lord be my Helper. After stopping a while, we went together in company to Boston, to the house of Mr. S., brother-in-law to the Rev. Dr. Colman, who long since had sent me an invitation. Several ministers and other gentlemen came in to pay their respects. My heart was but low, and my body weak; but, at the request of one of the ministers, I gave thanks to our gracious God, for bringing me in safety, and prayed that my coming might be in the fulness of the blessing of the Gospel of Peace. We then parted. After supper I retired, beseeching the Lord to raise my heart, and make His power known in the hearts of His people. Amen.

BOSTON: Friday, September 19. I was visited by several gentlemen and ministers, and went to the Governor's with Esquire Willard, the Secretary of the Province, a man fearing God, and with whom I have corresponded some time, though before unknown in person. The Governor received me with the utmost respect, and desired me to see him as often as I could. At eleven, I went to public worship at the Church of England, and afterwards went home with the Commissary, who had read prayers. He received me very courteously; and, it being a day whereon the clergy of the Established Church met, I had an opportunity of conversing with five of them together. I think, one of them began with me for calling "that Tennent and his brethren faithful ministers of Jesus Christ." I answered, "I believed they were." They then questioned me about "the validity of the Presbyterian ordination." I replied, "I believed it was valid." They then urged against me a passage in my first *Journal*, where I said, "That a Baptist minister at Deal did not give a satisfactory answer concerning his mission." I answered, "Perhaps my sentiments were altered." "And is Mr. Wesley altered in his sentiments?" said one; "for he was very strenuous for the Church, and rigorous against all other forms of government when he was at Boston." I answered, "He was then a great bigot, but God has since enlarged his heart, and I believed he was now like-minded with me in this particular." I then urged, "That a catholic spirit was best, and that a Baptist minister had communicated lately with me at Savannah." "I suppose," said another, "you would do him as good a turn, and would communicate with him." I answered, "Yes," and urged "that it was best to preach the new birth, and the power of godliness, and not to insist so much on the form: for people would never be brought to one mind as to that; nor did Jesus Christ ever intend it." "Yes, but He did," said Dr. Cutler. "How do you prove it?"

"Because Christ prayed, 'That all might be one, even as Thou Father and I are One.'" I replied, "That was spoken of the inward union of the souls of believers with Jesus Christ, and not of the outward Church." "That cannot be," said Dr. Cutler, "for how then could it be said, 'that the world might know that Thou has sent Me?'" He then (taking it for granted that the Church of England was the only true apostolical Church) drew a parallel between the Jewish and our Church, urging how God required all things to be made according to the pattern given in the Mount. I answered, "That before the parallel could be just, it must be proved, that every thing enjoined in our Church was as much of a Divine institution as any rite or ceremony under the Jewish dispensation." I added further, "That I saw regenerate souls among the Baptists, among the Presbyterians, among the Independents, and among the Church folks, — all children of God, and yet all born again in a differnt way of worship: and who can tell which is the most evangelical?" "What, can you see regeneration with your eyes?" said the Commissary, or words to that effect.

Soon after, we began to talk of the Righteousness of Christ, and the Commissary said, "Christ was to make up for the defects of our righteousness." I asked him, "Whether conversion was not instantaneous?" He was unwilling to confess it, but he having just before baptized an infant at public worship, I asked him, "Whether he believed that very instant in which he sprinkled the child with water, the Holy Ghost fell upon the child?" He answered, "Yes." "Then," said I, "according to your own principles, regeneration is instantaneous, and since you will judge of the new birth by the fruits, pray watch that child, and see if it brings forth the fruits of the Spirit." I also said, "That if every child was really born again in baptism, then every baptized infant would be saved." "And so they are," said Dr. Cutler. "How do you prove that?" "Because the Rubric says, 'that all infants dying after baptism before they have committed actual sin, are undoubtedly saved.'" I asked, "What text of Scripture there was to prove it?" "Here," said he, (holding a Prayer Book in his hand) "the Church says so." We then just hinted at predestination. I said, "I subscribed to the seventeenth Article of the Church in its literal sense with all my heart." We then talked a little about falling away finally from grace. I said, "A true child of God, though he might fall foully, yet could never fall finally." "But," said he, the Article says, "'Men may fall away from grace given.'" I answered, "But then observe what follows 'and by the grace of God they may rise again.'" Several other things of less consequence passed between us. Finding how inconsistent they were, I took my leave, resolving they should not have an opportunity of denying me the use of their pulpits. However, they treated me with more civility than any of our own clergymen have done for a long while. The Commissary very kindly urged me to dine with them; but, being pre-engaged, I went to my lodgings, and in the afternoon, preached to about four thousand people in Dr. Colman's meeting house; and afterwards exhorted and prayed with many who came to my lodgings, rejoicing at the prospect there was of bringing many souls in Boston to the saving knowledge of the Lord Jesus Christ. Grant this, O Father, for Thy dear Son's sake! Amen.

Saturday, September 20. Was refreshed with several packets of letters sent to me from different parts of England and America, giving me an account of the success of the Gospel. Yet I was a little cast down to find some English friends had thrown aside the use of means, and others were disputing for *sinless perfection* and *universal redemption*. I know no such things asserted in the Gospel, if explained aright. Lord, do Thou cause even this to work for good, and give me grace to oppose such errors, without respect of persons, but with meekness, humility and love. Amen.

Preached in the morning to about six thousand hearers, in the Rev. Dr. Sewall's meeting house; and afterwards, on the common, to about eight thousand; and again, at night, to a thronged company at my lodgings. I spent the remainder of the evening with a few friends, in preparing for the Sabbath. Oh that we may be always in the Spirit on the Lord's Day!

Sunday, September 21. Went in the morning, and heard Dr. Colman preach. Dined with his colleague, the Rev. Mr. Cooper. Preached in the afternoon, to a thronged auditory, at the Rev. Mr. Foxcroft's meeting house. Immediately after, on the common, to about fifteen thousand; and again, at my lodgings, to a greater company than before. Some afterwards came up into my room; and though hoarse, I was enabled to speak, and could have spoken, I believe, till midnight. To see people ready to hear, makes me forget myself. Oh that it may be my sleep, and my mèat and drink to do the will of my Heavenly Father! Oh that all who press to hear the Word, may take the Kingdom of God by force! Amen and Amen.

Monday, September 22. Preached this morning at the Rev. Mr. Webb's meeting house, to six thousand hearers in the house, besides great numbers standing about the doors. Most wept for a considerable time. Sometime after, I received a letter, wherein were these words: —

"But what I must give the preference to was that gracious season at the New North, the Monday following, where there was more of the presence of God through the whole visitation, than ever I had known through the whole course of my life. Justly might it have been said of that place, 'it was no other than the House of God and the Gate of Heaven!' O how dreadful was the place, and yet how delightful! The Lord Jesus seemed to be visibly walking in that His golden candlestick, to try some of the many thousands who were prepared for so holy an inquisition! I am sure I know none who could not but be humble at the thoughts of it. And who, indeed, could help crying out, 'Woe is me, for I am undone, because I am a man of unclean lips for mine eyes have seen the King, the Lord of Hosts.' The Spirit of God, indeed, seemed to be moving upon the face of the waters at that time, and who knows, but that to a great many souls, God was pleased to say, 'Let there be light, and there was light.' "

In the afternoon I went to preach at the Rev. Mr. Checkley's meeting house; but God was pleased to humble us by a very awful providence. The meeting house being filled, though there was no real danger, on a sudden all the people were in an uproar, and so unaccountably surprised, that some threw themselves out of the windows, others threw themselves out of the gallery, and others trampled upon one another; so that five were actually killed, and others dangerously wounded. I happened to come in the midst of the uproar, and saw two or three lying on the ground in a pitiable condition. God was pleased to give me presence of mind; so that I gave notice I would immediately preach upon the common. The weather was wet, but many thousands followed in the field, to whom I preached from these words, "Go out into the highways and hedges, and compel them to come in." I endeavored, as God enabled me, to improve what had befallen us. Lord, Thy judgments are like the great deep. Thy footsteps are not known. Just and Holy art Thou, O King of saints!

In the evening, I was weak in body, so that I could not say much at the house where I supped; but God, by His Blessed Spirit, greatly refreshed and comforted my soul. I drank of God's pleasure as out of a river. Oh that all were made partakers of this living water: they would never thirst after the sensual pleasures of this wicked world.

Tuesday, September 23. Went this morning, with Dr. Colman and the Secretary to Roxbury, three miles from Boston, to see the Rev. Mr. Walter, a good old Puritan. He and his predecessor, the Rev. Mr. Eliot, commonly called the "Apostle of the Indians," now with God, have been pastors of that congregation a hundred and six years. I had but little conversation with him, my stay being very short.

At eleven we returned, and I preached in the Rev. Mr. Gee's meeting house, but not to a very crowded auditory, because the people were in doubt where I would preach. Dined at the Secretary's; preached in the afternoon to a thronged congregation, and exhorted and prayed at my own lodgings. Lord, let Thy Presence always follow me, or otherwise I shall be but as a sounding brass or a tinkling cymbal.

Wednesday, September 24. Went this morning to see and preach at Cambridge, the chief college for training the sons of the prophets in New England. It has one president, four tutors, and about a hundred students. The college is scarce as big as one of our least colleges at Oxford; and, as far as I could gather from some who knew the state of it, not far superior to our Universities in piety. Discipline is at a low ebb. Bad books are become fashionable among the tutors and students. Tillotson and Clark are read, instead of Shepard, Stoddard, and such-like evangelical writers; and, therefore, I chose to preach from these words, — "We are not as many, who corrupt the Word of God." A great number of neighboring ministers attended. God gave me great boldness and freedom of speech. The President of the college and minister of the parish treated me very civilly. [In his edition of 1756 Whitefield wrote: "In my former Journal, taking things by hearsay too much, I spoke and wrote too rashly of the colleges and ministers of New England, for which, as I have already done it when at Boston last from the pulpit, I take this opportunity of asking public pardon from the press. It was rash and uncharitable and though well-meant. I fear, did hurt."] In the afternoon, I preached again, in the court, when, I believe, there were about seven thousand hearers. The Holy Spirit melted many hearts. A minister soon after wrote me word, "that one of his daughters was savingly wrought upon at that time." Lord, add daily to the Church, such as shall be saved! Paid my respects to the Lieutenant-Governor, who lives at Cambridge; and returned in the evening to Boston, and prayed with and exhorted many people who were waiting round the door for a spiritual morsel. I believe our Lord did not send them empty away. O Blessed Jesus, feed them with that Bread of Life Which cometh down from Heaven.

Thursday, September 25. Preached the weekly lecture at Mr Foxcroft's meeting-house; but was oppressed with a sense of ingratitude to my Savior, that Satan tempted me to hold my tongue, and not invite poor sinners to Jesus Christ, because I was so great a sinner myself. But God enabled me to withstand the temptation; and, since Jesus Christ had showed such mercy to, and had not withdrawn His Holy Spirit from me, the chief of sinners, I was enabled more feelingly to talk of His love. I afterwards found that one stranger in particular, was in all probability convinced by that morning's sermon. After public worship, I went, at his Excellency's invitation, and dined with him. Most of the ministers of the town were invited with me. Before dinner, the Governor sent for me into his chamber. He wept, wished me good luck in the Name of the Lord, and recommended himself, ministers, and people to my prayers. Immediately after dinner, I prayed for them all; and then went in his carriage to the end of the town, crossed the ferry, and preached at Charleston, lying on the north side of Boston. The meeting-house was very capacious, and quite filled. A gracious melting was discernible through the whole congregation.

In the evening, I exhorted and prayed as usual, at my lodgings; and I found a great alteration in my hearers. They now began to melt and weep under the Word. Oh, that the Lord may beat them down with the hammer of His Word, till the heart of stone be entirely taken away! Amen, Lord Jesus.

ROXBURY: Friday, September 26. Preached in the morning at Roxbury to many thousands of people, from a little ascent. Several came afterwards to me, telling how they were struck at that time under the Word; and a minister wrote to me thus: —

"Reverend and Dear Sir, — I return my hearty thanks for your good services yesterday, and expecially at Roxbury, my native place. I cannot but admire, and greatly rejoice in those extraordinary gifts and graces, which it has pleased the Father of lights to confer upon you, and, to see how much the intention of them is answered, in your flaming devotion, and zealous and indefatigable endeavors to do good to souls, and thereby advance the Kingdom and interest of our Lord. I think I never saw a more attentive audience, or more weeping eyes than yesterday and Monday. The Holy Spirit, the Author alone of all spiritual life, seemed in a very wonderful manner to be moving upon the waters of the sanctuary, breathing upon the dry bones. For my own part I was much affected, and gave our glorious Lord the praise."

Dined at Judge Dudley's. In the afternoon, preached from a scaffold erected without the Rev. Mr. Byles' meeting-house, to a congregation nearly double that in the morning. Gave a short exhortation to a great crowd of people; and spent the remainder of the evening at Mr. Deacon H's. After supper, we sang psalms, one of the ministers prayed, and then we took our leave. O that the Lord may answer our request, and revive His work in the midst of the years! We wait for Thy salvation, O Lord; O let Thy Kingdom come!

Saturday, September 27. In the morning, preached at the Rev. Mr. Welstead's meeting-house; in the afternoon, on the common, to about 15,000 people. Oh, how did the Word run! It rejoiced me to see such numbers affected; I could scarce abstain from crying out, "This is no other than the House of God and the Gate of Heaven." After sermon, I visited and prayed with two persons who were much hurt in the late fright.

Sunday, September 28. Preached, in the morning, at Dr. Sewall's meeting-house, to a very crowded auditory, and 555 pounds currency were collected for the Orphan House. Was taken ill after dinner with a vomiting fit; but was enabled to preach, in the afternoon, at Dr. Colman's, to as great, if not a greater congregation than in the morning. Here 470 pounds were collected. In both places, all things were carried on with great decency and order. People went slowly out, as though they had not a mind to escape giving; and Dr. Colman said, "it was the most pleasant time he had enjoyed in that meeting-house through the whole course of his life." After sermon, I had the honor of a private visit from the Governor, who came to take his leave of me for the present. At their request, I then went and preached to a great number of Negroes on the conversion of the Ethiopian, (Acts 8); and, at my return, gave a word of exhortation to a crowd of people, who were waiting at my lodgings. My spirits were almost exhausted, and my legs ready to sink under me; but the Lord visited my soul, and I went to bed greatly refreshed with Divine consolations. Oh, what am I that I should be thus daily fed with Heavenly Manna! Lord, Thou fillest my soul with marrow and fatness. Oh let me praise Thee with joyful lips!

MARBLE HEAD, SALEM AND IPSWICH: Monday, September 29. Set out at seven in the morning, for Marble Head, a large town twenty miles from Boston. About eleven I preached to some thousands in a broad place in the middle of the town. Dined with Rev. Mr. Bernard, one of the ministers of the place. Rode to Salem, four miles from Marble Head, and preached there also, to about two thousand. Here, one was struck down by the power of the Word; and, in every part of the congregation, persons might be seen under great concern. Salem is the first settled and largest town (next to Boston) in all New England; and, as far as I could see and hear, rather exceeds it for politeness. I found the inhabitants had been sadly divided about their ministers, and God was pleased, before I knew their circumstances, to direct me to a suitable subject. Lord, heal their divisions, and grant that with one heart and one mind, they may endeavor to glorify Thy Holy Name. After the exercise, I immediately set out for Ipswich, another large town, sixteen miles (the way we went) distant from Salem. Two or three gentlemen came to meet me, and I and my friends were most kindly entertained at the house of the Rev. Mr. Rogers, one of the ministers of the place.

IPSWICH, NEWBURY AND HAMPTON: Tuesday, September 30. Preached at Ipswich, at ten in the morning, to many thousands. The Lord gave me freedom, and there was a great melting in the congregation. After dinner, set out for, and reached Newbury, twelve miles distant from Ipswich, about three. The power of the Lord accompanied the Word. The meeting-house was very large. Many ministers were present, and the people were greatly affected. Took ferry, immediately after sermon, and with the Rev. Mr. Cotton, minister of the place, who came to fetch me, went in a chaise to Hampton. I was pleased to see more plainness in Mr. Cotton's house, than I had seen in any minister's house since my arrival. His wife was as one that serveth. Oh, that all ministers' wives were so! Nothing gives me more offense than to see clergymen's wives dressed out in the pride of life. By this they bring a reproach upon religion. They generally live up to the utmost of their income; and, being above working, after their husband's decease they are of all women most miserable. From such a wife, good Lord, of Thy Infinite mercy, deliver me!

HAMPTON, PORTSMOUTH AND YORK: Wednesday, October 1. Preached in the morning, though not with so much freedom as usual, at Hampton, to some thousands in the open air. The wind was almost too high for me. Some, though not many, were affected. God's Spirit bloweth when and where it listeth. After dinner, rode in company with many to Portsmouth, fourteen miles from Hampton. Got there in about an hour and a half, and preached to a polite auditory, and so very unconcerned, that I began to question whether I had been preaching to rational or brute creatures. Seeing no immediate effects of the Word preached, I was a little dejected; but God, to comfort my heart, sent one young man to me, crying out in great anguish of spirit, "What shall I do to be saved?" Crossed the ferry, immediately after sermon, and went over a very stony way to York, thirteen miles from Portsmouth, to see one Mr. Moody, a worthy, plain, and powerful minister of Jesus Christ, though now much impaired by old age. He has lived by faith for many years, having no settled salary; and has been much despised by bad men, and as much respected by the true lovers of the blessed Jesus. He came as far as Hampton to meet me; but getting before him in our night traveling, a physician, his neighbor, who also came to meet me, received us into his house, and kindly entertained us. Some of our fellow-travelers lost their way, but came to us sometime after our arrival at York. As I came along, I was surprised to see such improvements made in a place of a hundred years' standing, and could not but fancy myself in Old England. Surely, God is a God keeping covenant. He has blessed this generation for their fathers' sake, with all temporal blessings. Lord, with these temporal, give them spiritual blessings; otherwise, prosperity will destroy them.

YORK AND PORTSMOUTH: Thursday, October 2. Preached both morning and evening. Was comforted to hear good Mr. Moody tell me "that he believed I should preach to a hundred new creatures this morning in his congregation." And, indeed, I believe I did. When I came to preach, I could speak little or no terror, but almost all consolation. The hearts looked plain and simple; and tears trickled apace down most of their cheeks. One thing put a damp upon my soul. Mr. Moody has a son, a minister, who was once full of faith and joy in the Holy Ghost, and walked in the Light of God's countenance and made full proof of his ministry; but for these two years last past, has walked in darkness, and seen no light. He has an inexpressible gloominess, and cannot apply any of the promises to himself. I was assisted to pray for him; and did so the more earnestly, not knowing but his case might be mine hereafter. Lord, let me not be high-minded, but fear. Deal with me as it shall please Thee. Justly mayst Thou take every comfort from me: for I have wretchedly abused Thy loving-kindness. God be merciful to me a sinner!

Left York at four in the evening, and reached Portsmouth by night. Conversed and sang psalms with my friends. Rightly is Jesus called Immanuel: He is God not only in, but with us. Oh, that I may never provoke Him to depart from me.

PORTSMOUTH, HAMPSTEAD AND NEWBURY: Friday, October 3. Preached this morning, at Portsmouth, to a far greater congregation than before; but, instead of preaching to stocks, I had now reason to believe I was preaching to living men. People began to melt soon after I began to pray, and the influence increased more and more during the whole sermon. The Word seemed to pierce through and through, and carried such conviction with it, that many, who before had industriously spoken evil of me, were ashamed of themselves. Mr. Shutlif, the minister, when he afterwards sent me 97 pounds, collected at this time for the orphans, wrote thus: "You have left great numbers under deep impressions, and I trust in God they will not wear off; but that the convictions of some will be kept up and cherished, till they have their desired effect." Amen and Amen.

After dinner, I hastened to Hampstead, and preached to several thousands of people with a great deal of life and power. Collected 41 pounds for the orphan children, and set out directly for Newbury, which we reached about eight at night; and was kindly entertained at a gentleman's house with all my friends. My heart was filled with joy. In the way two old disciples came to me, acquainting me what sweet refreshing times God had vouchsafed them under my ministry. Lord, not unto me, but unto Thy free grace be all the glory!

NEWBURY, ISPWICH AND SALEM: Saturday, October 4. Lay at the house of Mr. L., minister of the place. Preached in the morning to a very thronged congregation. Collected 80 pounds. Hasted to Ipswich. Preached to a larger congregation than when there last. Collected 79 pounds for the orphans. Got to Salem about eight at night, where I was kindly received by Colonel P., and also favored with a visit from the minister belonging to the Church of England.

Sunday, October 5. Preached, at eight in the morning, in the meeting-house, at the minister's request. Read prayers, and assisted at the Sacrament, in the Church of England; but thought matters were not at all carried on with decency and order. Preached again, in the afternoon, in the meeting-house; and collected 72 pounds for the orphans.

SALEM, MARBLE HEAD, MAULDEN AND BOSTON: Monday, October 6. Set out from Salem at nine this morning. Preached at Marble Head about eleven; and the Lord attended His Word with such mighty power, that I trust it will be a day much to be remembered by many souls. I was upon the mount myself. The two ministers presented me with 70 pounds for the Orphan House, which they had voluntarily collected yesterday, in their own private meetings. Was most affectionately received and entertained by Colonel M. At the request of the Rev. Mr. E., Son-in-law to dear Mr. Moody, we went to Maulden, fourteen miles from Marble Head, where I preached, but not with so much power as in the morning. Here the Secretary and several friends from Boston gave me the meeting. I set out with them, immediately after sermon, and got privately into Boston about seven at night. Had the satisfaction of hearing that brother Seward had arrived safely in England. The Lord prosper the work of his hands! My health has much improved since I left Boston. Though I had ridden a hundred and seventy-eight miles, and preached sixteen times, yet I was not in the least wearied. I went to rest, full of peace, and desiring to be thankful to the Lord, for causing me thus to renew my strength. Oh, what a good Master is Jesus Christ!

Tuesday, October 7. Preached, both morning and evening, in Dr. Colman's meeting-house, with much power. People seemed greatly rejoiced at my arrival, it being reported I had died suddenly, or was poisoned. Visited a true disciple, who had been sick for a long season. The Lord has made his bed in his sickness, and he has been enabled to rejoice in the truth. Who would but be a Christian? Gave a word of exhortation to many people, at a house which I trust the Lord will visit with His salvation. Wherever I go, people will follow me; and I now, almost hourly, receive letters from persons under convictions, and visits from many children of God, Who causes me to triumph in the felicity of His chosen.

Wednesday, October 8. Went with the Governor, in his coach, to Mr. Webb's meeting-house, where I preached both morning and evening, to very great auditories. Both times, Jesus Christ manifested forth His glory. Many hearts were melted down. I think I never was so drawn out to pray for little children, and invite little children to Jesus Christ, as I was this morning. I had just heard of a child, who after hearing me preach, was immediately taken sick, and said, "I will go to Mr. Whitefield's God." In a short time he died. This encouraged me to speak to little ones; but, oh, how were the old people affected, when I said, "Little children, if your parents will not come to Christ, do you come, and go to Heaven without them." There seemed to be but few dry eyes. I have not seen a greater commotion since my preaching at Boston. Glory be to God Who has not forgotten to be gracious! Went with the Governor, in his coach, to my lodgings. Gave a word of exhortation to a great crowd of people, and afterwards slipped out privately, by a back door, and went to a man's house, whose wife and sister, as well as himself, I trust the Lord will visit with His salvation. Amen.

Thursday, October 9. Every morning since my return, I have been applied to by many souls under deep distress, and was grieved that I could not have more time with them. Gave, this morning, the public lecture at Dr. Sewall's meeting-house, which was very much crowded. When I came near the meeting-house, I found it much impressed upon my heart, that I should preach upon our Lord's conference with Nicodemus. When I got into the pulpit, I saw a great number of ministers sitting around and before me. Coming to these words, "Art thou a master in Israel, and knowest not these things?" the Lord enabled me to open my mouth boldly against unconverted ministers; for, I am persuaded, the generality of preachers talk of an unknown and unfelt Christ. The reason why congregations have been so dead is, because they had dead men preaching to them. O that the Lord may quicken and revive them! How can dead men beget living children? It is true, indeed, that God may convert people by the devil, if He chooses; and so He may by unconverted ministers; but I believe, He seldom makes use of either of them for this purpose. No: He chooses vessels made meet by the operations of His Blessed Spirit. For my own part, I would not lay hands on an unconverted man for ten thousand worlds. Unspeakable freedom God gave me while treating on this head.

After sermon, I dined with the Governor, who seemed more kindly affected than ever. He told one of the ministers, who has lately begun to preach *extempore*, "that he was glad he had found out a way to save his eyes." Oh that others would follow him. I believe, they would find God ready to help and assist them. In the afternoon, I preached, on the common, to about fifteen thousand people, and collected upwards of 200 pounds for the orphans. Just as I had finished my sermon, a ticket was put up to me, whereon I was desired to pray "for a person just entered upon the ministry, but under apprehensions that he was not converted." God enabled me to pray for him with my whole heart. I hope that ticket will teach many others not to run before they can give an account of their conversion; if they do, they offer God strange fire. Went to a funeral of one belonging to the Council; but do not like the custom at Boston of not speaking at the grave. When can ministers' prayers and exhortations be more suitable, than when the corpse before them silently assists them, as it were; and, with a kind of dumb oratory, bids the spectators consider their latter end? When the funeral was over, I went to the almshouse, and preached on these words, "The poor received the Gospel," for near half an hour; then I went to the work-house, where I prayed with and exhorted a great number of people, who crowded after me, besides those belonging to the house, for near an hour more; and then, hearing there was a considerable number waiting for a word of exhortation at my lodgings, God strengthened me to give them a spiritual morsel. Soon after, I retired to rest. Oh, how comfortable is sleep after working for Jesus! Lord, strengthen me yet a little longer, and then let me sleep in Thee, never to awake in this vain world again.

CHARLESTON AND REDDING: Friday, October 10. Was still busied, from the very moment I arose until I went out, in answering those that came to me under great distress. About nine, went with Mr. Cooper over Charleston ferry, where I preached with much freedom of spirit, and collected 156 pounds for the orphans. I dined at Mystick, at the house of Mr. R., a rich young man, who has seemed to be much affected for some time. Oh, that he may not lack one thing! Immediately after dinner, we hastened to Redding, twelve miles from Charleston, where I preached to many thousands, and collected 51 pounds 5s for the orphans. A considerable moving was discernible in the congregation. Felt very weak in body; but was refreshed to hear of a poor girl, who was found sitting at the gate in the cold. Upon being examined by a friend, he found she was under strong convictions, and had followed me from Roxbury. She said, "she wanted nothing but Christ, and Christ she would have." Blessed are they who hunger and thirst after righteousness, for they shall be filled. Lord, let this promise be fulfilled in her heart!

CAMBRIDGE AND BOSTON: Saturday, October 11. Was weak in body, having taken cold. But preaching, I find, is a constant remedy against all indispositions. Went again to Cambridge, four miles from Mystick, and preached, at the meeting-house door, to a great body of people, who stood very attentively (though it rained), and were much affected. It being a university town, I discoursed on these words, "Noah, the eighth person, a preacher of righteousness"; and endeavored to show the qualifications for a true evangelical preacher of Christ's righteousness. I spoke very plainly to tutors and pupils. One hundred pounds were collected for the orphans. After sermon, the President kindly entertained me and my friends. About four, we reached Boston, where I preached immediately, in Dr. Sewall's meeting house. I exhorted a great number afterwards at my lodgings; and then was employed, till near midnight, in settling my private affairs, answering letters, and speaking to those under conviction.

Sunday, October 12. Spoke to as many as I could, who came for spiritual advice. Preached, with great power, at Dr. Sewall's meeting house, which was so exceedingly thronged, that I was obliged to get in at one of the windows. Dined with the Governor, who came to me, after dinner, when I had retired, and earnestly desired my prayers. The Lord be with and in him, for time and eternity! Heard Dr. Sewall preach, in the afternoon. Was sick at meeting, and, also, after it was over. Went with the Governor, in his coach, to the common, where I preached my farewell sermon to near twenty thousand people, — a sight I have not seen since I left Blackheath, — and a sight, perhaps never seen before in America. It being nearly dusk before I had done, the sight was more solemn. Numbers, great numbers, melted into tears, when I talked of leaving them. I was very particular in my application, both to rulers, ministers, and people, and exhorted my hearers steadily to imitate the piety of their forefathers; so that I might hear, that with one heart and mind, they were striving together for the faith of the Gospel. After sermon, the Governor went with me to my lodgings. I stood in the passage, and spoke to a great company, both within and without doors; but they were so deeply affected, and cried so loud, that I was obliged to leave off praying. The Governor took his leave in the most affectionate manner, and said he would come and take me in his coach to Charleston ferry the next morning.

The remainder of the evening was almost entirely spent in speaking to persons under great distress of soul. I believe, the poor girl that followed me from Roxbury, got a saving knowledge of Christ this morning; for when I preached on these words, "The Lord our Righteousness," she was enabled to say, "The Lord *my* Righteousness," and that she was not afraid to die. I found upon inquiry, she could not read, which shows the sovereignty of God's electing love, and confirms what the Apostle says, "that the Lord chooses the foolish things of this world to confound the wise." Charity will incline me to take her to Georgia; for she is cast out already, in effect, for Christ's sake. Blessed be God! for what He has done in Boston. I hope a glorious work is now begun, and that the Lord will stir up some faithful laborers to carry it on.

Boston is a large, populous place, and very wealthy. It has the form of religion kept up, but has lost much of its power. I have not heard of any remarkable stir for many years. Ministers and people are obliged to confess, that the love of many is waxed cold. Both seem to be too much conformed to the world. There is much of the pride of life to be seen in their assemblies. Jewels, patches, and gay apparel are commonly worn by the female sex. The little infants who were brought to baptism, were wrapped up in such fine things, and so much pains taken to dress them, that one would think they were brought there to be initiated into, rather than to renounce, the pomps and vanities of this wicked world. There are nine meeting houses of the Congregational persuasion, one Baptist, one French, and one belonging to the Scots-Irish. There are two monthly, and one weekly lectures; and those, too, are poorly attended. I mentioned it in my sermons, and I trust God will stir up the people to tread more frequently the courts of His house. One thing Boston is very remarkable for, viz., the external observance of the Sabbath. Men in civil offices have a regard for religion. The Governor encourages them; and the ministers and magistrates seem to be more united than in any other place where I have been. Both were exceedingly civil during my stay. I never saw so little scoffing, and never had so little opposition. Still, I fear, many rest in a head-knowledge, are close Pharisees, and have only a name to live. It must needs be so, when the power of godliness is dwindled away, where the form only of religion is become fashionable among people. However, there are "a few names left in Sardis, which have not defiled their garments." Many letters came to me from pious people, in which they complained of the degeneracy of the times, and hoped that God was about to revive His work in their midst. Even so, Lord Jesus, Amen and Amen. Yet Boston people are dear to my soul. They were greatly affected by the Word, followed night and day, and were very liberal to my dear orphans. I promised, God willing, to visit them again when it shall please Him to bring me again from my native country. The Lord be with thy ministers and people, and grant that the remnant, which is still left according to the election of grace, may take root and bear fruit, and fill the land!

BOSTON AND CONCORD: Monday, October 13. Took an affectionate leave of many dear friends, especially of my kind host and hostess, who have been exceedingly kind to me and mine, and wept at my departure from them. Went with the Governor, in his coach, to Charleston ferry, where he handed me into the boat, kissed me, and with tears bid me farewell. About noon, I reached Concord, eighteen miles from Boston, where I preached to some thousands in the open air. The hearers were melted down. About 45 pounds were collected for the orphans. The minister of the town being, I believe, a child of God, I chose to stay all night at his house, that we might rejoice together. The Lord was with us. I wrestled with God in prayer for my friends, especially those then with me. Brother B., the minister, broke into tears, and we had reason to cry out "it was good for us to be here." O blessed be Thy Name, O Lord! for these sweet refreshings in our way towards the Heavenly Canaan.

SUDBURY, MARLBOROUGH AND WORCESTER: Tuesday, October 14. Reached Sudbury, six miles from Concord, about ten. Preached to some thousands, and observed a considerable commotion in the assembly. Got to Marlborough, eight miles from Sudbury, about four, where I preached to a large congregation. At first my heart seemed dead, and I had but little freedom; but before I had finished, the Word came with such demonstration of the Spirit, that great numbers were melted down. When I came into the meeting house, to my surprise, I saw Governor Belcher there; and, though it rained, and he was much advanced in years, he went with us as far as Worcester, fifteen miles from Marlborough, where we got about eight at night. Here we were kindly entertained at the house of Colonel C. We spent the remainder of the evening very agreeably with the Governor, and after prayer retired to rest. Oh, that I may prove myself a disciple of that Master, Who, while tabernacling here on earth, had not where to lay His head!

WORCESTER AND LEICESTER: Wednesday, October 15. Perceived Governor Belcher to be more affectionate than ever. After morning prayer, he took me by myself, and exhorted me to go on stirring up the ministers; for, said he, "reformation must begin at the house of God." As we were going to meeting, he said, "Mr. Whitefield, do not spare rulers any more than ministers, no, not the chief of them." I preached in the open air to some thousands. The Word fell with weight: it carried all before it. After sermon, the Governor remarked, "I pray God, I may apply what has been said to my own heart. Pray, Mr. Whitefield, that I may hunger and thirst after righteousness." Dinner being ended, with tears in his eyes, he kissed me, and took leave of me. O that we may meet in Heaven! Preached, in the afternoon, at Leicester, six miles from Worcester. Got to Brookfield by night, and was upon the mount, indeed. My soul was upon the wing. I was exceedingly enlarged, and was enabled, as it were, to take the Kingdom of God by force. Oh, what precious hours are those, when we are thus strengthened, as it were, to lay hold on God. Oh, that we should ever cast ourselves down from there! God be merciful to me a sinner!

BROOKFIELD AND COLD SPRING: Thursday, October 16. Preached, with little freedom at first; but, at the last, many were melted down. After dinner, was much enlarged and strengthened to wrestle strongly with God, for a revival of His work in these parts. Preached at Cold Spring, fifteen miles from Brookfield, at the house of Mr. L., to three or four hundred people. Spent the evening with my fellow travelers. I was somewhat cast down, but afterwards recovered freedom of soul, by retiring and pouring out my complaints and petitions before the Lord Jesus. Oh, the sovereign, distinguishing freeness of God's grace! If it were not for the consideration of that, my soul must be continually pierced through and through with many sorrows.

HADLEY AND NORTHAMPTON: Friday, October 17. Set out as soon as it was light, and reached Hadley, a place where a great work was carried on some years ago; but lately the people of God have complained of deadness and losing their first love. As soon as I mentioned what God had done for their souls formerly, it was like putting fire to tinder. The remembrance of it caused many to weep sorely. After a little refreshment, we crossed the ferry to Northampton, where no less than three hundred souls were saved about five years ago. Their pastor's name is Jonathan Edwards, successor and grandson to the great Stoddard, whose memory will be always precious to my soul, and whose books entitled "A Guide to Christ," and "Safety of appearing in Christ's Righteousness," I would recommend to all. Mr. Edwards is a solid, excellent Christian, but, at present, weak in body. I think I have not seen his fellow in all New England. When I came into his pulpit, I found my heart drawn out to talk of scarce anything besides the consolations and privileges of saints, and the plentiful effusion of the Spirit upon believers. When I came to remind them of their former experiences, and how zealous and lively they were at that time, both minister and people wept much. In the evening, I gave a word of exhortation to several who came to Mr. Edwards' house. My body was weak, and my appetite almost gone; but my Lord gave me meat, which the world knows nothing of. Lord, evermore give me this bread! Amen and Amen.

HADFIELD AND NORTHAMPTON: Saturday, October 18. At Mr. Edwards' request, I spoke to his little children, who were much affected. Preached at Hadfield, five miles from Northampton, but found myself not much strengthened. Preached at four in the afternoon to Mr. Edwards' congregation. I began with fear and trembling, but God assisted me. Few eyes were dry in the assembly. I had an affecting prospect of the glories of the upper world, and was enabled to speak with some degree of pathos. It seemed as if a time of refreshing was come from the presence of the Lord.

NORTHAMPTON: Sunday, October 19. Felt great satisfaction in being at the house of Mr. Edwards. A sweeter couple I have not yet seen. Their children were not dressed in silks and satins, but plain, as become the children of those who, in all things, ought to be examples of Christian simplicity. Mrs. Edwards is adorned with a meek and quiet spirit; she talked solidly of the things of God, and seemed to be such a helpmeet for her husband, that she caused me to renew those prayers, which, for some months, I have put up to God, that He would be pleased to send me a daughter of Abraham to be my wife. Lord, I desire to have no choice of my own. Thou knowest my circumstances; Thou knowest I only desire to marry in and for Thee. Thou didst choose a Rebecca for Isaac, choose one to be a helpmeet for me, in carrying on that great work which is committed to my charge. Preached this morning, and good Mr. Edwards wept during the whole time of exercise. The people were equally affected; and, in the afternoon, the power increased yet more. Our Lord seemed to keep the good wine till the last. I have not seen four such gracious meetings together since my arrival. Oh, that my soul may be refreshed with the joyful news, that Northampton people have recovered their first love; that the Lord has revived His work in their souls, and caused them to do their first works!

WESTFIELD AND SPRINGFIELD: Monday, October 20. Left Northampton in the evening, and rode eighteen miles to Westfield, where I conversed with a poor woman on a sick bed, who gave an account of our Lord's redeeming love to her. Met with a little book, written by Dr. Cotton Mather, entitled, "The Ornaments of the Daughters of Zion," which I would recommend to all, especially the Boston ladies. Preached the next morning to a considerable congregation. Hastened to Springfield, ten miles from Westfield, crossed a ferry, preached to a large auditory, and then returned and preached to those who could not get over the ferry, by reason of the wind. The meeting house was full. After I left Springfield, my horse, coming over a broken bridge, threw me over his head, directly upon my nose. I was stunned for awhile, my mouth was full of dust, and I bled a little; but, falling upon soft sand, I got not much damage. After I had recovered myself, and mounted my horse, God so filled me with a sense of His sovereign, distinguishing love, that my eyes filled with tears; but they were all tears of love. Oh, how I wanted to sink before the High and Lofty One Who inhabiteth eternity. I felt myself less than nothing, and yet knew that Jesus was my All in All. We stopped at a friend's house, about four miles from Springfield; and, after refreshment, went to rest, desiring to be thankful for the peculiar favors conferred upon me the past night. Lord, they are noted in Thy Book. Oh, let them be also written on the tables of my heart!

SUFFIELD AND WINDSOR: Tuesday, October 21. Set out for Suffield, which is about eight miles from the place where I lay. Reached there, and preached at eleven o'clock to several thousands of people. Meeting with a minister in the way who said "it was not absolutely necessary for a Gospel minister, that he should be converted," I insisted much in my discourse upon the doctrine of the new birth, and also the necessity of a minister being converted, before he could preach Christ aright. The Word came with great power, and a strong impression was made upon the people in all parts of the assembly. Many ministers were present. I did not spare them. Most of them thanked me for my plain dealing. One of them, however, was offended; and so would more of his stamp, if I were to continue longer in New England. Unconverted ministers are the bane of the Christian Church. I honor the memory of that great and good man, Mr. Stoddard; but I think he is much to be blamed for endeavoring to prove that unconverted men may be admitted into the ministry. How he has handled the controversy, I know not; but I believe no solid argument can be brought to defend such a doctrine. But the best of men are permitted to err, that we may know they are but men. A sermon lately published by Mr. Gilbert Tennent, entitled, "The Danger of an Unconverted Ministry," I think unanswerable. As I was riding to Windsor, after dinner, an old man came up to me, saying he "knew what I had preached in the morning was true," for he had felt it. "I was under the spirit of bondage twenty years," he said, "and have received the spirit of adoption twenty-three years." The people of God seemed much revived at Windsor, where a converted man is minister. As soon as sermon was over, I rode a mile and a half, and preached to a thronged congregation belonging to old Mr. Edwards, father of Mr. Edwards of Northampton. After exercise, we supped at the house of old Mr. Edwards. His wife was as aged, I believe, as himself, and I fancied that I was sitting in the house of a Zacharias and Elizabeth. I parted from him and his son (who came with me thus far) with regret; but, blessed be God, we shall meet in eternity! Lord, grant that I may always comfort myself with this thought!

HARTFORD AND WEATHERSFIELD: Wednesday, October 22. Preached, in the morning, to many thousands, with much freedom and power; and, in the afternoon, to about the same number, at Weathersfield, three miles from Hartford. Here I was refreshed by the coming of Messrs. Wheelock and Pomeroy, two young, faithful, and zealous ministers of Jesus Christ. This morning I intended to go and preach at both their places, and also to Plymouth, Rhode Island, etc.: but, after prayer and consultation with my friends, I resolved to proceed directly to New York. Accordingly, at night, I rode to Middletown, ten miles from Weathersfield, and was entertained at the house of Mr. Russell, the minister of the place.

MIDDLETOWN AND WALLINGFORD: Thursday, October 23. I was much pleased with the simplicity of our host, and the order wherewith his children attended their family devotions. Preached to about four thousand people at eleven o'clock, and, again, in the afternoon at Wallingford, fourteen miles from Middletown. I then rode to New Haven, fourteen miles further, where I was affectionately received by Mr. Pierpoint, brother-in-law to Mr. Edwards of Northampton.

NEW HAVEN: Friday, October 24. Was refreshed with the sight of Mr. Noble of New York, who also brought me letters from Georgia. Blessed be God, the Orphan House affairs go on prosperously. I declined preaching in the morning, because it was wet, the people had no notice of my coming, and I had much private business on my hands. Preached in the afternoon, and it being the time in which the Assembly met, the Governor, the Council, and the members of the Lower House were present. After sermon, two youg ministers came to converse with me; and, in the evening, I expounded at my lodgings to a room full of people. Oh, who would but travel for Christ!

Saturday, October 25. Was refreshed this morning by the sight of Mr. Jedediah Mills, the minister at Ripton near Stratford. He wrote to me some time ago. I felt his letter, and now also felt the man. I could not help thinking God would do great things by him. He had a remarkable work in his parish some time ago, and talked like one who was no novice in Divine things. With him I dined at the Rev. Mr. Clap's, Rector of New Haven College, about one-third part as big as that of Cambridge. It has one Rector, three Tutors, and about a hundred students. I hear of no remarkable concern among them regarding religion. I preached twice, and there were sweet meltings discernible both times. I spoke very closely to the students, and showed the dreadful ill consequences of an unconverted ministry. Oh, that God may quicken ministers! Oh that the Lord may make them a flaming fire! Amen and Amen.

Sunday, October 26. Preached both morning and evening to much larger congregations than before; and in the afternoon especially was the presence of God felt in the assembly. Many, I believe, were comforted and quickened by the Holy Ghost. I trust this will be an acceptable year of the Lord. After sermon, I waited on the Governor, whom I had observed much affected under the Word. When I came in, he said, "I am glad to see you, and heartily glad to hear you." His heart was so full that he could not speak much; and tears coursed down his aged cheeks. He also said he "was thankful to God for such refreshings in our way to our rest. Food does us good, when we eat it with an appetite"; and, indeed, I believe he had fed upon the Word. The Lord support him when his strength fails, and bring his grey hairs with comfort to the grave! In the evening, I expounded to a great number of people at my lodgings, and collected upwards of 35 pounds for the orphans. About eight at night we left New Haven. The moon shone bright, and, after we had ridden three miles, we arrived at a house, which, as a minister had told me before, "was full of God." The mother and three daughters were converted persons.

["While in the house I gave a word of advice to the fourth daughter, God blessed it as she told me herself last year when I was at New England; and she is now married to a worthy minister of Jesus Christ. *Who would but drop a word for God?*"]

God gave me to wrestle with Him in prayer; and my friends said at departing they were never in such a house before. It was a sweet time indeed. God made His power to be felt and known. After I had given a word of exhortation, that they should study to adorn the Gospel of our Lord in all things, we went forward on our journey, and got to Milford, ten miles from New Haven, about ten at night. The Lord's Name be praised from the rising of the sun unto the going down of the same! Amen.

MILFORD AND STRATFORD: Monday, October 27. Preached this morning at Milford to a large assembly. Many ministers were present, and they could not help glorifying God. Mr. Mills, who came again to meet me this morning, was much affected; and, as I was riding out of town, a gentleman met me, and with tears said, "I never felt God's Presence in the sanctuary like this before; it has been a blessed time to my soul." In the afternoon, I preached at Stratford, four miles from Milford.

FAIRFIELD AND NEWARK: Tuesday, October 28. Got to Fairfield, eight miles from Stratford, about ten last night. The weather was very cold, having snowed a great part of the afternoon; but the Lord brought us on in safety. Preached, in the morning, to a considerable congregation, and in the prayer after sermon, I scarce knew how to leave off. In the afternoon at Newark, twelve miles from Fairfield, I was much restrained both in prayer and preaching. It rained greatly, so that we had not a very large congregation. However, some were affected. I believe my Lord never lets me preach in vain.

STANFORD AND RYE: Wednesday, October 29. Came here last night in safety, though dark and rainy. Was somewhat dejected before I went from my lodgings, and distressed for a text after I got up into the pulpit. But the Lord directed me to one, and, before I had preached half an hour, the Blessed Spirit began to move the hearers' hearts in a very awful manner. Young, and especially many old people were surprisingly affected. At dinner, I spoke with such vigor against sending unconverted ministers into the ministry, that two ministers with tears in their eyes, publicly confessed, that they had laid hands on two young men without so much as asking them, "whether they were born again of God, or not?" After dinner, I prayed, and one old minister was so deeply convicted, that calling Mr. Noble and me out, with great difficulty, (because of this weeping), he desired our prayers, "for," said he, "I have been a scholar, and have preached the doctrines of grace a long time, but I believe I have never felt the power of them in my own soul." Oh, that all unconverted ministers were brought to make the same confession! After having by prayer recommended him to God, I took horse, rejoicing exceedingly in spirit, to see how our Lord was getting Himself the victory, in a place where Mr. Davenport, a native of Stanford, a minister of the blessed Jesus, had been slighted and despised.

Here I think it proper to set up my Ebenezer, before I enter into the Province of New York, to give God thanks for sending me to New England. I have now had an opportunity of seeing the greatest and most populous part of it. On many accounts, it certainly excels all other provinces in America; and, for the establishment of religion, perhaps all other parts of the world. The towns all through Connecticut, and eastward toward York, in the Province of Massachusetts, near the riverside, are large and well peopled. Every five miles or perhaps less, you have a meeting house; and, I believe, there is no such thing as a pluralist or non-resident minister in both provinces. Many, nay most that preach, I fear, do not experimentally know Christ; yet I cannot see much worldly advantage to tempt them to take up the sacred function. Few country ministers, I have been informed, have sufficient money allowed them to maintain a family. God has remarkably, at sundry times and in divers manners, poured out His Spirit in several parts; and it often refreshed my soul to hear of the faith of their good forefathers, who first settled in these parts. Notwithstanding they had their foibles, surely they were a set of righteous men. They certainly followed our Lord's rule, "by seeking first the Kingdom of God and His Righteousness," and all other things God added unto them. I think the ministers preaching almost universally by note, is a mark that they have, in a great measure, lost the old spirit of preaching. Though all are not to be condemned who use notes, yet it is a symptom of the decay of religion, when reading sermons becomes fashionable where *extempore* preaching did once almost universally prevail. When the spirit of prayer began to be lost, then forms of prayer were invented, and, I believe, the same observation will hold good as to preaching. The civil government of New England seems to be well regulated; and, I think, at the opening of all their courts, either the judge or a minister begins with a prayer. Family worship, I believe, is generally kept up; and the Negroes are better used than in any other province I have yet seen. In short, I like New England exceeding well. Send forth, O Lord, Thy light and Thy truth, and for Thy infinite mercy's sake, show Thou hast a peculiar delight in these habitable parts of the earth! Amen.

RYE IN NEW YORK PROVINCE: Being kindly invited by a minister of the Church of England, after dinner I went to Rye, eleven miles from Stanford. I read prayers and preached to a small congregation. Was civilly entertained by the minister, and then rode ten miles further to East Chester. Here I spent an agreeable evening with my dear companions in travel. God filled me out of His own Divine fullness, and made me to drink of His pleasures as out of a river. I think I know what our Lord means when He promises, "He that believeth on Me, out of his belly shall flow rivers of living water." Lord, evermore give me this water!

KING'S BRIDGE AND NEW YORK: Thursday, October 30. Preached in the morning to about three hundred people. After dinner rode six miles to King's Bridge, where I preached from the steps of a public house to about five hundred. Several New York friends came here to meet me. I talked with them on the way, of the things of God, till we arrived at the house of my dear friend, Mr. Noble. After supper, the Lord filled my heart, and enabled me to wrestle with Him in prayer for New York inhabitants, and my own friends. To add to my comfort, the Lord brought my dear brother Davenport from Long Island, by whose hands the blessed Jesus has of late done great things. In a letter to his mother, he writes thus: "The Lord has, in infinite mercy, given me, in my parish, near twenty, in a little more than two months' time. In almost all these the work of conversion seemed very clear." Let God have all the praise. Amen.

NEW YORK: Friday, October 31. Met with a bitter pamphlet written against me by some of the Presbyterian persuasion, and found freedom given me to answer it. I long since expected opposition from that quarter: I believe it is increasing daily. The Lord will make me more than conqueror through His love. I also met with two volumes of sermons published in London, supposed to have been delivered by me, though I have never preached on most of the texts. But Satan must try all ways to bring the work of God into contempt. Blessed be God, Who enables me abundantly to rejoice in all things that befall me. Preached at Mr. Pemberton's meeting house in the morning. Two or three cried out. Mr. Noble could scarce restrain himself, and, look where I would, many seemed deeply wounded. At night the Word was attended with great power. Alas, how vain are the thoughts of men! As I came along yesterday, I found my heart dejected, and told Mr. Noble I expected but little movings in New York; but he bade me "expect great things from God," and likewise told me of several who were wrought upon by my ministry when there last. O Lord, let these things humble my soul.

Saturday, November 1. Finished my answer to the pamphlet. God enabled me to write it in the spirit of meekness. O Lord, give it Thy blessing. Preached twice, as yesterday, to very crowded auditories, and neither time without success. The Lord seemed to show us more and more, that a time for favoring New York was near at hand. O wherefore did I doubt! Lord, increase my faith!

Sunday, November 2. Preached in the morning with some freedom, but was dejected before the evening sermon, and when I came into the pulpit, I could have chosen to be silent rather than speak. After I had begun, however, the Spirit of the Lord gave me freedom, and at length came down like a mighty rushing wind, and carried all before it. Immediately, the whole congregation was alarmed. Crying, weeping, and wailing were to be heard in every corner; men's hearts failing them for fear, and many were to be seen falling into the arms of their friends. My soul was carried out till I could scarce speak any more. A sense of God's goodness overwhelmed me. A little boy was much concerned, on the pulpit stairs. One of my friends asked him why he cried. "Who can help it?" he said, "Mr. Whitefield's words cut me to the heart." After I came home, I threw myself upon the bed, and in awful silence admired the infinite freeness, sovereignty, and condescension of the love of God. I was called down to the marriage of Mr. P., whom I met at Rhode Island, and who with his wife are going as my assistants to Georgia. Never did I see a more solemn wedding. Jesus Christ was called, and He was present in a remarkable manner. After Mr. P. had married them, I prayed, and my soul was enabled to wrestle with and lay hold on God. After this, Divine manifestations flowed in so fast, that my frail tabernacle was scarce able to sustain them. My friends sat round me on the bedsides. I prayed for each of them alternately. I continued in this condition for about half an hour, astonished at my own vileness, and the excellency of Christ; then rose full of peace, and love, and joy. Oh, how am I obliged to my enemies! God has remarkably revealed Himself to my soul, ever since I have seen the pamphlet published by the Presbyterians against me. O how faithful is He that promised, "It shall bruise thy heel, and thou shalt bruise his head." Lord, enable me to lay hold on this, during the time of my soujourning here on earth.

Monday, November 3. Preached both morning and afternoon, and perceived the congregations still increase. There was a great and gracious melting among the people both times, but no crying out. Near 110 pounds currency was collected for the orphans; and, in the evening, at seven, we took boat, and reached Staten Island about ten. A dear Christian friend received us gladly. We solaced ourselves by singing and praying, and about midnight, retired to sleep, still longing for that time when I should sleep no more. Lord, keep me from a sinful and too eager desire after death. I desire not to be impatient. I wish quietly to wait till my blessed change comes. Amen and Amen.

STATEN ISLAND AND NEWARK: Tuesday, November 4. Preached from a wagon on Staten Island, to about three or four hundred. The Lord came among them. One young man in the greatest distress, came to me after sermon, beseeching me "to pray that he might be converted." Many rejoiced to see me again. One gray-headed man came and told me how God had brought him from darkness to light, when I was here last. I was much refreshed with the sight of Mr. Gilbert Tennent and Mr. Cross. The former has lately lost his wife, and though dear unto him, yet he was enabled with great calmness to preach her funeral sermon, while the corpse was lying before him. This put me in mind of Melancthon, who, at the news of his wife's death, said, "My Kate, I'll come after thee ere it be long." Since his wife's decease, Mr. Tennent has been in the West Jerseys and Maryland, and told me how remarkably God had worked by his ministry in many places. Mr. Cross has also seen great and wonderful things in his congregations, so great that when I came to desire a particular account, he said, "It directly answered the account given by Mr. Edwards of the work of God in Northampton." What is the Lord Jesus about to do! If the beginning is so great, what will the end of these things be! Rode, after sermon, to Newark, about ten miles from Staten Island, where I preached to a considerable congregation; but it being dark before I concluded, I could not see what impression the discourse had made. However, at night the Lord manifested forth His glory; for, on coming down to family prayer, where I lodged, and seeing many young men around me, my soul was melted down with concern for them. After singing, I gave a word of exhortation. Oh, how did the Word fall like a hammer and like a fire! One poor creature in particular was ready to sink into the earth. His countenance was altered, till he looked, as it were, sick to death. At length he said, "What shall I do to be saved?" Others were dissolved in tears around him; and one of my fellow travelers was struck down, and so overpowered, that his body became exceeding weak. He could scarcely move all the night after. God, I believe, was working powerfully in his soul. For my own part I was almost spent. Passed the remainder of the evening in hearing Mr. Tennent give an account of his late excursion. Oh, he is a humble minister of the Gospel! May I follow him as he does Christ. Amen.

BASKINRIDGE: Wednesday, November 5. Set out at eight in the morning, and got to Baskinridge, the place where Mr. Cross exercises his stated ministry, about one o'clock. At the house where I waited in the way, a woman spoke to me under strong convictions, and told me "she was deeply wounded by my last night's discourse." When I came to Baskinridge, I found Mr. Davenport had been preaching to the congregation, according to appointment. It consisted of about three thousand people. I had not discoursed long, when, in every part of the congregation, some one or other began to cry out, and almost all were melted into tears. A little boy, about eight years of age, wept as though his heart would break. Mr. Cross took him up into the wagon, which so affected me, that I broke from my discourse, and told the people that, since old professors were not concerned, God, out of an infant's mouth, was perfecting praise; and the little boy should preach to them. As I was going away, I asked the little boy what he cried for? He answered, his sins. I then asked what he wanted? He answered, Christ. After sermon, Mr. Cross gave notice of an evening lecture in his barn, two miles off. There we went, and a great multitude followed. Mr. Gilbert Tennent preached first; and I then began to pray, and gave an exhortation. In about six minutes, one cried out, "He is come, He is come!" and could scarce sustain the manifestation of Jesus to his soul. The eager crying of others, for the like favor, obliged me to stop; and I prayed over them, as I saw their agonies and distress increase. At length we sang a hymn, and then retired to the house, where the man that received Christ continued praising and speaking of Him till near midnight. My own soul was so full that I retired, and wept before the Lord, under a deep sense of my own vileness, and the sovereignty and greatness of God's everlasting love. Most of the people spent the remainder of the night in prayer and praises. It was a night much to be remembered.

BASKINRIDGE AND NEW BRUNSWICK: Thursday, November 6. After breakfast this morning, at the desire of Mr. Cross, I went and gave a word of exhortation to, and sung and prayed with, a few people in the barn. Before I mounted my horse, many came to me under great concern of soul. A lad about thirteen years old, told me, "he never felt sin till yesterday." A poor Negro woman said "she was filled with a love of Christ," and, being too fond of the instrument, would fain have gone with me. Her master consented; but I bid her go home, and with a thankful heart serve her present master. When I was upon my horse several women came to shake me by the hand. I asked one "whether she knew Christ?" She said "Yes." "How long?" "Three years the third Sunday in next March," she answered. I asked another the same question. She replied, "Yes, but I am waiting for a fresh breathing from the Blessed Spirit." I took my leave of them, and rode in company with many children of God to New Brunswick, twenty-three miles from Baskinridge. Here letters awaited me from Savannah, acquainting me that there had been a great mortality among the people of that place, though the orphans continued very healthy; and that a minister was coming over to supply my place at Savannah. This last much rejoiced me, having resolved to give up the Savannah living as soon as I arrived at Georgia. A parish and the Orphan House together are too much for me; besides, God seems to show me it is my duty to evangelize, and not to fix in any particular place. In the evening I preached in Mr. Gilbert Tennent's meeting house. A little after, Mr. B. (a young minister, who, I hope, will hereafter come fairly out for God) preached for about an hour, and then, at the desire of Mr. Tennent, I concluded with a word of exhortation. And after sermon, in private prayer with my friends, oh, how did my loving Savior cause my cup to overflow! He permitted me to talk with Him as a man talks with his friend. This I take to be that freedom of speech which St. Paul speaks of, and through the Lord Jesus believers have access to the Father. Oh, the happiness of those who are born again of God.

NEW BRUNSWICK AND TRENTON: Friday, November 7. I had some thoughts of going to Freehold and Shrewsbury, but was prevented by the coming of Mr. William Tennent, whom I wanted to consult about his brother Gilbert going to Boston. He (diffident of himself) was at first unwilling, urging his inability for so great a work; but afterwards, being convinced it was the Divine will, he said, "the will of the Lord be done." With him also, Mr. R. is to go. He is a young minister, one of the tutors of Cambridge College, whom I brought with a view that he should return with Mr. Tennent. God has been pleased to work upon his heart by my ministry. I cannot but think he will be a burning and a shining light. It being the last time we should be together for a long season, we thought it best to spend some time in prayer together. Mr. Gilbert was our mouth to God. Many were greatly affected. About eleven o'clock we parted in tears, but with a full assurance that we should see and hear great things before we met again. I then went on towards Trenton, in company with Mr. Davenport and some others. The Lord was with us on the way. I retired as soon as I came to Trenton, and lay silently before the Lord. He heard the cry of my heart, and filled it with His abundant presence.

TRENTON AND PHILADELPHIA: Saturday, November 8. Preached this morning in the meeting house, though not to a very large or much affected auditory. Set out immediately after dinner, and was very providentially preserved in going over two creeks, which lay in the way, and were much swollen by the rain. In one of them two of my fellow travelers, in all probability, must have perished, had not a woman cried out, and bid us stop. A man who had been reached by my ministry, hearing my voice, came and swam our horses over the other creek, and conducted us safely over a very narrow bridge. About eight o'clock we reached Philadelphia, though the night was very dark indeed. Some friends were just come in, who had been another way to meet me. Several, with great joy came to salute me. We sang and prayed.

PHILADELPHIA: Sunday, November 9. Several came to see me, with whom I prayed. Preached at eleven in the morning, to several thousands, in a house built for that purpose since my departure from Philadelphia. It is a hundred feet long, and seventy feet broad. A large gallery is to be erected all round it. Both in the morning and the evening, God's glory filled the house. It was never preached in before. The roof is not yet up, but the people raised a convenient pulpit, and boarded the bottom. Great was the joy of most of the hearers when they saw me; but some still mocked. Between the services I received a packet of letters from England, dated in March last. May the Lord heal, and bring good out of the divisions which at present seem to be among the brethren there. Many friends being in the room, I kneeled down, prayed, and exhorted them all. I was greatly rejoiced to look round them, because there were some who had been marvelous offenders against God. I shall mention two only. The first is a Mr. Brockden, recorder of deeds, etc., a man eminent in his profession, but for many years a notorious Deist. In his younger days, he told me, he had some religious impressions, but coming into business, the cares of the world so choked the good seed, that he not only forgot his God, but at length began to doubt of, and to dispute His very Being. In this state he continued many years, and has been very zealous to propagate his deistical, I could almost say atheistical, principles among moral men; but he told me he never endeavored to make proselytes of vicious, debauched people. When I came to Philadelphia this time a year ago, he had no curiosity to hear me. But a brother Deist, his choicest companion, pressing him to come and hear me, to satisfy his curiosity he at length complied with his request. It was night. I was preaching at the Court House stairs, upon the conference which our Lord had with Nicodemus. I had not spoken much before God struck his heart, "for," said he, "I saw your doctrine tended to make people good." His family did not know that he had been to hear me. After he came home, his wife, who had been at sermon, came in also, and wished heartily that he had heard me. He said nothing. After this, another of his family came in, repeating the same wish; and, if I mistake not, after that another, till at last being unable to refrain any longer, with tears in his eyes, he told them that he had been hearing me; and expressed his approbation. Ever since, he has followed on to know the Lord. Though upwards of threescore years old, he is now, I believe, born again of God.

The other is Captain H . . . l, formerly as great a reprobate as ever I heard of; almost a scandal and reproach to human nature. He used to swear to ease his stomach, and was so fond of new oaths that he used to go on board the transport ships, and offer a guinea for a new oath, that he might have the honor of coining it. By God's grace, he is now, I believe, a Christian. Not only reformed, but renewed. The effectual stroke, he told me, was given when I preached last spring at Pennytack, though he had been under good impressions before. Ever since, he has been zealous for the truth; stood firm when he was beaten and in danger of being murdered some time ago by many of my opposers; and, in short, shows forth his faith by his works. I mention these cases in particular, because I think they are remarkable proofs of the doctrine of God's eternal election and everlasting love. Whatever men's reasoning may suggest, if the children of God fairly examine their own experiences, – if they do God justice, they must acknowledge that they did not choose God, but that God chose them.

And if He chose them at all, it must be from eternity, and that too without anything foreseen in them. Unless they acknowledge this, man's salvation must be in part owing to the free will of man; and if so, unless men descend from other parents than I did, Christ Jesus might have died, and never have seen the travail of His soul in the salvation of one of His creatures. But I would be tender on this point, and leave persons to be taught it of God. I am of the martyr Bradford's mind. Let a man go to the grammar school of faith and repentance, before he goes to the university of election and predestination. A bare head knowledge of sound words avails nothing. I am quite tired of Christless talkers. From such may I ever turn away. Amen.

Monday, November 10. Preached morning and afternoon to very large congregations. Many came afterwards and told me what God had done for their souls thereby. All the vacant time before and after preaching, I employed in answering my English letters.

Saturday, November 15. Preached twice every day this week, in the new house, one morning excepted, when I preached in Mr. C's meeting house, on account of the snow. On that occasion the Word seemed to smite the congregation like so many pointed arrows. Many afterwards told me what they felt; and, in the evening I was sent for to a young woman, who was carried home from meeting, and had continued almost speechless. I prayed with her, and heard afterwards she was in a more comfortable state. I cannot say we had one dry meeting. The least moving, I think, was one afternoon, when I was unaccountably carried out to talk against reasoning unbelievers. At dinner I had not fixed upon a text. When I was going to preach, I was so ill that some of my friends advised me to go home. I thought it best to trust in God. I went on, began preaching, and found my heart somewhat refreshed; but, all on a sudden, my soul was so carried out to talk against depending on our natural reason, that my friends were astonished, and so was I too; for I felt the Holy Ghost come upon me, and never spake on that wise before. As I was going home, I said to a friend, "Surely some reasoners were in the congregation." Upon inquiry, I found a number of them present, and then I knew wherefore I was so assisted. Oh who would but trust in God! One of these reasoners a little after, meeting Mr. B., said, "What! Mr. Whitefield could not make the people cry this afternoon." "A good reason for it," said Mr. B., "he was preaching against Deists, and you know they are a hardened generation." Lord, take from them a heart of stone, and give them a heart of flesh!

Another afternoon, there was such a universal commotion in the congregation, as I never saw in Philadelphia before. Numbers wept so sorely, that I broke off prayer after sermon sooner than otherwise I should have done. I preached on these words, "What shall I do to be saved?" — and, as I afterwards found, was providentially directed to that subject: for a Mrs. P., as I have it in a paper taken from her own mouth, went to Mr. Cummins to know why I should not preach in the church? He, after several invectives against me, said, "He could not answer his oath to the Bishop of London, if he did give me leave," and cautioned her against going to hear me, adding, "that if she followed or adhered to what I said, she was in a woeful condition." "Nay," said he, "you are damned if you do." He also told her, "He was distressed in his soul for her, because she was a good liver, and been brought up under pious parents." Mrs. P. asked, "If she, by God's assistance, lived up to the doctrine and example of our Savior and the Apostles, as laid down in the New Testament, should she not do well?" He answered, "Yes." "Then, sir," she replied, "I must believe in Mr. Whitefield's doctrine." "There now," he said, "you are running on again; I tell you, you are mad. Go home and hear him no more, and you'll do well enough." "No, sir," said Mrs. P., "I cannot stay away; and seeing so many people admire Mr. Whitefield's doctrine, and you so bitter against him, 'What must I do to be saved?' for you are enough to distract me between you." "You are good enough," replied Mr. Cummins, "and may dance or play at cards, and be in a far better way than Whitefield or his followers. For my part, I will wash my hands of your blood, and will leave you." "No," said Mrs. P., "you love money too well, sir, to leave this place." After a great deal more conversation, Mrs. P. left him, in great distress of mind, and often repeating to herself, "Lord, what must I do to be saved?" Contrary to Mr. Cummins' advice, she went in the afternoon, says the paper before me, to hear Mr. Whitefield, and he providentially preached on the trembling jailor's words, "What must I do to be saved?" — which gave the gentlewoman so much comfort, that she is thankful to God for having an opportunity of hearing that text explained, is much strengthened, and will by God's grace, follow His commandments. Lord, for Thy mercy's sake, work in her both to will and to do, after Thy good pleasure! Amen.

It would be almost endless to recount all the particular instances of God's grace, which I have seen this week past. Many who before were only convicted, now plainly proved that they were converted. My chief business was now to build up and to exhort them to continue in the grace of God. Notwithstanding, many were convicted, almost every day, and came to me under the greatest distress and anguish of soul. Several Societies are now in the town, not only of men and women, but of little boys and little girls. Being so engaged, I could not visit them as I would, but I hope the Lord will raise me up some fellow laborers, and that elders will be ordained in every place; then we shall see a glorious church settled and established in Philadelphia. Hasten that time, O Lord. I cannot leave off giving an account of this week's work, without mentioning another instance of God's grace. About the middle of the week I was called to visit one Mrs. D., then lying on a sick bed, who had been brought home to God when I was at Philadelphia last spring. Her husband was then at sea, and on his return home, greatly persecuted his wife, denying her spiritual friends leave to visit her. God now inclined his heart to let me come and pray with her, according to her desire. When I went the first time, he was not called up to join us. The next day he himself met me in the street, and gave me an invitation. I complied, and visited his wife several times. Never before did I see a soul so exult in God, or talk so touchingly of the love of Jesus, though sometimes in extremity of pain. Sometimes she was so full of God that she could not speak; and at other times, when she could not speak, and I bid her lift her hands if all was well, she stretched them with great earnestness. As soon as she recovered breath, she would talk of Jesus, saying that His love was above her pain, that she longed to be dissolved, but was willing to tarry the Lord's leisure. When I told her that I wanted to be gone too, she said, "No, you must stay longer, and bring home some more souls to Christ." My soul was much enlarged to hear a creature talk with such assurance just upon the brink of eternity. Her husband and other friends stood weeping by. God gave me great assistance in prayer; His presence filled the room, and some, I thought, would have cried out. Oh that this sickness may be a means under God of saving her relations' precious and immortal souls! After my departure, when one of my friends asked her, "What she thought of the righteousness of Christ?" she replied, "My soul is wrapped up in it!" Lord Jesus, let her repose her confidence in Thee even to the last. Into Thy hands I commend her spirit: for Thou has redeemed it.

Sunday, November 16. Preached, both morning and evening, and collected both times about 105 pounds sterling for the orphans. In the afternoon, I publicly baptized five adult women, who had undergone a strict examination. Before sermon, I gave them an earnest exhortation. They melted under the Word, and every thing was carried on with great solemnity. I preached from these words of St. Jude, "But ye, beloved, building up yourselves on your most holy faith, praying in the Holy Ghost, keep yourselves in the love of God, looking for the mercy of our Lord Jesus Christ unto eternal life." The congregation was very large, though I think not so large as when I took my leave last spring. There was abundance of weeping when I came to the conclusion of my discourse. Great numbers flocked to my lodgings; some under distress, some to give thanks for what God had done for their souls, and others to present me with something for the poor orphans. One that was baptized brought three children. I baptized them, prayed, and gave a word of exhortation with a melting heart to many dear souls. In the evening I went with Mr. Noble to take a final leave of Mrs. D., who was still rejoicing in God. Visited a poor distracted woman, and afterwards went to the Boys' Society. I then returned home, and at last went to bed, quite weary as to my outward man, but inwardly rejoicing in God my Savior. Oh that I could do more for Jesus Christ! He is kinder to me every day. Praise the Lord, O my soul.

GLOUCESTER AND GREENWICH, WEST JERSEYS: Monday, November 17. Was much melted at parting from my dear friends. Had it much impressed upon my mind, that I should go to England, and undergo trials for the truth's sake. These words, "The Jews sought to stone Thee, and goest Thou thither again?" with our Lord's answer, have been for some time lying upon me; and while my friends were weeping around me, St. Paul's words came into my mind: "What mean you to weep and break my heart? I am willing not only to be bound, but to die for the Lord Jesus." After fervent prayer, I took my leave of some, but having agreed to preach at Gloucester in the West Jerseys, others accompanied me in boats over the river. We sang as we sailed, but my heart was low. I preached at Gloucester; but found myself weighed down, and not able to deliver my sermon with my usual vigor. However, there was an affecting meeting, and several (as I heard afterwards) who had been in bondage before, at that time received joy in the Holy Ghost. With abundance of tears, after dinner, most of my Philadelphia friends who came over the water took their last farewell. I rode on in company with several to Greenwich, and preached to a few. In the evening, we traveled on a few miles; but my body was more out of order, and I thought God was preparing me for future blessings. It is good to be humbled. I am never better than when I am brought to lie at the foot of the Cross: it is a certain sign God intends that soul a greater crown.

PILES GROVE: Tuesday, November 18. Was somewhat better in the morning. Preached at Piles Grove, in the afternoon, to about two thousand people. At night, where I lodged, God was pleased so abundantly to refresh my soul, as to make me forget the weakness of my body. I prayed with and exhorted the family where I lodged; and visible impressions were made upon the hearers. O that they may be abiding! Ate a little; but was enriched plentifully with that Bread Which is Meat indeed and Drink indeed.

COHANSIE, 18 MILES FROM PILES GROVE: Wednesday, November 19. Had two precious meetings today at Cohansie. Preached to some thousands, both morning and afternoon. The Word struck the hearers till the whole congregation was greatly moved, and two cried out in the bitterness of their souls, after a Crucified Savior. My soul was replenished as with new wine. At this place, Mr. Gilbert Tennent preached some time ago. At his, as well as the people's request, I came here. Blessed be God, His Gospel spreads more and more! Amen.

SALEM, 18 MILES FROM COHANSIE: Thursday, November 20. Preached twice here this day: in the morning, in the Court House; in the afternoon, in the open air, before the prison, to about two thousand. Both times God was with us. After service, two or three came to me weighed down with the burden of sin. I gave them what advice I thought proper, and about five left Salem. O that the Prince of Peace would come and take possession of the inhabitants' hearts!

NEWCASTLE, 13 MILES FROM SALEM, AND WHITECLAY CREEK IN PENNSYLVANIA: Friday, November 21. Got here with some little difficulty, about midnight. Preached in the morning, in the Court House. Observed some few affected, and some few scoffing. Met Mr. Charles Tennent, and went with him to Whiteclay Creek. As we passed along, Mr. A . . . n, the Presbyterian minister who opposed me last spring at Fagg's Manor, met us. Thinking he intended to go by, I did not stop, but only pulled off my hat. He, turning about, said, "What, will you not shake hands?" I gave him my hand. He then asked me to have a conference, as he desired when last at Fagg's Manor. I told him, "Since he had begun by sending the queries in public, I was resolved to decline all private conversation." This, I found afterwards, highly offended him. There were many thousands at Whiteclay Creek waiting to hear the Word. I have not seen a more lovely sight. I sang the 23rd Psalm, and these words gave my soul unspeakable comfort.

> In presence of my spiteful foes,
> He does my table spread.

The melting soon began, and the greatest part of the congregation was exceedingly moved. Several cried out, and others were to be seen weeping bitterly. After sermon, I went three miles, and lay at Mr. Charles Tennent's house, who has lately married a young lady whom God was pleased to awaken by my ministry. Here I had conversation with Mr. Blair, and Mr. Craighead; but being taken ill, I was obliged to retire to rest. Blessed be God, there is a time coming, when all these interruptions shall be done away.

> O may I worthy prove to see
> Thy saints in full prosperity,
> That I the joyful choir may gain,
> And count Thy people's triumphs mine.

FAGG'S MANOR: Saturday, November 22. Preached in the afternoon to many thousands, when God was pleased to own His Word. I was taken ill after preaching. Straining caused me to vomit much. I rode about twelve miles, and thought it advisable to retire to bed immediately. But God's Presence so filled my soul that I could scarce stand under it. I prayed and exhorted and prayed again, and soon every person in the room seemed to be under great impressions, sighing and weeping. At last I was quite overpowered. A dear friend undressed me. The Lord gave me sweet sleep, and in the morning I arose with my natural strength much renewed. Blessed be the Lord my God, from Whom alone comes every temporal gift, as well as my eternal salvation!

NOTTINGHAM: Sunday, November 23. Rode four miles, and got to Nottingham about ten. It raining much, and the people thereby being prevented gathering so soon, I preached at one to a large congregation, who seemed in no wise to regard the rain, so that they might be watered with the dew of God's blessing. Immediately after sermon, we set out in a great company for Bohemia in Maryland, near thirty miles from Nottingham; and, to my pleasing surprise, as we were riding along, met with Captain G . . . n, whom I sent over with Mr. Seward to England. He arrived at Newcastle, in the morning, and came to me in the afternoon. I have been waiting for letters (that I knew were sent me) for some weeks.

BOHEMIA IN MARYLAND, AND ST. GEORGE'S IN PENNSYLVANIA: Monday, November 24. Got here about eleven last night, and was most kindly received by old Mrs. B . . . d, a true mother in Israel. Read my

English letters, and thought it was the will of God that I should embark for my native country next spring. Preached, in the afternoon to about two thousand, and have not seen a more solid melting, I think, since my arrival. Some scoffers stood on the outside, but the Holy Spirit enabled me to lay the terrors of the Lord before them, and they grew more serious. Several wanted to go with me, and many of their hearts seemed ready to break. My soul rejoiced in the Lord to see salvation brought to Maryland. I parted from good old Mrs. B . . . d in tears, and rode with my friends about ten miles to a place called St. George's, where a kind and courteous Quaker received us into his house. Here God showed me more clearly the way wherein I should go. Lord guide me with Thy counsel till Thou dost bring me to everlasting glory.

REEDY ISLAND: Monday, December 1. Came to Reedy Island last Tuesday morning. Several of my Philadelphia friends came to take their last farewell. All were melted down, I believe, when I preached in the evening. On Wednesday, Saturday, and Sunday I preached again. The Lord was with us every time. I was greatly delighted to see the captains of the ships, and their respective crews come constantly to hear the Word on shore, and join with us in religious exercises on board. Captain H . . . l, Matthew-like, was very busy in bringing his brother sailors to hear the glad tidings of salvation, and he rejoiced my heart with the news that some of them felt the power of God. This morning, the wind springing up fair, we set sail from Reedy Island. But before I go on, stop, O my soul, and look back a little on the great things the Lord has done for thee during this excursion. I think it is now the seventy-fifth day since I arrived at Rhode Island. My body was then weak; but the Lord has much renewed its strength. I have been enabled to preach, I think, one hundred and seventy-five times in public, besides exhorting very frequently in private. I have traveled upwards of eight hundred miles, and gotten upwards of 700 pounds sterling in goods, provisions, and money for my orphans. Never did God vouchsafe me such great assistance. Never did I perform my journeys with so little fatigue, or see such a continuance of the Divine Presence in the congregations, to whom I have preached. All things concur to convince me that America is to be my chief scene for action. May the Lord prepare me for every good thing He has appointed for me to do and suffer, and then I need not fear, being more than conqueror through His love.

CHARLESTON IN SOUTH CAROLINA: Wednesday, December 10. Had a pleasant passage, and arrived at Charleston last night. As we came over the bar, I was informed of a fire, that broke out about three weeks ago, and destroyed three hundred houses in the best part of Charleston in the space of three hours. The news much affected me, because I loved the people, and I preached to them this morning from Isaiah 1:9, "Except the Lord of hosts had left unto us a very small remnant, we should have been as Sodom, and we should have been like unto Gomorrah." In handling the subject, I endeavored to show what were the sins which provoked God to punish the Israelites in that manner. I drew a parallel between them and the Charleston people, and then made an application suitable to the solemn occasion of my preaching, May the Lord grant it may produce the desired effect, and be a means of preserving the inhabitants from being cast into that fire which never shall be quenched!

BETHESDA IN GEORGIA: Sunday, December 14. Preached again at Charleston on Wednesday evening. Went on board on Thursday, and reached Savannah on Saturday about midnight. Preached this morning, and arrived safely at Bethesda this afternoon. My soul was much touched with a sense of God's mercies. When I came to pray with an old Christian in our infirmary, I was quite overwhelmed.

Monday, December 29. Enjoyed a very comfortable Christmas at Bethesda, having God often with us in my public ministrations among the family and laborers. One woman received Christ in a glorious manner; and several others were brought under strong convictions. On Christmas Day I married Mr. Periam to one of the schoolmistresses whom I brought out from England; and last Saturday I married Mr. Habersham to Mr. Bolton's daughter whom I brought with me from Philadelphia, and who was converted some time ago at Savannah. Both times the Bridegroom of the Church was present with us; and many, I hope, felt a union between Jesus Christ and their souls. Having appointed Mr. Barber to take care of the spiritual, and Mr. Habersham to superintend the outward affairs of the Orphan House, and settled all things to my satisfaction, finding my call clear to England, I, last night, took a sorrowful and affectionate leave of my family; and this day went to Savannah, but narrowly escaped being shot by a laborer walking behind me with a gun under his arm. The gun went off unawares, but the mouth of it was providentially towards the ground; otherwise, I and one of my friends, in all probability, would have been killed; for we were directly before and not above a yard or two distant from it. We ought to live in such a state as we would not fear to die in! For in the midst of life we are in death.

In the evening I preached at Savannah, and took my final leave of the people, it being inconsistent with my other affairs to act as their pastor any more. Another minister is not yet come, but is expected daily. I gave the Trustees notice January last, of my design to give up the parsonage. Blessed be God! I am now more free to evangelize and go wheresoever the Lord shall be pleased to call me. I yet hope well of Georgia, though, at present, it is in a very declining and piteous state. It will flourish, I believe, when settled upon a religious foundation. Till then, God will bring the counsels of men to nought. It was so with New England: I am persuaded it will be so with New Georgia. Glory be to God! I leave behind me some who love the Lord Jesus in sincerity.

MR. JONATHAN BRYAN'S PLANTATION NEAR PORT ROYAL IN SOUTH CAROLINA: Thursday, January 1, 1741. Left Savannah on Tuesday, in the afternoon. Arrived here this morning about two o'clock, with some more friends in Mr. Jonathan Bryan's boat, who, with some others, came to Bethesda, in the hope of my returning with them. I trust, he and two or three more since our last meeting have accepted Christ. In the afternoon, I preached at his house to several of the neighboring people. The Lord made it a Bethel. In the evening came Mr. Hugh Bryan, his brother, lately converted at Savannah. His wife died some time ago; in what frame, the following letter, which he sent to a niece of his, now at Bethesda, will best testify.

"Dear Child, — Under written are the dying words of your aunt, which I send for your satisfaction and information. She died October 7, between the hours of nine and ten in the morning, being filled with the full assurance of faith in Christ, and a joyful hope of eternal salvation through His merits and mediation.

"As your aunt and I were praying to our Lord Jesus, to give her the comforts of His Holy Spirit to support her under the agonies of death, she replied, 'I see Him! I see Him! Now I see light.' After this, she continued in prayer about half an hour; but her speech failing her, we could not during that time understand what she spake, only we could hear the Name of Jesus often, and 'Come Jesus! Come Jesus!' Then again she spake out plainly, and said, 'Who would die without God? Now I see light.' Then she lay in an agony about half an hour, and again spake out, and said, 'God has let me see great and glorious things which would not be believed, if they were told.' Then your uncle R . . . s coming into the room, spake to your aunt S . . . s, and your dying aunt hearing his voice, called him to her, and when he was come, she spake to us and said, 'Mind what I say to you; for hereafter you must all give an account of what I now say to you. God has enabled me to speak to you before I go, (for I am just going).' Then she said, 'God is a just God as well as merciful. Be diligent in searching your hearts. Brother, tell Mr . . . he is in the wrong. My pain is great, but Christ is sufficient for me.' And she repeated that 'God had let her see great things that would not be believed, if they were told.' She said also, 'Follow Whitefield, God will bless him, wherever he goes. Don't speak lightly of him. Bless him. Bless him. God has enabled me to speak to you before I go. I am just going. Farewell, Farewell. God be with you!' Then she composed herself, and lay about half an hour, and neither moved nor groaned, except her lips and tongue, and the heaving of her breast in breathing, seeming to be in her perfect senses till about a minute before she died. She looked round at each of us that were about her bed, and then departed in quietness."

Thus far Mr. Bryan. I shall only add, "O death, where is thy sting! O grave where is thy victory" over true believers! What fools are they who count their lives madness.

CHARLESTON: Sunday January 4. Came here yesterday, in company with both the Mr. Bryans, and several other friends. Had the satisfaction of meeting with my brother the captain, and hearing from him some account of affairs among the brethren in England. The Lord enable me to steer a wise and steady course, when I come among them! Preached twice this day, and expounded in the evening to large auditories. Was affectionately entertained at the house of Mr. F., and enjoyed much of the Divine Presence and consolations in my soul. Happy they whose lives are hid with Christ in God.

Saturday, January 10. Preached twice every day this week, and expounded frequently in the evening, to a great company at Mr. F's. The Holy Ghost applied the Word with power. Several had acquainted me what God had done for their souls; and one was so filled when Christ manifested Himself to her soul, that she continued a whole night praying and praising God. Some have fallen away, but, blessed be God, the greatest part continue steadfast. Enemies are more enraged. As a proof of it, take the following instance. When Mr. Jonathan Bryan came to Georgia, he showed me a letter written by his brother, Mr. Hugh Bryan, in which it was hinted that the clergy break their canons, and this he desired me to correct for the press. I did. It was published this week. Immediately, Mr. Bryan was apprehended and bound over; and, being asked, frankly confessed that I corrected and made some alterations in it. This evening a constable came to me with the following warrant.

"South Carolina Sf.
"By B . . . W . . . , etc.
"Whereas I have received information upon oath, that George Whitefield, clerk, hath made and composed a false, malicious, scandalous, and infamous libel against the clergy of this Province, in contempt of His Majesty and his laws, and against the King's peace;

"These are, therefore, in His Majesty's name, to charge and command you and each of you forthwith to apprehend the said George Whitefield, and to bring him before me to answer the premisses. Hereof fail not, at your peril. And for your so doing, this shall be your and each of your sufficient warrant.

"Given under my hand and seal this 10th day of January, in the fourteenth year of his Majesty's reign, Anno Domini, 1741.

"B . . . W . . ."

"To all and singular the Constables of Charleston."

I went before the C . . . J . . . , confessed that I had revised and corrected Mr. B's letter for the press, and gave security to appear, by his attorney, at the next general quarter sessions, under the penalty of 100 pounds proclamation money. Blessed be God for this further honor! My soul rejoices in it. I think this may be called persecution. I think it is for righteousness' sake. Oh, how gently does the Lord deal with me, and by these little trials forewarn, and, I trust, prepare me for greater ones!

Sunday, January 11. Preached this morning, upon Herod's sending the wise men to find out Christ, under a pretense that he intended to come and *worship* Him, when in reality he intended to *kill* Him. I endeavored to show from there how dreadful it was to persecute under a pretense of *religion*. Mr. W . . . d telling me that what he did was out of a *sense of duty*, and that binding me over to the Sessions was *no persecution*, led my thoughts this way. In the afternoon, I preached from these words, "They proclaimed a fast, and set Naboth on high among the people, and there came in two men, children of Belial, and sat before him. And the men of Belial witnessed against him, even against Naboth, in the presence of the people, saying, 'Naboth did blaspheme God and the king.' Then they carried him forth out of the city, and stoned him with stones that he died." (I Kings 21:12,13.) My hearers, as well as myself, made the application It was pretty close. I especially directed my discourse to *men in authority*, and showed them the heinous sin of *abusing the power* which God had put into their hands. In the evening I expounded on the story of Orpah and Ruth, and exhorted my hearers to follow the Lord Jesus Christ, though His cause be never so much persecuted and spoken against. Lord Jesus, keep us from being ashamed of Thee or of Thy Gospel! Amen and Amen.

Thursday, January 15. Received several encouraging letters from my friends at Boston; among whom Secretary Willard, an honorable Councilor, writes thus: "Mr. Webb tells me, that divers young men in this town, who are candidates for the ministry, have been brought under deep convictions by your preaching, and (as he hopes) are carried off from the foundation of their false hopes (their own righteousness) to rest only upon Christ for salvation." The Rev. Mr. Cooper writes thus: "I can inform you, that there are many abiding proofs that you did not run in vain, and labor in vain among us in this place. I could much more than fill this paper with the accounts I have received from the persons who have been impressed under the Word preached by you. But I can only now say in general, some have been awakened who were before quite secure, and, I hope, a good work begun in them. Others, who have been under religious impressions, are now more earnestly pressing into the Kingdom of Heaven; and many of the children of God stirred up to give diligence for the full assurance of faith. There is a great flocking to all the lectures in the town; and the people show such a disposition to the new Tuesday evening lecture, that our large capacious house cannot receive all who come. I am sure your visit to us has made a large addition to the prayers that are going up for you in one place and another, and, I hope, also, the jewels which are to make up your crown in the Day of the Lord." Mr. Welch, a pious merchant, writes thus: 'I fear I am tedious, but I can't break off till I just mention, to the glory of the grace of God, and for your comfort and encouragement, the success your ministry of late has had among us. The impressions made seem to be abiding on the minds of many. The doctrines of grace seem to be more the topic of conversation than ever I knew them. Nay, religious conversation seems to be almost fashionable, and almost every one seems disposed to hear or speak of the things of God. Multitudes flock to the evening lecture, though it has sometimes been the worst of weather. Ministers seem to preach with more *life*, and the great auditories seem to hear with solemn attention; and, I hope, our Lord Jesus is getting Himself the victory over the hearts of many sinners." Others write to the same effect. All love, all glory be to God!

> For this let men revile my name,
> No cross I shun, I fear no shame;
> All hail reproach! and welcome pain!
> Only Thy terrors, Lord, restrain.

Friday, January 16. Preached twice every day this week, and expounded in the evening as usual. Congregations much increased since Saturday night last; and I never received such generous tokens of love from any people as from some in Charleston. They so loaded me with sea stores, that I sent many of them to Savannah. Having now all things finished according to my mind, I preached my farewell sermon last night, and spoke at the burial of a Quaker woman, at the desire of her surviving friends. I this day went on board the *Minerva*, Captain Meredith, in which I took passage for myself and some others to England. Thou God of the sea and the dry land, be with us on our voyage, and prepare me for the many perils and mercies that await me among my own countrymen! Amen and Amen.

ON BOARD THE "MINERVA": Sunday, January 18. Continued on board these two days, to settle our ship affairs, and dispatch some other business. The winds being contrary, many friends came from Charleston, and we spent the afternoon together. I preached, and the Lord was with me. Towards the evening our friends left us, not without hopes of seeing each other hereafter in the land of everlasting rest, if not on this side eternity. Blessed be God, that there is such a rest remaining for His people!

Sailed over Charleston bar, January 24, and arrived at Falmouth on March 11. About three days after we set sail, we had a violent storm, which continued about four hours. During the rest of the passage, we had pleasant weather and fair winds, till we came very near upon soundings. Afterwards, God was pleased to detain us near a fortnight; but the weather was pleasant, and, through the bounty of our dear Charleston friends, we had all things richly to enjoy. In the beginning of the voyage, my body was weak, and my spirits low; but afterwards, God was pleased to strengthen me both in body and soul. These words came one day with great power upon my heart, "Arise, go to Nineveh, that great city, and preach unto it the preaching that I bid thee." At another time, the Lord spoke to me by these words, "Take the foxes, the little foxes, that spoil the vines: for our vines have tender grapes." This part of Joseph's blessing was one night brought home to me with a sweet power: "The archers have sorely grieved him, and shot at him, and hated him. But his bow abode in strength, and the arms of his hands were made strong, by the hands of the mighty God of Jacob." At another time, when my soul was dejected at a sense of my own weaknesses, and the number and greatness of my impending trials, the Lord raised and comforted me with this promise: "Fear not thou, for I am with thee. Be not dismayed, for I am thy God: I will strengthen thee, yea, I will uphold thee with the right hand of My righteousness." The books of Genesis and Exodus, which I expounded in course, morning and evening,

were much blessed to my spiritual comfort; and the Lord has been pleased
to give me freedom to write down some of my extempore discourses, which
I hope He will bless for His own Name's sake. In short, this voyage has
been a profitable voyage to my soul, because of my having had many
opportunities for reading, meditation, and prayer. I cannot but adore the
Providence of God in favoring me with such blessed retirements I have
frequently enjoyed on the great waters. I dared not expect to meet with
such success as He has been pleased to give me abroad; and I doubt not, I
shall yet see greater things there, as well as at home. I never had such a
variety of trials and changes of life lying before me as at this time; but I
throw myself into the hands of the blessed Jesus, and shall conclude this
further account of God's dealing with me, with a hymn composed by my
dear and honored friend, Mr. Wesley.

> Ah, my dear Master! Can it be
> That I should lose by serving Thee?
> In seeking souls should lose my own,
> And others save, myself undone?

> II   Yet, I am lost (shouldst Thou depart)
> Betrayed by this deceitful heart,
> Destroy'd, if Thou my labour bless,
> And ruined by my own success.

> III   Hide me! if Thou refuse to hide,
> I fall a sacrifice to pride;
> I cannot shun the fowler's snare,
> The fiery test I cannot bear.

> IV   Helpless, to Thee for aid I cry,
> Unable to resist, or fly;
> I must not, Lord, the task decline,
> For all I have and am is Thine.

> V   And well Thou know'st, I did not seek,
> Uncall'd of God, for God to speak;
> The dreadful charge I sought to flee,
> "Send whom Thou wilt, but send not me."

> VI   Long did my coward flesh delay,
> And still I tremble to obey,
> Thy will be done, I faintly cry,
> But rather — suffer me to die.

> VII   Ah! rescue me from earth and sin,
> Fightings without, and fears within,
> More, more than hell myself I dread,
> Ah, cover my defenceless head!

VIII   Surely Thou wilt. Thou canst not send,
And not my helpless soul defend,
Call me to stand in danger's hour,
And not support me with Thy power.

IX   Lord, I believe the promise true,
"Behold, I always am with you;"
Always, if Thou with me remain,
Hell, earth, and sin shall rage in vain.

X   Give me Thine All-Sufficient grace,
Then hurl your darts of rage or praise.
Jesus and me ye ne'er shall part,
For God is greater than my heart.